THE BOOK OF ANGELS
THE DIVINE COUPLE

The Origin of Angels, Signs & Symbols

Kaya
Christiane Muller

● UNIVERSE/CITY MIKAËL (UCM)
TEACHING & RESEARCH CENTER

● UNIVERSE/CITY MIKAËL (UCM)
TEACHING & RESEARCH CENTER

International Headquarters
53, rue Saint-Antoine
Sainte-Agathe-des-Monts, QC
Canada J8C 2C4

E: org@ucm.ca
W: www.ucm.ca

To organize a lecture, seminar, or workshop: org@ucm.ca

Discover Kaya's webinars on dreams, signs, and symbols: www.ucm.ca

English translation: Blanaid Rensch
Revision: Haritha Nayak, Deborah Kukreja, Dru Delmonico
Proofreading: Martine Thuillard, Johanne Ouellette, Hélène Lacoursière,
Nicolas Lacoursière, Susan Lloyd-Piralli, Alan Coombs, Nancy Smithers
Cover: Anthony Di Benedetto
Graphic Designer: Nadia Poirier and Ke Thien Nguyen
Coordinator: Maryvonne Denis

1st edition : 2nd terms 2017

Legal deposit: 2nd term 2017
National Library of Quebec
National Library of Canada

ISBN: 978-2-923654-74-4

Printed in Canada

PERMANENT   100%   BIO GAS   Ancient Forest Friendly™
ENERGY

Printed on Rolland Enviro 100, which contains 100% recycled, post-consumer
fiber, and is certified Ecologo, Processed Chlorine Free and FSC recycled, as
well as manufactured using biogas energy

Table of Contents

The reader will better understand the language
used in this book if he bears in mind that apart
from the preface and introduction, this is the
transcription of oral teaching.

Kaya

This book has been produced from extracts of lectures
that my husband and I prepared and that I gave
in public in Canada and United States.

The love that unites us is the very breath of my words.
In all simplicity, I invite you to discover our daily life
as well as that of other people who follow this
Ancient Path of Knowledge

Christiane Muller

Note: To facilitate reading, we have used the masculine pronoun
when referring to individuals – male and female – in general.

PREFACE

As a young child, as I observed and slowly moved my fingers; I used to wonder why was I in a body, why human beings were on Earth, and what was the meaning of Life. This questioning was so intense that at a very young age, I accepted the existence of a Divine Force surrounding us and looking after us, looking after the world.

Despite this, things in my childhood didn't go as I'd expected at all. This led me to read books on spirituality in my teenage years. Through these books, I was on a heartfelt quest to find out why I'd suffered so much in childhood, what these ordeals meant, and above all, how I could remedy this.

During this research period, I came across several people and various books that led to some Knowledge. However, Up Above made sure that I went beyond this first stage.

At the age of 16, when I was completely focused on the piano, my right hand began to work less well than my left. I was so buoyed by my ambitions and desire to succeed that I concentrated all my efforts to understand why my right hand was so limited. After several years of physiotherapy and re-education, I managed to heal my hand but a few months later, the symptoms came back. I wanted to have a career as a concert pianist, nothing else really interested me. Although I was already a qualified primary teacher, that didn't seem as important to me. Even my couple and desire to found a family had become secondary.

The events of my childhood and inability to be a concert pianist led to depression and a great quest for truth. I started psychotherapy at about the same time as I attended one of Kaya and Christiane Muller's conferences. I went up to speak to them at the end because I sensed that the message they conveyed through The Traditional Study of Angels was different from anything I had ever heard thus far.

I'll always remember the first time I became aware that memories – unconscious memories – that I thought were normal, were erroneous and the root of great blockages. I said to myself, 'It is incredible that memories lodged in my unconscious can have such an influence on my life without my realizing it. If only people knew that a great deal of our experiences come from our unconscious!'

After this revelation and the discovery of *The Book of Angels*, I received the keys that would allow me to work on my conscience. Not only did The Traditional Study of Angels provide answers to questions I'd been asking since early childhood, but it also provided a synthesis of everything I'd learned up until then. I knew that this Knowledge would lead me much further, much deeper.

The wonderful, extraordinary aspect of The Traditional Study of Angels is that it offers a complete work method that it is as powerful as psychotherapy for our whole conscience, with the added advantage of going deeper, taking all of our lives into consideration. It allows us to develop our own spiritual autonomy.

Since I started working intensely with the 72 Angels, I've observed transformations in my life on all levels. On the spiritual level, analyzing dreams and symbolic language help me explore and understand myself better and better on the causal level every day. Angel Work helps me purify and better master my thoughts and emotions. On the physical level, it teaches me to materialize in a divine manner.

Materialization has affected my life on all levels. On the couple level, it is such a deep, happy joy for me to evolve alongside my wife, Sophie, who has been following the Teachings of Universe/City Mikaël for several years. On the professional level, although I still play the piano, now, as a Teacher and

Assistant Director in a school, I am totally devoted to helping children. Today, I realize how much I evolve in their presence and how important it is that they receive a spiritual education as young as possible. I now know that my place is at their side instead of seeking fame and glory above all else.

The Traditional Study of Angels leads to long list of changes! Kaya and Christiane are marvelous examples. Through the wonderful testimonials and analyzes in this 2nd volume of *The Book of Angels, The Divine Couple*, the number of people who feel called to follow an initiatic path is growing daily. The Knowledge offered by the Authors of *The Book of Angels, The Divine Couple* represents a new era of conscience that engenders numerous transformations on all levels. This new book will help you understand how, thanks to these transformations, as we journey along our Path of Destiny, we learn to materialize in the right, just, Divine way, to fuse our inner and outer couple, our receptivity and emissivity, to marry Spirit and matter in all aspects of our daily life.

I am happy you have found this book... probably as though by magic in a bookstore, on the Internet, on the advice of a friend, or, quite simply, as the follow-up to Volume 1, *The Book of Angels, The Hidden Secrets*. We have all experienced the same phenomenon of having been truly guided toward *The Book of Angels*, published by Universe/City Mikaël (UCM). If you attend a lecture, workshop or seminar one day, you will hear anecdotes and true life stories that lead each participant to discover this initiatic Teaching that has existed since time immemorial. You will discover the marvelous ways Heaven guides those who intensely seek answers to their existential questions and who are ready to receive Knowledge. The stories and testimonials in this book show that each soul touched by this Teaching can have access to true revelations and experience an expansion of conscience that surpasses ordinary imagination. Becoming an Angel is not easy...but it is the Destiny of each and every one of us and my heartfelt wish for you.

Eloi Delmonico

Assistant Director & Teacher

INTRODUCTION

The Path of Destiny that leads to the Divine Couple

Through the events in my life, the Path of Destiny has guided me to an absolutely wonderful life of truly profound happiness! The beautiful, fairytale world where dreams come true, where prayers are answered, where we meet our soulmate and live happily ever after really does exist! You'll see...

Many years ago when I was living alone with my son, I had a dream. At that time, I didn't know The Traditional Study of Angels or the interpretation of dreams via symbolic language, but I paid great attention to my dreams. In that dream, *I saw something fall from the sky and explode on Earth. Then I saw a man fire a bullet into the gasoline and everything went on fire.* And I woke up, deeply affected by this dream since, for the previous three weeks or so, I had seen many signs showing me the death of a child near me.

In the middle of the night, I sat up in bed to meditate and, a few seconds later, in my meditation, as though in a dream, I saw a sage sitting on a chair in the middle of a starry sky, pointing his finger at a star, telling me, "It's time. Keep yourself free for an encounter...your mystical husband is on his way."

The next morning, a thought persisted in my mind. 'Don't go to the sea, go to the mountains.' I heard this several times, 'Don't go to the sea, go to the mountains.'

That morning I was meeting a friend and the plan was to go for a picnic by the sea. When he arrived, I explained that we had to go to the mountains and not the sea. He asked,

"Where in the mountains?" "I don't know... wherever you like," I answered.

He chose to bring me to the Alps. At the end of the day, before driving me home, he suggested we stop for something to eat in a mountain lodge in the Lure mountain (Lure means Light, the Mountain of Light).

Shortly after our arrival, the owners of the lodge received a phone call from the police. The woman learned of the death of her ex-husband and one of her young daughters. Both of them had been killed in a plane crash. Her ex-husband, who was paraplegic, had been flying a small plane and, just after take-off, the plane had crashed into a tank of gasoline, which had exploded. I understood my dream and my signs. Seeing me, the woman asked me to stay with her during this ordeal, and I immediately accepted this angelic mission, without the slightest hesitation. I wasn't even surprised by her request because it was clear to me that Heaven had sent me there.

Two days later, I went back home to get some clean clothes and toiletries. On my return Joel, the owner of the lodge, told me that his wife was being treated by Patrick. They were in the Berber tent that had been erected just a little further on in the lovely mountain pasture. It was a beautiful sunny day and the flowers and great big trees all around were bathed in the warm sunshine. I saw outside at the wooden table with the tent in view. When I saw Patrick come out, a voice in my mind said, 'It's him!'

I watched this tall man walk across the field toward me. And when I saw his eyes, I knew he was the man Heaven had sent me.

Today, Patrick is my beloved husband. Ever since our encounter in the Mountain of Light, we have lived each day like a dream. I thank Heaven for guiding me to him through dreams and signs. Together we discovered the power of Angel

Work and Symbolic Language. And dreams and signs continue to guide, inspire and help us evolve to better serve.

At the beginning of this wonderful adventure with Angel Work, I received a dream in which I was told I was going to work in the depths of my being. Here is the dream: *Seven divers were about to go down very, very deep. They went through a sort of great time funnel without dying or losing their capacities. There was a team of scientists with a woman scientist in charge of directing operations. As they descended, they passed several levels. Measures were taken at each level to check that everything was okay. At one point, the divers were all in a line and they dived together. They weren't wearing any clothes. In front of them there was a long corridor of shallow water. As soon as they were in this water, they immediately adopted the fetus position, as though they were asleep. Then the team of scientists observed their reactions as, one after another, they woke up. I gave something to each of them. When it was the 7th diver's turn, he suddenly opened his eyes and handed me a piece of paper with a drawing of the seal of Solomon – two equilateral triangles forming a star. The seal was inside a circle. Then the gradual descent process with surveillance of all the parameters continued.*

This dream and many others, activated by my intense work with The Traditional Study of Angels, were true revelations. They helped me heal my deep wounds and understand my past. You'll see how.

Dear readers of this book, I've chosen to share my life experience with you in order to deliver a message of hope and to testify to the fact that with this Teaching, everything is possible. My heartfelt wish is that my sharing will encourage you to keep going, never to despair, even if you are going through very difficult ordeals. The Light is always there, waiting for us to find It. After many years of Angel Mantra practice, my life is now so wonderful, I give thanks to God for this Teaching every single day. Angel Work enables us to cleanse the negative memories of our soul, to get back on our feet, to advance and evolve. This extraordinary Work can change everything in our life. It helps us become a new person, a better soul; it helps us heal all of our hurts and wounds. Thanks to the Angels, I have a wonderful, beautiful life that I happily share with my beloved spouse as we work together to become a more and more divine couple. I am a living example of what this Work can do.

Before achieving an angelic life, however, my life program had preordained my coming face to face with a concentration of negative memories that I had to cleanse and transform. These memories were mostly related to distorted forms of the Qualities of Angel 39 REHAEL, the Angel of submission, which are: *insubordination, rebellion, lack of listening and receptivity, crime against parents and children, parental projection onto their children of what they didn't achieve, violence, cruelty, authoritarianism, imposing obedience with severe cruelty, mental illnesses, emotional problems, anxiety, depression, suicide.*

I believe I experimented all of these distortions in previous lives of mine and consequently bore the memories of them engraved on my soul. Through my father, I was led to experience life situations directly related to these distortions. I had brought back negative karma from my previous lives and I had to fully, deeply integrate what it was like to experience them so as never to repeat them. It was ordained in my Program and the Divine Law that evil, wrong-doing, what hurts is educational took on its full meaning for me in this life. It was time for me to reap what I had sown in other lives.

To better understand the context of my life, here are a few details. My father's parents didn't allow their son, my father, to continue his schooling even though he was very intelligent and a gifted learner. My paternal grandparents were farmers who were poor on many levels. Like the very difficult life they led, they were very hard on my father and their entourage.

Régine at 6 months and at 6 years old

My father contracted tuberculosis (TB) at a very young age. When he married my mother, he was 22 and she was 18. While he was being treated in a sanatorium, my mother gave birth to my brother in a hostel for single mothers. A little later, I came into the world. My father went to night school at technical college and attained a diploma in industrial drawing. However, with the events in 1968 in France, his diploma wasn't validated. Discouraged, he succumbed to TB again and was obliged to go to a sanatorium for a much longer stay. We had to move to a region in France that was reputed for good air.

While my father was in the sanatorium, a Jesuit priest drove my mother, my brother and me to this new region. This man was in charge of the mathematical research department at the National Center of Scientific Research and, as a priest, he also led discussion groups. That's where my mother met him. Already this was a sign indicating what I was going to experience in this new place: mathematics of my conscience that would lead me to carry out deep, spiritual work. Whenever we think of scientific research, we know that lots of experiments of all sorts are carried out to see and test the results obtained and to draw constructive conclusions. When positive, it is generally a process that serves the evolution of mankind.

We lived in a magnificent place. There were mountains, streams and a nearby spa, well-known for treating respiratory illnesses. Symbolically, this indicated that there were a lot of emotional memories within me, related to erroneous ways of thinking, that needed to be healed. In this place, I was going to begin cleansing, rectifying and healing. But, of course, I wasn't aware of this at the time.

The first time I saw my father again, I was about 5 years old. He was very weak and still coughed a lot. My mother warned us that we weren't to tire him. For my brother and I it was like seeing a stranger, but at the same time, we were happy to have a dad.

My learning program regarding submission was activated the summer I was 6 years old. One day, my mother, brother and paternal grandmother were going shopping. I was playing and my mother let me stay at home because my father was there. Just after they left, my father told me that I had to learn about my anatomy, my genital anatomy. I didn't want to because I wanted to continue playing. He told me that if I didn't do it then, I'd have to do it in front of everyone when they came back. He added, "It's as you like!" So although I thought it wasn't going to be very pleasant, I thought that if I had to do it, it was something that everyone had to do it. My father told me to take off my underpants and to get up onto the bed. Then with a mirror and a small spoon, he showed me every part of my genitals telling me the name of each part. I felt really bad and I wanted to put my clothes back on. Afterwards, he said to me, "If you tell the others, you'll get a fatal thrashing!" I was shocked and terribly frightened because I understood that fatal meant death. I experienced an awakening of conscience, as though something deeply buried or dormant in me had just been awakened. Without understanding, I realized that I had submitted to something wrong, that I'd had to obey no matter what. A program had been activated, a program related to the above-mentioned distortions: *imposing obedience with cruel severity, lack of listening and receptivity, and mental illnesses*. I bore resonance with these distortions within me, and that day a program of intense purification was set in motion because I began to suffer from asthma and various respiratory problems and allergies.

Then came school and I was in what was called preparatory class, the class when children learn to read and write. We regularly brought our notebooks home to be signed by our parents and to show them our progress. One day, I made several mistakes so the teacher gave me a bad mark. It was the first time my father beat me violently. He told me to bring him one of his shoes and to stand in front of him in my underpants. Then, holding me by the arm, he hit me with the shoe. I was so surprised and the pain was so intense that I fell to the floor screaming. He pulled me up by the arm and went on hitting me. After this experience, I became afraid of bringing home bad marks.

Thanks to *The Book of Angels, The Hidden Secrets* I've been able to understand that I had memories that resonated with my father's personal failures. When I read: *parental projection of what they didn't achieve onto their children and violence*, I understood how deep my father's inner suffering regarding his failed schooling had been for him to hit his young daughter so violently.

Toward the end of the school year, my parents told me I had to have my hair cut so as not to get too hot in summer. I didn't want to. I had long hair that my mother brushed and plaited every morning. I didn't understand why that particular summer I was going to feel warmer than the previous summers.

My parents brought me to a small barber shop and left me there while they went off shopping. The barber was a big, elderly man who looked more like a butcher in his white coat than a hairdresser. I felt very uneasy but I didn't say anything. I didn't move. He began to cut my hair and he cut and cut and cut. When he finally stopped cutting, all that remained was half a centimeter of hair all over my head. He had given me a buzz cut – a military haircut. I looked at my shorn head in the mirror and tears slowly flowed down my cheeks. That was my only reaction because I saw there was nothing to be done. I was experiencing submission through obligation. Of course, at that time I didn't know that Cosmic Intelligence had planned this experience in my learning program to help me work on my over-imposing inner fire, on my too strong emissivity, on my rebellious thoughts, and lack of respect for Hierarchy.

Cosmic Intelligence had me go through this experience because in my past lives, I had over developed the *yang* aspect, my masculine polarity. It was a barber – a man's hairdresser – who had cut my hair. The fact that he had given me a soldier's buzzcut indicated that symbolically I needed to submit to the cutting of my former thoughts of rebellion and absence of respect for authority and hierarchy that I had had in a past life or lives. Soldiers are not required to have very short hair merely for practical, hygienic reasons, but also as a mark of submission, to make them understand that rebellious thoughts and emotional overflow will not be tolerated.

Three years later, when I was 9 years old, another striking incident in my life occurred. One day, I had to bring home a dictation exercise for my parents to sign; I'd got zero points because of mistaken plural forms. For my father, this was inexcusable. I was so scared that I pretended to have stomachache on the appendix side. I'd once heard of appendicitis and I remembered it well. My fear had drained all color from my face, making me so pale that I was believed. My mother brought me to the doctor and after examining me, referring to my appendix, I clearly remember him saying, "It's still okay but as she says she's in pain, we'll operate." The next day, I found myself in theatre, ready for the operation. I told myself I had won this time but I couldn't use this pretext again.

Throughout our schooling, my brother and I lived in fear of failure and my father's reaction to it. This clearly points to our having unconscious memories that resonated with perfectionism, intransigence and extremism. It was to help us work on these memories that Cosmic Intelligence had chosen such a father for us. My brother and I also needed to work intensely on our structure, as the following experience shows.

When I was 11 years old, my parents bought an old house quite far from where we lived. And guess what? We had to do all the renovation work on it ourselves. For several years, we worked on it during the school holidays and on weekends.

As my father had back problems, he could only do a limited amount of work. So my mother, my brother and I did the work under his orders. We camped on the site and before beginning to rebuild the house, we first had to gradually take down the old structure. It was very hard work in difficult conditions that we had to carry out no matter the weather or our mood. This renovation work lasted until I was 16 years old. Over all those years, I learned the true meaning of hard work. I needed these intense experiences to be able to rectify the old memories that permeated my inner structure. I had to learn that before rebuilding, we first need to undo, to remove the old, useless aspects, and to cleanse whatever is still worthwhile in the former structure. It was a very profound lesson related to one of Angel 39 REHAEL's Qualities: *regeneration*.

One day, when I was much older and my hair had grown very long again, my father decided he would cut 2 centimeters off it for every mark I got that was below average. This time, I'd had enough, and I said, "No! That's out of the question." There was no hesitation in my voice and my father didn't say anything. I myself was surprised at my answer. It was as though someone else had spoken for me.

I'd been strong enough to say no because Cosmic Intelligence had allowed me not to submit this time. It was no coincidence that my father had said 2 centimeters. He could have said 3 or 4 centimeters, or any other figure. Number 2 symbolizes relationships with others in the concrete, outer world of action as well as with ourselves. For my father, any mark below average was synonymous with failure. Anything that reminded him of his own school failures was unbearable for him. His desire to cut my hair, which symbolizes thoughts and self-esteem on the positive level, revealed his inner desire to cut off his own thoughts and self-esteem that had reactivated these painful emotions in him.

Régine as a child and as an adult

Another time, I came home from high school, happy to tell my father that I had got 18 out of 20 in Math, his favorite subject. I was really happy and looking forward to his congratulations. I was expecting this mark to result in lots of praise and acknowledgment. I was sure my father would be delighted with me and I anticipated basking in his praise and pride in me. However, number 18 refers to Angel 18 CALIEL. Among the human distortions of this Angelic Field of Conscience are: *seeks to win, seeks flattery*. You'll see how Heaven made me work on no longer nurturing this distortion, on no longer seeking good results in order to be loved, to be acknowledged.

We lived on the second floor of an apartment block. Full of enthusiasm, I raced up the stairs, opened the door and delightedly announced, "I got 18 in Math!" to my father who was standing there just in front of me. Without batting an eyelid, he said, "You've forgotten something." I replied, "No, no. I haven't forgotten anything." He insisted, "Oh yes you have." So I went outside, looked around and went back in again. Once again, he said, "You've forgotten something." I didn't understand. I went back downstairs and looked all around before going back up to our apartment again. I told him I hadn't found anything, and that I didn't understand. He only replied, "Get out! You forgot something outside!" I went back out and sat there crying. When my mother came home from the store, she spoke to my father and came back to tell me, "You forgot to greet your father first; you didn't say hello to him when you arrived." My father's behavior taught me a beautiful lesson: do not strive or do favors to please others; do not expect anything in return.

My father's rigidity was so strong that it manifested right down onto the physical level. At one point, – I remember, I was 13 years old at the time – he had a slipped disk and had to have an operation. Laser operations didn't exist then. It was a very heavy procedure. Two 10-15 centimeter metal bars were inserted into my father's back and screwed onto either side of his spine; he'd have to keep them there for life.

On the metaphysical, symbolic level, the fact that my father could no longer physically bend revealed his great rigidity on the inner level, on the level of his thoughts and emotions. He was incapable of tolerance, forgiveness and gentleness. Needless to say, if I had such a father, it meant that I had strong resonance with him on the level of my inner man. The following incident shows the extent of harsh thoughts and inner coldness I had accumulated on the mental level throughout my previous lives.

One morning, as I was getting ready for high school, my father burst into my room like a canon ball and smacked me across the cheek with incredible force. The force of this blow knocked my head against the wardrobe door which split, and the mark of his hand was imprinted on my left cheek. I was stunned and completely bewildered; my left cheek was on fire and I felt sharp, violent pain in my head. I sat down on my bed in a daze. I didn't understand what had just happened. Why?! I was crying and praying, asking, "God, what's going on? Why is this happening to me?" Later, I realized that I never once prayed for it to stop. I never thought of it. Somewhere inside me, I knew that I had to go through all of these experiences even though they weren't easy.

For as long as I can remember, I knew that if I experienced difficult things, it was because I had surely done wrong before. Even before going to school, I had the inner certainty that we lived several lives. It was clear and obvious to me that we weren't merely a body made of matter. This awareness gave me great inner strength. Heaven didn't leave me without inner resources to face the ordeals I had to go through. The certainty that we have several lives gave me great inner fortitude and prayer was a great help to me. For me, God was my Father; He was the one I spoke to, He was the one I asked if my deeds were right and good. The Name REHAEL means *receptivity to God*. I also experienced that Quality.

Throughout our childhood and adolescence, our parents did their best to provide their children with everything they hadn't had themselves. They wanted us to succeed at all costs. They bought us books and encyclopedias. We did sports and music. Music became a wonderful outlet for me but, at the same time, using it as such, I developed a distortion. You'll see how. I began studying music at the age of 7. I wanted to learn the piano but I was told a piano was too big and too expensive. So I chose the classical guitar. I strove so much to please that very quickly I became a gifted pupil. I had excellent marks and I skipped several levels and was admitted in the advanced guitar classes. My father left me alone when I practiced and I took great advantage of that. At the College of Music everyone was kind and I felt a certain admiration for me. I nurtured that admiration because it restored my self-esteem. I needed to be loved and acknowledged so much! I wasn't even scolded for my poor marks in music theory. I was very quickly allowed to play in a concert and I heard my father exclaim with exaggerated pride, "That's my daughter!" This attitude of his clearly reflected the distortion: *parental projection of what they haven't achieved onto their children.* I remember the deep disgust I felt regarding his attitude, which reveals the strong resonance I had with pride. I still had work to do.

The following incident shows how Cosmic Intelligence can intervene and call a halt to ordeals and difficult situations when we have paid and settled most of the negative karma ordained in our program; because my testimony today is a pale reflection of all the cruelties and abuse I experienced in my childhood. The day my father, mother and I were called to appear before the children's magistrate, it was my father's birthday. My father was celebrating his 44th birthday, which is deeply symbolic because Angel 44 YELAHIAH is his Guardian Angel on the physical level. My father embodied several distortions of this Angelic Field of Conscience, which often manifested in his behavior. These included: *extremism, aggression, brutality, demonic forces, injustice.*

I remember that day very well. I was waiting in the Court House corridor. The Court House was an old, dark building and I didn't feel at ease at all. A boy sitting beside me asked me the name of the judge I had to appear before, and when I told him, he said, "You're lucky. That judge is really nice. The other one is mean; he doesn't like children!" That day, the judge put me under the protection of Social Services. That very day, I no longer had to go home. The phase of my life where I had to submit to ordeals and violence was over. From then on, my life was much calmer. Through that judge, Cosmic Intelligence had sent me a protector who applied Divine Justice in the vibration of Angel 44 YELAHIAH, the Warrior of Light and Universal Protector. For me, it was as though God had declared, "That's enough now; it's time to move on."

Throughout my childhood, I prayed and prayed; I prayed every day. And each time I prayed I asked to be happy. For me, being happy meant that there was no suffering on Earth, that no one suffered. Today, I know that this wish of mine to see everyone on Earth set free from pain and suffering was a reflection of what I was going through on the inside, in my inner Earth. I wanted every part of me to be freed from suffering. By working on myself with *The Book of Angels* and through the study of my life and dreams in the light of the Law of Resonance and symbolic language, my prayer was answered. I am now at peace with my past because I understand it. Considering it with the understanding and lucidity that Knowledge has given me, I sometimes feel as though it all happened to someone else. Since then, a lot of things have evolved. My father has evolved. He has changed so much that when I see him now after all these years, it's a different person that I meet. He constantly helps everyone around him and is always doing other people favors. I've been able to tell him, in all serenity, that I love him and that I've forgiven him.

A dream showed me that Work with The Traditional Study of Angels would lead me to beautiful, deep understanding of events. *I found myself in India, in Kullu, at the foot of the Himalayan mountains. My aunt Danielle was with me and Patrick was standing at my side. We were in a building that was built at the end of the world. Instead of the wall, there was a great bay window. We could see the Universe, above and below. Both of us sat there looking at the stars that were so close to us. Particles of matter went off into space. We witnessed the birth of a star. It was really beautiful. Danielle exclaimed, "Oh! That one is so beautiful!"* In concrete reality, my aunt Danielle has been living in Kullu for many years in order to follow a spiritual teaching. I've been close to this aunt of mine since childhood and we are very close in age. For me, she represents spirituality.

I'd like to end this introduction by sharing with you a message I heard in a meditation a few years ago, which is a good illustration of the principles of this Teaching that comes from the Kabbalah: *I saw my body covered in painful thorns and I heard a voice say, "Healing your body won't help; you need to take out the thorns."*

That is exactly what Angel Work helps us do. By doing Angel Mantra Recitation, we uproot the causes of our suffering. In other words, we transform the distortions – the thorns – that engender it. Slowly but surely our suffering, the pain, goes away.

Régine with her son

Heaven also gave me the extraordinary gift of a wonderful son who helps Patrick and myself grow on the Path of our mutual Destiny. He has become a young adult, journeying along his own Path of Destiny, accompanied by the Angels and his angelic spouse. He followed his dreams and signs and met the love of his life at the young age of 18. Together they form a Divine Couple who have chosen to devote their lives to serving God through sharing the Teachings of the Traditional Study of Angels and through their example of what it means to live as an angelic couple. I am now fulfilled on all levels and I thank God for all the Divine Love that accompanies me in my daily life, and which guided me to this beautiful, liberating Teaching.

Régine Thomas

Angel 48 Mihael

The Inner Couple
Before the Outer Couple

To get to the numerous places on our Western Canadian lecture tour last spring, my husband Kaya and I sometimes traveled by plane. One day we were invited to two different radio interviews on the same day, one in Calgary and the other at the University of Winnipeg. We decided that I'd take the very early morning flight to Winnipeg and Kaya would do the interview in Calgary. It was the month of June, during Angel 18 CALIEL's reign.

On the plane, I was given seat number 18. I was very happy with this lovely synchronicity. I started to tidy away my bag and straightaway a flight attendant came over, eager to help me. Beyond her kindness and professional service, I felt an affinity with this woman on the energy level; through this clairsentience, I knew that she was a spiritual person. The plane took off and I went back to doing inward Angel Mantra Recitation with Angel 48 MIHAEL in preparation for the lecture on the inner couple.

As soon as she had a free moment, the flight attendant came to talk to me. She told me about her job, where she came from and I listened. After she'd been by a few times, she asked me, "And why are you on this flight?" I explained to her that I gave lectures on dreams, signs and the Angels. She looked at me intensely, clenched her fists, and exclaimed, "Oh! As soon as I've finished serving, I'll be back to talk to you!" She explained to me what she was going through. "Six months ago, my 42-year-old husband told me that he was leaving. Without giving me any real reason, he told me he was tired of our relationship and that he wanted to experience a different sort of life. We have two daughters. His decision really upset me but it also propelled me onto a spiritual path."

I listened as she told me about her spiritual path and her belief in reincarnation. Perceiving and understanding her interest, I said to her, "Among the 72 Angels, there's one you could work with: Angel 48 MIHAEL. Angels represent states of conscience and Angel MIHAEL helps us rediscover *harmony and marital peace.*" The flight attendant went on to confide in me, "I feel I'm changing and I can also feel my husband is coming closer. He thinks I'm more interesting and that I'm a better wife. I think I'm getting him back." So I warned her, "If you work with Angel MIHAEL that doesn't necessarily mean you'll get your husband back. By doing Angel Mantra, your spirit will visit the negative memories you have in your unconscious that led to this outer manifestation, namely a possible separation from your husband."

During the flight, I virtually gave her an introductory lesson on both the Traditional Study of Angels and Angel 48 MIHAEL. I explained how to invoke an Angel, how effective and beautiful Angel Mantra is, and the numerous opportunities available for her to do it – for example at work, when she didn't have to concentrate on something particular or when she didn't have to talk to passengers. I explained that invoking an Angel would activate the unconscious memories she'd accumulated over her many lives, and that during the night she'd receive dreams corresponding to the Angelic Field of Consciousness she invoked. She also needed to understand that she'd visit the corresponding human distortions, too. Men who appeared in her dreams revealed aspects of her inner man, of her masculine principle, and women, aspects of her inner feminine principle. Her dreams would allow her to observe how these two principles interact in her inner world. Beautiful dreams would show her qualities, whereas more difficult dreams would reveal human distortions. So she would have direct access to the true colors of her inner couple. She'd gradually come to understand that the situation she was going through on the outside was the consequence of the distorted memories she had on the inside.

During the flight, I had time to tell her about the three Guardian or Birth Angels. I told her how to identify Them and what They represent. This woman's great interest reminded me of a sign I'd received at the beginning of this trip, just before catching the flight. Checking through my bags for the last time, I noticed I had a copy of *The Book of Angels, The Hidden Secrets*. Since I didn't need it on the plane, I took it out, intending to put it into one of the suitcases that would be going into the hold. But just as I was about to do this, I heard my little inner voice say, 'No, don't! Keep it with you!' And I obeyed even though there was no obvious reason for my keeping it in my hand luggage. But now I understood why that book was to stay close at hand.

It is essential to always respect other people's level of evolution. So I inwardly asked her soul if she was ready to receive this book. At the same time, I also asked God if it was right for the evolution of her soul for me to give it to her. Just a few seconds later, the flight attendant said, "It's funny you know, ever since I've had these difficulties with my husband, key people have been put on my path. Shortly after my husband announced his intention to leave me, I had to fill in for a deceased colleague. During that flight, another stewardess on duty gave me a spiritual book that helped me a lot." Hearing this, I knew her soul had just answered my question. That's why it's important to practice analyzing everything we see and hear using symbolic language. We train ourselves to analyze everything that happens around us as if it were in a dream. This is how we develop the capacity to tune into and perceive the messages and answers Up Above sends us. In this particular case, the answer was direct. So I offered this woman *The Book of Angels* and I told her how it had come to be in my bag. She was deeply moved.

A little later, on my way to the lavatory, I saw she was already reading it as she sat having her meal. Not only was she nourishing herself physically, but also metaphysically. She was hungry on all levels and I could feel she was being nourished. When I came out of the toilet, she looked up at me and said, "I've found my three Birth Angels – Angels 7, 9 and 60. I understand so many things now!" I was moved to see her as freshly enthusiastic as a young girl. Later she came and told me, "I've found my husband's Angel: it's Angel 6. I understand the human distortion, *multiple personalities*." She said this nicely, kindly, without any criticism or judgment. I could see she was a lovely person.

I saw her mention the book to her steward colleague. This man went past without looking at me; he was very serious and respected the rigorous aspect of this job. Toward the end of the flight, she came up to me to say a few last words, while her colleague was standing just behind me. He very delicately put his hand on my shoulder and said, "You made her day!" He still didn't look at me, but I felt he was truly happy for her, for her soul. At the end of the flight, she said, "Thank you. Maybe we'll see each other once again at one of your lectures. I've got four hours free before my next flight, I'm going to read *The Book of Angels* and invoke Angel 48 MIHAEL."

In Winnipeg, I rented a car to drive to the radio station downtown. When the car rental assistant handed me the papers with the technical details and type of vehicle, I first noticed *blue car*, then the license number *EYS 450*. I was deeply moved again by the synchronicity because 45 is the number associated with Angel SEALIAH, and the theme of the lecture we were giving throughout this major lecture tour, covering more than 85 cities and towns, was directly related to this Angel. This lecture tour was the most intense tour we had experienced so far and it was widely covered by the media. Cosmic Intelligence had organized several events, including some difficult situations where we'd had to transform evil into good. This particular lecture tour was very successful, thanks to the magnificent work of the organizing team that I thank with all my heart and soul. It is beautiful to see so many souls open up and so many destinies change, such as this flight attendant's.

In all, we gave this lecture in 250 French-speaking, English-speaking and German-speaking towns and cities in Canada, the USA, and Europe. Just imagine how I felt driving a car whose license plate read *EYS 450: eyes + Angel 45 SEALIAH,* whose main Qualities are *right motivation and purity of intention.* That Up Above had been so thoughtful moved me to tears. Such signs give us wings! The car rental assistant said, "You asked for a vehicle with a large trunk for your luggage. This one is actually smaller that you requested, but we have another model with a more suitable trunk, if you like." I replied, "Oh no! No thank you! This one is absolutely fine!" Some people might have been angry, but for me, it was a gift.

A mission inspires and uplifts the person who fulfills it. I felt no stress at all on the drive to the University of Winnipeg even though the numerous radio and TV interviews throughout the tour required our getting up very early and going to bed very late. One of the flight and accommodation organizers thought it was sometimes too much. So I told her about the flight attendant I'd met and she was very moved. I said to her, "Yes, I had to get the 6:30 am flight, but a person's destiny has just changed." When we are offered such an angelic mission, we no longer count our efforts. That's what being a human angel on Earth is. I had wings! I didn't feel tired at all and I was sure I'd arrive on time.

Whenever we follow the pace set by Up Above, when we *dance to Heaven's tune,* we no longer force ourselves, we no longer put any pressure on ourselves, we simply concentrate on accomplishing each of our tasks and we no longer waste any energy. It's our distortions that lead us in all directions, scattering and dispersing our energy. We need to be aware of this, and remember it, especially during initiations.

When I arrived at the university, I had so much energy that instead of taking the elevator up to the interview room on the top floor, I took the stairs. And on my way up the stairs, another synchronicity: I met the radio presenter coming down to meet me. He introduced himself as 'Mikael' – MIKAËL! At the University! I knew his name was Mikael, but the match with Universe/City MIKAËL meant so much to me and once again, I was very moved. The interview went off very well and the presenter was so interested in the subject that our meeting was prolonged. I was deeply touched by this because I *read* it symbolically: what happens on the individual level always has repercussions on the collective level. All the different aspects of this trip showed me this: the airplane, which symbolizes the world of thoughts; the flight attendant who was ready to embark on an initiatic path. The situations experienced on this trip allowed Angelic waves to come down to Earth and be broadcast. In a dream, a university symbolizes high, advanced studies of conscience, so realizing all the symbolic meaning of this on the concrete level really moved me.

Another event occurred on my return. At the office, a member of the volunteer staff there told me that the journalist from Winnipeg University had called to say that part of the interview hadn't been recorded properly, and that he'd like to do the interview all over again, but by phone. Now a person in an ordinary conscience might have complained about the waste of time and energy and the poor result. But with an Angelic conscience, such thoughts and feelings no longer exist. It wasn't the journalist's fault, even if he was annoyed and put out by these difficulties. Knowing that this situation had been orchestrated by a Guide from the Parallel Worlds, I wasn't in the least annoyed or angry; I reacted with kindness and respect, without making him feel guilty, aware that such an attitude would help him, and would leave a positive mark.

Some journalists covered the subject matter of our lectures rather superficially, but we adapted to them. It is important to adapt to the other person's needs and level of conscience, and always remain sympathetic and kind. Such an attitude may help them prepare their next interviews with more depth. Anything's possible. Maybe in the future, one of them may be promoted, and even become the CEO of a major radio or television channel. Although he may have done thousands of interviews, he'll always remember the reaction he received to his misaction. It is vital to understand the Divine Law that teaches us that evil is educational, that wrong-doing, what hurts, and all misactions have their rightful place in the scheme of things because they help us become aware of our distortions. We can then purify and transcend them. We must always bear in mind that evil is educational and it serves Good. Its true purpose is to help us develop qualities and virtues and become better people, better souls.

The same journalist called back several times to be sure I'd be there; a beautiful interview took place in July and all went well. We can measure the importance of keeping right, just, qualitative motivation and checking to ensure the purity of our intentions, no matter the circumstances, since Up Above sees to it that we are justly rewarded.

I'd like to share with you another event Kaya and I experienced after the final lecture of our Western Canadian tour. On our way to the airport in Calgary, we stopped off at a restaurant to have a vegan pizza. When we came back out to the car, Kaya clicked the electronic key to open the car door but it didn't work. He tried several times but to no avail. So we checked the license plate just to make sure it was indeed our car, and we read: *Friendly Manitoba EYS 054*. The numbers were reversed! Imagine just how subtle Heavenly Guides can be! Two cars, parked side by side, the same model, the same color, showing us the mirror effect through symbolic language.

What is Above has its likeness below and what is below has its likeness Up Above; Heaven is reflected here on Earth; the microcosm reflects the macrocosm; we were being shown that our lecture tour had reflected and embodied Divine Will; our motivation was a reflection, a mirror image of Divine Motivation; the Angel teachings we taught throughout our lecture tour would echo in the hearts and souls of those who attended and Angel Knowledge would spread. Our car number was *EYS 450* and the other car was *EYS 054*. It truly was a mystical experience! Kaya and I were both speechless in the face of such synchronicity. We looked at each other, deeply moved by this beautiful sign from Up Above, this seal of approval from Up Above through the magical mirror image. This is how we live, constantly accompanied by the metaphysical world. We constantly feel its presence. It is a very concrete way of life, through which human beings install Angelic Conscience on Earth by manifesting Qualities, Virtues and Pure Divine Powers.

Now I'd like to share several life experiences that help us understand certain human distortions of this Angelic Field of Conscience, including jealousy and competition.

Here's what a woman shared with me: "Since I began working intensely with the Angels, I've become jealous. It doesn't make any sense. Before this, I sometimes felt a little jealous when my husband flirted a little, but that's not his worst fault. And I didn't consider my jealousy to be an important distortion to work on. But ever since I've started invoking the Angels, every time a woman comes near my husband, I become like a jealous tiger, even though there's nothing physical going on. I feel like I'm regressing and sometimes I find it difficult to contain my anger." I explained to her, "That's normal. Your reaction reveals that you have memories of jealousy in your unconscious. As long as these memories were dormant, you didn't realize how much jealousy you had within you. But now, your intense work with the Angels has awakened these memories and you feel this jealousy in you in these situations.

To develop Angelic qualities and an Angelic conscience, we have to visit the distorted memories we've accumulated during our many lives. We cannot experience Love in its Highest state, in its purest form, if we haven't transcended sadness, jealousy and competition. Angel MIHAEL will help you carry out this purification work in great depth; Angel MIHAEL is the Angel that helps us deep-cleanse such distortions."

I saw this woman a few months later and she told me about three dreams she'd had. Here's the first dream and what she thought it meant. *I saw a man sitting in an armchair, in what seemed to be the sitting room in a house. He was a handsome black man in a business suit and looked like President Obama except a bit thinner. When I got close, I saw he was wearing red lipstick. I said, 'Gosh, what are you doing? Why on earth are you wearing lipstick?' And I woke up. Meditating on this dream, I told myself my inner man was depolarized, that his wearing lipstick showed that he wanted to seduce. This dream encouraged me to work on my seduction."*

Let's analyze this dream in detail. The man that this woman saw in her dream represents part of her inner man, who shows her how she sometimes behaves when in action. The man is seated; that shows he's receptive. The fact that he's wearing a business suit in a sitting room shows that his receptivity is concentrated on matter. This woman is receptive when she materializes but she adopts an attitude of seduction and power, symbolized by the red lipstick and the business suit. She wants to please too much. Red symbolizes matter. Through this dream, this woman was being shown that there is a certain degree of depolarization in her that has been caused by material needs. This manifests itself, on the one hand, through an exaggerated receptivity on the physical level, and on the other hand by reduced mental, intellectual, spiritual emissivity.

The next day, this woman told me another dream. *I saw my husband sitting down with his legs spread open. He was dressed and a young woman was sitting in his lap. She was not sitting with her back against his chest; she was facing him, sitting astride him in white trousers. She was fully dressed and she was beautiful. He was stroking her hair. Observing this scene, I felt jealous.* Then she added, "What really affected me is that immediately after this scene, I didn't receive any more images but I experienced deep vaginal pleasure. It was so intense that it woke me up. It was more intense than when my husband and I make love. What does that mean?"

I explained to her that this very interesting dream touches on the world of pleasure – not just pleasure created by the sexual act on the physical level, but pleasure or deep enjoyment generated by forces in her unconscious memories. It is surprising to learn that some people have more pleasure during the sexual act when there are distortions such as crude language or external stimuli like films, objects, thoughts, etc. When everything goes well and the sexual act is calm and serene, people in an ordinary conscience eventually get bored and feel attracted to what they don't have. How many people think about their ex-husband or ex-wife or forbidden, inexperienced fantasies during sex in order to reach orgasm? Taken to extremes, there are even people who play sadomasochist games to obtain physical, sexual pleasure. Through negativity, through domination, through power games of repulsion-attraction, they feel intense pleasure, but whenever they find themselves in a healthy, harmonious, tender sexual relationship, they feel totally bored.

The way our conscience with its multiple facets works is really very special. The way we live and initiate, activate, stimulate actions and reactions, sow emotions and reap responses, gestures that may be positive and/or negative in our daily life too. We are nice and kind and we make love to our spouse regularly, we look after him or her, etc. and all of a sudden, he or she tells us our love life is boring. It lacks spice! *It lacks spice*, what does that mean? Well, this woman's dream can help us better understand.

She was shown parts of herself where there is infidelity in her intimate life and this excites her. She is jealous, but at the same time, she likes this cat and mouse game. In some of her distorted memories, infidelity has been recorded, and in others, there are memories of a forbidden attitude and guilt, etc., when she's with a man. She is actually jealous because she herself has forces within her that could deceive her spouse. That's why she's jealous. Her soul contains memories of infidelity and all sorts of needs. These attitudes bother her and her conscience wants to rectify them, because thanks to her spiritual path, she now knows that infidelity, jealousy and competition don't lead to happiness.

The reason why there were no more images at the end of her dream is because she is not yet ready to see all of her memories tainted by these distortions. Negativity may be as stimulating as positivity. In her unconscious, there are forces that enjoy and take pleasure in these distortions; they love them and want more. Her physical, sexual pleasure was very intense because she had been in contact with a block of condensed memories. When we record one or two little sensations, we don't necessarily feel them being recorded in us. But once these sensations have accumulated over years, over several lives even, then they condense into a great big block of memories. In this dream, Cosmic Intelligence reactivated a reservoir of memories of excitement related to numerous infidelities and passing pleasures; this is what led to the intense physical pleasure she experienced.

The Law of Resonance teaches us that in the outer world, we automatically attract situations, people and events that resonate with what we have on the inside. There is a strong duality between our conscience that refuses evil and wrong-doing and the unconscious forces that encourage and push us into nourishing ourselves on the sensations that are so desired in spite of ourselves. Such duality makes us feel torn and gives rise to difficulties that complicate our life and prevent us from experiencing happiness. The Law of Resonance, which applies at all times, in all dimensions, means that we can see beyond visible appearances to what the other person emits on the metaphysical level. For example, if someone has memories of infidelity and seduction in his inner *luggage*, if he himself doesn't express them, his spouse will, or else he'll attract someone who'll stir up ill-feeling in the couple's relationship even if there haven't been any instances of infidelity or seduction. That's why it is so important to work on our inner couple. So many people seek all sorts of *recipes* to help them advance, but dreams like this woman received are real Godsends; they are true gifts from Heaven. Through such dreams, Cosmic Intelligence sends us personalized *recipes*, created specially for us. All of the ingredients we need to carry out inner Work are contained therein in the form of symbols.

This woman, who works for a multinational company, received another dream the following night. *I was preparing a report in English for my boss. I had to give a presentation in front of my boss and a panel of executives, but I couldn't do it. I arrived late; it was difficult; I was no good.* Then, just like after the last dream I had, the scene disappeared and I was woken up by very powerful feelings of intense physical, sexual pleasure."

When we study symbolic language, it is important to get used to making the connection between the elements that appear in our dreams and what they represent for us in concrete reality. It is essential to proceed like this because Cosmic Intelligence often uses elements from our personal life to show us parts of ourselves. Hence when we see people, places, animals, pets that we know in real life, on the concrete level, we ask ourselves what they represent for us, how we perceive them, how we'd describe them, what characteristics we'd give them.

So I asked this lady what her boss represents for her and she said, "He wants to succeed in the world, in matter. He's always competing with others."

By using her boss as a symbol in her dream, Up Above wanted this woman to understand that she has deep resonance with competition, and when she feels she is no good, then she will automatically compensate with seduction to try to stay on top of the situation. We may think that this kind of situation is not frequent but, in actual fact, people who are attracted by power and greed always act like that. If they lose, then they either become very angry or overly gentle, excessively nice in order to re-arrange things and ensure they can win again. So let's continue to analyze this dream; it is so interesting.

She was to give a presentation in English but she couldn't do it. Angel 48 MIHAEL, whose main Quality is *fertility* also touches on growth and a capacity to expand, of course, because fertility doesn't only relate to the physical procreation of a child but also to the materialization of any project. The competitive forces that dwelled in this lady limited her potential for expansion and her capacity to materialize divinely, angelically. We can see also that she is ready to do anything to succeed. If she were poor, she might even do prostitution with a dream like that – because simultaneously she experienced ill-being due to her limitations as well as pleasure from the competitive forces she unconsciously nourished. This kind of dream could be sent to many, many people, because competition and the need to succeed in order to have material pleasure are widespread distortions, both in the workplace and in all forms of prostitutions, and also in a couple's relationship.

Married life is so often difficult because both spouses want to be right, and often sexual intercourse ends up done not with divine love and pleasure but power games! There's competition every time one spouse claims to be the best, to have succeeded in doing something better than the other spouse. For people in ordinary conscience, this is common and seems quite normal to live alternatively in a complex of superiority and inferiority. But over several lives, a person accumulates so much pleasure at having won these competitions, that one day, these memories inevitably turn against him. This is why we say often: opposite attracts. We want to have what the other has, or positively, we are inspired and want to integrate the potentialities that we find in the other person. This woman's dream confirms how intensely such memories can resurface but through the negative aspect in her case. Hence we can understand why Cosmic Intelligence programs limitations in a person's life.

Let's take another example. A man tells his wife good news about a promotion or a good opportunity at work. His wife may be happy and yet simultaneously unhappy or put out because she needs failure and limitations. What a paradox! She pushes and encourages her husband to succeed because her own, inner memories of failure and insecurity are active, but when he has to go away on a two-day training course, she's unhappy. That's the whole ambiguity of such a situation. Unlike so many theories, a dream shows us the long-term consequences of our actions. That's what's so wonderful with the Traditional Study of Angels. When applied to our daily life, it helps us become aware of each and every one of our thoughts. Through Angel Work, we catch hold of our little, negative pleasures, our little, negative *material orgasms*, and we transform them. Gradually, the memories of jealousy and the need for competition disappear, both at home in our couple and in the workplace. We can then experience true happiness.

Now I'd like to continue with another subject: the metaphysical dimension of body language. The body *speaks* and always expresses, *translates*, unconscious aspects of ourselves. As an example, let's take a closer look at the way President Barack Obama and his wife Michelle greeted each other in public by knocking each other's fists, during the presidential campaign.

Symbolically, this gesture, introduced by an American basketball player, has both positive and negative aspects. In concrete reality, this greeting reveals a cool president and the photo of himself and his wife exchanging this cool gesture was published worldwide, and it particularly moved the young. It also reveals aspects of communication in this couple. Wonderful, beautiful changes have occurred in the United States following the election of Barack Obama as president. However, as extraordinary as this president may be, like everyone, he too has his positive and negative sides. It is vital to always use our discernment and analyze each act, each gesture in the light of symbolic language.

Let's analyze this greeting. Knocking our fist against another person's fist doesn't procure a very pleasant feeling; in fact, it may actually hurt. Hands symbolize giving and receiving, as well as a capacity to create and make things. Even if this situation was pre-planned and desired, it was no coincidence either. It means that giving and receiving in this couple sometimes include clashes and power struggles.

During the same public appearance, President Obama gave his wife a smack on the bottom, which is not the most appropriate gesture, is it? If my husband Kaya did this to me in public, I wouldn't say anything right then, but as soon as we were alone I would gently discuss the cause behind such a gesture. What does it mean to give someone a smack on the bottom? What does this gesture reveal? It is a sign of domination, of possession and belongs to dynamics of attraction and repulsion. But this doesn't mean we shouldn't touch each other of course! My husband has the right to give me a few gentle, loving caresses in public; it's very pleasant. But a macho-type gesture like this would certainly be called into question.

In the past, at the beginning of my spiritual path, I frequented a spiritual milieu that advocated certain rigid concepts that I applied. Later, when I met Kaya, he helped free me from such unnecessary rigidity by deliberately showing his love for me by touching me gently and lovingly in public. His expressing his love for me like this helped show me the importance of our relationship, of our couple, and my need to free myself from such restraint. A spiritual couple doesn't display too much intimacy in public, but a gentle, loving spontaneous testimony of the love felt may become a source of inspiration for the couple themselves and for others too, if it is done appropriately and not to show off. Body language is so eloquent that it is vital to analyze it using symbolic language to decode its true meaning.

To go on with body language, let's analyze a very common gesture: a wink. Winking in a right, just, qualitative way is an art! Winks, especially between a man and a woman, must not be used indiscriminately. People sometimes refer to a *wink from Heaven*. In such cases, it refers to divine manifestation, orchestrated synchrony. It's better not to popularize winking when we don't know what this gesture emanates on the metaphysical level because it is non-verbal language that is induced by memories. In some countries, a wink expresses a romantic or even sexual invitation, which is not harmless. In China, winking is considered very vulgar and is very much frowned upon.

To illustrate the importance of this gesture, let me give you an example. During one of our lecture tours, I noticed that the male volunteer helper accompanying us often specifically winked at men and women. While I was talking to him, a person came up to us and began to talk about what we had just been discussing. The man winked at me. I later explained to him the metaphysical meaning of this gesture. I said to him, "I'd like to explain something to help you. You need to become aware of the subtle effect of your winks. The wink you gave me earlier wasn't right. If you happen to be with a woman who feels lonely or who has affective, emotional needs, your wink will arouse and titillate her and create a misaction and a disguised request for more."

This man is a therapist. He is on a spiritual path and employs various spiritual techniques. He questioned me about this subject regarding winking, and I explained, "As a therapist, you have great responsibility. Through your winks, you transmit a certain seductive energy to your patients. Some of them may be very vulnerable women experiencing a great opening of their unconscious. Do you understand the responsibility you have as a therapist? And think of all that your wife may feel when you wink at other women; it reactivates all the memories she has related to the acts of infidelity you committed with other women in the past. Your infidelity really hurt her. Of course, there were things she needed to understand and learn from that situation. She is now on a spiritual path and she is cleansing her memories. She has done great work regarding her suffering, her pain and she forgave you which is rare as you know. You are truly cherished by Up Above since she stayed with you after all you did. You haven't yet fully realized that your winking is too intimate a gesture; it stimulates others and engenders situations that are conducive to infidelity. Even if you stop winking on the physical level, the memories that incite you to wink are still present and active on the metaphysical level. You need to be vigilant about this because we can stop drinking when we are an alcoholic but it doesn't mean all our memories are healed. The more your wife's conscience opens, the finer her perception of what is happening on the subtle levels will be. So you shouldn't be surprised if your wife gets angry, and refuses you; or, in the name of spirituality, holds back and doesn't dare say anything to you. To truly be able to help others as a therapist, and to have a right, just attitude toward your wife, you for sure have some cleansing to do in your memories and you need to stop these unconscious games of seduction if you want to become a great initiate."

After addressing this rather delicate issue, this man continued to wink at me several times on the lecture tour. He'd catch himself doing so and blush each time; his ego was suffering big time. He was shaken and upset. Once, he even winked at Kaya. We all laughed warmly and good-naturedly, but he was really embarrassed and uncomfortable because it was beyond his control and he didn't know what was happening. His ego was winking at us even more than usual. He kept apologizing. It had become like a nervous tic. It was very special how Up Above orchestrated all this during the tour to help this man transform his ego. My husband and I understand that we are a strong, sometimes intense mirror; it is not the first time that we've encountered this kind of situation. People, especially therapists, sometimes feel the unconscious need to compete with us on the spiritual level. That man will long remember this initiatic lecture tour during which Cosmic Intelligence provided him with intense teachings.

One day, during that same period, I put a cooler box on warm rather than cold and we had to throw out the food. This man found it very difficult to accept my misaction because he tended to put us on a pedestal. I could read his thoughts and I felt that he looked down at me because of this incident. He began to speak differently to me; he sometimes used a rather haughty tone as though to let me know he held me in less esteem now. At the end of the lecture tour with us, he shared his experience with a friend. He told her he'd felt judged, and that he thought we were too rigid, too strict. We understood what this man was going through and we had a lot of compassion for him. Especially as we had been told in dreams that he would experience great initiations during this tour, and that it was going to be difficult for him to call himself into question in any depth.

Another volunteer helper who accompanied us at the same time, and who shared a room with this man, discreetly confided in us that he'd behaved very inappropriately. He kept wanting to give him energy healings, telling him that his heart chakra was ill. This volunteer helper hadn't dared say no, and the man had almost forcibly put his hand on his heart. At times, this other volunteer helper felt so bad and was so upset by this behavior of a man who called himself a therapist that he sought refuge by withdrawing to the bathroom. We know this man has a beautiful soul and great potential, but as a therapist, he has a long way to go.

On the last night of his week with us, before going to sleep, this man asked Cosmic Intelligence if it were right for him to go and leave flyers advertising his energy healings in the stores of the towns we'd lectured in. We knew it wasn't appropriate but we waited for him to receive his own reply in a dream or through signs because of course he was free to do whatever he wanted. During the night, he received the following dream: *He saw a person selling drugs in a mall and there were corrupt policemen who weren't able to arrest him.* The next day was a rest day. Before leaving, he went off for a long run to try to digest his dream. He came back with the idea that maybe it wasn't the right time to distribute his flyers in the stores in this town. Then he asked Kaya to help him better interpret his dream, to help him gain a deeper understanding of what it meant. Kaya explained, "Drugs symbolize dependence on the mind or spirit level. This means that in your exchanges with others, you create and nourish spiritual dependencies. Your inner police and your sense of justice that should normally incite you to put a stop to this behavior are incapable of doing so because they are corrupt."

This man, who worked for a long time for the police force, was really touched and shaken by this dream. He never thought that he had this in him. As the three of us were discussing this, he kept winking at me non-stop. He couldn't stop himself. It was as though he'd been switched onto automatic pilot, that the wink button had been pressed on; he was speechless at what was happening. Each involuntary wink made him more and more ill-at-ease. I said to him, "We understand what you're going through; we feel deep compassion for you. Work on your winks. If you really need to wink, you can wink at your wife." My husband explained to him, "Look how closely related the energy of seduction and corrupt power are. I'm sitting right here beside you and you're winking at my wife, in spite of all the explanations and teachings you received this week. You see how deeply rooted it is in you? Another man could really hold it against you, you know. And this is the tip of the iceberg, what you are experiencing right now in terms of seduction." He was on the verge of tears. It was time for him to leave. His initiatic week was over; he'd had his dose of initiation.

Now I'd like to move on to a TV commercial for Coca-Cola Light. At first sight, and in an ordinary conscience, we may find this advertisement funny and even positive. When we watch it with a vertical conscience though, taking into consideration the metaphysical, symbolic dimension of the elements in it, we realize that it reflects and nourishes distortions.

In this commercial, we first see *a young woman wearing a light, summer dress, walking her dog along a beach by the sea. In one of her hands, she's carrying her shoes, and in the other, a can of Coca-Cola Light. Then, she catches sight of a handsome man in swimming trunks coming out of the water. We can see she's attracted to him. Their eyes meet and we can feel seduction intermingle. Turning his back to the woman, the man begins to get dressed. First he pulls on a pair of jeans, then a black shirt. When he turns around again, the woman sees that he's wearing a priest's collar. Very surprised, she adjusts one of the straps of her dress that had fallen off her shoulder. The man, continuing to look seductively at her, draws close and takes her can of coke, helps himself to a drink and goes off with the can. She lets him do this, smiling all the while.*

Let's analyze this commercial using symbolic language as if it were a dream. The man and woman at the seaside represent the masculine and feminine principles faced with their emotional *luggage*. The woman is walking her dog. As the overall scenario is not positive, we have to consider the negative symbolic aspect of a dog, which is its tendency to excessively display its instinctual needs and affective, emotional dependency. The woman sees the man up the back, and the back in general symbolizes the past. This indicates that both of them are under the influence of their emotional memories.

The fact that the man – a priest who has vowed to celibacy and sexual abstinence – uses his powers of seduction, reveals memories where spiritual charisma was used for seduction. Clothes symbolize the aura and black represents hidden aspects. This means that this man's spiritual communication on the social level contains numerous hidden aspects. As a symbol of what is occulted, unknown, it may be positive when circumstances aren't suitable for the revelation of hidden elements, but this is not so in the situation between this man and woman. The fact that the man takes the woman's drink and helps himself shows that he uses his spiritual charisma to quench his thirst for women's emotions, to nourish his need for female emotions. Coca-Cola doesn't symbolize the best emotions, does it? This means that this man nourishes his emotional level without discernment and irresponsibly. He acts under the influence of distorted memories and he creates this way the abuse of power. He plays with the *light* aspect: *Coke light – Have a great break!* It's as though, regarding his spiritual work, he's telling himself to take a break. And what does he do during his break? In a very light-handed manner, he steals women's emotions. Of course, such behavior only succeeds with women, who, as in this example, also act under the influence of their instinctual, unfaithful forces. The Law of Resonance is always applicable.

When we commit to a spiritual path and our distorted memories still haven't been completely transformed, we sometimes have to impose rigor, even a certain rigidity in order to master our instincts. It isn't easy. Some people need a break after a while because the pressure exerted by the retained, repressed forces becomes unbearable. So they let themselves go a little, metaphysically, and sometimes even physically too, thinking there won't be any consequences since it's so slight; since it's *light...*

Let's analyze *light* drinks such as diet coke. Some so-called light drinks contain aspartame, which is a synthetic sweetener that causes side effects such as headaches, migraine, dizziness, convulsions, nausea, and weight gain. Many people believe that the absence of sugar means they won't put on weight and they drink large quantities of light drinks. Such excess leads to serious consequences since 75% of harmful reactions to food additives are due to aspartame. Even though this fact is known to the FDA (Food and Drug Administration), a US organization in charge of food and medicine quality control, the use of aspartame has yet to be officially forbidden, and few people are aware of its harmful effects.

Our role here is not to analyze aspartame but to show what this physical reality corresponds to on the metaphysical level. Excessive consumption of artificially sweetened drinks indicates affective, emotional lacks and a great need for gentle sweetness, which we try to assuage superficially, artificially, while sometimes knowing how harmful and illusory it is. Calling such drinks *light* nourishes the illusion of lightheartedness, ease, and the absence of serious consequences.

In this advertisement, the man takes the woman's can of Coke Light. She seems to be happy, but on the metaphysical level, she has been robbed of her energy.

Let's continue with a metaphysical experience related to Angel 48 MIHAEL's Field of Conscience. A woman shared with us that she felt attracted to a man who was working with Traditional Angelology and other methods simultaneously. They had talked together and shared their dreams, and several times, the man told this woman that he'd seen himself make love to her in his dreams. This woman is happily married, and she loves her husband and their children. As her encounters with this man continued, she began to feel ill-at ease and she talked to me about it. She said, "I felt as though he had gotten into my head. I didn't know what to do. He'd become an obsession, so I prayed and asked for help and one night I received a dream. *I saw this man and I told him straight that I was happy with my husband and that this had to stop.* When I saw the man the next day, I told him my dream and I explained what I was going through. I said, 'I'm in a distortion. The way you look at me bothers me and I've become obsessed about it. All that you keep telling me makes me feel most uncomfortable and ill-at-ease. I'm not at all happy about my friendship with you.' He was surprised."

After some time, we realized that he behaved like this with other women. This man is not in a relationship himself, and his tendency to tell women that he made love to them in his dreams had disturbed quite a few of them. He thought he was very evolved and didn't realize he was mixing his affective, emotional needs and Knowledge.

This example is interesting and very powerful. Whenever we undertake a spiritual path, we quite naturally tend to share what we are going through, including our dreams. But we must be vigilant between men and women because in dreams, we may see ourselves make love to different people in all sorts of situations. We mustn't take these dreams literally and project them onto the people concerned. Making love to someone in a dream shows us that we fuse with what that person emanates, with his/her character traits and behavior. Depending on the memories Up Above wants us to work on, the symbol we fuse with, positively or negatively, may be anyone or anything. It can be very surprising sometimes. It may be a neighbor, an acquaintance, a famous contemporary or historic character, even an animal, a landscape, a color, etc. By fusing on all levels of our being with the symbol presented, we become it. There is a fine line between positive and negative. We need to study the dream and situation well – hence the importance of understanding the symbolic meaning of fusion.

Thus it is also important to discern whether the symbol in our dream is positive or negative. When the person we fuse with in a dream is not married, and is presented as a beautiful, inspiring symbol, then there's no question of infidelity. However, if the person is married and we are aware of this in the dream, then such a dream reveals infidelity. The symbolic theme teaches us what we need to purify and transcend. Fusion with beautiful, inspiring symbols indicates that we are in the process of integrating the states of conscience and the qualities these positive symbols represent.

Later, this woman dreamed that *her husband was going to die and that her own father would be there*. Knowing that a father symbolizes action and the concrete world, this dream made her feel bad and it really destabilized her. During a dream-sharing session, she told this dream to her friends, including this man. He said to her, "That means that I might be the one to replace your husband and look after your children.' For her, this dream and this man's suggestion made no sense. She talked to her husband about it. At first he was annoyed and worried about this man's behavior. However, since he too works with Traditional Angelology, in the end, he reacted very well. He went to talk to the man in question. He said to him very nicely, "I understand that my wife is a beautiful symbol of a spiritual woman and mother for you, but she represents part of you, part of your inner woman, what you as a man would like to experience with a spiritual woman. Stop sharing disturbing dreams with her please. Your behavior is not right." But a week later, the man began again. This time her husband, very politely but firmly, said to him, "If you want to keep meeting our family and being friends with us, you absolutely must stop sharing your dreams like this." For this unmarried man, this kind of sharing had become true nourishment on the energetic, affective, emotional and power level.

It is essential to pay attention to certain aspects of dream potentiality. Angel Work gradually leads us to visit other people's souls and we must never play around with these powers. This man was acting all mysterious when he declared, "I dreamed about you." What was his intention? Because everything depends on our intention. When we are allowed to visit other people's souls in dreams, the purity and authenticity of our intention is of the utmost importance. Our intention must not hide any power games or emotional, affective needs. People who function according to the dynamics of power games use their Knowledge, as well as the other person's needs and dependencies, to attract attention and to seem important. That's how false gurus construct themselves: by hypnotizing those around them in the name of the great, beautiful principle of Universal Love, without having integrated it themselves. It is vital to understand this aspect to guarantee the healthy progress of our soul on the spiritual level.

Let's continue with a quotation from Albert Camus: *'Why must we love rarely to love deeply?'* What does the word *rarely* mean here? This quote is related to attraction-repulsion dynamics. Many couples experience this ambiguity in their relationships. They adopt behavior that makes them inaccessible, and the intimate act of fusion while making love becomes so difficult and rare that the relationship deteriorates. Sometimes, with a lot of humor, Kaya says, "If we only make love once a year on our birthday, it's perfectly understandable that the husband – or wife, as the case may be – feels famished!"

From time to time, a woman tells us that her husband is rather coarse and vulgar and the way he makes love repels her and leaves her feeling empty. To regain harmony, a weaning period may prove indispensable. It is important to gently explain to our spouses that certain gestures or attitudes are not pleasant for us. And when the sexual act goes well, it is just as important to encourage our spouses. We can also create a romantic atmosphere, we can light candles and put on beautiful, calm, gentle music, without, however, falling into the trap of wanting the conditions to be absolutely perfect and expecting the act of love to be perfect too. We mustn't become incapable of improvising. The time will come when spontaneity and light-heartedness dissolve the complicated aspect. Complications are caused by distorted memories; purification of these memories allows us to regain harmony. When we experience a true, authentic love relationship, it is so beautiful and fulfilling that questions like Camus' no longer arise.

We've talked in previous lectures about sexuality within the couple that can be so beautiful, replenishing, and regenerative. When Kaya and I are making love, it is so profound, it is such powerful, deep replenishment. It helps all our energies circulate and it is good for our health on all levels. Personally, it wasn't always like this for me before I cleansed my memories. In the past with my previous partners, I sometimes felt empty after making love. Why? Because of mine and my partner's distortions. The love we felt for each other was not unconditional; it was marked by expectations and unconscious competitive attitudes. Consequently the energy we exchanged was not pure. After having sex, I felt drained. In order for their sex life to be truly replenishing and regenerative, both partners need to undertake a spiritual path and consciously cleanse their memories marked by the following distortions: jealousy, infidelity, and fear of losing the other person. Then their purified vital energy will be able to circulate freely and beneficially.

Here is another quote that offers beautiful teaching in great simplicity: '*One day, thanks to having cleansed our memories, the fridge is always full.*' This is a quote from my wise husband, Kaya. For the fridge to be always full, we mustn't feel any lack. To better understand this, let's have a brief look at the symbolism of a fridge. Someone who suffers from lack, who is physically, emotionally, mentally and spiritually hungry, tends to devour whatever food he sees, and in so doing, he exhausts himself and empties his resources. This is the outer consequence of all sorts of needs and dependencies. In relationships marked by lack, both partners remain hungry while needs, deficiencies and dependencies proliferate. As long as we bear memories of lack, no matter how well stocked the fridge may be with physical nourishment, we won't know true happiness. We will always eat more than necessary and we'll put on weight. That's why it is so important to work on the distortions of our inner couple with Angel 48 MIHAEL. As soon as our distorted memories have been transcended, we attain a state of conscience wherein the fridge is always full and our resources well managed on all levels of our being. We feel well balanced, and we and our partner are always available for each other.

Let's continue with two other aspects of the Angel MIHAEL Field of Conscience: reproduction and growth. A man shared the following dream with us. *He saw himself with three childhood friends, one of whom is particularly intelligent. All three of them were holding their penises in their hands. They cut them open, took out and cleaned the inner canal, and then put them back in place. The dreamer wondered, "What has this got to do with me?"*

All of the elements of this dream represent parts of this man. First we see that there are only men, so it relates to excessive masculine energies acting intimately; it means also that he is too centered on outer action because the masculine polarity is related to exterior action and the feminine polarity to the inner world. The fact that there are a number of people explains that social life is too important and this creates problems with his intimacy. He was being shown that he was working too rigidly on the purification of his memories and that he tends to cut, to repress his sexuality because he is too much in the intellect. He goes about it too intellectually. This man emanates the energy of a former monk – he even looks like one – so we can understand how he can be tough with himself to avoid any intimate need with a woman, and all the blockages that it can create in his life.

A dream is so powerful. It reveals everything about the personality of the soul. The presence of the number 3 allows us to make a link with Angel 3 SITAEL, whose main Quality is *inner and outer construction*. The symbol of the penis is not only related to to the procreation of children on the physical level, but more generally to the great universal principle of creation – the great creative force that allows us to conceive and realize all sorts of projects. In his efforts to cleanse his memories in order to reconstruct himself, this man sometimes cuts himself off from his creative power. This automatically leads to difficulties in the process of materialization. The childhood friends represent memories related to his childhood in this life, and also to *luggage* or *baggage* recorded in his past lives. By overusing his intellect, this man experiences a discrepancy, which also manifests in his relationship with his wife.

This dream could also have been sent to a woman, because a penis as a symbol of the creative principle and the masculine polarity concerns women just as much as men. If a woman had received this dream, it would have shown her that she sometimes cuts herself off from her creative power, which renders her incapable of using her inner masculine polarity and being emissive when necessary.

Now I'd like to continue with a TV commercial that is also related to the penis symbol, but in a different context. We'll analyze it as if it were a dream. *First of all, we see two young nuns picking white flowers in the convent garden. The tune "Alleluia" is playing in the background. Then the young nuns walk around the garden with their flowers. They stop in front of a statue of a naked child. One of them notices that his penis has fallen off. We see her put her hand over her mouth to stop herself from saying anything. The other nun wraps the tiny piece of penis in a white handkerchief and they bring it to the Mother Superior. She unwraps the white hankie and when she sees the penis, she looks very attentively, intently and severely at the nuns. Then she opens up a drawer in her desk, where we see a tube of extra strong glue. We understand it is a commercial for this brand of glue. Just then, the bell strikes 9 o'clock. Throughout the whole advertisement, none of the nuns says a word. Then we see the Mother Superior head toward the statue, followed by the two young nuns. She applies the glue to the broken piece of penis and sticks it back on again, pointing downward. Then she leaves. As soon as she has her back turned, one of the two young nuns quickly turns the penis so that it is pointing upward.*

Although this commercial has funny aspects, a symbolic analysis reveals several negative aspects related to the repression of intimacy and sexuality. First of all, we see two nuns; the number 2 represents relationships with others. The two branches of white flowers symbolize the beautiful, spiritual feelings that they manifest to others. The statue of the nude child is a symbol of identification. The presence of statues indicates resonance with what the statues represent. We admire them, and would like to be or become what they symbolize. For the two young nuns, the nude child statue represents purity and innocence.

The nun's gesture of putting her hand over her mouth when she sees the broken penis clearly shows that she prevents herself from expressing what she feels. This gesture indicates the presence of repressed memories. There had always been a penis on this child statue, but seeing it severed became a trigger that awakened repressed emotions in the two young nuns. Their reaction is typical of rigidified, spiritual memories, marked by celibacy and forbidden sexual relationships; even though it was a child, we can feel this in the energy of the commercial. So we can understand why sometimes there are instances of sexual abuse with children in the Catholic Church, especially the multiplicity of scandals in the last years. This extreme way of forcing celibacy in spiritual practice was imposed long ago in order to apparently attain the highest levels of conscience. Whenever we bear such memories, a healthy relationship, and in particular, the intimate relationship between a man and a woman, will be so difficult. These memories will awaken and manifest, either in great urges and desire, or in punitive restraint. Such a concentration of memories is not easy to cleanse and it takes a long time, but it can be done with Angel Recitation. Angel 20 Pahaliah is an Angel used to cleanse these repressed forces to attain real transcendence of sexuality.

When the Mother Superior learns about the incident, she is not impressed. She looks intently and severely at each of the young nuns before opening a drawer containing a tube of glue among other things. She wants to give the impression that she is in charge of the situation and knows how to carry out her spiritual responsibilities, when in actual fact her creative force has been extinguished by too much rigidity. This can be seen in her facial features and read in her eyes.

Through the power conferred on her, the Mother Superior maintains this apparent mastery, which is in fact control. Nevertheless, she does want to repair it. She takes her tube of glue, and, followed by the two nuns, she sets off to stick the broken penis back on. But when her back is turned, one of the young nuns turns the penis so that it points upward. Symbolically, this gesture indicates sexual stimulation exerted by nudity.

If we watch this advertisement while in an ordinary conscience, it seems funny. However, it contains a considerable negative side through the fact that those who made it used a statue of a child. This advertisement may awaken memories of incest and pedophilia.

The symbolic meaning of incest refers to the stimulation of the vital, sexual energy of someone close to us, in our family or care, who is not mature and old enough for such stimulation. People – monks and nuns – who live in monasteries and convents often harbor a great number of repressed emotions, sometimes so rigorously repressed that all it takes is a minor trigger element for the repressed emotional force to emerge in a such an act. This kind of repression may also lead to acts of pedophilia.

Numerous scandals have muddied the Catholic Church these past few years. The fact that Catholic priests, unlike ministers in other religions, are not allowed to marry and have to live a life of total sexual abstinence is a source of great frustration and sexual repression. In the grip of these forces and under the influence of repressed, transcended needs, as well as the fact that they live in an exclusively male world, many priests and monks, consciously or unconsciously become homosexuals. The schisms the Catholic Church experienced in past centuries, which resulted in the Protestant movement, stemmed partly from the fact that marriage was forbidden for priests. In our society today, this subject is often a taboo because it upsets the naivety of those people who refuse to see certain major problems in the Church. However, one day, the memories and *karmic luggage* accumulated throughout the course of several past lives spent in a rigid, fossilized, religious structure have to be faced and purified. With the Power of Angel 48 MIHAEL, we can transform and transcend such memories and attain good balance and equilibrium in a love relationship. It will then be healthy and right, based on fidelity and the fusion of the two complementary polarities, and it will reflect marital harmony.

I'd like to continue with the subject of menstruation, which is related to fecundity, fertility, and is therefore also related to the Angel MIHAEL Field of Conscience. What follows will help men better understand certain changes in attitude their partners may have during their menstrual period. It will also help free them from any prejudice they may have regarding this subject. Menstruation is often a difficult time for women. Knowledge of the initiatic dimension of menstrual periods helps to live with them well.

While I was preparing the Angel 48 MIHAEL lecture and workshop and all the examples had been chosen, I received a message from a young 23-year-old woman who is on an intense spiritual path. She wrote to me, saying, "I know we ought to develop spiritual autonomy, but I feel I should share this with you." This young woman follows signs from Heaven and she was right. As soon as I read her story, I knew it should be included in our books since it could truly help women and the new generations to understand the metaphysical and spiritual role of menstruation.

Here is what she shared. After separating from her boyfriend, this young woman decided to stop taking the pill, and since then her menstrual periods had stopped. She understood the disappointment, sadness and depression she felt were due to this separation. Her life had become dull and insipid. She linked what she was feeling with the fact that her periods had stopped. She reacted by doing intense spiritual work on her memories, and gradually, her enthusiasm and joy for life returned – but not her periods! She told me she felt ashamed not to have her periods, but didn't understand why she felt ashamed. Angel 48 MIHAEL is her Guardian Angel on the physical level, so she invoked Him intensely to discover the profound cause behind the absence of her periods. Through the dreams and signs she was sent, she'd managed to understand a lot of things, but she needed to deepen her understanding.

During the period of time she was working intensely on the symbolism of menstruation with Angel 48 MIHAEL, her landlord asked her to turn on the self-cleaning function of the oven in her apartment. She activated this function and immediately the oven made a noise as though refusing to carry out this cleaning work. Straightaway, she made a link between her own inner work and the oven.

As a receptacle, an oven symbolizes the feminine principle, receptivity, warmth and love that transforms. In this case, it was an electric oven. Electricity represents the fire element, therefore, the spirit and the masculine principle. Let's analyze the technical aspect of a self-cleaning oven. The oven must be empty and heated to a much higher temperature than used for cooking or baking. This young woman made the link between the symbolism of an oven and the womb. She understood that she harbored memories of lack of love, which were preventing her from transforming and cleansing certain distortions.

She also made the link with the expression sometimes used regarding pregnant women: *she's got a bun in the oven.* Although she had a general understanding of this dynamic, it remained rather abstract. She needed to understand the links in greater depth. Feeling the benefits of Angel Recitation, she continued to work intensely with the Angels. Simultaneously, she asked to be given access to the world of causes in order to understand why her periods hadn't come back.

One evening, she ate out with a friend who was going through a separation with his wife. Of course, she was aware that this man represented part of her inner man. Before meeting him, she had an intuitive feeling that Cosmic Intelligence was going to send her a message through this friend. She listened to him attentively as he shared his current difficulties. Among other things, she learned that both his daughters were ill. He had also confided in another friend, who had told him he was in the process of dealing with a large knot or blockage. This young woman explained his situation in the Light of the Teachings of Traditional Angelology. "You are experiencing an awakening of a great block of unconscious memories." The man had realized that he had a right to love but that he unconsciously refused this right. When the young woman heard that, she was deeply moved. She became aware that she hadn't allowed herself the right to love either. She asked me for advice.

I returned to her short, but very judgmental, sentence: "I'm ashamed not to have my period." I explained to her that she too was visiting blocks of memories. Her very intense spirituality came from her past lives. We'll see and understand what was awakened in her and what caused this awakening. When I myself was in deep initiation, I sometimes had very lengthy, abundant periods with blood clots. At other times, it was the very opposite, and my periods stopped for several months. Whenever a woman goes through deep initiations, she can expect to experience this kind of phenomena because working on our memories causes upheaval in our physical body and in our hormonal system. Of course, it is advisable to consult a gynecologist to ensure there is nothing seriously wrong on the physical level.

Let's analyze the symbolism of menstruation. What is menstruation on the physical level? It is the monthly bleeding that occurs in women when the uterus eliminates the inner lining tissues that had been formed to welcome a fertilized egg. When fertilization hasn't taken place, menstruation begins in order to allow for the renewal of these tissues. This renewal occurs periodically, in a discontinuous fashion, unlike the continual renewal of our skin and other mucus membranes.

On the metaphysical level, menstrual problems relate to innumerable memories. Many traditions, including Christian, Jewish, and Hindu used to impose – and in some regions in the world, still impose – the quarantine of menstruating women. Considered impure during their period, they didn't have the right to enter sacred places. When memories of such prohibitions awaken, revealing old ways of thinking, the situations and soul-states or moods we go through may be very difficult to bear.

I explained to this young woman that memories of forced reserve and shame, accumulated over many lives, had awakened in her. In other lives, she may have been a man. She could have subjected women to this kind of quarantine. Erroneous concepts related to menstruation are deeply buried in the collective unconscious. She may then have had lives as a woman in religious contexts, which inculcated shame regarding menstruation and the feeling of being impure. In her present life, she is being called upon to work on this reservoir of distorted memories.

Nowadays, in some societies where there is no true spirituality, this outdated concept of impurity persists, since a woman who has her period is momentary proof of failed fecundity. Long ago when it was necessary to populate the Earth, it was important to have a lot of children, who, at the same time, guaranteed the workforce, hence the family's survival. Since women mostly went from one pregnancy to another, each followed by a long period of breastfeeding, they had hardly any periods. Hence a menstruating woman was considered impure and infertile.

Knowing the symbolism of menstruation, we can reconsider its physical and metaphysical role and offer young girls and boys right, just, appropriate sexual education.

When Kasara had her first period, I explained to her, "Kasara, your period is a beautiful sign of femininity and fertility. It is telling you that you now have the power of fecundity; you are now capable of having children and thus participating in the process of the creation of human life. Simultaneously, your periods are a means to purify you. It is important to understand the role they play and the various phenomena related to them. If you knew how many women I've met who no longer have their periods, who have become sterile, and how desperate they are about it!"

For Kasara, the highest, utmost, ultimate project of hers is to have children, to found a family. It's inscribed in her Program. No one ever notices when Kasara has her period. It doesn't affect her mood. Only unexpectedly catching sight of a small sanitary towel in the waste-bin allows me to guess. I deepened the subject and said, "Menstruation is purification *via* blood. And as you know, blood represents vital energy. In some women, the distorted memories they harbor in their unconscious, as well as the erroneous or deficient education they received about menstruation, leads them to a difficult experience of their period. Each month, they are confronted with memories that awaken, and if they don't have Knowledge to understand the phenomena they are going through, nor the tools to work on these memories, it can be very intense. They may feel and even manifest aggression toward themselves and others. This purification period should be welcomed as a positive phase for inner cleansing and renewal. We always feel better afterwards, remember that..."

Initiates, both men and women, constantly visit memories. On the physical level, a man doesn't menstruate, but on the metaphysical level, he too goes through corresponding cycles and processes. Menstruation represents powerful purification of vital energy that affects memories related to the first chakra, which particularly concerns our roots and functioning on the physical level.

When the unconscious opens and negative memories are reactivated, for some women this manifests in difficult, painful periods. A woman in an ordinary conscience will say that it's her period that causes her to feel unwell, whereas it is actually her negative memories that are the true cause.

Let's analyze the link with blood. At the sight of blood, our mind and spirit may enter into contact with memories related to accidents, death, illness, lack of fertility, and all sorts of difficulties. It is important for women to agree to go through initiations that involve purification. Instead of referring to impurity, a female initiate is glad to have her period because she knows purification is taking place. She welcomes this purification because it will allow her to attain the highest levels of conscience. Such awareness completely transforms the erroneous vision that people often have regarding menstruation.

As we have seen, menstruation is related to fertility. The first time a teenager has her period is a time for rejoicing because it is a sign that she is fertile and that she is now entering a new stage of life. However, we mustn't neglect the fact that although the beginning of the menstrual cycle indicates the beginning of maturity for the physical body, it does not mean that the girl has reached emotional and psychological maturity.

Menstruation is periodically inhibited when a woman becomes pregnant, and disappears completely at the menopause, a stage in life that people in an ordinary conscience tend to associate with sterility. How many women have cursed their periods and then, on reaching menopause, would love to maintain them only because menopause is considered a sign of sterility and old age!

Women who value the material level and physical aspects will find it difficult to accept the absence of menstruation and being infertile. But spiritual women understand that fecundity is not limited to the physical level. It manifests in their relationship with a man on the level of thoughts, emotions, actions, and projects. Fecundity is as vast as the Universe! It is important to know that in its positive, multi-dimensional aspect, menopause symbolizes the transcendence of procreation, which allows women's creative potential to be elevated to other levels. It is often positively referred to as the *change of life*.

A lot of women going through menopause have hot flashes. Let's analyze this phenomenon that I too experienced, although not for long. Why do hot flashes occur? They are an emergence of unpurified memories and accumulated tension. It is vital to know and understand that, apart from the physical aspect I've just explained, the mood we feel during our period or menopause is always related to our memories. Women who aren't on a spiritual path, who haven't worked on themselves, arrive at menopause with an overload of memories and no means of understanding what they are experiencing on the metaphysical level. On the inside, blockages activate the mind and spirit's fire, and materialize as disturbing hot flashes. When we know how to work on these blockages, and how to cleanse, purify, transform and transcend negative memories, hot flashes and other symptoms associated with menopause disappear.

We need to observe when hot flashes occur. In my case, they always manifested when certain thoughts were re-awakened at particular times, during particular events. Those hot flashes were a call for me to purify. While menopause is a symbol of infertility and old age for some women, for the women who undergo this change of life well it can become a period of great liberty in the couple's intimate relationship. I personally bear witness to the fact that it is the most beautiful time in my life regarding sexuality. Work on distortions, such as jealousy, infidelity, fear of losing the other person, led to my inner completeness. It allowed me to experience great liberation, rejuvenation and increased vital energy through spirituality. It is true that initiations engender fatigue or ill-being, but we must realize that it is for our own good, that they help us improve. I can assure you that the more time goes by, the better I feel, nourished by inner wisdom that leads to true happiness. This state of conscience is formed on the level of our inner couple. Even people who do not have a spouse or life partner at the moment can do this inner work on themselves. It will lead them to true happiness and inner completeness.

This understanding quite naturally leads us to consider the menstrual cycle as renewal instead of death because the egg hasn't been fertilized. This also explains why for women who have their period, Cosmic Intelligence sometimes orchestrates a visit to memories that have nothing to do with pregnancy, but which concern death in a more general way as the end of a cycle or stage that precedes renewal or rebirth: dying to be reborn. The person who doesn't know this concept may be overwhelmed with sadness and depression, whereas anyone who knows this initiatic process rejoices in the renewal and transformation it will bring about. That is why things go well when menstruation is considered as a reflection of femininity and experienced as purification.

A metaphysical understanding of menstruation and the menopause is not only beneficial for women but also for men, the couple and family life in general. It offers the new generations a different vision of fertility. What wonderful reprogramming that will help them avoid a lot of turmoil and many inner and outer conflicts!

Now let's move on to another issue related to the inner couple. Sometimes people wonder whether they have finished their apprenticeship with their spouse, whether their spiritual path has led to their no longer having any resonance. Such a question is very important and must be considered for each individual case. Indeed, it mainly depends on the memories of both people concerned, and we cannot trust appearances. Each case is different but the process of awareness is the same: before making any decision regarding separation, we ask for dreams and signs to find out if there is still something we need to learn with our spouse.

Let me give you a concrete example. A woman who had been married for 6 years told me that she had never had any affinity with her husband on the spiritual and intellectual levels; they existed on the physical and emotional levels. Her husband is a good person but she found life with him boring. She tried to help their relationship evolve but he didn't change. So she understood that the evolution she desired and needed wasn't part of her husband's program. Although he was a very nice, gentle person, their relationship engendered conflict.

This woman is a psychologist, working in the field of health. Having specialized in mutual aid, she shared her knowledge in radio programs. She told me that their attempts to have a child remained fruitless. The couple tried all sorts of therapies but no baby answered their call. Then, when the couple gave up all the treatments, she became pregnant. However, she lost the baby after a few months. She took this as a sign asking, "Are we really made for one another? Is it right for us to have a child together?" In a climate of beautiful communication, the couple decided to give themselves a year to regain harmony. If nothing had changed in a year's time, they would separate.

During that year, the woman came to know the Teachings of the Traditional Study of Angels. She already dreamed a lot and she'd used her dreams to help her make this decision. At an opportune moment, she asked, "Is it right for the evolution of my soul to remain with my husband, or is it right for us to separate?" She received the answer in a dream. *She saw herself on a magnificent horse with a beautiful, luminous man, a truly handsome prince, radiating Light. She saw her husband on the ground. He had an extra tooth in his palate and he wasn't happy. My husband Kaya was there too. She heard a voice say, "You have the choice of staying with your husband or leaving with this man."*

In this dream, Cosmic Intelligence offered this woman a choice that affected her spiritual dimension since Kaya was present. For people working with The Traditional Study of Angels and symbolic language, my husband symbolizes spirituality applied on the concrete action level. The dream reveals to her what creates her duality.

All of the elements of the dream represent parts of the dreamer; not only the radiant prince. Teeth symbolize the structure of wisdom and also, given their usefulness when we eat, our primary needs. The fact that there is an extra tooth that isn't in the right place indicates that the woman has too many primary, instinctual needs in her masculine energy while she also has a great spiritual potential with the radiant prince. It's because of these needs that she attracts this kind of husband. A horse symbolizes vital energy and determination to advance. Two currents seem to be in opposition and she has to choose between them, and the prince is not yet in her life. She isn't told what to do. Why not? Because there are residual memories and she isn't sure of her choice. She wishes for a highly spiritual relationship but she has forces that stop her change, her evolution, to become this new relationship with the radiant prince. The duality is a 100% in her. She feels very happy and not happy simultaneously.

Finally, the couple decided not to separate. First, the woman moved into a cottage on a campsite in order to take a step back to review their situation and see what it's like to live alone. This woman shared with me how difficult it was for her to decide because her husband is a kind, devoted man who does everything for her, but she finds their life together uninteresting. She tried to interest him in Angel Teachings and Angel Work, but in vain. Intellectually, he hasn't much to say and he is continually absorbed by sports on the TV. She was very affected by this situation.

One night, this woman received another dream wherein *she saw a white winter coat on the side of the highway. A voice said, "The owner of this coat has been chosen by ..." and she heard the name of a man she knows in concrete reality. He's a man who is on a spiritual path. She looked at the label and saw her name written there. Then she found herself at her parents' home and her husband was there. However, he was awkward and ill-at-ease as though he was no longer in his rightful place, as though there was no room for him there anymore. Her brother couldn't believe his ears when she announced that she was the happy chosen one. Then in the car her brother heard a cassette where the man in question was talking and he said that she was his chosen one. After that, she saw the man, radiant, who said, "In a minute." She saw him a minute later. Then another man appeared. He was handsome and emanated wisdom, like a Guide in the parallel worlds. He brought her down into the basement. When they came out, he showed her a huge building site under construction.* What does this dream mean?

I told her that were two possible interpretations. She may have visited the soul of the man in question, and in that case, she was being shown "Yes, it's him." Or, she was only being shown parts of herself. We need to be vigilant with this kind of dream and always remember that, even if we visit a person's soul in a dream, all of the elements shown also represent parts of ourselves. God showed her what kind of energy she conveys and strives toward, but also what aspects she still needs to work on. Up Above, They are excellent pedagogues. Whenever a difficult phase is planned in a person's program, They send the person a dream like this to encourage them. Up Above, They know how difficult solitude may be, especially when our faith isn't strong enough.

I warned this woman that the man in the dream is not necessarily the man who will replace her husband –that he might be only a symbol. The winter coat on the side of the highway represents her capacity to keep warm during the times she goes through cold soul-states while advancing toward others in her search for spiritual love. The fact that the coat is white indicates that this capacity stems from her spirituality. Then she is in her parents' home; her parents are premonitory symbols regarding action. Why premonitory? Because, in a way, our parents are our origin, the beginning of something, the co-creators of our physical body, thanks to which we can act in matter, on the action level. Their presence in this dream indicates that this woman is concretely committed to a stage where she is going to change partners. It is not only an inner stage she's going through. New behavior regarding life is being born in her and she is almost ready to transcend and to activate a new masculine energy in her that could eventually lead to meet a new man. We see that her husband no longer has his place in this woman's intimate, family, and personal life. The woman's brother, who is like a protector for her, is also present in the dream and he is happy to hear that his sister is heading toward a new relationship. The presence of her brother indicates that the new energy emanated by the dreamer is beginning to radiate in her, in her inner family. It also means that her capacity to decide is getting stronger because it is validated on the family level.

By saying, *In a minute*, she is being told that the time for meeting her chosen one is close. I explained that she could have been told a month or ten years. They chose a minute to encourage her, but a minute may sometimes last a lot longer than we expect. In the meantime, the man who resembled a Guide from the parallel worlds brings her down into the basement, which symbolizes the subconscious. There she sees work in progress on a huge building site. This represents the extent of reconstruction work that is going on in her conscience so she will be ready to welcome this new spiritual love. While she carries out this work, she needs to be patient because the minute won't necessarily be the shortest minute of her life.

I asked this woman how she had asked her question. She told me she had asked that question in a moment of dismay and despair when she'd felt all alone in her cottage on the campsite. She'd cried while doing Angel Recitation, praying and wondering if she was deluded. She thought of the many couples who put up with an ordinary relationship and stay together even though they find their life colorless and uninteresting. As there are still few men on a spiritual path, she thought she was deluding herself that she could have a spiritual spouse. She still had a lot of doubts.

She was sent this dream to encourage her. Although he may well be, it is not at all sure that the man in the dream is the person destined for her. We need to be very careful when we receive a symbol of a person in a dream. It can only announce that someone with this type of energy will come in our life and Up Above uses a symbol because it is more easy to say it will be this new man when the dreamer doesn't have any reference to understand what type of person or kind of situation it will be. We have seen this very often with men and women who were experiencing these kinds of dreams, on the verge of changing their lives, evolving to a new relationship without having met the exact person. A dream is always true and real, but it can be so on many levels – sometimes on the spiritual level, or on the intellectual, emotional or physical level. The most important thing is to develop divine qualities. And this can take many forms. So when in doubt, it is important not to do anything, not to project our needs and expectations onto others so we will not create an illusion of love, a projection of our desire onto others. If a man or a woman is not interested in you, and you are in love in dreams, it can only indicate that you tend to love people that do not want you. You have opposition in your memories that create these types of dualities. When the right person is announced in a dream, all the stars are aligned... not only in dreams but also in reality. We then receive confirmation in dreams of the steps that we can take toward the person. This woman knew it was most unlikely that the man in her dream was her destined spouse because he lives in another country and their encounter was limited to a few spiritual conversations. She was almost certain that he was only a symbol for her, that he was a symbol of her coming aspiration. We need to use dreams as scientists. Dreams are much more logical than we could imagine, even if they present a distant future that is not ready to manifest yet.

However, given all the changes she was going through and all that she had called into question, she felt disorientated because she had too many needs. She was not detached enough from her wish to meet someone. It was an obsession for her and it shouldn't have been. We need to put in first place the notion of developing divine qualities. Once we have them in us, it is absolute that divine love and wisdom will manifest in the incarnation of our twin soul. She was almost 40 years old and her ardent desire to have a child also was putting pressure on her. I explained to her the importance of accepting her program and to do the best you can simultaneously to make it evolve but without forcing of course. Biological maternity and paternity are not planned for all of our lives. In some of them, we may have to work on our nun and monk *luggage*, and our program provides us with an opportunity to help others by developing a capacity to love, as well as all the qualities of a spiritual mother or father. When we develop the state of conscience of altruistic love and a planetary family, we consider all children on Earth as our children. The key to happiness is the acceptance of our Life Plan, our Life Program. The principle aim of our life plan is not to procreate and materialize, but to go through the various, pre-ordained stages as virtuously as possible. What's important are the memories recorded in our soul. Being able to accept our program means we are able to accept life as it is, without asking for anything else.

This woman also shared a repetitive dream. In this dream, *she sees herself with her ex-husband. He dies and is reborn and she goes back to him.* I explained to her that through this dream, because her ex-husband was not a good symbol for her, she was being shown she needed to die to a certain kind of relationship. To do so, she needed to cleanse the memories related to it. As long as this work wasn't done, she risked attracting the same kind of man and having the same kind of relationship.

In another dream, *she saw a woman measuring a fat-bellied man's waist. It measured 53 inches. The woman told him he needed to change that; he needed to undertake therapy, otherwise he'd no longer be insured.* This dream revealed aspects of the dreamer's inner man. So you see that the radiant prince and the duality with her present husband was really there.

Symbolically, being fat-bellied means that we've overeaten, that we are too heavy, and have too many primary needs. The number 53 refers to Angel 53 NANAEL. The list of human distortions of this Angelic Field of Conscience includes: *refuses spirituality and Knowledge, difficulty achieving our aims and communicating, difficulty living as a couple.* When we receive a number in a dream, it does not mean we have to work with its corresponding Angel. The number is simply part of the symbolism of the dream. Checking the Angelic Qualities and human distortions associated with the number allows us to become aware of other aspects of ourselves that we need to develop or rectify.

In this dream, the dreamer was being told that if she doesn't work on these aspects, she will no longer be insured. Here it's a question of Celestial, Heavenly Insurance. What does that mean? Celestial Insurance is the Insurance we have on the metaphysical and spiritual level when we respect Divine Laws and behave qualitatively in a right, just manner, and take right, just, qualitative action; i.e., when we live in accordance with qualities and virtues. This Insurance forewarns us of the concrete consequences we will have if we behave in a distorted manner or if we make the wrong decision due to too many needs on the masculine, concrete level, in our emissive energy mixed with spirituality, because of the 53 inches in her case. When a person sometimes very stubbornly resists opening up to spirituality and refuses to rectify his erroneous behavior, Cosmic Intelligence has to orchestrate ordeals and difficult events in his concrete reality to incite him to reflect on his behavior and way of living. In such cases, the person no longer has any Celestial Insurance. No matter how many earthly insurance policies he may have, they won't prevent his experiencing the ordeals he has to go through in order to learn.

The dreamer was experiencing this duality and her great inner suffering made this transition period very difficult. Her dreams showed her a change of program, a new stage. She needed to be patient and continue working on her memories and her inner couple. When God decided the time was right, the path to follow would appear.

Here is an example another woman shared with us. In her family, everyone except her husband works intensely with the Traditional Study of Angels. This woman had been on a spiritual path for several years and she was in despair. She told me, "My husband doesn't want to hear about Angels. He's too active in matter and sometimes it bothers me." I explained to her that her husband was a part of her, of her inner man, and that she shouldn't forget the Law of Resonance. We have met this man. He's a doctor, who has beautiful values and who is truly devoted to his patients. He is attentive and takes time to listen to them. Generally speaking, he has a good approach and communicates well. I asked this woman, "Don't you think you might have some catching up to do with your husband? Maybe he is more evolved than you on some levels." She looked at me, surprised, but she had understood.

This woman had a lot of rigidity. However, over the years, she has changed. She has become more feminine, which is also manifested in the way she dresses. I said to her, "Don't talk to your husband about Angels, but be inspiring and radiate Angelic Qualities! Don't expect quick results, and, above all, no comparisons! Some people and relationships evolve faster than others due to initiations set off by Angel Work. Other people's evolution is activated thanks to our becoming a beautiful, inspiring model for them when we know how to manifest spirituality in a qualitative way instead of being emissive or imposing."

When initiations lead us into difficult zones of our unconscious, we aren't very attractive or capable of being inspiring examples at that time. So it is important not to complain. But it is also true, especially in our intimate life, that we cannot hide our state, which may lead our spouse to make remarks such as, "What's the point in you being interested in all those things? Look at the state you're in!" In spite of our uninspiring soul-states, we must be patient and tell our spouse we love him/her, that we are working on transforming ourselves to become a better person, a better spouse. We need to reassure our spouse that he/she is not responsible for our bad mood, for the difficult soul states we are going through. Angel Work takes time and we can't skip stages. At times like this, instead of wanting to impose our spirituality on others, we must remain humble and explain to our spouse that the state we are in is due to deep, intense inner work. That will help our spouse understand and it may even become inspiring. Modesty, simplicity, and humility are attitudes we should always have when sharing our dreams with our partner; they'll help him/her to accept the physical manifestations that occur. Generally speaking, a man needs concrete examples, whereas, due to her emotional side, a woman follows her intuition, her feelings first of all. As time goes by, the husband will realize his wife is changing positively. By becoming a better person, she becomes a source of inspiration and happiness for him.

A few months later, I saw this woman again. She told me she had had a wonderful weekend with her husband. They had gone off as lovers for a walk in the mountains, which was an opportunity for beautiful sharing. During the weekend, her husband received the following dream. *He saw himself with a pneumatic drill for digging up the road, but he didn't know whether he was going to dig it up or simply patch the surface.*

It was an easy dream to interpret. She said to her husband, "This dream shows you that you have the ability to dig. A road symbolizes advancing and digging it up means you have the potential to discover memories buried in your unconscious and to transform them. If you dig deep, it will slow down your capacity to advance. All we have to do is transpose the situation to concrete reality: if we want to repair a road, we can either dig down deep to do it well or only patch it up on the surface." Her husband was very moved by the veracity of this interpretation, which reflected exactly what he was going through. He was also moved by this woman – his wife – who had become so much freer, even regarding her sexuality. She has changed a lot over the past few years. Now she is a woman who has blossomed and who radiates beautiful energy; it's wonderful to see her angelic evolution. She has become a source of inspiration for her husband.

The Monday after their weekend in the mountains, this man returned to work in his medical practice. When he came back that evening, his wife lovingly welcomed him home and asked him if he'd had a good day. He replied, "I had a wonderful day because last night I had a beautiful dream." What had he dreamed? He dreamed *he saw himself and his wife holding hands and flying. They flew over the high buildings of a town or city. It was really enjoyable. They flew on a builder's large pencil, and instead of an eraser on the end, there was a little, red jet engine. She wanted to do some shopping so they stopped to do so and then they flew off again.*

All of the elements of this dream represent parts of the dreamer. He was being shown the states of conscience he had experienced with his wife in the mountains. Seeing ourselves fly symbolizes the elevation, capacity to soar and global vision we acquire when we rediscover our Angelic nature. The fact that he was flying with his wife over high city buildings reveals his connection and symbiosis with his feminine principle; it is in connection with a great intelligence, a great communication with a high level of conscience in the relationship. This connection allows him to rise above all physical activities in matter, as symbolized by the city. The whole concrete, physical aspect – matter – had lost its importance to leave room for *takeoff*, elevation, communion, and fusion.

They flew on a builder's pencil. A pencil symbolizes the materialization of ideas and thoughts. When we think, emotions are generated that incite us to act, to manifest and materialize our ideas. During the weekend, this couple had exchanged beautiful, elevating ideas. These ideas allowed this man to fly, to rediscover the freedom and vision that exists in the causal world.

Instead of an eraser, there was a red jet engine. Red symbolizes matter and energy on the concrete, physical level, and a jet engine frees us from gravity. So the jet engine instead of an eraser is a very positive aspect. It means that erasing past memories by transforming them helps us to advance. This man has seen his wife and children all change, one after another. And he realizes that these changes have a beneficial, elevating influence on him, which helps toward the renewal of his life in his relationship with his wife and with his children.

He has become aware of his capacity to repair. He is moved because he understands that he can *write*, construct a new life. It's no coincidence that he's a doctor. Anyone who chooses to become a doctor needs to learn to heal those parts of himself that are ill. While he cares for sick people in the outer world, he does the same work in his inner world, very often without realizing, without knowing that each patient reveals suffering parts in himself. A doctor's job is to repair the consequences experienced in the body caused by negative thoughts and emotions. Physical illnesses and blockages are engendered by our states of mind and soul and our negative memories. In this man's dream, we see that he was very moved by the new intelligence his wife was developing thanks to Angelic Knowledge. For him, her interpretation of his dream was concrete, as was the fact of seeing how gentle, loving and respectful she was. This man's wife is reaping the fruit of her patience and the beautiful work she has accomplished by always referring back to herself each time she felt put out. Knowing that her husband represents part of her inner man, instead of projecting the cause of her annoyances onto him, she identified the resonance and cleansed her memories.

This woman shared this story with me two years ago. While I was preparing this lecture on Angel 48 MIHAEL, the couple's daughter sent me an email telling me her news and sharing her great joy regarding her parents' evolution. Two years after the dream we've just discussed, her father started to do Angel Recitation. The first Angel he invoked was Angel 60 MITZRAEL, whose main Quality is *reparation*.

It is rare to begin with this Angel. Usually, people begin working with the Angel of prosperity or success. This doctor understood that by integrating the Qualities of Angel MITZRAEL – which facilitate *the practice of psychology and psychiatry, and which favor the healing of mental illnesses* – he would be even better able to understand and help his patients. The wonderful quality of patience allowed this woman to set an example for her husband, and he was able to follow and begin to materialize what had become logical for him, thanks to this Teaching. This was part of their program and we are very happy for them. However, we also need to understand and accept that sometimes a couple's program follows a different plan; other things may have been preordained for them.

Now I'd like to talk about a song by Natasha St-Pier called "J'avais quelqu'un" – "I Had Someone." This artist sings some nice songs, including "Je n'ai que mon âme" – "I've Only Got My Soul", which is truly wonderful on the spiritual level. The song we are going to discuss explains inner problems regarding the couple. I suggest you listen to it and analyze it using symbolic language if you understand the language it is sung in. Otherwise, I suggest you listen to the various tones of voice and, if by any chance you see the accompanying video-clip, closely observe the singer's body language; you'll be surprised at how much you understand regarding the singer's true intentions and the ambiance created. Indeed, it's a very good training exercise to listen to lyrics and music we like with a vertical conscience, as if we were in a dream. The tone of voice (as well as the scenario and singer's body language in their video clip) is often very revealing too.

Natasha St-Pier's video clip for "I Had Someone" shows this young woman's very emissive social side that looks after others better than she does her partner. She is too much on the outside and doesn't listen enough to her inner world or her lover's. Although the lyrics express regret that their relationship failed, her smile and body language do not. When she sings, "I had someone...," we can see her jaw is a little twisted, and metaphysically, we perceive that she is in contact with distorted memories. There is a lack of depth and authenticity in what she emanates. We can feel that the singer is a little lost in matter and fame, and this is transcribed in her songs.

The song mentioned awakens and brings to light certain states of conscience that we may experience when a love relationship crumbles because we don't take time for the other person. We don't acknowledge them; we don't really grant them a place in our life. We take their presence for granted and end up considering them as part of the furniture. We spend hours on the phone talking to others, and the rare times we listen to our partner, we only half-listen. Hence, hurt and frustration accumulate, discrepancies grow and the rift widens. It's the kind of situation a lot of couple's experience when both partners are too focused on the outside, work, friends, social activities and leisure. In an ordinary conscience, very often the relationship begins flamboyantly and rapidly evolves into great passion. As time goes by, passion fades, the relationship crumbles, becomes boring, and ends in separation; or, the couple accept an inert relationship, solely focused on the children, paying off the mortgage for their home, and a humdrum daily routine.

When we are in a couple relationship and we work on ourselves through Angel Recitation and dream analysis, we must be careful to look after our love relationship and family well. We need to remain vigilant because our dreams can be very destabilizing. Whenever we are shown distorted aspects of ourselves, we mustn't project them onto our partner; we must remain attentive to him. When we transform ourselves and become an example, they will gradually feel incited to create changes in themselves. However, if nothing happens and if we receive dreams that they are no longer the right person for us, then we take our courage in both hands and we end the relationship.

When a couple are both on a spiritual path and are working together on their inner couple, then the process is inverted. The more the relationship advances, the more the partners communicate and intensify work on their inner couple, the better they love each other. It's an absolute fact! What's more, like absolute Truth, it leads to infinite expansion.

Listening in symbols enriches and develops profound listening. While the other person is talking, we don't start thinking, 'I have to do this or I didn't do that yet...' We are deeply sensitive and tactful, and we listen with all our soul, even if the other person isn't right, isn't at his best. We listen and we are conscious that what we do to others, we do to ourselves. All that we think, say and do is inscribed in us. We reap all that we sow. That's the Law of Return. And like the Law of Resonance, it applies all the time, in all circumstances and situations.

By working on ourselves, we learn to be unconditional. A woman has the capacity to create atmospheres and ambiances; this comes from her particularly powerful emotional side. The atmosphere and ambiance created in the home have a very powerful effect. However, it is very important to create them, without any expectations, without wanting anything in return, and not pride ourselves on them or become possessive. In our dreams, we can be confronted with these aspects, revealing our expectations, possessiveness, and relentless pursuit to have everything perfect and just the way we want.

Let's move on to another subject: twin souls. How can we find our twin soul?

A woman received the following dream. *She saw herself in her kitchen. There was food in brown bags. She told herself that her husband hadn't tidied the food away. Then she went into the sitting room. Her husband was sleeping and he woke up. When she went back into the kitchen, there were two pink-fleshed fish on the worktop and there were two stones near the fish. A cat came along and ate the head of another cat. Only its paws were left. Then she saw her husband go outside. He was carrying a tree.*

Two days later, her husband told her he was leaving her, and four months later, he moved in with another woman. It was a complete shock for this woman who has two children with this man.

In this dream, she didn't visit her husband's soul. She was shown her own program and what was going to happen. The kitchen is a symbol of preparation. There are resources but not yet tidied away. The sitting room represents her masculine principle on the social level. Through the symbol of her husband sleeping and then waking up, she was shown parts of her inner man, who, inspired by social intimacy, were in the process of waking up and becoming active. The negative memories related to the couple were reactivated. Then she goes back into the kitchen where she sees two fish, two stones and two cats. The number 2 represents the relationship with others. In Traditional Angelology, it refers to Angel 2 JELIEL.

As an animal that lives in water, a fish symbolizes primary or instinctual energy associated with emotional needs. The fish were dead so we need to consider the negative aspect of this symbol. The two stones refer to the mineral kingdom, which symbolizes the deep unconscious, memories of very old, ancient actions which have become crystallized, petrified. Through the cat symbol, she was being shown that she has a tendency to nourish the negative aspects of this animal in her, i.e., too much independence in her relationship with the man. A cat comes and goes as it pleases; it may also be very capricious, sneaky, and hypocritical. The independence this woman nourishes on the thought level in order to feel good is not right independence. It is not true independence. She uses it as a protective shell to flee the relationship. But this shell also prevents her from being intimately involved in her relationship. Through the image of her husband leaving and carrying a tree, she is being told that she will feel uprooted on the action level. The cause of this uprooting is to be found in her excessive independence and the fact that she continues to feed on old, dead emotions on the affective, sentimental level. And that's exactly what this woman felt.

She had just begun a spiritual path with the Teachings of Traditional Angelology when she received this dream. She was in the process of doing great work on herself. The separation from her husband meant the house, which was in joint ownership, had to be sold. She also had to change jobs and find an apartment, which was difficult for her. She received another dream, wherein *she was looking for an apartment with her husband – her ex-husband.* I explained to her that she was being shown that she was trying to rebuild her life – find an apartment, create a home for her children, etc. – with the same kind of negative masculine energy, the same state of mind, of conscience that she had functioned with before. Even though the separation from her husband had set in motion a whole series of changes in her outer world, she still needed to do great cleansing in her memories. The move she was forced to do in concrete reality also had to be accomplished on the metaphysical level, i.e., she also had to change her mentality, her state of conscience.

Time went by and one evening this woman made a request to the Angels: she wanted to meet her twin soul. She described the kind of man she was looking for. During the night, she received this dream. *She saw three women and one man. One of the women said to her, "This man is your twin soul." She turned round and she was disappointed because the man had a big nose. The woman went on to tell her that the man's mother worked with Traditional Angelology. Then, another woman, who in concrete reality also follows the Teachings of Traditional Angelology and who had found her twin soul, told her, "Your English teacher has blue eyes and he's a homosexual." She was standing beside a stairway. The dreamer went up to the teacher and saw that indeed he had blue eyes. He gave her a black file but she would have liked a yellow one.*

This is a very interesting dream. Why? Because people often make requests of the Universe, repeating non-stop, "I want this, I want that, I want, I want, I want..." If a person is sufficiently evolved to receive an evaluation, a profound diagnosis of himself, the Universe, either in dreams or through signs, shows him the memories and aspects of himself that he needs to cleanse and rectify before being granted his request.

The number 3 corresponds to Angel 3 SITAEL, the Angel of inner and outer construction. There were 3 three women so it refers to inner construction. Regarding her inner construction, the dreamer is shown memories of her past, symbolized by the man in the background. His big nose symbolizes overly instinctual needs. This organ calls to mind an animal's snout and concerns the sense of smell, which is related to the first chakra. This man's mother works with Traditional Angelology. Generally speaking, a mother symbolizes the inner world. This confirms for the dreamer that at this stage, she would attract a spiritual man, but that he was still too instinctual. She was being told that great purification work and development of qualities was in progress, but not yet completed.

Then she meets another young woman, who in concrete reality also works with the Traditional Study of Angels and who has already found her twin soul. This means that on the spiritual level, part of the dreamer has already contacted – is already in contact with – her twin soul. This young woman introduced her to her English teacher. Symbolically, English corresponds to expansion, but in this dream, it refers to expansion within the couple. So she needs to give priority to work on her inner couple, and more particularly on the memories that this English teacher represents. His blue eyes symbolize spiritual vision. Hence he represents part of her inner man that has already been on a spiritual path. The teacher is homosexual, which indicates a depolarization. Given his spiritual eyes, this teacher part indicates that she needs to study, in the Light of Initiatic Science, those aspects of her inner man that lead to discrepancy regarding expansion. It is a serious discrepancy that has led to the manifestation of homosexuality. Many homosexuals have great qualities, sometimes much greater than many heterosexuals. We have encountered several during our lecture tours and some of them have told us about their deep wounds.

Homosexuality manifests in people who have been deeply hurt and wounded by the other polarity. These wounds come from this life or from many past lives. By becoming homosexual, they unconsciously seek to flee former, difficult behavior experienced in relationships as a couple or in the family, where the burden of responsibilities prevented them from satisfying their personal needs. As homosexual relationships are naturally childless, this allows them to concentrate on their need for material expansion and worldly pleasures. We all have memories, percentages, at various levels in our unconsciousness of homosexuality. Many people that are not homosexuals received dreams about that subject. We mustn't judge these people, because whenever we harbor memories of experiences with the other sex that bitterly disappointed us and profoundly hurt our soul, it sometimes takes one or several lives to get over them. Understanding this allows us to have compassion for homosexuals. For the soul, homosexuality is an experimentation like so many others.

This dream shows this woman that she needs to face up to memories she has that are marked by depolarization, which affects both symbols of English and homosexuality, hence a desire for expansion, the satisfaction of material needs and worldly pleasures. The black file that the homosexual teacher holds out to her symbolizes hidden aspects related to the difficulties mentioned. She would have liked a yellow file – yellow symbolizes confidence. Hence she was being shown that she'd like to acquire confidence immediately without studying hidden aspects of herself; her unconscious memories are more focused on material expansion than seeking her twin soul. Now, however, she is sufficiently evolved to do the necessary work. This beautiful dream is an encouragement that stimulates Angel Work and patience to, one day, find Love with a capital L.

Here is another very revealing dream that is full of teaching. On one of our trips, just as I was thinking about a dream I had received, we were overtaken by a car whose registration number was 488. For me 488 meant Angel 48 MIHAEL and Angel 8 CAHETEL that represents Divine Materialization. It was a very beautiful dream.

I was with Kaya on a beach. The sea was a beautiful, sky blue. It was a beautiful sunny day and a dune on our left sheltered us from the wind. A light breeze created a very pleasant atmosphere. I was holding Kaya's hand and he said to me, "Come on, let's fly." And we both took off. It was so beautiful, so pleasant! We were flying in the air! As we flew, I recalled a dream Kaya had received several years ago. In that dream, he was told that the Teachings of Traditional Angelology were 4000 years ahead of present day human consciousness. We had been given a certain power and it was important not to reveal it. But I could see that it didn't bother anyone because people in a solely material conscience couldn't believe it. This ensured our tranquility while allowing us to continue our evolution. Still flying, I continued my reflection and said to myself, 'It would be so nice to be able to travel like this in concrete reality during our lecture tours.' Then, I immediately corrected myself, saying, 'No, no, there's concrete physical reality and all the boxes of books and material to be transported. It is important to respect this dimension.' And I agreed with my thoughts. We landed in front of a hotel. Arm in arm, we tenderly went into reception, where a very nice man handed me a mauve file.

In this dream, I was shown my inner couple and my thoughts regarding Divine materialization. A couple flying symbolizes the intellectual and spiritual fusion of both polarities and, in this case, there was also fusion on the work level. The mauve file symbolizes studying the spiritual dimension right down onto the physical level because we had already landed when I received the file from the man at the hotel reception. From a positive point of view, a hotel is a place of rest, vacation, renewal and replenishment, or a stopover on a journey.

Kaya and I are happy to spend 24 hours a day together without ever tiring of each other. We are always happy to be able to discover each other continually, because whenever we are on a spiritual path, we are constantly changing, transforming. Each day, we discover new changes in the other person as well as in ourselves. That's why our relationship as a couple becomes more and more beautiful and leads us ever farther on the path of Destiny. In such a relationship, we also learn to use body language with a spiritual conscience. We feel at ease to manifest the love and tenderness we feel for the other person because it's always done gently and is never exaggerated.

Kaya's dream revealed that the Teachings of Traditional Angelology were 4000 years ahead of our time. It is true that we mustn't show off our powers and it is wise to remain discreet and humble. That's also why we mustn't reveal the dreams we receive about other people or projects we are working on. I've only shared this dream here as an example of the goal we may all reach one day when we have cleansed our memories. Angel Work transforms us so much that it's difficult to find words to describe it.

In the metaphysical dimensions, the perception of time is different. We can do things there, set projects in motion that will have great repercussions in concrete, physical life. We can help people and participate in the activation of life plans. Everything is possible. On the metaphysical level, things evolve very rapidly and they are programmed a long, long time in advance. However, we also have to respect the various factors of evolution that prevail in physical reality. Whenever we move, become active and carry out projects on the concrete, physical level, a certain amount of time and space is required. We cannot get around this. But we should know and understand that everything that is realized and manifested on the physical level is first decided in the Parallel Worlds. Whenever something is planned and part of the Divine Plan, everything begins to move and evolve in a way that allows for its materialization. Of course, physical reality is slow, but there's a reason for this. Its sole purpose is to lead us to develop Qualities, Virtues and Divine Powers.

During the intermission, some of you shared with me that the work we've done so far has aroused a lot of things in you: sadness, a feeling of abandonment, and fear for some; for others a feeling of emptiness, or other distortions. This is perfectly normal because Angel Work always has powerful effects. Angel 48 MIHAEL represents fertility, fecundity, hence the capacity to engender life. When a person experiences this Field of Conscience in a distorted way, symbolically speaking that means sterility, death, emptiness, a void.

I'd like to give you the following advice: "Live your moments of distortions well, live them consciously. Accept yourselves when you don't feel good, when you are sad and feel lonely and abandoned. Be compassionate toward those parts of yourselves that you discover; know that when old memories are reactivated, they can plunge us into all sorts of states that are sometimes very difficult. So be kind and gentle with these aspects of your inner man or woman, for those parts of you that have been hurt and that manifest in a distorted manner. It is with love and understanding that you can best heal and transform them."

Now let's analyze a commercial for a bank. We shall use symbolic language and analyze it as though we had received it in a dream or experienced it in concrete reality. As we watch it, we shall ask ourselves, "What would this mean if I had seen these events in a dream or if I had really experienced them?" This exercise will help us understand a lot about our two polarities, as well as certain aspects of the Angelic State of Conscience of Mihael. It is an excellent exercise to get to know ourselves better, as well as to keep a causal vision of things and hence not be influenced by commercials that push us to buy or that sometimes deform reality. It's also excellent training practice in how to read our daily life in symbols and so better understand the signs we are sent.

Here is the story presented in the commercial. *We see a young English tourist with a street map and a camera visiting a little village in Italy. Going into a bakery, he bumps into a young Italian woman on her way out. He apologizes in English and continues to watch her leave on a small, white moped. Without any kindness, the baker lady interrupts him briskly and harshly asks him what he wants. From inside the bakery, we see a sign in the shop window saying, "Pane e Dolci" (Bread and Pastries).*

In the next scene, the young Englishman is sitting having a soda on a café terrace when he catches sight of the young woman walking along carrying her shopping. She's wearing a black dress with little flowers. The man jumps up, puts money on the table and goes to meet her. He greets her and asks her in English if he can help carry her bags. She says yes in Italian. Then we see them walking together to her house. An old neighbor, hanging up washing on her balcony, looks at them disapprovingly.

In the third scene, we see the young Englishman leave a bouquet of white chrysanthemums on the young woman's moped that is parked in front of her house. At the same time, we hear a man's voice explaining that different flowers have different meanings, that in Italy chrysanthemums are associated with funerals and grieving. Then we see quite a rough looking workman reverse his van, knock over the moped and the bouquet of flowers, and drive off without looking back. Seeing the overturned moped and the chrysanthemums, the elderly neighbor immediately thinks the young woman is dead. Then we see several villagers all leave a bouquet of chrysanthemums in front of the young woman's door. When the young woman comes out, she stops, surprised and dismayed to see all the bouquets of chrysanthemums on the ground. Just then, she catches sight of her neighbor, who, on seeing that she is alive, drops her shopping and stands there open-mouthed in shock.

Now let's analyze it in detail. It starts with a man – an Englishman, who's traveling in Italy. He's walking around with his camera and a map. This would mean we are actively visiting some of our old memories, an as of yet unknown area of our conscience that concerns the collective memory and mindset of Italy. From a positive point of view, a camera allows us to study the past. Thanks to photos and films we've taken, we can go back and study the past. From a negative point of view, it represents nostalgia, possessiveness and attachment – in this case, emotional attachment to the past.

Then in a bakery, the man encounters a beautiful Italian woman and he feels attracted to her. This is linked to relationships between two people, in a couple, and love. Symbolically, the plus side of Italy represents love, *joie de vivre*, spontaneity and enthusiasm; from the negative point of view, it represents exaggeration, overflowing emotions and passion that can become dangerous. Unmastered emotions often lead to all sorts of conflict, tension and difficulties.

We can see the man in the advertisement is English – from England. From a positive point of view, England symbolizes a capacity for expansion. It differs from the United States by also symbolizing a certain refinement, a little like France differs from the French part of Canada, Québec.

The negative side of the English is that they want to give the impression that they are masters of their emotions, whereas in actual fact it's not true mastery but control and repression of their emotions. They also sometimes have problems with a haughty attitude and superiority complex.

This commercial shows us an encounter between two distortions: on the one hand, Italy with its passion and overflowing emotions, and on the other hand, the English mentality with its repressed emotions and the resulting rigidity which manifests itself on the action level.

The man meets the young woman in a bakery or cake shop. We can see it's called *Pani e Dolci* – which means Bread and Pastries – *sweet pastries*. Bread is a staple food but it also symbolizes transformation. It is the result of a mixture that has to be kneaded, left to rise, then baked in the oven – that means exposed to heat which mustn't be too high or too low. In a bakery or cake shop, we can also buy pastries and they too represent nourishing energy but on the emotional level. Generally speaking, food represents the energy we need to be active.

The bakery is in an old building, which symbolizes old structures and old memories. The buildings nearby are also old and run down. The meeting between the young man and woman is the result of their bumping into each other as he's going into and she's coming out of the shop. This indicates that old memories concerning life as a couple are being touched on here... old memories of when both polarities meet, there being a mixture of love, sweetness and... bumps! That means a mixture of instinctual, emotional and aggressive energies, which of course creates difficulties.

Don't forget when we analyze a dream or real life event or situation, we must always consider all of the elements – people as well as objects – as parts of ourselves. Therefore, the baker-lady whose attitude doesn't show any kindness, understanding or compassion for the young man, represents the rigid, arid parts of our being. On the one hand, since she prepares and sells bread and pastries, she offers essential food and sweetness, but on the other hand, she isn't able to do so with love and kindness because of the rigid, dried-up parts she has within.

In the following scene, we see the young man seated at a table, having a drink on a café terrace. We don't know exactly what he's drinking but since it's a liquid, it is related to the emotional level. This scene reveals his need to satisfy himself on the emotional level. Then we see the young woman walking along the street carrying shopping bags. She's wearing a black dress with little flowers. Clothes symbolize our aura, the way we emanate, project and radiate what we are onto the outer world, on the social level. The fact that the dress is predominantly black is revealing, not only regarding this woman but also regarding the man's inner woman. From a positive point of view, black symbolizes hidden aspects – that means hidden information that it's not the right time to reveal just now. The negative aspects of black symbolize aspects we want to hide or keep hidden for negative reasons. It also represents darkness, obscurity, the dark side where's there's no light, hence no understanding. From a negative point of view, black clothes indicate there are aspects within us that we want to hide from others.

The man is attracted by what the young woman emanates, what she radiates. He offers to carry her bags and she accepts. Apparently everything is fine; it looks good, but we later see that this gesture triggers a whole series of incidents and misunderstandings that will reveal the hidden aspects of their being, which also show us what can't work on the relationship level.

When the man sees the woman for the first time, she's on a moped. Since we sit astride it a little like how we would sit on a horse and we don't need to make any effort (unlike a bicycle that we have to pedal), and as we are in direct contact with the air and our environment, it symbolizes freedom of movement. Her moped is white. White symbolizes spirituality. However, the fact that the moped gets knocked over by a van indicates there are parts within us that when involved in a social situation both create and suffer accidents. The van driver acts negligently and irresponsibly. Of course, reversing can be positive, but in this example, the symbolism is negative. In general, this accident indicates there are things that need to be rectified in the way we advance or reverse so as to be able to offer the other person beautiful feelings – symbolized by the bouquet of flowers – and so as not to lose our warm, spiritual side nor the feeling of freedom we have in our relationships with others.

The fact that the young Englishman chose a bouquet of chrysanthemums, without knowing that in Italy these flowers are associated with funerals and death and are often put on graves, shows us how important it is to think about the symbolism and consequence of our gestures. For the Italian neighbor, the sight of the knocked over moped along with the bouquet of chrysanthemums automatically triggered the association: accident + chrysanthemums = death. So, for her, the young woman was dead. Whereas in Japan, for instance, a chrysanthemum figures on the old imperial emblem and is not at all considered a symbol of death.

However, if we deepen our analysis of the symbolism of chrysanthemums, we can reach a better understanding of the state of consciousness this flower symbolizes. To do so, I looked up and studied chrysanthemums on the Internet. They are beautiful flowers that exist in different colors and flower late in the fall, throughout the month of November, at that time of year when all other flowers have already withered. So they're a natural choice when it comes to decorating graves on All Souls' Day, a religious celebration of the dead which takes place in November. Furthermore, the fall – when the leaves fall off the trees and all Nature rests – symbolizes the end of a cycle as much in the outer world as on the metaphysical level, in terms of conscience. Some people love the fall, while others do not. When we don't like this season, what does it mean? It indicates the presence of conscious or unconscious memories of sadness when confronted with the end of a cycle of life or indeed the end of any cycle. Such a person fears death; he doesn't understand that life and its evolution are made up of cycles, of a succession of deaths and rebirths. He finds it difficult to end things and go toward the new. Once we've integrated the deep, profound meaning of the cycles of life, we no longer talk of death and rebirth, because we know, we are fully aware that Life continually renews itself. At each change of cycle or situation in life, we say to ourselves, 'Something is ending, something new is on the way, I'm evolving...'

So, from a positive point of view, chrysanthemums symbolize a capacity to face change with beautiful feelings, a capacity to encounter death, winter and cold ambiance with confidence and serenity on both the concrete, physical level as well as in the subtle dimensions.

Let's go back to the advertisement and analyze chrysanthemums as if we'd seen them in a dream, conscious that all the elements in a dream represent parts of ourselves: both the man who offers the young woman those lovely flowers of beautiful feelings as well as the elderly neighbor who misinterprets what she sees. What made her jump to the conclusion that the young lady was dead without having the slightest concrete proof? It was her own memories of experiences marked by accidents, loss, sadness and a feeling of abandonment that led her to such a conclusion. Since she hasn't got Knowledge, she doesn't realize that she projects onto the outside everything she bears within.

Cases like this offer us opportunities to learn, to put Knowledge into practice. Whenever a situation awakens intense emotions in us that drive us to imagine things and jump to conclusions, we should always refer back to ourselves – i.e., take a few minutes or seconds to go within and check if our evaluation is right given what we've just seen or heard, or if it's based on a personal, emotional reaction. And if we only realize later that we misinterpreted a particular situation, then we should also go within, apply the Law of Resonance and analyze everything using symbolic language. Proceeding like this helps us to gradually become aware of difficult memories lodged in our unconscious. In the light of Angel 48 Mihael, we can have access to these distorted memories that are directly related to our inner couple and cleanse them.

We can easily train ourselves while traveling in a car with someone. My husband, Kaya, and I have often done this and it has led to our creating beautiful symbiosis. Now, when he's driving and I happen to say to him, "Look out! A car's coming..." or "Watch out, there's this or that...," with beautiful honesty, he replies, "Oh! Thanks! I didn't see it." Kaya has a great number of things to organize and coordinate. The symbiosis between us allows me to perceive moments when his mind is preoccupied. It's as though I were in his mind, his body, his very being. We complete each other quite naturally and effortlessly. This symbiosis helps him at busy times like this. But it wasn't always the case. In the beginning, when I said, "Watch out! A car's coming!" Kaya always replied gently, "It's OK, Christiane, I saw it. There's no problem. This time, it wasn't your intuition speaking, it was inner fears of yours." So I would say to myself, "I badly evaluated the situation. I'm the one who has a problem. It's my inner accidents that made me react. What was I thinking about? Is there any relationship with the dreams I had last night?" I systemically applied the Law of Resonance and symbolism until I managed to understand why I had badly evaluated the situation.

Today, the wonderful symbiosis that exists between us is the result of lots of training in all sorts of situations. Sometimes a man reacts impatiently if he's driving and his wife often tells him to be careful, unnecessarily exclaiming, "Watch out!" I saw my mother, who's Italian, do this all her life. When I was young, she used to do it, and when she panicked in the car like that, my father would get angry. Neither of them was right, but my mother didn't evaluate situations well because she didn't have access to Knowledge that would have helped her react differently. Car trips are a great opportunity to practice and hone our evaluation skills, and see how close we are to achieving symbiosis.

During a lecture tour, my husband and I were in the car and there was a program on the radio where several guest speakers spoke about reading signs. I was moved to hear well-known personalities talk about the teachings we receive through signs and premonitions. One man said, "Yes, yes, me too! I travel by plane quite a lot and sometimes I have premonitions. It's true that signs exist. I agree with you that they exist. But I've often been afraid to take the plane because I had a premonition that something was going to happen, and nothing happened. Here we are talking about the times it works, when premonitions turn out to be right. But what do we do when they don't work, when our premonitions are wrong?"

I found his question very interesting because the Teachings of the Traditional Study of Angels allow us to explain such cases via the Law of Resonance and the existence of unconscious memories that are reactivated in the presence of appropriate trigger elements. We can then understand what we are going through and tell ourselves, "I was scared, but my fear wasn't justified; I didn't anticipate the situation well. That means I reacted under the influence of my memories. I'm going to cleanse them with Angel Recitation, Angel Mantra Recitation. That will help me always remain well focused and able to truly perceive what is happening on the subtle levels, what is about to materialize. My intuition and premonitions will then be right. Until then, I won't get angry when I'm mistaken. I'll consider it as training practice."

Let's go back to the young Italian woman in the commercial. We now understand that the knocked over moped and flowers on the ground in front of her door indicate that in her unconscious, she harbors memories that resonate with this kind of situation. She attracted these events. Whether in a dream, in concrete reality, or as inspiration for a commercial, the Law of Resonance always applies. And analysis with symbolic language leads us to deep understanding that englobes all the levels of our being. Regarding the couple, this incident, this kind of event would be a sign announcing difficulties, which would result in memories of abandonment and fear of losing the other person – difficulties that are to be found among the human distortions of the Angelic Field of Conscience of Angel 48 MIHAEL.

How many people experience all sorts of fear because of unsettled *baggage* they bear in their memories! Every time we are afraid of losing the other person, instead of denying or repressing this fear, we do Angel Recitation and deep cleanse the corresponding memories, thanks to the Power of the Angel. By working on our unconscious memories like this, the day will come when we feel beautiful harmony and great serenity in our inner couple. Everything I've told you can be put into practice in all circumstances, because both principles –masculine and feminine – are found in everything, absolutely everything.

Now I'd like to continue with another true story that is also related to Angel MIHAEL's Field of Conscience. A woman in her sixties, who had just had breast surgery, shared her experience with me. "Twenty-seven years ago, I decided to have breast implants to increase my breast size. Of course I now regret doing this, but at the time I wasn't on a spiritual path and I didn't know any better. Just recently, I was told that these implants were cracked, so I decided not to have them replaced but rather to have them removed, and simultaneously do inner work to cleanse the memories related to this experimentation."

This woman works with the Teachings of Traditional Angelology and before the operation, she did Angel Recitation very intensely. The operation went well but she developed breathing difficulties. She could no longer breathe and lacked air. Because of this incident, she was kept under observation in the hospital a week longer. "After getting out of the hospital," she continued, "Everything went well physically. I even thought of my hospital stay as a beautiful gift. I felt fine there. Seeing other women with so many problems helped me surpass myself. I tried to help them. It was an important step for me. Back home, I couldn't raise my arms and I felt completely exhausted. It was as though I was going through inner death. And I was hungry, terribly hungry. I ate non-stop and it wasn't good, healthy food. In my dreams, I was shown that I wasn't nourishing myself well. I received all sorts of dreams. Even last night, I had a dream where *I saw myself with a tray full of cakes and cookies. Then I saw a man arrive with another tray of them and even though my arms were full, I wanted more. He gave them to other people, not to me. I wasn't happy at all about that. Imagine!"* This woman understood what she was going through.

Let's analyze this dream where Cosmic Intelligence put her in contact with memories inscribed with lack of sweet energies. The cakes and cookies she was eating and excessively desired reveal affective, emotional deficiencies. This woman didn't realize that her memories marked by affective lack had been aroused by the fact that after the operation, she had smaller breasts again. Through this dream, she was being told, "Look, you want to eat so as to be able to nourish others, to be loved; but as long as you don't cleanse the memories that push you to want bigger breasts, you will never have enough. You will still have lack and be unable to share with others. You won't be able to be altruistic or truly love others, because the only thing that will count for you will be the satisfaction of your own needs, which will be camouflaged in an exaggerated desire to nourish others. That's the reason why, as well as the seductive aspect, you wanted to have bigger breasts."

I asked her a question. "Do you remember what happened when you decided to have breast implants?"

She replied, "Yes, I had just been through a break up. My husband left me to go and live with my best friend. It was a complete shock, a very difficult, painful experience. But I didn't know the Law of Resonance then; I didn't have access to Knowledge. At that time, I began to consider having breast implants because I didn't want to have drooping breasts when I was 50. That was my goal at the time."

I explained to her, "Now you know that people undergo this kind of surgery to compensate for inner lack. Of course we don't feel well when we are going through a break-up. If we don't have the Knowledge that allows us to deeply understand what we are going through, we can feel ugly, hopeless, and lose all our self-esteem. We may feel that we are becoming decrepit and old. You experienced betrayal by your husband and your friend. Since you didn't know the Law of Resonance, you couldn't know that you had to experience this betrayal in order to understand that in your unconscious, you harbored memories that correspond to this situation; that you too betrayed others, not necessarily in this life. But you mustn't drown in guilt and blame yourself; it was an experimentation.

We have all done all sorts of experimentations in the course of our many lives and we bear memories of these experimentations in our unconscious. When the time comes to become aware of them, Cosmic Intelligence orchestrates outer events, such as betrayal, as in your case, or abandonment, illness, bankruptcy, an accident, and so on, in order to awaken latent memories that resonate with the outer event. It is important to know that what we go through, whatever we experience, always corresponds to our program of evolution."

This understanding is essential for the new generations, because at the present time, there are a great many young women who choose to undergo such operations without knowing the symbolism behind their desires or all that's involved in their choice. Of course, breast surgery has its rightful place in both increasing and decreasing breast size. It is justified whenever someone has had a serious accident or had a breast removed following cancer, as well as when the weight of a person's breasts causes serious back problems. In all these cases, surgery and implants help the person remain functional. In a way, they represent a second chance.

However, when such surgery is only chosen for the sake of appearances, esthetic reasons and seduction, as well as because of excessive emissivity on the affective, emotional level, then it is a distortion. An initiate, who has Knowledge, knows that true beauty comes from the inside and that we can't solve emotional, affective difficulties, or meet an evolved man by artificially modifying the size of our breasts.

We may have the most beautiful, plastic breasts in the world but they won't be of any use when Cosmic Intelligence reactivates our distorted memories and shows us our lack of authenticity. On the contrary, they may even intensify the discrepancy between what we are going through on the inside and what we look like on the outside. The more our unconscious opens, the more aware we become of the contradictions that exist between our physical appearance and what we really are deep down. We then understand that manipulating our outer aspect doesn't help. Change has to come from within. If we work on ourselves, one day, we will reach the point where the size and outer aspect of our breasts don't bother us any longer. But as long as we feel unhappy and bothered by our breasts, this indicates that there is something we need to understand regarding femininity and maternity.

On the symbolic level, whenever a woman has small breasts and is bothered by this, it means that she isn't maternal enough, that she is depolarized. Her masculine polarity is too strong. If she is not put out by the size of her small breasts, it means that she lives her femininity well. Everything is a question of inner attitude.

And what do breasts that are too big symbolize? For women, breasts are a symbol of maternal nourishment. Naturally, a mother breastfeeds her child. In sexual relationships, a man also feels nourished by her; he rediscovers the essence of beautiful, loving connection with the feminine Energy of God, and the pure feelings of being like a problem-free child, nourished on pure Love and Wisdom. It is amazing how breastfeeding a child is so powerful on the unconscious level because through the mother's milk, which is white and therefore related to spirituality, a child can live solely on this nourishment. You can imagine how powerful the symbol of the breast is in terms of conscience and of divine qualities! That's why a man is attracted by his wife's breasts during their intimate relationship. He is seeking that total plenitude and fusion of abundance on all levels. So we can understand that this symbolism doesn't only apply on the concrete level when a mother breastfeeds her child or a wife nourishes her husband with love; it is valid for all women because they constantly nourish and nurture others on the energy level with their thoughts and emotions. And it also applies to men because every man has his feminine polarity within; every man has an inner woman. We all have both polarities and should work on developing the beautiful, innate, divine, angelic qualities of each polarity.

The nurturing, emotional, affective function of breasts symbolically represents the gift of self, God's manifestation, nothing less! Generally speaking, oversized breasts indicate an exaggeration of this function. An overdeveloped maternal and spiritual side symbolically corresponds to affective, emotional, and energy overfeeding. We want to nourish and nurture others too much because we want them to prosper so we can get something in return. And where there is excess, there are always lack. We can see this in cases where large-breasted people refrain from giving. There are memories of distorted giving as well as fears of missing something, of not receiving love and affection as well as divine connection and nourishment from the Source and Fountain of True Love and Wisdom.

Let's go back to this woman's dream. She was visiting memories that showed her difficulty giving sweetness. She didn't want to give any cakes or cookies to other people; she held onto them. That's the meaning behind her having a tray of cakes and cookies in her arms and wanting more. 'You give, but in fact it is only to receive in return; it is not unconditional.' What's more, she was angry because the man gave some to the others but not to her. This indicates memories of a lack of emotional, affective energy. She was also shown that in her unconscious, she harbors memories of lives where she didn't emotionally nourish others enough. Hence she experienced the same thing herself. She too lacked the energy of love.

The betrayal she experienced with her husband and best friend reveals that in her unconscious, there are memories of betrayal and infidelity: certain forces in her took other people's affective, emotional resources. This woman is in the process of deep cleansing these memories with the keys offered by the Traditional Study of Angels. During the course of this cleansing, she has to die to her old memories to be reborn in a new conscience. That's why she felt so exhausted. It was the effect of the inner death she was going through on the affective, emotional level.

Then this woman talked to me about her second husband who is a very agreeable, kind man, who is spiritual in his own way. Listening to her, I sensed that she didn't appreciate him as he deserved. She was aware of this but wasn't able to change the situation. Regarding this, she said, "During my operation, my husband was always there at my side. He who is more of a builder and workman, he did everything for me, even the cooking, which he had never done before! In fact, he doesn't know how to cook but since I couldn't raise my arms and was so tired and depressed, he really took care of everything. Whenever I massaged my breasts because I was in pain after the operation, he was at my side. He accompanied me in all I had to go through and I became much more grateful to my husband." She went on to say, "Do you know what I did several times? I prayed really intensely never to forget these times, to always remember what my husband did for me."

What enabled this woman to develop such understanding and gratitude for her husband? Of course he doesn't only have qualities; he also has distortions, just as she has. So why was she suddenly able to appreciate him so much? Because she had worked on herself. The operation to remove the breast implants and the ensuing difficulties had made her more aware and led to a greater opening of her conscience. She had cleansed part of her memories of superficiality, abandonment, betrayal and infidelity that had previously prevented her from totally committing to her second husband and acknowledging his beautiful qualities. As she changed, her husband changed too.

This example shows how each negative situation bears positive elements. We don't always see them immediately, especially when we don't yet have the Knowledge that allows us a deep understanding of all we go through.

Here is another true story that is also related to esthetic operations but in a very different context. It's the story of a very intelligent, beautiful, wealthy woman who used to be a model. She was in her twenties when she had a very serious accident, which she came out of alive but completely disfigured. She had to have multiple operations to rebuild her face. Regarding this experience, she told us, "If I hadn't had that accident, if I hadn't been through all of those ordeals, I wouldn't be where I am now. I wouldn't have journeyed so far spiritually speaking. I know now that the accident was a gift from Heaven, a true Godsend."

This woman has great charisma. She emanates great intensity as much in her expression of qualities as distortions. She is working with the Traditional Study of Angels, which has helped her understand her life story. Like many people, this woman is seeking her twin soul. For a certain period of time, she did particularly intense Angel Recitation and she received the following dream. *She was with her daughter and the two of them were sitting at a table in a magnificent garden, in which there was a wonderful tree. There were also two men, but she couldn't see them clearly. She heard a voice announce, "The count has arrived." The count walked up to her, kissed her on the mouth and said, "I love you." She replied, "But how can you love me? We've only just met." He replied, "I have always known you," and kissed her again, saying, "You are beautiful."*

It's a very beautiful dream, which shows her the encounter of her inner couple. After such a dream, we feel exalted, that's for sure.

Let's analyze the symbolic meaning of this beautiful dream. The woman was sitting in a magnificent garden with a very beautiful tree. This means that she was receptive to beautiful feelings and that she also had Knowledge of the process of materialization because, among other things, a tree symbolizes the different cycles of Divine materialization. She was with her daughter. She symbolizes her future, her inner child who is growing and learning. Then she was told the count had arrived. He represents her inner man. The fact of his being a count symbolizes nobility of soul, mind and spirit. Generally speaking, this also applies to all royal titles, such as king, queen, duke, duchess, etc. In the context of this dream, this symbol appears in a positive light, hence its positive symbolism. The count loves the woman for what she is on the inside, for her essential self. He doesn't stop at outer appearances. He represents a truly noble heart. Even though throughout the history of humanity, royalty and nobles often experimented with distortions, exploited and abused the material resources and power they had, their true role was to serve their people, to guide, protect and help them with the abundant resources at their disposal.

The aim of such a dream is to encourage and validate the beauty of the soul and divine riches. Cosmic Intelligence was telling this woman, "You see, that's how you will feel if you cleanse the memories that limit you on the inside. It's not your physical appearance that is important but your inner beauty: the beauty of your soul, the quality of your thoughts and the rich abundance of your sentiments, your altruism. If you feel good on the inside, everything will be fine on the outside too, and you will be able to know true love. You will feel complete and fulfilled in your inner couple, you will no longer be upset by the fact of living alone and not having found your twin soul yet. You will trust Up Above because you know that your twin soul will come along at the right time, when you are ready to encounter him. This will happen when you have understood the value of inner beauty and repaired old past life behavior when you exploited and abused beauty and power."

I said to this woman, "The state of conscience and well-being you are experiencing thanks to this encounter with your inner man in your dream will help you make good use of the time that's necessary before encountering your complement in the outer world. By continuing to transform yourself, you'll see the whole world will change. You need to learn to use the wait to continue to work on yourself instead of desperately wanting someone in your life. Your twin soul will appear one day, in this life or another. You just have to be patient."

A very beautiful example regarding this is provided by the Walt Disney film, *Beauty and the Beast*. The Beast is actually a prince who was put under a spell for being mean and horrid to others. He had to rediscover noble love before recovering his own beauty. He had to live alone, unwanted in his material kingdom, until the day he meets Beauty, who succeeds in reactivating his inner beauty so that his heart of stone melts and all bitterness and criticism are gone. It's a wonderful story!

In the State of Conscience of Angel 48 MIHAEL, we do not materialize with the aim of achieving physical, material goals, such as carrying out projects exclusively for the money they will make. What matters is the way we materialize. We learn to materialize divinely by remaining focused on qualities.

The following example will lead us to a deep understanding of a dismissive sentence we quite often hear: *That's your problem!* A woman in her fifties told me that she'd always had difficulties in her emotional relationships. They'd never really worked. She said, "In my last relationship, I was involved with a man who'd been separated from his ex-wife for years. He saw her again from time to time and that didn't bother me. But, as time went by, I realized he was still having sexual intercourse with her. So I put a stop to our relationship. Just recently, I received the following dream: *I saw him arrive in the backyard. He came and lifted up a handful of earth. He told me he was still in love with me and he kissed me. So I asked him, "Are you free now?" He replied, "That's your problem."* She asked me, "What does this dream mean?"

I gave her the two possible interpretations. "You may have visited his soul and been shown where he is in his evolution. Or all of the elements in this dream represent parts of yourself. But what matters most is that even if you were allowed to visit his soul, this dream reveals that you still resonate with this man. The fact that in your dream you accept his kiss shows that you have resonance, that you are still attracted to him."

Let's analyze the symbols in this dream. The man arrives in the backyard of her house. The front of a house, the façade, that everyone can see, represents what we emanate in the outer world, what we choose to reflect about ourselves, our public facet, so to speak. The backyard of a house symbolizes the intimate aspects of ourselves; it's a symbol of inner renewal and replenishment on both the individual and social levels (since we usually share a house with other members of the family).

Generally speaking a man symbolizes action in the outer world. This ex-partner, who has just arrived and lifted up a handful of earth, simultaneously represents aspects of this woman's inner man. The pile of earth symbolizes aspects of her inner earth that is taken from her by this former relationship, the kind of attitude that says, 'I can come into your life and take your earth. I want what you have.' Next, we see in the dream that he kisses her and that he wants her back, but he doesn't want to change. That's what he means when he says, "That's your problem." This is the attitude both the ex-partner and this woman's inner man share.

Through this dream, the dreamer was being told that she still has this unfaithful duality within her and that she needs to work on it so as to be able to attract a problem-free relationship. Even if in the concrete world, this woman doesn't behave like the man did – she didn't have sexual intercourse with her ex-husband while she was in a new relationship – but on the level of her unconscious, she still has similar memories recorded there. These memories prevent her from committing fully. It is these memories that make her emotional relationships difficult.

Studying dreams is very interesting and revealing. If we have exes – ex-husbands, ex-boyfriends, ex-life partners – they can appear in our dreams. But that doesn't mean they are actually going to come back into our life on the concrete level. Using them as symbols, Up Above wants us to understand that we still resonate with them; we still have resonance with particular aspects of their being. And if we want our next relationship to be better, if we want to be able to commit ourselves fully, we need to transform these aspects in ourselves. One day, we evolve by cleansing memories in relation to our exes and when they re-appear in our dreams, they are totally different; they appear radiant, kind and right. With time, we can even receive dreams where we visit them so as to understand what stage they have reached in their evolution. One day, in dreams, we can even become a guide for our exes and help them without their knowing. However, we are only granted this kind of dream when we have no more negative resonance with them. As long as we haven't transcended our personal needs, we cannot truly help others, either in dream reality or indeed in concrete reality.

Through her dream, this woman was being told, "Continue to work on the resonance you have with this man. When you think of him, remember what you went through with him, and apply the Law of Resonance and symbolism. Cleanse your memories so you won't attract the same kind of relationship again."

Here's an example of a dream that touches on the symbolism of the animal kingdom in both the outer world and in our inner world. Animals symbolize our primary, most basic needs, our instinctual vital energy, and also the way we manage this energy on the sexual level. A woman shared the following dream. *In a restaurant, where the pastry chef makes wonderful cakes, a crocodile was always placed as a decoration on the cakes. The crocodile was energetic and multidimensional – there are none like this in concrete life. She knew it wasn't right, but said, "This crocodile has great potential." The person with her asked her to go, but she can't make up her mind to leave. She felt attracted to these pastry crocodiles, the pastry chef, and this place.*

What does this dream mean? Let's have a look at the symbolism of a restaurant first. In concrete reality, a restaurant is a public place where food is offered and a certain number of people are welcomed, so it is related to the social level and the way we nourish others. Transposed to the metaphysical level, the symbolism of a restaurant shows us how we welcome and nourish different parts of ourselves, and also what sort of welcome and what sort of physical, energetic subtle nourishment we offer others. It's the whole interplay of maternal and paternal nutrition on the social level.

The fact that there was a pastry chef in this restaurant who made wonderful cakes decorated with a live, energetic crocodile shows the dreamer the kind of sweetness with which she nourishes parts of herself and others in her actions. She is aware that the crocodile's presence isn't right, especially given its multidimensionality. It isn't just a physical decoration in the form of a crocodile but the state of conscience this animal emits. It's like comparing a human being to an extraterrestrial, or physical senses to subtle ones. A human being represents the physical level whereas an extraterrestrial symbolizes multidimensionality on the metaphysical and intelligence levels. The dreamer feels the strong attraction that the crocodile state of conscience exerts over her. She can't leave. She is fascinated by the potential the crocodile represents.

Let's take a closer look at the symbolism of a crocodile. It is an aquatic reptile, which in its negative aspect, reminds us of a snake and coldness. A crocodile symbolizes old, aggressive, emotional memories related to vital energy. Crocodiles live as much in the water as on land and we know that these two elements represent, respectively, the world of emotions and the world of action. This animal is capable of remaining motionless, without food for very long periods of time. It lives in still waters such as slow-moving rivers, swamps and muddy waters in warm climates. In terms of conscience, this indicates that the heat generated by emotions seems to be under control. It doesn't cause any waves; there's no tsunami. But this powerful potential that's held in check can manifest itself suddenly and very rapidly. A crocodile can act with great speed and agility and its powerful strength allows it to attack very strong animals such as lions or sharks.

Through this dream, this lady was being told, "Look how you nourish others! You emanate tranquil strength and you give the impression of being in control. But under the surface, in your inner earth and waters, there's a crocodile that can spring forth all of a sudden and manifest very aggressive, destructive energy. What's more, we can see you like aggressive sweetness."

This woman had already told me that whenever she ate too much sugary food, she suffered from deep anxiety, real anguish during the night. After that, she'd start fasting and would forbid herself sugar in all its forms. She often went from one extreme to the other. She even told me she was convinced she'd been a prostitute in another life because she had forces within her that liked that. Although she now looks like a nun, she's actually married and has three children. Therefore, she sometimes becomes rigid in order to retain these forces, which have not all been cleansed yet. I told her, "After this dream, now that you've become aware of your inner crocodile, you can better understand why you experienced those anxiety attacks and your attraction to aggressive sweetness."

Whenever we overeat, whenever we need too much sugar, it means we're touching on memories. When we sometimes feel excessively hungry and stuff ourselves with cakes, sugary things and sweets, even if they are good quality and organic, when it's not a healthy hunger or a moderate dose of sugar, then we have to know we are in a distortion. We are visiting memories marked by a lack of energy, sweetness and tenderness. I said to this woman, "No doubt you've already eaten sugary things without having any anxiety attacks afterwards." She agreed and I added, "That means that you only make a mad rush for sweet things when something symbolically activates your inner crocodile. That's what creates a mixture of aggression and gentleness in your energies."

This lady's husband is spiritual and he radiates a certain sweet gentleness, but in the face of his wife's emissivity and power, it's difficult for him to develop his masculine polarity well and to take his place. I said to this woman, "You'd like your husband to be a leader, but for him to be one, you need to let him take his place. With what you've been shown in this dream, you may sometimes feel attracted to a man who, like you, has a mixture of tenderness and crocodile aggression. But if you had a husband like that, you couldn't bear him."

Sometimes this woman also had dreams wherein *she saw good, spiritual, altruistic people bringing her healthy, organic food, people she knew in the concrete world. She could neither accept it nor eat it. That food made her vomit even though it wasn't in excessive quantities.* Regarding these dreams, I told her, "Up Above wants to help you understand that your inner crocodile memories prevent you from receiving true sweetness, true gentleness. As long as you haven't cleansed these memories, good food and beautiful energy will make you vomit. Your inner crocodile doesn't want them, because it needs very instinctual, aggressive energy. It can't bear when things are too sweet, tender and meek."

We all aspire to tenderness and good nourishment on all levels of our life. But before being able to digest and assimilate them, we need to cleanse our unconscious memories. We need to transform our crocodile memories that symbolically want to feed on lions and sharks.

As I mentioned, this lady often had dreams wherein *she saw herself as a prostitute.* She understood that through the symbolism of prostitution, she was being told that in other lives, she'd granted too much importance to matter, to the material world. She'd given it priority. In her present life, she tends to be quite nun-like and manifests a lot of rigidity. She has a family with children but sometimes it's very difficult. She just can't contain all her distorted forces so every now and again, she explodes.

In other dreams, *she sometimes saw herself making love to a cat-man; a man with hair just like a cat's. And she liked that.* When we see ourselves making love to someone in a dream, it is very important to understand what this means in terms of conscience. Generally speaking, making love means we are ready to fuse with whatever the other person represents. We fuse with his way of thinking, feeling, behaving; we fuse with his way of being. The cat-man in this dream reveals that this woman's masculine polarity is too instinctual, too animal-like. The cat-man symbolizes aspects of her inner man that are manifested through the negative characteristics of a cat, which includes hyper-independence. A cat comes and goes as it wishes. It receives and gives caresses only when it suits it. Transposed to human behavior, this shows human behavior that keeps others at a distance and that feeds on energy generated by independence. However, this form of independence is not true independence. It's more a form of inaccessibility that increases the other person's emotional dependency.

Dreams like this are great gifts. They are like detailed maps allowing us to locate the inner regions we need to work on. Doing this work leads us to experience true harmony in our inner couple and, sooner or later, the results will also manifest themselves on the outside. The Law of Resonance is absolute. Everything comes from the inside. On the outside there are only consequences that serve as a mirror and as trigger elements to bring us back to the causes that are to be found within us. This lady has great spiritual potential but, for the moment, she can go from one extreme to another. Knowing this, I am convinced that she has the capacity within herself to attain the highest levels of evolution. As I've already said to her, "You are far from passive or lackadaisical, you are an intense, determined person, that's why everything is possible on the positive level if you cleanse your memories with the Angels!"

The following dream examples are particularly related to fecundity. When we refer to fecundity or fertility, it's not only a question of a woman's physical capacity for fertility, but fecundity as a universal characteristic of the feminine principle (which exists in men and women, of course, since everyone has both polarities). Fecundity refers to our capacity to materialize ideas, to incarnate feelings, to conceive and materialize projects, to conceive and materialize divinely, i.e., by manifesting Qualities and respecting the Cosmic Laws. The realization of a project also involves associations and partnerships, of course.

A woman, who has immense financial resources at her disposal on the physical level, received this dream. *She sees her sister who has taken fertility pills and had seven babies. Both her sister and one of the babies die after the birth and it's the dreamer who has to look after the other babies.* What does this dream mean?

Understanding this dream was a revelation for this woman who was already on a spiritual path before encountering Work with Traditional Angelology, symbolic language and the Law of Resonance. It's interesting to analyze the kind of dreams Cosmic Intelligence sends people who have great material abundance.

This dream indicates the presence of memories that push this woman to create, to continually launch projects. Her sister symbolizes part of her inner world, and the fact that she took fertility pills means that she absolutely wants to be fecund, fertile. She creates one project after another and never has enough. This also indicates that there are parts in her that fear sterility, that her unconscious also harbors memories marked by the opposite of fertility: sterility.

There were seven babies so we can link this to Angel 7 ACHAIAH, whose main Quality is patience, which becomes impatience in the distorted aspect. Whenever we create with a lot of impatience, the projects and their initiator risk failure. The mother and one of the babies die. The initial nurturing energy is not available and someone else has to take care of the remaining projects that were launched. How does this kind of dream materialize?

Whenever a person, who has a lot of resources at his disposal, launches several projects simultaneously, and then some of them are aborted because managing them has become too difficult, the person may tend not to worry about this. Her abundant resources allow her to immediately replace the aborted project with another one. If the person hasn't had a spiritual awakening and developed deep self-awareness, he cares little about collateral damage, i.e., the damage caused to the other people involved in and affected by the aborted project. He may react like a spoiled child regarding a broken toy. He simply discards it because he knows he'll receive other toys. He doesn't learn to take care of or repair it because there are employees paid to do so. These employees do their best,

86   Angel 48 Mihael

mostly without realizing, to maintain a structure, which is not divine but solely functional. Of course, they share resonance with their employer(s).

We interpreted this dream for this woman and it was clear that she wasn't used to hearing the truth that our dreams reveal to us, but she was very receptive. On several other occasions, she asked us for other dream interpretations, and then we didn't hear from her for a couple of months. She needed time to digest all that she was learning about herself. When she got in touch again, we could feel that she had integrated deep understanding of the aspects that had been revealed. She was ready to receive more Knowledge.

This woman dreams a lot and the majority of her dreams are related to her power of materialization. They reveal that, generally speaking, for the time being, in spite of all her good will, she doesn't yet materialize in a right, just manner. Here is another dream of hers.

A party or gala has been organized above her doctor's garage – in concrete reality, this doctor is a friend of hers. – It's a gala for charity. The doctor tells her that the party cost two million dollars but they only made $2,600 profit. The dreamer replies that it wasn't a good idea but it was fun. The doctor agrees with her that they had really enjoyed themselves at this party. Then the dreamer says to the doctor, "We organized a golf tournament that cost two million dollars with only $170,000 profit."

She received this dream while sleeping on a plane bound for Japan, where she had a business appointment for her company. The presence of the doctor indicates that this woman wants to materialize concrete projects to help others heal. The way she goes about it shows that she makes poor use of her resources, on the level of both her polarities. Both the doctor, who represents part of her inner man, and herself as a woman, spend exorbitant sums to have fun on the pretext that it is for charity. The underlying intention is not true altruism.

Regarding the two references to two million dollars, we can link them to Angel 2 *Jeliel*, an Angel that is related to *altruism and providential associations*. In the context of this dream, these Angelic Qualities are distorted. After such expenditure, the benefits made are minimal. We can deepen the symbolic analysis of the figures quoted by referring to Angel numerology, which means that the $2,600 refers to Angel 2 JELIEL and Angel 60 MITZRAEL (*reparation through awareness*), or if we read it as 26 hundred, Angel 26 HAAIAH (*discretion and a sense of organization*); and in the case of the $170,000, Angel 1 VEHUIAH (*Divine Will*) and Angel 70 JABAMIAH (*alchemy that transforms evil into good*).

Let's have a look at what golf symbolizes. The positive aspects of golf are the development of qualities such as concentration, precision, accuracy, and a capacity to pursue a goal. It is very popular sport with business men and women who like to set aims and objectives and attain goals. However, if our only aim in playing is to put the ball in the hole to win, in other words, if the pursuit of goals is limited to the physical, material level, then our behavior is distorted. What matters is never the score at the end of the course, but the intention of our action, as well as the motivation and attitude we manifest throughout the game. It's the same in the business world and the realization of projects, associations, partnerships, and the world of work in general. What matters most is to behave in the material level with the intention of developing Qualities, Virtues and Divine Powers.

Dreams are important. Their language is the language of Truth. They reveal to us our true intentions and they show us what really and truly motivates us. Of course all of these revelations deeply affected this woman, but she was ready to hear the truth.

In another dream *she saw clowns in a kind of spa. There were water jets. A male alcoholic told her he loved her, but she didn't love him. Then she saw the sea at low tide and numerous pairs of shoes. Then the clowns were up in the air.*

Once again, all of the elements in this dream represent parts of the dreamer. The clowns indicate that parts of her inner man tend to use humor as a mask behind which this woman hides certain aspects of herself, including the sadness she sometimes feels. In the context of a spa, the clowns being up in the air refers more specifically to her way of thinking and her emotions. A spa can be a positive symbol if we use it to restore calm in ourselves, to relax, renew and replenish our energies. Due to the clowns, the water jets and the alcoholic, the context becomes negative. This woman is being told that she only seeks well-being, comfort, consolation and distraction on the physical level. What's more, the alcoholic telling her he loves her reveals another part of her inner man. This part suffers from affective, emotional dependencies, which are transposed into the way she behaves and does things. The woman doesn't love him. She doesn't want that in her life so she rejects him. This indicates relationship difficulties, which will eventually manifest in her outer couple, if they haven't already done so.

In this context, the sea at low tide is a negative symbol indicating the withdrawal of emotions. Then, there's the shoe symbolism. Shoes, sometimes even shoe factories, are frequent symbols in the dreams of wealthy people. Shoes symbolize the way we advance on the social level. A large number of shoes indicates the presence of a multitude of forces used to advance on the social and personal level. We can easily imagine the mass production of distortions this can lead to if these forces begin to advance and behave negatively.

After hearing Kaya's interpretation of this dream, this woman told me about her life. She told me that her husband, a very wealthy man, had sold all of his businesses and all he wanted to do was to retire and spend his life on an island, playing golf, organizing parties where alcohol flows abundantly. She can't bear it anymore. After a week there, she felt exhausted. There were always arguments because he wanted to stay on the island and she didn't. This woman, who has a doctorate in law, has set up a beautiful health food company, with an ecological dimension. Her company is her baby and through this project, she tries to materialize in a right, just, spiritual way. But her motivation and commitment to this work create clashes with her husband.

I explained to her, "Everything you reproach your husband for is the reflection of distortions you bear within yourself. The worldly, jet set society, the alcohol, parties and fun are resonances that you now find superficial. All of that is revealed in your dream via the clowns, spa and alcoholism. These memories haven't been cleansed yet, that's why you still have to experience this situation. You needn't participate frequently, but when you are exposed to this kind of event or encounters, don't feel obliged to talk. People are so happy to be listened to in depth. Observe them consciously while remaining aware and receptive to what is going on within yourself. Study your resonance and whatever upsets or annoys you and take advantage of this new awareness to cleanse your memories. Hence, you will gain access to a new stage of conscience." This woman is so open that being exposed to this kind of event awakens her own superficial and materialistic memories. She doesn't feel well and becomes exhausted. I advised her to do Angel Recitation, to learn to love these people who symbolize parts of herself. By invoking an Angel non-stop during these festivities, she will feel fewer needs and gradually, with natural synchronicity, changes will take place.

The situations we go through in the outer world serve to help us become aware of our distortions so we can transform them. If we carry out this work within ourselves, sooner or later, the outer situation will change. It's an absolute fact. Only work on ourselves leads to metamorphoses. I'm personally convinced

Angel 48 Mihael

of this since I've witnessed it at first hand for myself, and then for thousands of others too.

After listening attentively to me, this woman said, "I understand why my husband is like that. I have to experience this. My mother was an alcoholic and didn't take care of us in our childhood." She understood the process of reincarnation. I agreed with her and told her that if she had attracted an alcoholic mother, it meant she had been an alcoholic herself in other lives. She may have been too active regarding her projects and neglected her children. She had attracted this mother to work on herself, to transform her distorted memories.

When we set out on an initiatic path, we mustn't want to feel good at all costs. Visiting our memories is not an easy task, especially in the case of large blocks of distorted memories. As the purification of our unconscious gradually progresses, and our understanding evolves, the difficult phases are reduced and become easier to get through.

This woman, who is very fecund on the material level, shared another dream. *I had six babies. I brought them to church and I told the priest that he'd soon be baptizing them. The babies were transformed into white candles. Then they were alternately babies and candles. On the way home, one of the babies transformed into a frog that got out of the car and jumped around in all directions. I told my son to catch the frog before it was lost. My son managed to catch it and put it into a sealed box. There were as many boy babies and girls.*

This dream expresses fecundity, new inner children, new projects and possibilities. 6 corresponds to Angel 6 LELAHEL, *Divine Light that heals everything, lucidity, clarity and understanding* but on the negative side it is related to *ambition, masks, multiple personalities, tendency to take everything for granted, focused solely on the material aspect of things and people, etc.* This woman, who now works consciously with Traditional Angelology, has become used to establishing links between the numbers she sees in her dreams, or that are presented to her as signs, with the numbers associated with Angels. Moreover, she has seen the number 6 in several dreams and even if this dream is negative, she has extraordinary qualities and she is a wonderful soul. But this dream is important to her because she is very spiritual but sometimes she mixes spirit and matter selfishly. She is also very intuitive and open on the third eye. A link may also be made with Angel 6 LELAHEL and the sixth chakra: opening of the third eye. Her spiritual work favors the opening of the third eye. She wants to consecrate her babies to her spirituality, i.e., to consecrate her new projects to a spiritual dimension but in this case it is a little too much and she can tend to be extreme sometimes and disconnected from realities. Their alternating with candles means that she is seeking understanding and Knowledge since a candle symbolizes light and understanding. It is also a symbol of rituals used to create an atmosphere, an ambiance but it is not normal that a baby transforms into a candle. The meaning of this connects with the fact that she is too materialistic on the spiritual level. She can tend to use or abuse others, even her own children, to have time to meditate and pray, like rich people do sometimes with their children when they give them to a nanny while they escape in their business illusions. In a spiritual dimension, carrying out rituals offers us an opportunity to go deeper within ourselves, to become more meditative, but in this case we understand that she is prepared do anything to be able to pray like a nun who decides not to have children and to consecrate her life to celibacy.

Through her new projects, the dreamer is forced to apply the spiritual knowledge she has acquired to matter, but she can misuse her future potential also. Symbolically, this explains that she is so used to abundance that she can lose her perception of realities and others. Rich people often behave like that, having so many projects, and so many employees that they even forget they exist sometimes. They live in a world that is so easy that family or employees can suffer. While driving home, one of the babies transforms into a frog. Very stimulated by learning symbolic language and reading signs, this woman is beginning to understand that parts of herself still behaves like a frog. What does a frog represent? As an animal that lives in water, it symbolizes emotions and instinctual needs that incite the dreamer to become scattered and agitated like a frog that jumps all over the place. She is obliged to imprison, to limit this part of herself as long as her needs and their related emotions haven't been transcended. A symbol like that will also create a lot of discrepancies between spirit and matter.

Here is a final dream concerning this woman. *My aunt tells me that I'm going to receive 3,000 diamonds from my deceased sister. There are diamonds everywhere, small ones and big ones. There are diamonds for different quality rings. I'm sitting on the toilet, gathering up beautiful, big precious stones. The bathroom is covered with them.*

Precious stones and diamonds are usually beautiful symbols but in the context of this dream they become negative. Why? Because as they are in the toilet, they are not in their right place. From a positive point of view, a diamond, which is a mineral, is made from cut or sculpted quartz and symbolizes great transformations of the unconscious. During the different stages of its transformation, this mineral goes from its initial stage as black coal to finally become a diamond that manifests bright, luminous purity. In the negative context of this dream, it represents the emergence from our unconscious related to memories where numerous resources at our disposal were misused or used in illusion.

The figure 3,000 may be related to Angel 3 SITAEL, *master builder on the inside as well as on the outside*. But we can also link it to Angel 30 OMAEL, whose Qualities include

multiplication, materialization, expansion and fecundity.
Well, this woman is a *multiplier*. In her dream, her aunt tells
her, *"There are lots of diamonds and you can have more from
your deceased sister."* The dreamer didn't mention what her
aunt and sister represent for her. We can deepen the meaning
of her aunt's words even without this information because
they reveal that the dreamer has memories and a program
of experimentation regarding material wealth. As long as we
haven't integrated the state of conscience of inner wealth,
inner prosperity, that is obtained through the development
of Angelic Qualities and Virtues, no matter how wealthy we
are on the outer level, we will never feel satisfied.

The positive aspect of this dream lies in the fact that the
dreamer is sitting on the toilet, which is a symbol of
purification. That means that she wants to purify misactions
due to an abundance of resources that were misused. This
woman is going through great inner transformations. She has
been able to accept and digest the memories visited in her
dreams and the interpretations she received. This has allowed
her to go through several stages: her recent dreams bear
witness to this. In one of her recent dreams, *she saw herself
flying through the air with her mother.* The transformation
she is going through thanks to the purification of her distorted
memories related to ill-used wealth will gradually lead her to
conceive and materialize projects in the state of conscience
of inner wealth and prosperity.

In the beginning, it is essential to accept all of our limitations
and to be able to consider them as gifts. The passage in the
Bible that says *it is easier for a camel to get through the
eye of a needle than for a rich man to enter the Kingdom
of God*, contains great truth. Indeed, an overabundance of
material means may cause a person to get lost. That's why we
must always be vigilant and set ourselves goals that allow us
to develop altruism and put it into practice. When the time
comes, Cosmic Intelligence may say to us, "Yes, we can grant

you abundant resources because we Know that you will use them in a right, just, altruistic way."

Now, let's talk about jealousy. This emotion is often associated with affective, emotional aspects. In the life of a couple, jealousy is often caused by fear of losing the other partner. However, great needs for power are often hidden behind jealousy. The film *Cleopatra*, starring Elizabeth Taylor as Cleopatra and Richard Burton in the role of Mark Anthony, provides us with a very good example of the mechanisms and power games that we may implement and take part in.

It takes place in Ancient Egypt. Cleopatra was queen of Egypt and had a number of lovers, including Julius Caesar, the Roman emperor. This fact touches on ancient collective memories related to both Egyptian and Roman aspects, and their qualities and distortions. Egyptians, in their negative aspect, honored deities with far from praiseworthy aims. They used their spiritual knowledge to acquire absolute power on the material level.

An excerpt from the film, described below, shows how Cleopatra, the queen, uses jealousy in her power games when concluding a political and romantic alliance with Mark Anthony. Let's analyze this excerpt as if it were a dream. If you watch the film, notice the effect of power, which is clearly emphasized. What may be engendered by a thirst for power? It creates jealousy, competition, and comparison, all of which are human distortions of the State of Conscience of Angel 48 MIHAEL. Notice the statues and the ambiance as well. What memories do they awaken in you?

The scene reveals a lustful, drunken, greedy feast in Cleopatra's palace. Queen Cleopatra and Mark Anthony are sitting side by side but each at own table. To Cleopatra's right there is a large gold statue of a crocodile. The animal's mouth is open. Mark Anthony is already drunk and is clearly bored. Cleopatra notices this and makes a gesture with her right hand. On her orders, a pompous chariot appears bearing a man disguised as Caesar. Behind him appears a woman who resembles Cleopatra. Then we see the false Caesar and the false Cleopatra kiss each other passionately. This makes Mark Anthony so mad with jealousy that he rushes toward the chariot, pulls the woman out of the arms of the false Caesar and kisses her himself, while looking toward real Cleopatra's table. He sees that she has left the room. He lets go of the woman and runs to find Cleopatra. He finds her in her bedroom, lying on her bed. They have a very intense discussion and Mark Anthony expresses his jealousy and envy of Caesar. He thinks that Cleopatra still loves Caesar although he's dead and that he, Mark Anthony has only ever been Caesar's right hand and in his shadow. Part of him wants to stop loving Cleopatra, but simultaneously, he knows he'll never be able to leave her. We see that Cleopatra is moved by Mark Anthony's suffering and inner struggle. Their kiss reveals the mixture of attraction/repulsion that dwells in them.

In the following scene, we see them in bed together talking about love. That's when Cleopatra tells Mark Anthony that she has loved him since she first saw him, when she was only 12 years old.

This extract shows a great many distorted memories that they both harbor regarding love, relationship as a couple, glory, riches and celebrity.

These memories belong to the human distortions of Angel 48 MIHAEL: *lust, passion, seeking sensual pleasures to compensate for the absence of a spiritual life, feelings of attraction and repulsion.* Jealousy is related to emotional needs and a desire for power. The gold statue of a crocodile symbolizes these distortions. From a positive point of view, gold indicates Divine Materialization; from a negative point of view, a crocodile that lives both in the water and on land, symbolizes very old, primary emotional needs under whose influence a person can attack both on the emotional level and in the world of action. Distorted aspects are also manifested in the way Mark Anthony embraces Cleopatra: with tenderness, aggression and possessiveness all at the same time. His behavior and energy expresses this mixture of attraction/repulsion and protection/threat that we sense in situations where power games are going on.

An interesting metaphysical aspect is depicted in the creation of the illusion and the effect it has on a person. Caesar was assassinated, but with the false Caesar on the chariot, Cleopatra creates a scenario as though she were still with Caesar; so she was playing and mixing power and love in a very negative way. Jealousy is a very complex force of love, possessiveness and anger. Mark Anthony's extreme reaction to this illusion shows us how a person may become prey to mirages as long as he hasn't cleansed all of his distorted memories. This scene plunged Mark Anthony's mind and spirit into an accumulation of memories marked by the emotions of jealousy, envy, lack, ambition, comparison and duality, which he then expresses in Cleopatra's bedroom.

Regarding the phenomenon of illusion, it is important to remember the Divine Law that says that illusion is educational. This Law is essential for us to understand the multiple realities that people have to experiment before discovering true Wisdom and Love. Illusion creates grounds for an apprenticeship wherein the person believes he is right even though he isn't. Hence he creates so-called extraordinary experiences for himself through which he advances positively, and very gradually discovers that he is not right. Without illusion, it would be impossible to be motivated to experiment because we would be constantly confronted with our distortions. We wouldn't see anything else and we would lose all hope. It is fascinating to understand the true meaning of hope.

In this scene, Cleopatra is wearing a white dress. From a positive point of view, white symbolizes a person's inner spiritual dimension. This isn't the case in the scene we're analyzing because in the context of this film, spirituality only serves the conquest of material riches and powers. Likewise, the numerous statues of deities highlight spiritual power that is not used to materialize divinely, but to satisfy earthly ambition. We can also see the phenomenon of comparison that is very clear in this scene when Mark Anthony compares himself with Caesar. The triangle of comparison, jealousy, and competition often manifests in couples when memories related to power are awakened and create conflicts. In such a context, if the people do not have access to Knowledge that allows them to refer back to themselves and become calm before expressing themselves, a liberating, constructive dialogue is impossible.

Let's analyze the memories of comparison. Comparing ourselves with others only leads to discontent and permanent dissatisfaction. Envy and a need to compare ourselves with others are signs that our memories related to past situations haven't been settled yet. This is often the case when we begin a new relationship, like the woman who told me, "When I made love to my husband, I could feel that the past hadn't been settled. Sometimes, I had flash images of my husband's ex-wife." In actual fact, it turned out that her husband used to think about his ex-wife when he was making love.

It is very important to work on past memories to purify them well and to transcend them. If we are living alone at the moment, instead of envying those who are in a couple, we work on our inner couple.

In many relationships, power games are not only fueled by comparison, but also by competition. In such cases, the lovers don't want their partner to have loved anyone else before them. It has to be the first time they've loved, which indicates great egotism. Their competitive spirit makes them want to know who fell in love first. Such memories can be so grotesque that it is all the more important to cleanse them.

Let's talk about jealousy and the memories that activate this distortion. A woman told me that she and her spouse were working with Traditional Angelology. She went on to say, "When he told me about his past, which was marked by infidelity and jealousy, that made me think. Moreover, as he's working intensely on himself, I sense things about him on the metaphysical level. He's promised me that it was nothing physical, that there was nothing on the concrete level. But I'm scared. I really don't feel well sometimes. I still remember when my mother was 45 years old and my father left her for another woman. She never got over it. I'm afraid of going through the same thing as her."

I said to her, "You aren't in the same situation as your mother but if your spouse still has infidelity on the metaphysical level, if he doesn't cleanse these memories and forces, it can lead to concrete future infidelity. Your fears reveal your resonance with what your mother went through. Use your fears to cleanse the unconscious memories that engender them but make sure that you act right with your man and that you take good care of him. I am sure your mother was probably like those women who, with time, become distant with their husband. Why would a man or woman stay with a spouse who doesn't love them? Why should we stay and suffer in a relationship that is not right, where there is no intimacy, no sexuality as an expression of our love and fusion? Why do we need to maintain the illusion of a couple? We have many erroneous concepts about love. Love is a garden and we need to take care of it if we wish to have a good harvest, a beautiful life. So many married couples suffer in a fake relationship. So every time you feel afraid, instead of trying to convince yourself that you won't go through what your mother did, accept the fact that you harbor similar memories in your unconscious and change to become a wonderful lover. Do everything you can that is right and just and profoundly, divinely loving so you will not have any regrets if, one day, he chooses to leave. That will only mean that this man was not for you. However, usually, when we take good care of our spouse, we do not lose him or her. This is an absolute, logical fact. As you are committed to an initiatic path, Cosmic Intelligence is offering you an opportunity to transform these memories and forces that your mother accumulated and experienced. Learn the lessons and grow from them. That's the true purpose of your mother's experience and what you are going through with your present companion; that's the purpose they serve – to help you evolve and become a better person, a better soul, who understands, knows and seeks to materialize true, unconditional love and divine fusion on the inside and on the outside."

This woman, who is working intensely on herself, sometimes goes through initiations that create ill-being. Regarding this, she said to me, "I don't feel good with my partner. I cannot look after him. I sense that he's withdrawing because he doesn't feel good either. And I know that if I don't look after him, there's an even greater chance he'll go off with someone else."

"Up Above has planned and organized your program well, you can trust that, but of course you need to take care of him if you want him to be with you. Unconditional Love doesn't mean we do not do anything in Love," I replied. "Of course, the negative aspect of your partner, his minus side, is not right, but his minus becomes a plus for your minus. Let me explain; that's mathematics of our conscience. This means that his negative aspect of having been unfaithful stimulates your negative aspect of not looking after him well enough in your relationship. Your fears create the opposite and you need a plus to transform a minus. He wants your love but you reject him. It is normal that you should be afraid of losing him. It is an alarm signal that you sense in you. Being too focused on the outside and not changing inside, creates problems in your intimate relationship. If you do not take good care of him, then you are already preparing and programming that you will lose him. You need to trust your life plan. You don't know what's going to happen in this relationship yet so trust God, trust the Program He has chosen for you. Do your best for the relationship to work and develop in a well-balanced way. Work on your fears. If you trust what Cosmic Intelligence has orchestrated for the good of your evolution, then you will be able to go through events with causal vision and deep understanding of what you need to change in yourself. The reason why Up Above chose this man for you is because of your resonance with him, with his qualities and his distortions. Since his distortions activate your fears and worries and hence lead you to work on yourself, then his minus should become a plus for your evolution."

This woman shared several of her dreams with me, which I explained to her. I told her, "Your dreams confirm that you still nurture feelings of passion. There are forces in you that enjoy passion. If you had a very evolved spouse right now, you wouldn't appreciate him because of those forces; he wouldn't play passionate power games and you'd eventually get tired of him; you'd feel bored. We mustn't think that initiates have necessarily cleansed all of their distorted memories. An initiate knows that this work is long and is carried out in stages. He told you what he did in the past; at least he was open and fair with you. Now give him a chance to change and transform yourself at the same time. You need to be persevering, patient and determined. If you revel in these forces because of the stimulation they provide you with, you will tend to put off cleansing them, and they'll continue to exert their influence on you. One thing is sure: if you cleanse your memories, you will attain emotional, affective stability. How? With whom? On the physical level, we rarely have access to all the data, thank God! We surely wouldn't be ready to face all of the aspects. Up Above always takes our pace of evolution into account and conceives our learning programs and initiations accordingly. If we apply the Law of

Resonance and the other Divine Laws in our daily life, we can rest assured that harmony and happiness will feature in our life. You should consider yourself cherished to have an initiate as a partner who's working intensely on himself and doing his best. You need to work on your fears and resonance and trust in the Program God has established for you. Remember it is precious to have a spiritual man evolving with you. Do not take him for granted because it is normal that if you do not love him well, he will eventually find another person. Take care of your couple and remember also that without divine sexuality, without pure intimacy, there is no real couple."

From one initiate to another, I'd like to tell you that when our unconscious opens, large blocks of memories are sometimes activated. Their activation is intentional; Up Above knows you are capable of overcoming and transforming them. At any time on your journey, people can be placed on your path who will play the role of disturbers and trigger metaphysical events and situations that will seem unfair to you. Initiates must never project their negative feelings, emotions, thoughts or behavior onto others no matter how unfair or mean they are. This is what makes the difference between a person in an ordinary conscience and an initiate. Sometimes, Up Above deliberately sets certain circumstances and certain people on our path. If you still can't transform a particular evil aspect, and if you can't resist projecting the negativity you feel onto these people, pray to God and ask Him to help you: "Dear God, please ensure that the energy emanating from me isn't projected onto this person who is causing me to suffer at the moment. Please help me to consider him as a symbol in a dream. Please, help me!"

When we pray to Heaven, we invoke the Highest Levels. Up Above will answer by adding one layer after another to help us move on to another stage. Sometimes it can become very intense, very powerful. A single person can set off a whole block of memories. The actual person is insignificant compared to the reservoir of memories he activates. He is merely an instrument to trigger these memories. In order to learn to remain stable and imperturbable in all circumstances, initiates have to train themselves to transform considerable concentrations of negativity. Remember these very important aspects when you are going through trials and ordeals. This will help you move on to another stage without recording new karmas. Not hurting the other person when he isn't right or fair is Wisdom that needs to be immediately acquired in the process of purifying memories and transforming evil.

Here is an example that another woman, who is working with this Teaching and looking for her twin soul, shared with us. She was very happy with the following dream of hers. *I see myself in a tidy attic. There isn't much in this attic. Then I see myself making love with an ex-partner that I'd lived with for three years. Next I see myself in a wedding dress. I go up the stairs in a tower and at the top, there's an eagle that seems to be protective.*

I asked her what her ex represented for her. She replied, "I lived with him for three years but I'd never go out with an entrepreneur again!" It was clear from the way she pronounced *entrepreneur* that she still admired his attitude and work. She explained to me that as time went by, they'd experienced a lot of duality and had become like two competitive bosses. Their relationship hadn't worked. He wasn't spiritual and wasn't interested in working on himself and walking a spiritual path.

Let's analyze this woman's dream. An attic represents a place where we tidy away our memorabilia, symbolically speaking, our memories. The dreamer was happy because everything seemed nice and tidy. However, even though the attic was tidy and not encumbered with lots of things, the attic symbol was used to show her that she still nourished herself on certain past memories. She was making love with her ex. That means she still fuses with his way of thinking, feeling, behaving. The wedding dress indicates that on the inside, she is ready to marry this type of energy, that she is very attracted to men who focus on material competition. Going upstairs symbolizes a desire and search for elevation, but the symbol of the materialistic entrepreneur, who is a boss with no spiritual dimension, taints everything else. In this context, the eagle she sees at the top of the stairs, even if it seemed to be protective, becomes negative. As an animal that belongs to the world of air, this bird represents instincts (animal) and also thoughts (air). From a positive point of view, it symbolizes loyalty and fidelity as well as a capacity to raise ourselves up very high and to see very far. But we mustn't forget that it is a bird of prey. In this dream, it reflects the duality this woman is going through: on the one hand, her desire to raise herself up spiritually; on the other hand, her unconscious desire to maintain and protect past energies.

This woman is on her own at the moment. She is on a spiritual path and she wants to find her twin soul. Through this dream, she was shown why she can't meet him right away. Even if on the conscious level she is on a spiritual path and aspires to life in a couple with her spiritual complement, on the unconscious level, she harbors untranscended memories that push her toward the kind of energy that her ex represents. She continues to maintain and fuse with energies and thoughts that give priority to matter. By using her ex-entrepreneur-spouse as a symbol, Up Above was showing her, "You want to encounter your twin soul, you want to have a spiritual spouse, but look at the kind of memories you still have in your attic! You may want him on the conscious level, but these unconscious memories get in the way; they are an obstacle. They sabotage and cancel your efforts. You need to transform them if you want to move on to the next stage."

I said to her, "If you were introduced to a spiritual man who doesn't fully assert his masculine dimension yet, he wouldn't attract you. You wouldn't be able to help him construct himself and develop his full potential. You wouldn't want him." She thought about this, named a few examples of spiritual men, and said," That's so true! When I first saw them, I wasn't in the least attracted to them. Now they are in relationships and live as a couple, I've seen them change and become beautiful." This woman needs to understand the importance of purifying her memories so as to prepare a place for the man that Cosmic Intelligence has in mind for her.

Since our discussion, she has now received lots more dreams, including nightmares because Up Above has opened doors onto other zones of her unconscious. She is visiting very negative memories, but she is very happy to do this purification work. She knows that by working on her inner couple, she is also preparing her outer couple.

Let's move on to another example a different woman shared with us. This woman has accepted to share her story, which is a life story that helps us understand that although it may be difficult to be alone, it's better to wait and continue to work on our inner couple.

This woman, who is a gym teacher, told us the message of one of her dreams and the reality she is going through by speaking symbolically as follows. *I did a backward somersault without going through any of the necessary stages, in spite of all the ill-being and uneasiness my soul felt that I didn't listen to. Then I found myself, hands tied to a man, locked in the trunk of my car. Thank God, part of me came back to set me free!*

Let me go back briefly to the beginning of her path.

She got married for the first time, and had two miscarriages and difficulty conceiving. When she was 28, she separated from her husband, a strict, rigid man. During the same period, her sister lost a child. She was deeply affected by the death of this child. Then she met someone else. After six months in this new relationship with a man she didn't know very well, she discovered she was pregnant. She immediately decided to keep the baby. She didn't know then, but it was a girl. Afterwards, she said, "I was so afraid of never having children that I knew immediately that I was going to keep that baby. And my husband agreed."

She defined her husband as follows. "He's originally from Morocco, where he was a rich aristocrat. He had land and had been to university. He still hadn't received the necessary certificates of equivalence for his studies and diploma to be allowed to teach in Canada, but he was able to fill in as a substitute teacher. While he was a fine, refined, intelligent genius, he also had phases where he didn't want to do anything at all. The university where he worked used to call me to inform me of his absence. As he didn't work, money problems and difficulties followed. Over time, his financial difficulties got worse because he wasn't able to transfer money from Morocco. Gradually, a certain misery ensued. When we decided to separate, I was terrified he'd take our child to Morocco. But he didn't. He seemed to simply abandon his child. I never heard from him again. Being with my daughter is the most beautiful experience I've ever had in my whole life."

Her daughter is now 23 years old. For her mother, this period corresponds to 20 years, 15 of which she has been without a spouse. She had difficulties in relationships. After this Moroccan, she had a partner for five years, without him really being a partner. At the very outset of their relationship, he said to her, "I don't want to commit myself. We're friends who have sex, that's all." For those five years, she was literally obsessed with this man.

This woman began working with Traditional Angelology in May 2005. Shortly afterwards, this man announced, "Our relationship is over because I've found the woman of my life." This came as a great shock to her. She realized that she needed to grieve, and that she'd had to go through this situation; she had karmas to settle. Between May and October 2005, this woman received quite a few premonitory dreams, and in October she met another man.

She kindly shared her story to help all those who are still waiting to meet their twin soul, their complementary spouse. Her testimonial shows us how important it is to follow Heaven's Guidance well, and not let dependencies and emotional, affective needs make our decisions for us when it's a question of forming a couple.

Here is the first dream she received. *I was in a big hotel by the sea. It was a beautiful place. The hotel was luxurious and the sea was sky blue. I was with friends. I was introduced to a man called Sir Paul William. (I didn't know him in concrete reality.) He was very tall and very nice. I was sitting on a couch and he was sitting on my left. He was talking to someone and his right shoulder and arm were against me. I leaned my head on him in all confidence and closed my eyes. I felt really good even though I hardly knew him. I trusted him and felt confident. We got up to go in to dinner. Other people arrived. I sensed a threat for this man. Among the newcomers, there were some people who wanted to steal something. I felt that they were ready to do anything to get what they wanted. But what was it? Sir Paul William wanted me to sit beside him at the dinner table. He showed me a bottle of wine, a very, very old bottle. I took it into my hands and closely examined it. As I was looking at the bottle, I became aware of the threat. I realized there was a seal on back of the bottle. I knew that was what the men were looking for: this seal was very valuable. I managed to take off the seal and I hide it in my right hand. Sir Paul William understood. I gave him the seal and discreetly we managed to put it into a safe for safekeeping. I knew that those men were ready to kill to obtain this seal.*

All of the elements of this dream represent parts of the dreamer, but we shall only analyze the main aspects.

Through this dream, she is being shown memories that are ready to do anything to obtain a seal that's supposed to be very valuable. The incident takes place in a luxury hotel, which is a symbol of wealth and pleasure. The attraction the dreamer feels for Sir Paul William reveals memories related to notoriety, refinement, and worldly pleasures. This is what the father of her daughter represents on the concrete level; he was a rich, noble, intelligent, distinguished Moroccan.

Sir Paul William could have been a positive symbol, and so could the seal, the wine and the hotel. However, in this dream, all of these elements become negative because of the presence of forces that intend to steal and are even ready to kill to get what they want. The seal on the bottle of wine becomes negative because it was granted too much importance. Concretely, all we have to do is to imagine what the seal on a wine bottle represents. She was shown forces in her that are ready to do anything to get hold of and possess what wine represents. From a positive point of view, wine symbolizes emotions and an atmosphere or ambiance that activates certain states of conscience such as joy, pleasure, sharing, and moments of social relaxation.

However, here it is the negative aspect that is predominant and manifested by a worldly atmosphere. The old wine bottle and its seal indicate the presence of old memories of great emotional dependencies. This woman was seeking a certain emotional quality in a love relationship. But this type of relationship is an illusion since it is based on notoriety, worldly pleasures and superficiality.

The energies and ambiances in our dreams enable us to diagnose what is going on within us and so we can know what we are going to experience on the outside. Let's go back to the dreamer. She received another dream that she described as insignificant. In actual fact, it was a very meaningful dream for her. Here it is. *I saw my daughter doing gymnastics; she was on the beam. She was practicing a backflip, a backward somersault on the beam. She was finding it very difficult. I offer to help her because she was not going about it the right way. I told her she needed to proceed in stages. She needed to start again from the very beginning and relearn the basics. Then, we'd move on to the thrust of the legs to form the back bridge, hands on the beam. I repeated how important it was before the leg thrust to first memorize exactly where the beam is to ensure her hands have a solid grip.*

In this dream, her daughter symbolizes part of the dreamer herself. Gymnastics symbolize learning qualities in action. The beam represents maintaining balance, equilibrium. Everything that happens behind our back concerns the past. The backward somersault on the beam means that she needs to learn well how to make a jump back into the past in conditions that require mastery of balance and the apprenticeship of the various stages necessary for her new actions to take place in all security. She is being told that she is going to activate the forces of her past and that she needs to be careful if she wants things to go well. She needs to watch her equilibrium and learn to return to her past while respecting each stage.

Legs are a symbol of action and moving around on the concrete, physical level. Before thrusting her legs toward actions related to the past, the gymnast first has to position her hands solidly. Hands symbolize giving and receiving. They are also a tool for creating and making things.

Returning to the past requires respect for each stage. That's the beauty of initiations. We can activate memories and purify them without the negative needs that they contain manifesting on the physical level and upsetting our life. This dreamer wanted to do a backward somersault without paying heed to the advice received in her previous dreams. She was shown that she will have difficulties if she doesn't take the time to integrate the lessons learned at each stage on the way.

This respect for each stage applies to work on our inner couple too. Whenever we notice distorted parts of our inner man – or our inner woman – they needn't manifest on the outside. Just imagine the Godsend it is to be able to become aware of them and work on them in the metaphysical reality of our dreams without having to go through difficulties in our relationships in physical reality.

Let's go back to the month of October when this woman met a man. She met up with him two or three times and chatted with him on the phone. Hesitatingly, she said, "I felt reticent on the soul level; something was going on. The minute I was in contact with him, one of my dreams from a few years ago came to mind: *A man came up to me. He was very handsome and really luminous but I kept putting him off. Afterwards, I let myself go and we were able to fly. It was wonderful!*"

She made a link with this dream even though the man she'd met had nothing in common with the man in her dream. She thought, 'Maybe I'm reticent because I have negative memories.' She questioned herself and, one evening, before going to sleep, she asked Up Above a question. The way she formulated it will show you that she did her backward somersault. She didn't ask if the man was the right person for her evolution, she asked, "Is it time for me to go ahead with this man?" Up Above, They know how to interpret our questions correctly. The dream she received in reply to her question disconcerted her. We'll understand why it is very important to correctly interpret the symbolic meaning of our dreams and signs.

Here is her dream. *I was with friends. My cell phone rang. It was a woman asking me for help. She wanted information about a man that I knew at work. This man was interested in her and she wanted to know what I thought of him. I moved away from the group to be better able to talk to her because I understood how deep and important her question was. I headed toward a restaurant terrace and sat down. I explained to her that he was a good man and it would be worth her while getting to know him. I told her that I had quite often seen him at various evening events, and sometimes I'd seen him offer women a drink, but he'd never gone home with any of them. I even asked him out of curiosity why he did that. He explained that his aim wasn't to seduce those women, but rather to get to know them and to talk with them. At another event, we were all surprised by his talent when he began to play the guitar and sing. I said to her, "I know he's not as handsome as you'd like, but I can assure you he's worth getting to know. You won't regret it. And anyway, he's been in love with you for ages but you never realized." I added, "I understand you. I'm going through the same thing with ... – she named the man she asked Up Above if it was time to go ahead with – but I can assure you that he's worth getting to know; he's a good man." All this time, I was sitting on the terrace and a group of people asked me if I could move so that they could sit together. I moved. There were also people who wanted to set up a rain shelter. I had to go over this shelter. I surmounted these obstacles while talking on my cell phone. At the end, I repeated, "It would really be worthwhile your giving this man a chance for you to get to know him. You won't regret it." I said goodbye. I turned off my phone and to my great surprise, the woman materialized in front of me, her cell phone in her right hand, just like me. She took me in her arms, hugged me, and thanked me.*

This woman, who had been feeling reticent about the man in question, took this dream as a decision of Up Above's to encourage her, telling her, "Yes, he's the right one for you; you can go ahead."

Let's analyze this dream where she is told, 'He's worth getting to know.' The words used and the symbols that appear in dreams are never a mere coincidence. Everything is mathematically precise. Let's look at them in detail. It takes place on a restaurant terrace, which is related to the social aspect. The woman who calls her asking for her help is part of herself. During the phone conversation, she talks to that part of herself and makes comparisons. The man she talks about gets to know women by offering them a drink, an alcoholic drink.

Wanting to get to know someone by offering him or her an alcoholic drink reveals emotional dependency. It may seem beautiful, but when we analyze it, other aspects are brought to light. The dreamer made a link with this when she said, "He's not very handsome but he's worth getting to know."

Very often people begin a relationship without having any profound affinities. Others get married on the same basis. This way of creating our destiny and living love as a couple cannot lead to magical relationships.

As the dreamer was talking, she was asked to move by a group. She was being shown that she wasn't in her rightful place. The group set up a rain shelter that she had to go over. So many obstacles! But she remains convinced and she's also the one convincing. In a dream, it's always important to analyze who is talking. We have to learn to discern if it is a Guide from the Parallel Worlds, or someone we know who is being used as a symbol to show us aspects of ourselves. This analysis is just as important when we are the one talking in the dream.

This requires self-analysis: "What does this symbol represent for me? What am I feeling at the moment? Am I feeling emotionally dependent?" This introspection helps us interpret dreams, signs and symbols more correctly; it helps us avoid misinterpretation and subsequent misactions.

In this dream, the woman is convincing herself. She needs a man so much that even if he causes her pain, she doesn't mind... She'd asked Up Above persistently and a man had turned up in her life. But as the Law of Resonance is constantly at work, the man who manifested could only be the reflection of memories of emotional, affective dependencies and needs that this woman still harbors.

Up Above synchronized such an encounter because she needed to experience this situation. She had already begun working with the Traditional Study of Angels at the time. As she was talking to us, we could perceive her great spiritual potential behind her words. We listened to her with a lot of love and without any judgment. She told us that the man loves good food, going out, etc. Moreover, he's a hunter. Of course, like all human beings, hunters have a potential for transformation and evolution, and what they do with it depends on their state of mind and spirit and what motivates them. On the metaphysical level, hunting has a very precise meaning: it refers to man's attitude to animals. Animals symbolize the instinctual dimension of our vital energy. A hunter behaves as a predator. In other words, instead of integrating the qualities of his inner animal world and transcending his distortions, a hunter acts with the intention of tracking and killing his inner animals to then feed on them. This is true physically when he ingests their flesh, and also emotionally, through the pleasure, feelings and sensations he experiences during and after the hunt.

At that time, we didn't explain the symbolism of hunters and hunting to this woman. It would have been too much for her. Our listening to her did her good but we felt that she didn't want to hear any opinion that differed from hers. The time hadn't come for her to move on to the next stage.

Later, this woman received a very clear dream that allowed her to understand that she'd had to go through this experience. Here is that dream. *I was with a woman. She was in danger. I tried to set her free from a man who was holding her hostage. Her hands are tied behind her back. I lock her into the trunk of a car for her safety. I'd go back and get her out later. But as I closed the trunk, I become the woman in the trunk with her hands tied behind her back. I realized that I'm not alone. The man had anticipated my intention and he'd hidden himself in the trunk. I was caught and there was no way I could get out of this predicament.*

All of the elements of this dream represent parts of the dreamer. She is being shown her own forces that tie her up. They are related to her two principles: her feminine polarity and her masculine polarity. She became involved in a relationship with a man she met and it was a very difficult relationship. At first, everything was fine and beautiful. She gave that man her most beautiful feelings and sentiments. She gave him everything right down to the physical level. She flowered his garden. After a while, it became so difficult that the Angels were left by the wayside, as Kaya would say. She made so many concessions for the relationship to work that she completely set her spiritual path aside. At one point though, her natural character reasserted itself and she could no longer go on like this. Such a dream shows that we mustn't blame others because we are the ones who create our dependencies and prisons.

This relationship lasted three years. The man turned out to be aggressive, strict and rigid, especially with this woman's daughter, who still lived at home because she was studying. Her daughter is a beautiful soul. She is one of the new children. But he hated her and he showed her all his hatred. It was hell. And it was her love for her daughter that incited this woman to break off her relationship with him.

Since the end of this relationship, everything in her life has changed, including her job. She is in the process of regaining her Angelic light-heartedness. Beautiful things are in store for her. In this new phase of her life, she received the following dream.

I was at my mother's home. There was a family reunion or party, I'm not sure which. There were people I knew and others I did not. I observe a man from the corner of my eye because I didn't know him but I wondered who he was. In the beginning, I didn't think he was very handsome, but the more I looked at him, the more handsome he seemed to become. I walked from room to room, observing the people there. I was a little cold. I arrived in a small sitting-room where a couch-bed was open and covered with beautiful, warm blankets. Since nobody was there, I decided to lie down under the blankets to warm up. The man I observed earlier came in, and to my great surprise, he came over and lied down beside me. I was a little confused, but I didn't sense any bad intention. He took me in his arms and said, "Come on, I'll warm you up." So I let him. He took me in his arms and kissed me tenderly. I let him do this but I was a little uncomfortable because I didn't know him. However, once again, I only felt kindness and authenticity in his gesture. He looked at me and said, "I know you are working with Angel 1 at the moment."

I replied, 'It's Angel VEHUIAH, Divine Will.'

"Yes, it is."

"It's not easy, is it?"

"No, it's not easy."

I felt great compassion for him, for his soul. I understood just how difficult his work was. I knew how hard it was to materialize in accordance with Divine Will. I observed his face, which was really close to mine as we were still lying in each other's arms. I thought that, in spite of the difficulty of his work, his face was beautiful, luminous, and harmonious. I knew he was going to succeed in transforming himself and in better materializing Divine Will.

Up Above sent her this beautiful dream, which is also true encouragement. The only hitch is that she didn't know him and that she tends to become intimate too fast when a man approaches her. Despite this, the dream shows that she has reached another stage and that she has the potential to attract more spiritual, evolved energies on the affective level. This woman has changed her tune; she reasons differently and she has greatly changed. She told us, "Now, I understand. My present aim in life is to succeed in my inner couple." She was truly sincere when she said this because she has been marked by her difficult experiences. She will remember them for several lives. At present, she can fully succeed in doing her backward somersault, and she does it step by step, stage by stage. As for her happiness, it is already present in the wonderful relationship she has with her daughter, a beautiful soul, who is evolving spiritually. Thanks to intense work on her inner couple, this woman is on a beautiful, truly evolutive, spiritual path.

For our final example, we are going to symbolically analyze a commercial by Rogers AT&T, entitled *Express Wedding*. We shall analyze it as though it were a dream.

It begins with a yellowish-orange tent set up in a remote spot high up in the mountains. It's winter. A young couple are camping. It's a special occasion. We see the young man offer a ring to his beloved. We understand that he's proposing to her. Then we see the young woman alone in the tent looking at her ring. At the same time, she's talking to someone on her cell phone, a chef. In the next scene, we see a large crate fall out of the sky behind the young man outside. When the panels open, we see an organ. Almost immediately afterwards, a yellow helicopter arrives and an old priest steps out of it. We also see a wedding-dress arrive on a sledge pulled by huskies. People crowd in from all over the place, all dressed for a wedding. There are also several bridesmaids, none of whom are very slim, all of whom are squeezed into fuchsia pink dresses. Everyone seems happy to be there for this occasion, except the young man. The final image is of the young man's sad, disappointed, resigned face.

It is quite easy to understand the symbolic message contained in this situation. On the conscious level, the couple aspire to simplicity, purity, and a natural, romantic setting. But, under the influence of unconscious memories, their reality is quickly transformed into just the opposite. Hence the necessity to discover and get to know each other before beginning a relationship. It is essential to find out if there is any possibility of forming an evolved couple, who share spiritual ideals, thoughts and values.

Before committing physically to a person, it should be a priority to receive dreams to confirm if it is the right person, the right soul to fuse with, for our spiritual evolution on Earth. We should always use our angelic power and ask God to send us Divine confirmation. Tell this to all the new generations. Teach them to live their life angelically.

Angel 37 Aniel

How to get out
of old behavioral patterns

A woman shared the following dream with me. She said, *"A Tai Chi teacher was showing me a posture, and she said, 'Two steps back are more important than one step forward.' I didn't understand. I looked at her and asked why."*

All of the elements in this dream represent parts of the dreamer. The action of stepping backward may be positive or negative; in a dream, it may be showing us that forces from the past are holding us back and preventing us from advancing, from making progress in terms of conscience. In this dream, however, it is the positive aspect. This woman was being told, 'At the moment, it is important for you to return to your past to learn to reconstruct your relationships with others.' Everything that is behind us, in the background, as well as our back, represents the past.

Through the symbol of the Tai Chi teacher, the dreamer was taught that by returning to her past, she could rediscover ancestral wisdom. She would be able to cleanse and reprogram her memories and hence have access to a new stage of evolution. This evolution will allow her to enjoy her relationships better.

She could have been shown an airplane, train, or car reversing, or simply taking two steps back herself without any reference to Tai Chi. To understand this dream in depth, let's analyze the symbolic meaning of this very ancient martial art that comes from China.

Tai Chi differs from other martial arts by the slowness of its gestures that are carried out very gently and harmoniously, with absolutely no violence. A person doing Tai Chi simultaneously trains himself to be aware of his thoughts, emotions, and the vital energy circulating in him, as well as everything he emanates on the metaphysical level.

Tai Chi originated in China. Every population, every country has its + and −. At one time, China was famous for its ancestral wisdom. Nowadays, it is known as a great power of materialization and multiplication. The negative aspect is the loss of ancestral wisdom and spirituality. For decades, spirituality was forbidden, and it is still very controlled today. At the present time, the Chinese are almost solely focused on matter and their physical development. However, one day, we shall see a spiritual China once again. When it has sufficiently experimented in matter and experienced multiple problems caused by multiplication without conscience, its spiritual roots will re-surface. And the future will be radiant once again in China; human rights will be better integrated and respected.

The dreamer was told that the two steps back were more important than one step forward. What does this mean? The teaching she received is full of great wisdom. This woman was being told that when she consciously revisits her past, she will realize what isn't right or just in her. She can then bring about the necessary changes by cleansing and reprogramming her memories. Hence, she will advance in the right way, without constantly repeating the same erroneous behavior stemming from her past.

This woman was very moved by the interpretation of her dream! Her eyes lit up. She understood that it was a very simple dream containing great wisdom. Kaya suggested she work with Angel 37 ANIEL, because her dream reflected the manifestation of one of the aspects of this Angelic Field of Conscience. This Angel, bearer of the vibration of number

37, helps us work on our fear of change and of breaking old behavioral patterns. Angel ANIEL also helps us break the circle of dependencies that exist in our relationships with others. Consequently, we welcome new currents and new ideas. We change our mentality with greater openness on all levels.

Angel 37 ANIEL gives us the courage and strength to break old structures. It takes a lot of courage to rectify our flaws and weaknesses and to change bad habits that have been adopted and even crystallized in the course of our lives. Before being open to a new mentality, we have to break the old structures without letting ourselves be influenced, without feeling annoyed or disturbed by people who continue to function the old way.

How can Angel 37 ANIEL help us do this? By the Power and Strength contained in His Name. By repeating His Name as a mantra, we activate this Divine potentiality in ourselves. Everyone bears within himself the Qualities, Virtues and Powers of the 72 Original Angelic Essences as defined by The Traditional Study of Angels (Traditional Angelology). The 72 Angels constitute the Divine Nature, the 72 facets or faces of the Creator. In Traditional Angelology, the work method that is taught to reactivate our divine nature is *Angel Recitation* or *Angel Mantra Recitation* (cf. page 6). It is a very simple method that we can put into practice in all circumstances and at any age. It consists in repeating the Name of an Angel with great intensity, with pure intention and sacredness. We can do Angel Mantra practice while walking, doing housework or any other activity that doesn't require our total concentration. We can also sing or chant the Name of an Angel to a tune we like or that we invent as we go along. Whenever the context isn't suitable for us to do Angel Recitation out loud, we do it on the inside, and as often as possible throughout the day. We recommend working with the same Angel for at least 5 days.

Whenever we do Angel Mantra Recitation very intensely, we concentrate on the Qualities and Strengths that the Angel represents and we can better recognize the distortions we have regarding this Field of Conscience. Angel Mantra allows us to rectify our human distortions and integrate the Angel's potentiality. While we are working with the same Angel over a 5-day period – or more if beneficial – through dreams and daily life situations, we receive all sorts of teachings, the themes of which correspond to the Angel invoked. This gradually makes the understanding and interpretation of dreams easier. Beautiful dreams will reveal Qualities, and difficult dreams and nightmares, our distortions. In this regard, I'd like to share with you a situation experienced by a man who worked with this Angel.

This man invoked Angel 37 ANIEL for several weeks. One night he received the following dream:

"I'm in a place where, in the background, I see the watch factory where I work in concrete reality. I'm lying on the ground and there is a young colored woman by my side. She is beautiful and pure. We kiss and hug. I feel it is very pure. My ex-girlfriend is there, just beside this beautiful colored woman. I can read her thoughts. She is telling herself she'd like to get me back. I feel she is jealous. Then the young colored woman gets up and goes. As she leaves, she looks at me and says, 'I miss you.' Then a third woman arrives and I feel she is sad and jealous too."

Regarding the third woman, this man told us, "I know her in concrete reality; I had an affair with her."

It was easy for this man to validate that his dream was related to Angel 37 ANIEL, an Angel that *breaks the circle of addictions* and dependencies and confers *mastery when faced with intellectual and emotional impulses*. He knew the 3 women represented different personalities of his inner feminine principle. The watch factory is also an important symbol. He could have been shown the same 3 women in a scene where there was a completely different background, without this watch factory, his real life workplace.

How can we analyze this symbol? First of all, it is no coincidence that this man works in a watch factory. We only talk about coincidence when we don't know the Divine Laws and symbolic language. All jobs, professions, trades, activities, everything we do on the outside corresponds to inner work, which serves the evolution of our conscience. We analyze why we do such an activity, why we have the job we do, what it represents for us, how we feel when we do it, etc. In every situation, there is always the + and the −.

In this dream, the man could have been shown a watch factory even if he didn't work in one at all. The presence of this symbol accentuates the importance of the message he was being given. This is always the case when elements in our dream match our concrete reality.

Let's try and understand this symbol. What is made in a watch factory? Watches and clocks, of course! So it's an activity related to time. Through this symbol, this man was being told, 'Watch, pay attention to how you use your time on the personal and social levels! How do you spend your time? Positively or negatively? What do you devote your time to?'

He could have been shown a large watch or clock, couldn't he? But it was a watch factory he saw. This factory, the people who work in it, plus all that goes on there, symbolizes aspects of this man regarding his social behavior and the way he multiplies. Metaphysically, this watch factory symbolizes the state of this man's conscience. It shows that he spends his time repeatedly reproducing the same emotional, affective behavior based on jealousy. The fact that he was lying down also signifies something very important. We can see that he is too relaxed, too much based on personal pleasures when he is in a work environment. He can be lazy sometimes because he has too many emotional dependencies. This also means that he is too seductive when he works and in his social life. He may often create infidelities with women on the concrete level or metaphysical dimension. How can this be done? He will have a macho energy, smiling all the time at the secretaries, charming people he encounters, etc. He will behave and stimulate others to engender infidelities. So many people are like this. We can hear their seductive tone when they talk with each other, even if no physical infidelities occur.

The factory was in the background. Symbolically, everything in the background, everything situated behind us, means that whatever is shown is related to the past. It also represents this man's foundations, the origin of who he is, where he is coming from. In the scene featuring the 3 women, the presence of the watch factory reveals that this man spends a lot of time nourishing emotional dependencies with others. He's had this relationship pattern for a long time. Through the behavior of these 3 women, he was shown the past, the present and what lies ahead for him i.e. a beautiful relationship, like the one he has with the young colored woman in his dream. But this beautiful relationship cannot be stable. It will be shaken, potentially broken by the memories and multiple emotional dependencies that this man can engender.

When she says, 'I miss you,' as she's leaving, he is being shown that future relationships will also have emotional, affective dependencies. This man will express his affection and love in an apparently beautiful, pure way, but 3 distortions will re-surface: possessiveness, sadness, and jealousy. It's inscribed in his memories; he will attract that until he cleanses them. This dream reveals this very clearly. It can engender a lot of problems for him in the long term because of the symbol of the watch factory.

The diagram on page 5 shows a veil hiding a great number of memories that dwell in our subconscious and in the various layers of our unconscious. These are memories we have accumulated throughout our many lives, because everything we think, feel, and do is continually inscribed and recorded in us. They constitute our karmic *luggage*.

The Law of resonance allows us to understand that we attract all that we are, positive and negative. You may say, "But I don't know all that I am; I don't know what's in my unconscious." It's true and that's why it is so important to pay attention to our dreams; they reveal hidden aspects of ourselves. Hence, if we are shown a dream like this man's, it means that we cannot attract a beautiful, independent, autonomous person, capable of loving us with pure, unconditional love, without being possessive, or jealous, without games of seduction. The different essences presented in this dream will always be in connections, fused with each other. As long as we still harbor these memories, it's impossible, because the Law of Resonance is constantly in action. And this Law is absolute!

In actual fact, a person with this kind of memory in his *luggage* wouldn't even be attracted to someone without any dependencies. Of course, he would feel the inner beauty produced by independence and pure love. He might even be impressed by what such a person emanates, but there wouldn't be any magnetism to lead to their being together. If someone emanates waves of attraction and repulsion, and the other person doesn't have this kind of energy, there won't be, there can't be, any affinity and attraction between them. The Law of Resonance is mathematical and he will be always stimulated by beauty + attraction and repulsion, so with a typical type of women! It's not easy for someone with dependencies to encounter a person who is truly free to love him with pure love. If he had to spend his life with this person, he'd be bored because such a person wouldn't get involved in games of seduction, jealousy and possession to satisfy his expectations and emotional, affective needs. This would automatically create conflict and deep ill-being. In other words, two such people would be incompatible. We take a great step forward when we understand this!

This man's dream reveals that he goes from one relationship to another. As long as he hasn't cleansed his memories, he won't be able to have a stable emotional relationship. He'll continue to live with these two tendencies. On the one hand, he'll attract dependent, languishing, jealous women with a lot of expectations, whereas, on the other hand, he himself will be attracted to apparently inaccessible, independent women, but it won't be true independence!

Sometimes we say a person is independent but very often, there are hidden distortions behind this independence. An apparently independent person may not display possessive, jealous behavior and may seem to be above such behavior. However, it's not the true autonomy we acquire when we activate the Qualities of Angel 37 ANIEL in ourselves.

In actual fact, the independence displayed is often a protection which hides many unconscious hurts, wounds and jealousy patterns. The person has built a wall of protection and self-defense to prevent himself from feeling the painful emotions that he has repressed in his unconscious. This false independence also renders the person incapable of true commitment to another person. Yes, sure, he may feel attracted and in love, but it's not true Love with a capital L.

It is normal to receive this kind of dream before attaining a high level of conscience. We need to understand that we unconsciously activate a mechanism of avoidance that pushes us to change partners. We avoid being upset and working on the relationship because we have too many hurts and wounds buried inside us. What's more, we project onto the outside, saying things like, "He's never home; I miss him; he could spend some more time with me." Or, "He doesn't give me enough freedom. He is possessive and suffocating." There are all sorts of contradictory scenarios that a person goes through due to memories of difficult relationships.

For a woman, whatever bothers her regarding her husband or life partner's distortions reflects aspects of her inner man. This is true for what she experiences in dreams and in concrete reality. Whenever a woman's conscience is open, she can be shown her emotions and reactions toward her spouse. The same applies to a man who is bothered by a woman. The woman represents part of his inner woman. This is always true, in all circumstances, without exception.

Let's consider the case of a woman who thinks her husband is never home. This simple fact touches on memories of lack and emotional, affective dependency that she has accumulated over many lives. So, whenever we wish to evolve, we take two steps back, symbolically speaking, like in the example of the dream about Tai Chi. We evaluate our past, our memories, and when we realize we have committed misactions1, we refer back to ourselves and rectify with Angel Mantra Recitation. By reprogramming our distorted memories, we take one step forward, then another and another...Hence we avoid repeating the same behavior over and over again. It is a very powerful work method which is not limited to intellectual understanding. The important thing is to always apply it, every minute of our lives. It helps us catch distorted thoughts and emotions as soon as they arise and rectify them, one by one.

Another example shows how Work with Angel 37 ANIEL helps us recognize and rectify repetitive behavior.

A radiant teenager who works with the Traditional Study of Angels, shared the following dream with my husband, Kaya: *"I saw myself in underground galleries. I was very, very small. I was as old as I am now but I was really tiny in size. I was only 2 centimeters tall! I was frightened because a violent, aggressive, coarse, vulgar monster was running after me. As I was running away, I met a young blond haired man. He was the same age and as small as I was. He too was afraid of the monster. He ran and ran... Then I found*

myself in a car with a friend and her father who brought me
back to the underground galleries."

Kaya explained the meaning of the dream to her. "All of the elements of your dream represent parts of yourself. The underground galleries mean that you are connected with memories that exist in your unconscious, just below the veil. You are very open and you are working on yourself, so it's normal to be shown your memories.

"The presence of the young man and the number 2 regarding size indicates that this is related to the masculine, to your potential to be in a relationship and your emissivity. The fact that you are both so tiny reveals inferiority complexes in both polarities, in both the masculine and feminine principles, in your forces that create love and wisdom. The young man has blond hair and is in difficulty, so this symbol is related to parts of you that find it difficult to assert your luminous ideas and concepts. This is due to the fact that your negative parts, symbolized by the monster, are stronger than your positive parts."

We often receive this kind of dream when going through adolescence. We are in the process of full mutation; good and evil are fighting on the inside, simultaneously constituting our future adult personality. The memories of other lives are more acutely awakened during this phase because the program that leads us to encounter the karma we need to work on is activated. Adolescence is a very important stage in the developmental of our conscience.

Kaya went on to say, "The big, violent, aggressive monster running after you indicates feelings of superiority that in the past, incited you to act aggressively and violently with your needs. When we are shown distorted aspects of ourselves, we may indeed be frightened until we have managed to transform them. This kind of dream also indicates that whenever there are unfair situations with your friends, situations that are not right and just, you let yourself be impressed and flee. You are incapable of telling them you don't agree with them.

"In the second part of the dream, you are with your friend and her father, who drives you back to the same place. This means that you have major memories of violence, domination and control. These two people also symbolize parts of you. Your friend's father is a more global symbol than your friend, who is closer to you. Her father is related to what she represents for you. He represents a lot of memories related to action in regards to friendship and trust in others. Through this symbol, you are being told, 'Look how you actively behave when you are with others.' He brought you back to the same place, where there are negative, violent, aggressive forces, and inferiority and superiority complexes. With such a dream, you need to be vigilant because you may attract friends or boyfriends who will want to dominate and control you, and who are coarse and vulgar. As long as you daren't assert your convictions, you'll recommence the same karmic cycles."

The young woman looked at Kaya and exclaimed, "That's so true! When I'm attracted by a young man, it's always the same story. The men I'm attracted to don't resemble each other physically – sometimes they're blond haired, sometimes brown haired –, but they've always got the same type of character: they are controlling, dominating and vulgar. Exactly as you've just said!"

This young woman is very sweet, gentle and refined. But among the memories buried in the depths of her unconscious, there are memories that resonate with the behavior of the men she attracts. The Law of Resonance helps us understand what she bears on the inside.

Kaya told her, "You are young; you're still a teenager. Before committing to a relationship, I advise you to do great work on your memories. Deep cleanse them, and from today on, learn to assert yourself and express your convictions. Otherwise, you risk ending up with a violent, aggressive, boorish husband and you'll have a very difficult life. It's inscribed in your dream and in your inner program. You are privileged because your conscience is open and you have access to Knowledge, unlike many people who simply endure their program in ignorance. You can work on the causal level and change your destiny. If you transform your attitude to relationships, you can change your life program. When confronted with a person or a situation that isn't right, you politely say that whatever they propose doesn't suit you."

Understanding this gives us great motivation and the necessary courage to cleanse our memories. Of course, meeting our inner monsters isn't pleasant. But we need to know that these monsters correspond to inner forces that resonate with people in whose presence we don't dare assert ourselves. It's easier to say nothing than to give our point of view to help things evolve positively.

After receiving such a dream, the following day or days, we feel vulnerable, fragile, and afraid of everything and nothing; we withdraw into our shell and let negativity dictate our life. We feel incapable of activating our positive aspects and strengths. But it is better for us to encounter our monsters in dream reality rather than see these forces materialize in the form of a violent spouse and difficult trials and ordeals that could last for decades.

We can indeed change our destiny with mathematical precision if we become really and truly involved and committed to working on the causal level. By transforming our memories, we change the parameters of our destiny. Consequently we attract situations that resonate with the new data. The Law of Resonance is very precise and absolutely right for each of us. When we know this Law, instead of wanting to change others, or waiting for them to change, we work on the transformation of our own structures and inner programs. Then we will be able to act and express ourselves clearly and divinely, and sooner or later, we will see changes take place in the outer world. Needless to say, we need to be patient before seeing transformations materialize on the physical level. Many souls have accumulated heavy karma. Some people have a hard time, alternately struggling between the role of victim and aggressor for lives and lives.

Kaya said to this young woman, "I advise you to work with Angel 37 ANIEL. This Angel will help you break the circle of dependencies that keeps bringing you back to the same place." The young woman smiled at him and said, "That doesn't surprise me; I was born on September 24th, which means I have this Angel twice as my Birth Angel: it's my Guardian Angel on both the physical and emotional levels."

Whenever we have the same Birth Angel twice, it means that His Field of Conscience is particularly important regarding what we have to learn and integrate in our present life. This young woman has brought into her life, in her karmic *luggage*, the distortions and qualities related to Angel ANIEL. She is already very evolved for her age, but her dreams reveal that she has old concepts, old structures and circles of dependencies that need to be broken. With Angel 37 ANIEL she is well equipped to carry out this Work, and Cosmic Intelligence will provide her with the necessary situations for her to successfully complete the apprenticeships that have been planned for her life. Cleansing her memories will favor an opening of conscience. She will become more receptive to the higher levels and may receive new concepts. Hence, she will attain high levels of conscience.

When we have repeated certain behavior for several lives, it is very beneficial and liberating to do some very deep Work with Angelic Essence 37, ANIEL. Very often, we have important doses of negativity to be transformed, which requires the strength and force of character, willpower and courage that this Angel provides us with. We can tell ourselves, 'OK, I'm going through some very difficult issues at the moment and

I understand why. However, I know I have the capacity to transform the forces and memories that engendered these difficulties.' Here is an example.

A woman who attended a lecture told me, "We have four children. Our 13-year-old boy is a dysmorphic dwarf. His deformity is serious. Ever since his earliest childhood, he has taken up a lot of space in our family. In fact, his powerful energy takes up all the space! There's a lot of power in him, we can feel it. When he was only 2 or 3 years old, his eyes made me think of demon's eyes. He used to scare me at times! For several years now, he has had the same dream: *He sees himself in front of an enormous crowd, speaking about different subjects. Everyone listens to him. He behaves like a politician speaking to crowds of people. He also received a dream where he is in prison with a man and two children. Water gradually rises and floods the whole prison.*"

I explained to this woman, "It's certain that in a past life, or maybe even in several past lives, your son was a politician or orator who had a lot of power and influence on the masses. But he didn't use this power well. Memories of those lives are reactivated in his recurring dream where he is addressing crowds of people. Being born with a handicap in this present life means that in other lives, he created karma with serious consequences for himself. He may have manifested a lot of pride and had considerable feelings of superiority. He may have used his power to crush others."

Of course, if we applied this reasoning to all haughty people who show feelings of superiority, we might expect there to be more dwarves on Earth. How come this isn't the case? Before attaining high levels of conscience, we all have inferiority and superiority complexes to transform. In the case of someone born as a deformed dwarf, it indicates a great accumulation of this kind of negative energy. Whenever a person exerts a multiplying function, as in the case of a politician, the accumulation of memories happens very quickly. Such a person has power over thousands, even millions of people. Consequently, a great quantity of energy is added to his karmic *luggage* each time he speaks, decrees and decides something.

Whenever a multiplying factor leads to abuse of power on a collective dimension, the negative karma engendered is more serious than in the case of someone exerting his power abusively in a much more restricted environment, such as his own family. The karmic impact is not nearly as great. When we understand the responsibility a *multiplying* person has, we know that his behavior and actions had better be right and just! In some of his past lives, this soul, must have behaved very negatively and manifested a strong complex of superiority regarding others.

Both of the dreams reveal what is going on in this person's inner world. In the recurring dream, he is visiting his old memories of power which have not yet been settled. In the second dream, he is confronted with his inner prison. The two children represent his child aspect – i.e. joie de vivre, spontaneity, vivacity, etc. – in relationships with others. As for the water rising in his inner prison, it symbolizes emotions that invade and limit. Emotions are a powerful multiplying factor, both positively and negatively.

In his present life, he can no longer do what he did in his past lives; he no longer has the stature to do so. When we don't know the Divine Laws, when we don't know that Divine Justice is absolute, we may cry and lament, "Why is my child like this? It's so unfair!" The child himself may wonder, "Why was I born like this? It's not fair! My brothers and sisters all have normal bodies; they are beautiful and I'm small and deformed!" He may feel great rage and rebellion if he doesn't accept his limitations and work on his memories.

One day, we understand that every single life plan, every single program Cosmic Intelligence decides on is right and just. In this example, the recurring dream and the description this boy's mother gave, show that he would repeat the same erroneous patterns if he had a normal body. He'd repeat the same behavior; he'd crush others. Now, however, he isn't able to do so!

I gently explained to his mother, who is very open and wants to learn how to have a more Angelic approach and understanding: "Your Work consists in evolving through this situation, in acquiring Knowledge which will allow you to understand why your child has to go through this, and why you have had such a child. Little by little, you'll be able to lead your son to understand and accept his state. He can then use this life to cleanse his memories and liberate his karmas. It won't be easy, but cleansing is better than rebelling against your shared Life Program." This woman understood very well. She is very open and has beautiful humility. She is a beautiful person!

She looked at me and said, "My husband, this boy's father, the father of our four children, belongs to the illegitimate lineage of the king of Belgium, Leopold II. I've studied his family tree in detail." She seemed to think she had understood what this meant. The term bastard lineage means that Leopold II had mistresses who have children. This woman had made a link with her son.

As I didn't know anything about the history of Leopold II – I only knew he had been King of Belgium – I looked him up. History tells us that Leopold II was king of Belgium until 1908. During his reign, the Congo was the king's strictly private colony. Several countries have had colonies, but in this case, a whole country was the king's private colony! He used the resources of the Congolese and made them collect rubber, a product that was in fashion then. He behaved like many kings and sovereigns who exploited the people and resources of colonized countries. Among other things, Leopold II had many palaces built for him. What's more, he was very cruel; apparently he cut off the natives' hands. He was so barbaric that an international committee intervened! After that, the Congo became a Belgian colony and was no longer Leopold II's private colony.

Is this young boy born with dwarfism the reincarnation of Leopold II? His mother seemed to think so. Not necessarily. We mustn't fantasize over reincarnations. As long as we haven't received a dream wherein Cosmic Intelligence clearly tells us that we are the reincarnation of such a person who did such a thing, it's better to abstain from all fantasizing. A reincarnation dream has to be precise! It has to fulfill certain criteria. Even if we are given exact indications, we aren't necessarily being told, 'Look, you did this or that.' We are given the opportunity to be reborn to our former errors. Generally speaking, we shouldn't focus on a specific person either in concrete reality or seen in a dream, but on what he represents symbolically.

By working with Angels, we can know the broad outlines of what we were and what we did in other lives. Our attractions and annoyances show us. That's all that counts. Otherwise we'd be invaded with all sorts of historic details and information. Knowing the essence of the Work we need to do is sufficient. By working on one distortion, we can touch on several lives, because sometimes we nourish and transport a weakness or flaw from one life to the next!

This young boy may have nothing to do with Leopold II or Belgium, or the era in question. He may have been a leader or politician in other lives and other countries where he exerted a lot of power. He wasn't right or just; he felt superior; he may have cut off people's hands, been extremely cruel, and done all sorts of things. In his current life, he has reincarnated like this. It is important to understand the Cosmic Laws of Reincarnation and Karma in their essence.

Once again, we must never judge. Of course, the father, mother and children, and other family members have all been affected by this. But we must never evaluate other people's level of evolution according to outer circumstances! Some of his brothers and sisters may be very evolved. However, they all have something to understand and rectify. This boy may inspire others to high levels of evolution because his condition leads them to do great Work. Through his presence, they will be inspired to discover, consciously or unconsciously, right, just power and renown.

His mother told me, "One of his brothers is so evolved on the inside. He already has great spiritual power and he's learning how to use it well." This mother, this woman is such a beautiful person! We can already see she is highly evolved. Everything is symbolic and each symbol has its + and its −. It is important never to judge the members of a family when one of the members has a disability or deformity. Knowing the symbolic meaning of dwarfism, we must be careful to abstain from any discriminating judgment. If this young boy begins to do beautiful spiritual work on himself, he may become a source of inspiration for his entourage and all humanity. By living his condition well, he will evolve very, very fast. That's how handicaps should be lived: in total acceptance as an opportunity to undertake a beautiful spiritual journey, during which the person will transform his old memories and manifest his divine potentiality from within to without.

Let's have a look at another case that also concerns repetitive behavior. It's about a man who worked for the French army for many years. He was in the technical domain where he studied radars. One day, he felt a spiritual calling and experienced an opening of his conscience. From then on, he felt he couldn't stay in the army. He wanted to help others so he gave up his military career and left. This man did research in several fields. He studied certain methods of personal development. In addition to these, he became interested in the world of energy so as to be able to give energy treatments and activate healing.

One day, he and his wife came across The Traditional Study of Angels. For them, this Teaching corroborated their own awareness that to truly be able to help others, we must first deep cleanse our own unconscious. This man told us, "One day, after attending a lecture, I received a dream that night. *I was in a chic restaurant but I didn't have the money to pay for a meal. Suddenly I transformed myself into Churchill which impressed the clientele. Seeing how impressed they were, I went up to the restaurant owner and made a proposal. 'Let's make a bargain. I'll keep on being Churchill and talk to your customers, and in exchange, you'll give me a meal.' The restaurant owner agreed.* And I woke up."

The human distortions of the ANIEL Field of Conscience include: *Charlatan, perverted, misleading spirit.* This example is particularly related to *misleading spirit.* We need to be constantly vigilant because we may tend to repeat behavior that suits us but which isn't right.

The meaning of this dream was very clear for this man. A restaurant is a symbol of social behavior and the way we nourish others and ourselves. As well as nourishing the physical body, we also nourish ourselves energetically on the level of our thoughts, emotions, atmosphere and ambiance, etc. In this dream, the man was in a chic restaurant, which reveals that he nourishes needs for luxury and appearances. He didn't have the money to pay for such a restaurant, but he was so determined to satisfy his needs that he transfigured and transformed into Churchill.

Let's analyze what this British politician symbolizes. Churchill is a symbol of British determination during World War II. He was a man of power, with great charisma, as well as social and political standing. He is considered to have been a very ambitious person with strong will and great determination.

He was first a deputy, then a minister several times, and finally, prime minister. He is reputed to have been a great lover of whisky, champagne and cigars. All of these elements are contained in this symbol. As always, there is the + and the −. In this particular case, it is the negative aspects that emerge since the man who transfigured into Churchill was abusing the power he had to do this. He deceived customers to satisfy personal needs. Since Churchill was an important collective character, the abuse of power has a considerable multiplying effect.

When a person is able to transfigure, it means that he knows the energy and behavior of the person in question; in this case, the states of conscience represented by Churchill. The man who received this dream has great stature and charisma. He could easily have been a leader. He is fascinated by military history and the biographies of leaders, who, through their participation in the management of great conflicts, played key roles in the history of mankind.

As the history of mankind shows us, great vigilance is required not to be tempted to use power for personal ends. When we feel attracted to biographies of historic characters, we must remember the Law of Resonance. While reading such books, our spirit visits memories that resonate with the attitudes and behavior of the characters in question. Simultaneously, certain aspects and forces in our unconscious are aroused. Hence the need to evaluate everything we read with great discernment to ensure we maintain our divine values and principles instead of continuing to nourish former memories of conflict, glory and existential struggles. Lots of people discuss history or politics and express very strong, categorical points of view. They preach that we mustn't do this or that, that we mustn't let history repeat itself. But they themselves emanate energy that is just as intense as the energy of those they criticize and judge. They want to kill those who killed or who didn't make the right decisions. It is fascinating and very revealing when we listen to people in symbols because they are always talking about themselves in terms of consciousness; we really discover who the other person is in his deepest essence. We perceive the kind of memories he harbors and needs to work on to evolve in each of the *departments* concerned. Whenever a person talks about history, politics or any other situation, we discover his values and principles. We perceive his intention through the tone of his voice, his gestures, and the points of view he expresses.

After receiving this dream, this man knew what he had to work on before being able to give energy healings in the right, just, divine, qualitative way. Otherwise, he might present himself to patients as a Churchill. Without realizing, he could badly advise them, push them to change, exaggeratedly motivate them to transform. Of course, he wouldn't become Churchill in concrete reality, but in his relationships with others, he would emanate the state of conscience symbolized by Churchill, especially when in contact with patients who have social renown or material wealth, as well as those with serious problems; to such an extent that people who are sensitive to power, renown and charisma, would be attracted to him by his speeches and subjects of conversations and do all he'd ask. When we have such power, such charisma, we also have great responsibility. If we misuse it, we create serious karma while believing we are helping others. Work with Angel 37 ANIEL to break out of these old behavioral patterns is strongly advised in such cases.

It is necessary to break the old, crystallized structures and concepts that prevent us from having global vision and a deep, profound, multi-dimensional understanding of life. In Angel Work, we succeed in breaking out of these old patterns by doing Angel Mantra Recitation. This consists in repeating the Name of an Angel with the intention of activating His Qualities and Powers in us. Through this Work, we simultaneously cleanse and transform our flaws and weaknesses. We concentrate intensely on one particular Angelic State of Conscience for several days or even weeks. When we change

Angels, we enter another Field of Consciousness, another Angelic vibration. With time and practice, we get used to these changes of vibratory frequency. Those who work seriously with this Teaching know the powerful, transforming effects it has on us. That's what transfiguration Work to become a human angel consists in, i.e. the embodiment of the Qualities, Virtues and Powers of the 72 Angels of Traditional Angelology here on Earth.

However, before successful Angelic transfiguration, we first have to deal with our distorted transfigurations like this man who transformed into Churchill. As we gradually advance in the cleansing of our memories, we become more receptive, more meditative, and we can then consciously experience transfigurations. We hear voices within, we have visions, or feel as though we were in the body of someone we know. It's very special to feel this. It may even be destabilizing at the beginning, but we get used to it with time. Hence, we can suddenly hear ourselves speak exactly like someone we know. When this happens, we need to analyze the situation as we would analyze a dream. This allows us to identify the kind of energy we perceived and the resonance activated in us that made us speak as we did. At a more advanced stage, we know how others perceive us.

Transfiguration really does exist. Psychiatric patients often experience it but in a distorted way. The fact of not being understood in what they experience on the subtle levels disturbs them even more and aggravates their instability. It's the same phenomenon in the case of a receptive, spiritual person who experiences transfiguration consciously. Work with the Angelic States of Conscience helps us to gradually develop profound receptivity and the necessary understanding to experience these intense moments well.

The spiritual guides in the parallel worlds also do transfiguration. Just like people on Earth, there are spiritual guides that are more evolved than others. Some may appear in our dreams in the form of our grandmother or grandfather, as a teacher, an artist, a scientist, a public or historic figure; in short, in the form of anyone who is symbolically important to us.

Spiritual guides may even transfigure into a tree, a cloud, a puddle, etc. However, we need to know that at their level, they no longer have any resonance with negativity and that their work is supervised by Cosmic Intelligence.

It's certainly in our interest to rectify our distortions! Then, there won't be any more negativity to influence us as it does when we still resonate with other people's distortions. Knowledge of the phenomenon of transfiguration allows us to understand what happens in cases like the man who transformed into Churchill in his dream.

Let's take a closer look at this very interesting phenomenon. Sometimes when we are talking to someone, we suddenly think he looks like someone we know, maybe a family member, colleague, friend, or acquaintance. In the beginning, we wonder what's happening, "Why do I think he resembles such a person? Physically, they have nothing in common, absolutely nothing! Why does he remind me of this other person?" It's because, for those few seconds, that person emanated a similar energy or state of conscience as the other person we know.

Transfiguration is first of all a metaphysical phenomenon on the energy level. In the metaphysical realities of dreams and the subtle worlds, it is clear that we can have an integral experience of transfiguration, like the man who became Churchill. It is also possible to transfigure on the physical level. Look at a dog and its master. With time, a certain fusion occurs between them and they end up resembling each other. Such resemblances can sometimes be very funny.

Likewise, mimetism is also a type of transfiguration. It can be observed in couples who have lived together for such a long time that they end up physically resembling each other. Children's expressions and gestures may also resemble their parents'. Transfiguration is a very natural phenomenon in both physical and metaphysical realities. By perceiving the same states of conscience over a long period of time, we integrate them; they transfigure us and we then emanate them ourselves.

The transfiguration process also takes place on the level of countries. On the energy level, each country is a powerful egregore composed of certain states of conscience wherein its inhabitants are collectively immersed. This is why people in the same country have personality traits in common.

When we understand the multi-dimensional aspect of transfiguration, we are able to follow conversations and simultaneously perceive the multiple phenomena that occur, either consciously or unconsciously, on the subtle levels. Moreover, we manage to perceive the links and interpret the symbolism. Needless to say, quite a lot of training is required! However, this then opens us up to the multi-dimensions and to physical and metaphysical fusion. It is absolutely wonderful. Life and conversations become so vibrant, so alive! One day, we manage to maintain these high levels of conscience, in which we are always aware of what we and others emanate.

Let's have a look at a very interesting example that shows us what can lie hidden behind certain behavior, behind dependencies. As we've already seen, Angel 37 ANIEL breaks the circle of dependencies. For some people, it is easy to give up a dependency, whereas for others it is extremely difficult. How come?

When we see what goes on in people's unconscious, we are capable of feeling compassion for them. We feel, we sense, that behind a dependency there can be a great accumulation of difficult, painful things.

Here is the example. A woman told me she intended to get married. She has been living with her life partner for about ten years. For some time now, both she and her partner have been on a spiritual path with the Teaching of Traditional Angelology. This woman told me, "We've decided to get married to manifest an even deeper commitment as well as the fusion of our two inner principles, masculine and feminine." They fixed the date for the following year.

She told me, "Since we've decided to get married, I've been going through one initiation after another! Up Above are certainly ensuring that I do some deep cleansing! I understand it's in-depth preparation and that the concrete wedding is only the tip of the iceberg. We want to move on to a new stage. I've received several dreams. Here is one of them: *'I saw my partner and he didn't want to marry me. I asked him why and he replied that he preferred a Granola woman.'*

This couple live in Quebec, Canada. Let's analyze what a Granola woman means in this context. It's a little like the Peace and Love style of the 1960s, natural but also laid back, without much structure or many moral principles. However, in this dream, it wasn't the authentic natural aspect. Although I knew this, I asked her what a Granola woman represented for her. She replied that it was a natural person who doesn't wear makeup. She went on to tell me that she herself has been wearing makeup since she was 15. Some women wear light makeup, but this woman wears excessive makeup and cannot give it up. That's why she was sent this dream. Just seeing this woman, anyone, even someone who doesn't know how to interpret dreams, would easily understand the meaning of this dream. This woman is an example of dependency on makeup and she was aware of it. She knew that through her extreme, exaggerated use of makeup she was trying to mask certain aspects of herself; she was hiding things.

With the Teachings of the Traditional Study of Angels, we work on very subtle things that are related to the metaphysical levels. A person in an ordinary conscience is unaware of the existence of these levels.

I've known this person for some time now. In spite of her pronounced makeup, she sometimes emanates a certain freshness, a certain lightheartedness, like a child. Talking with her, underneath the makeup, buried deep inside her, hidden by the makeup, I could feel the presence of memories marked by great suffering. I have a lot of compassion for her and I understand her difficulty in giving up makeup.

I sometimes perceived that others judged this woman, without realizing all that she might be going through on the inside. In this spiritual domain, excessive makeup was out of place among the other women there. People could be heard thinking, 'How can anyone be on a spiritual path and wear so much makeup?' But this woman was doing her best. We never discussed this issue together even though several opportunities arose. I always respected her silence. Her makeup didn't bother me. It didn't prevent me from seeing the beautiful potential that was beginning to blossom thanks to the intense Angelic Work she was doing on herself.

This woman told me that her makeup problem stemmed from her childhood and past lives. She also told me that her mother had died young, but she didn't elaborate on this. Then she told me that she often had dreams wherein she failed exams.

What do exams represent in dreams? They reveal lack of self-esteem, of confidence also. Failing them indicates also memories of failures, of blockages, of not succeeding. She went on to say, "I recently received a dream where *I was to take an exam and I didn't manage to do so. So I told myself I was really stupid! Then I heard a voice repeating the name*

'Aurore' over and over again! Non-stop, I heard, 'Aurore, Aurore, Aurore!'" I asked her what Aurore represented for her. Of course, I already knew the answer because in Quebec, everyone knows! She told me Aurore represented the child martyr.

In Quebec, Aurore is a very well-known child who was martyred by her stepmother. This stepmother tortured Aurore until sheer exhaustion caused her death at the age of 10. This story was in all the headlines and it gave rise to a trial. In 1951, this true story inspired a novel and a film, which were very successful in Quebec. The film was even supported by the clergy, in spite of the fact that it denounced difficulties that the control and influence of the clergy had engendered for the people at that time.

This event revealed mistreatment of children, rigidity in their upbringing and education, as well as the sectarian traditionalists within the church. It deeply affected the imagination and conscience of the people of Quebec. All this emerged at a time when, in Quebec, the Catholic Church was undergoing great transformation, called the Peaceful Revolution, whereby Church and State were separated and public and religious powers were redistributed.

The first film relating the story of Aurore, the child martyr, was released at this time and greatly affected the collective conscience. In 2005, another version of this film re-awakened memories and emotions that resonated with this story. That's what Aurore represents for this woman.

Making the link between her dream and this child's true story, she told us that she too had memories of being a child martyr and also of a mean, cruel, abusive stepmother. In certain lives, she had more than likely been rigid and brutally violent with children, and in other lives, she had possibly been martyred. It is important to understand these dynamics. We are never a victim without first being an aggressor, a persecutor.

If you have seen this film, then you have surely felt how it stirs up memories. It is a very powerful film! However, the Law of Resonance helps us watch it with deep, profound, *vertical* understanding. When we know this great Cosmic Law, we know that whenever we feel put out, bothered, upset by anyone, or any event, incident, behavior, or anything whatsoever, it means that, on a certain level, to a certain extent, we have memories that resonate with what bothers, annoys or upsets us. It's an absolute fact! Sometimes we overhear verbal violence in certain parents. They are harsh and rigid with their children, and unconsciously, they martyr them on the energy level.

One day, we fully realize how limited we can be by blockages inscribed in ourselves, in our memories. We shall see how we can use this film to work on our memories of authority, submission and obedience. Of course, a situation such as Aurore's resonates very strongly in us. This resonance incites us to reflect, to call authority into question and to bring about change.

It is so important to face and confront our memories! It may be very difficult because they are sometimes extremely painful. Nevertheless, this is how we can open up to new currents, thoughts and concepts. As long as these memories exist, the fears and blockages inscribed in them will create obstacles.

Regarding this film, a man came up to see me to confess that he couldn't watch it. He simply couldn't watch a child being martyred. He told me about his own resonance with the situation. From early childhood and for years, he witnessed his uncle's violence as he beat his aunt and cousins. Once he'd grown up and become an adult, he told himself he could kill the aggressor that no one would see him, and so no one would know.

At that time, this man didn't know The Traditional Study of Angels. Now he is working with this Teaching, he knows the Divine Laws and symbolic language, which allows him to understand in depth. Just the fact that he so easily thought of committing such a fatal, murderous act and then camouflaging it reveals that he must have committed such an act in other lives. He is well aware of this. Then he declared that thanks to Knowledge of the Divine Laws, he'd never be able to think like that again. He asked me if young Aurore had purified karmas by being subjected to such a life. I told him that she hadn't reached the purification stage yet. She'd submitted without any conscience or true awareness, a little like an animal that doesn't know what to do. It is very different for someone who has Knowledge. When we persecute someone who has Knowledge, when we lack kindness and beat or mistreat him, he understands that he is going through this because he has memories to purify or a collective mission to accomplish. Hence, he manages to feel compassion and he transcends his karma.

Let's take the example of Jesus. We can read in the Scriptures that Jesus knew what was in store for him. He had seen it in dreams and he knew the reasons and long-term consequences of what he was going to go through in public. That great initiate knew the Law of Resonance, same as Gandhi or any great soul. Like them, we can apply it in our daily lives. Hence, when someone is unkind or does us wrong, or who is critical, mean and aggressive to us, instead of projecting outward, we refer back to ourselves. In doing so, we strengthen ourselves on the inside and we consecrate the difficult phases of our evolution.

On the other hand, if we don't have Knowledge, without realizing it, we experience the Law of Karma. A life like Aurore's is truly a karmic consequence. This man was very upset at the idea that a child could be mistreated like this. I explained to him that indeed we feel a lot of compassion for a child martyr. Nevertheless, when we have transformed our own resonance, we no longer feel pained or upset because we understand that everything is right and just. We know that a child martyr reaps what he sowed in his previous lives, even though he looks completely innocent.

I explained this subject in greater depth. I explained to this man how we can train and fortify ourselves in situations that upset us, where we feel pained and saddened by what the other person is going through. In such cases, we must remember that earthly justice has its role to fulfill through the different existing police and legal structures. In such structures, very important work is carried out to ensure that the wrong doing is dealt with. Divine Justice and the Law of Karma also apply through earthly, human laws. Above all, we must remind ourselves that Divine Justice is absolute. We mustn't forget this. It is accomplished in all sorts of ways.

Whenever a person reincarnates in very difficult life circumstances, we have to take into consideration his past lives. Then I told this man about the consequences for the uncle he hated so much that he'd wanted to kill him for mistreating his aunt and cousins. In a future life, this uncle may find himself in a situation like Aurore's.

These explanations helped this man understand the rigor of Divine Justice, which is enacted through earthly justice. If earthly justice is unable to play its role correctly, we need to know that there will be repercussions for those involved in a future life or lives. However, if we were a battered child, it is important not to consider ourselves monsters, because in doing so, we continue to hit ourselves over the head and we remain imprisoned in old behavioral patterns.

Personally, what really helped me when I was going through difficult things, was to say to myself, 'I did that too. That's why I'm experiencing it now.' Instead of sinking into the victim role, I went further. Things clicked into place and I was able to tell myself I was going through such and such an experience to settle my karmas, to close off loose ends and put a stop to vicious circles. I used to think about the enormous reservoir of my memories wherein gestures I had made and acts I had committed long before were recorded. Thus I set a program in motion that allowed me to cleanse these memories with global vision while simultaneously acquiring universal conscience. That's how we advance and stop mistreating ourselves and others. We become capable of accepting everything we may have gone through and experimented.

Sometimes, under the influence of feelings of revenge, we'd like to take the law into our own hands and punish the wrong-doer. But remember the example of the boy who didn't use his powers well in other lives and is now a dysmorphic dwarf in his present life. The logical follow-up of karmas that we create ourselves is so well thought out! Everything, absolutely everything is always wisely thought out and organized for the evolution of our soul, in accordance with the karmic *luggage* we have accumulated throughout our existence.

It is really comforting to know that whatever we may have done, we can rectify our karmas thanks to the Power of the 72 Angels. Of course, stirring up memories disturbs us, but we can cleanse everything. That's why we no longer mistreat anyone; we have a vision and understanding of a multitude of lives wherein we experimented all sorts of things. This vision favors an opening of conscience and serves the evolution of our entire being.

During an Angelica yoga workshop, a woman listened to people telling me what they experienced during the workshop. Some had experienced sensations, particular feelings and emotions, while others had had visions. The woman was frustrated because she hadn't felt anything on the metaphysical level. However, when she watched the extract from the film about Aurore, she felt a lot of emotions. At one point, it was so powerful that she thought she was going to vomit.

I explained to her that over the course of her lives, she had very probably erected shells or thick carapace and frozen her emotions so as not to feel anything in situations that risked arousing very painful emotions. It took something very intense, very powerful to help her reconnect with her deep emotions. I added that it was, of course, the same for positive emotions. The walls, shell or carapace we erect to protect us from negativity also cut us off from everything that is beautiful and positive. If we want to attain high levels of conscience and connect with the multi-dimensions, we have to face up to our painful, negative memories and transform them. With the keys the 72 Angels offer, we are well equipped to succeed in this Work.

I suggested that she could do an exercise at home. I suggested she choose a time when she feels good to settle comfortably and meditate for a while with Angel 37 ANIEL. Then, she should think about Aurore's story. Instantaneously her mind and spirit will connect with memories that resonate with what this child experienced. From a state of well-being, she'll be able to cleanse these memories one at a time by meditating on past lives and on the consequences of her misactions and experiences. As she very gradually does this deep-cleansing work, she will no longer feel the need to freeze her emotions and erect protective walls around herself. She'll be receptive once again to Cosmic currents and will be able to perceive the multi-dimensions.

Many people function with excessive emissivity; sometimes it's as though they were addicted to talking, to being active and busy, to socializing, and even when they sit still, their mind keeps on thinking about all sorts of activities and things. Indeed, this is a very common phenomenon in our society today, which is not only due to Facebook and other social medias; many people of all ages and generations find it very difficult to go within so they develop excessive emissivity. This excess is caused by powerful emotions of insecurity and all sorts of inner blockages that prevent unconscious memories from re-surfacing. Even when such people meditate, they remain too emissive in their thoughts, in their mind and spirit. However, if they persevere and keep their intention focused on rebalancing their emissivity and receptivity, they will obtain results, that's for sure.

The more we open up to the metaphysical dimensions, the more we are able to understand the teachings we receive through our dreams and symbols that appear in our meditations.

What is the difference between someone who physically assaults another person and someone who verbally attacks him? The accumulation of negativity is less for the person who is able to restrain himself physically. However, when people exclaim, "You're such a pain in the neck!" or worse, we can feel the violent, sometimes dangerous aggression in these words. In a dream or meditation, a person who said such a thing could be shown that, metaphysically, he hit the other person.

We weren't necessarily beaten in this life, and we may not have beaten anyone else either, but Cosmic Intelligence could send a dream containing the symbol of a child martyr to an angry parent who used words to violently strike his child, because even though he didn't physically strike him, he assaulted him with verbal aggressiveness, with negative energy.

Since seeing this film, and recording this symbolism in my inner library, when I encounter certain children, the image of Aurore, the child martyr, comes to mind. I know then through clairvoyance that these children are metaphysically beaten by their parents, on the energy level. For over 30 years now, new children have been arriving on Earth with a very, very open unconscious. They are hyper-sensitive and can very easily feel the intention behind words. They would be able to perceive them more consciously if we taught them to listen to and understand their feelings, to what they sense.

Some of these children arrive with very heavy *luggage*; we shouldn't deny this. They are not all enlightened beings. As their unconscious is very open, they sense the very slightest aggression that dwells in them, which resonates with any aggression they detect in others. That's why they so often react in anger and/or rebellion. Hot-tempered children sometimes resemble real little tigers, they are so intense and impulsive in their reactions to what we say or ask. Their unconscious is less and less veiled, which means that their spirit often visits great blocks of memories where they accumulated violence.

As they are very evolved and their unconscious is so open, others find it very difficult to function in old, habitual structures, making it difficult for the people around them to continue with their habitual ways of functioning, with their old methods of discipline and traditional ideas regarding children's upbringing. These new children are so sensitive and react so intensely to everything that it is very difficult for them and for their family and entourage. Some of them may become very introverted and reject others quite aggressively, whereas others may develop autistic tendencies and become afraid to manifest in everyday life. Children, parents, teachers, educators, pedagogues, psychologists, doctors, everyone involved feels more and more discrepancies when faced with these new children. It was intended! This phenomenon obliges our society to re-structure itself. The way we bring up and teach children needs to be called into serious question. In the years to come, great changes will be brought about in all areas of our society.

Due to their great openness, these children's reactions are totally different from those observed up until now. We now live in an era and have reached a point in time when it is essential to understand that everything comes from within. The metaphysical and physical levels cannot be dissociated. If we want to be happy and blossom in our life on Earth, we need to learn how these two levels work. Without this understanding and new concepts, we cannot help but react when faced with the current state of the world, social inequalities, the destruction of the environment, illness and disease, wars, etc. More and more, we feel discrepancies; we are more stressed. The general atmosphere and ambiance in life today is becoming more electric.

New children are arriving with new needs; they bear the potentialities of Angel 37 ANIEL. They are helping break the old structures in their family and in society. However, these children aren't angels yet! They too arrive with their *luggage*, which contains numerous distortions. Some of them rebel and indicate issues that need to be called into question. Their presence jostles and disturbs our resistance to change and this may manifest in very powerful ways! That's why it is sometimes so difficult with them.

To explain these dynamics, I'd like to share the true story of a man who has been following the Teaching of Traditional Angelology for many years now. He is a lovely person who has a recomposed family of four children. He had a dream about his 3-year-old son. In the dream, *he drove to an infirmary in a car shaped like a pill. As he was leaving, a nurse chained up his young son: he put chains all around his neck and arms. The father thought this was normal and he pulled on the chains to drag the child to the car. The child fell into the water and his father pulled on the chains to lift him out.* This man was horrified when he woke up. Although he's a strong person, he sobbed his heart out. He was so upset that, throughout the day, tears kept springing to his eyes.

All of the elements of this dream represent parts of this man. The infirmary, the nurse, and the pill-shaped car are related to healing. He was being shown what kind of energy and state of mind, of conscience he had when he tried to heal his child: he put chains on his son's manner of communication and manifestation. This caused his son to fall into the water, which symbolizes emotions. Through this dream, this man was being shown that he needed to be careful not to be too harsh in his efforts to heal his child. This man wasn't only harsh with his outer child, but also with his inner child, with his own capacity to learn and grow. Being less harsh and more clement, he would rediscover well-being and he'd know how to bring up his children in a right, just, loving manner both on the inside and on the outside.

Thanks to this dream, this man became aware of his inner violence. In his childhood, he received a very strict, harsh upbringing. Not wanting to subject his children to the same severity, he adopted a rather lax attitude with them. At the time of his first marriage, he hadn't begun his spiritual path. He was excessively tolerant with his first two children, so much so that they didn't have the benefits of any authority at all. He projected onto them all that he hadn't been able to do himself and he let them do what they liked. These children are now grown up and this man can see the poor results of such an upbringing. He realizes all that he didn't give them through such an upbringing. Now they have grown up and they are more mature but there was a time that he was really worried about them; especially with the growing Knowledge he was receiving inside him.

This man remarried and the two children he's had in this new union are new children – as are the other two, in fact – but these two younger children are really very intense! They are very open and intuitive. Behind each word, they feel what is hidden in their parents' unconscious very deeply.

They constantly push their parents' buttons, so to speak; i.e. they keep activating trigger elements. If the yes or no they are given is not clear and determined, they keep on until they are. It's not easy with them and sometimes this father feels himself getting angry. On the other hand, he knows he has to provide a good framework for his children and not let them do whatever they want. They don't need laxity; they need an upbringing founded on true love and right, just, qualitative authority. These children feel the least distortion and always react to it. This takes pedagogy on the highest levels of conscience, so not only do these children represent a very evolutive element for their parents, but also for the whole society.

Of course, it is difficult to exert right, just authority when we ourselves don't aspire to high levels of conscience, but it is important not to express violence or verbal aggression. A little smack may do some good, but it should never be given with rage. It's our intention that makes all the difference. When we say no, we must do so with rigor, not violence or severity.

As long as we haven't cleansed all of our memories, it's normal to feel angry. Children can push so many buttons and set off distortions! We mustn't hold this against ourselves but rather introduce the benefits of Traditional Angelology into their upbringing instead. Whenever it is necessary to speak to a child, we can take a few seconds to do Angel Recitation before we speak to him. This allows us to express ourselves and act with a higher level of vibration and conscience than when we are in the grips of anger or impatience.

Needless to say, repeating wise guidelines to ourselves and others is necessary when we want to replace old concepts and behavior with new ones. With repetition, we finally integrate them. One day, we understand that having to repeat over and over again to a child is a gift we offer ourselves at the same time. When we speak to the child, we also speak to parts of ourselves. Hence, we educate and re-program our inner and outer children simultaneously. Proceeding like this allows us to break old patterns that we may have repeated over many lives. It also allows us to abandon the old concept, "I'm the parent, you're the child, so keep quiet!"

It's the same for affective, emotional dependencies we may have experienced in our past lives. As we've already seen, Angel 37 ANIEL helps us break the circle of dependencies, which prevent us from communicating and manifesting well. We love our child so much we don't dare say no for fear he won't love us anymore. Or, we say no but in a vague, hesitant manner, which he feels and takes advantage of. Such an attitude is a reflection of our own fear of not being loved and appreciated by the other person.

Many spiritual people live their daily lives without being capable of saying a nice but determined no. They live in a perpetual circle of affective dependency in their family, at work, and in society. They are so afraid they'll be told no that they themselves don't dare pronounce this word. Our modern society is presently experiencing the yes syndrome. It is one of the main causes of growing problems in the family, at school, and in education in general. Even government representatives are afraid to say no, and sometimes legalize the very opposite of what they should, just to maintain power, to be liked. A lot of people don't understand the necessity to define limits at the very beginning of our apprenticeship as a child, family and society. As we gradually evolve and develop qualities, fewer and fewer limits are required until eventually none at all are necessary.

We can work on all dependencies with Angel 37 ANIEL. Let's have a look at three very common ones: alcohol, cigarettes, and drugs. Let's try and understand why these forms of dependency have become so widespread today.

Let's begin with addiction to alcohol. Alcohol is a liquid, consequently it is symbolically related to emotions. Cigarettes are related to the air element and represent difficulties on the thought level. Drugs are related to the mind and spirit and vital energy. A person who takes drugs has a very strong mind and spirit, and simultaneously experiences an opening of the unconscious and so encounters his distorted memories. At the same time, he perceives the distortions of other people that he resonates with. He tries to escape them and flees into illusory realities by taking drugs. This behavior is becoming more and more frequent, especially among young people, teenagers, and even children! It is very destructive! That's why it is so vitally urgent to provide them with Knowledge.

Work with The Traditional Study of Angels may even help a person who is addicted to hard drugs to set himself free from his addiction and to heal in depth on the causal level. It is a very evolutive healing that takes place on the metaphysical level, within the person, and allows him to get out of his prison of impasses and illusions forever. As soon as we understand multi-dimensionality and the deep meaning of existence, we develop a new interest in Life.

Earlier we saw the example of an addiction to, or a dependency on makeup. It's the same thing for a drug addict. Hidden behind his addiction, his dependency, are great blocks of memories that he is trying to flee. Although coming off drugs is useful, a drug addict needs to cleanse his memories, otherwise his problems will reappear one way or another. Deep healing requires us to cleanse our memories. That's how dependencies disappear; there are no more needs!

A young man shared his story with Kaya. He told him he was addicted to hard drugs. Yet his dreams showed that he was on the path to being healed. He was working with Traditional Angelology and did Angel Mantra Recitation regularly. This had triggered his dreams. He was really happy to live an initiatic life because it provided him with a lot of sensations. And initiatic life does indeed provide us with very powerful sensations! Today's young people seek excitement and sensationalism; they do extreme sports, not to mention all they seek and find via computer technology! However, all these sensations come from the outside and are often distorted.

The discoveries this young man had made touched him profoundly. He shared two of his dreams on this subject. Here is the first one: *"I'm with a friend who represents someone who likes to serve and help. We go into a big house. We open a door into a room where everything is clean and tidy. We open another door into a room where we come upon lots of people taking drugs. The fact that we surprise them causes them to flee, leaving all their drugs and paraphernalia on the floor. I realize I didn't come for the drugs; I came to see the people. Then a cleaning lady cleaned everything up. There was nothing left, everything was spick and span."*

Through this dream, Up Above were encouraging this young man, showing him the great Work he has done on the inside. The cleaning lady represents a part of him that has cleansed his need for drugs on the social level.

Here is his second dream. *He saw himself going through a very dark tunnel with his wife.* – In concrete reality, he doesn't have a wife. – *Coming out of the tunnel, the couple arrived in an enormous room full of vehicles and scooters that belonged to him, but they were all damaged. This man began to paint a car white and do his utmost to get it to start again.*

In this dream, he was being shown that he had just taken an important step. The tunnel symbolizes the unconscious, where dark, somber parts find a spiritual path difficult to follow. The wife represents his feminine principle as well as his inner world.

The vehicles symbolize his old ways of advancing, whereby he created accidents, not only on the physical level, but also in relationships.

Remember the Taï Chi example where the dreamer has to learn to return to her past? We must always return to past memories and rectify them. In his second dream, this man was repairing and painting a car white. In color symbolism, white represents spirituality. This dream reveals that this person truly wants to advance spiritually, to re-start his vehicles in a new way.

Here is another example that is related to the ANIEL Field of Conscience. It helps us understand other aspects and behavior of children who are presently incarnating on Earth. A woman asked Kaya to interpret her son's job; he's a fire eater in a circus. She wanted to know the symbolic meaning of this.

Kaya explained the deep meaning of this job. Fire is related to our spirit, and our mouth serves to eat, drink, speak, and kiss. In this job, we have to insert incendiary liquid into our mouth to be able to produce fire. Needless to say, it is not the positive meaning that prevails. In French, this job is called 'cracheur de feu,' i.e. fire spitter, which is a more accurate term for what the person actually does, and more clearly negative. On the metaphysical level, it means that the person's mind and spirit spits fire. And this kind of fire doesn't create a lovely, warm, harmonious atmosphere.

We usually spit out a mixture of saliva and mucus to clear our throat and respiratory tract. In this case, the symbolism of spitting may be positive provided we spit discreetly and respectfully. We spit to liberate whatever was obstructing our throat. The act of spitting is then part of a natural process of purification. But, we may also spit on someone or something to express contempt and scorn. Spitting in someone's face is a major offence. In such a case, spitting is negative. The job of fire eater or spitter is related to spectacular street or other shows; this woman's son, for example, performs in a circus. A fire eater wants to impress people. There's also the idea of danger: creating and braving danger. This choice of job reveals that the person still has very destructive aspects in the way he communicates his emotions and thoughts, as well as in the way he uses the creative power of his mind and spirit.

On hearing these explanations, this woman told Kaya that her son had had a lot of difficulties. At the age of 16, he became a punk and took drugs. Then he lived like a hermit in the woods and didn't want to know anything about the world anymore. From the age of 5, he used to look up at the stars and declare he had no business living on Earth. He said it wasn't his place, that he shouldn't be here.

This kind of attitude is characteristic of many new children. Like many of them, this woman's son has heavy *luggage*, a great many distortions in his unconscious. He doesn't know what to do with his inner destructive fire. As a child, he used to look at the stars, which symbolize Destiny and Guidance from Above. He wanted to be elsewhere, to have a different destiny, an easier fate, because when he incarnated in this life, he could feel the heaviness of his karmas. He didn't know the meaning of life on earth, but he had a premonition: he instinctively felt that programs would cause his negative memories to re-surface and that he'd have to face up to them. His soul already knew that it would be difficult; it had that feeling of foreboding and so his mind, his spirit refused to change. That's why he didn't want to be on Earth!

To end the symbolism of a fire eater or spitter, I'd like to mention the Walt Disney film, *Lilo & Stitch*. This very interesting film symbolically shows how new children function. They are sometimes hyperactive and destructive. When we don't understand them, and we don't know how to guide them, they destroy everything; it's in their program. This film, which also features a fire eater, is very educational for new children because it inspires them to learn to master their inner forces.

In the lecture I gave on Angel 30 OMAEL, I talked about the symbol of gremlins. Stitch is a little similar, he's a little extra-terrestrial animal. Like extra-terrestrials, new children are open to dimensions beyond the Earth. They are in contact with the multi-dimensions of the metaphysical worlds.

In this film, Stitch symbolizes that great, powerful, very intelligent, multi-dimensional force that is awakened and activated in new children, on the physical level. It can manifest positively, but in the film, it is negative at first. For example, in one scene, we see Stitch shoot a water pistol. Water symbolizes the emotional aspect. If we transpose this symbol to new children, it explains the emotional intensity they often express aggressively to communicate and obtain what they want.

I recommend you watch this film as though you were being shown a dream. That will help you enter the multi-dimensions and understand the intensity of hyperactive children. As you watch it, be aware that the different characters and their interactions represent parts of yourself, just like in dreams. Practice considering these characters as multiple facets of yourself.

In this film, little, turbulent, very intelligent, multi-dimensional Stitch meets the young girl, Lilo, who is aggressive and often fights because she feels misunderstood and unloved. The scenes containing water reveal the power and scale of the emotions these children emanate. We also see a school bus, which symbolizes advancing in learning on the conscience level. When we manage to master emotions, our apprenticeship goes well. There is also the fire eater/spitter who hasn't mastered his element at all. He sets fire to the ceiling, which symbolizes our mentality and the thought level.

If you watch this film while remaining aware of the metaphysical and symbolic levels, you will discover all of its deep, profound meaning. It really shows us the forces at work in people and how these forces can evolve. At the end of the film, Stitch, the extra-terrestrial, has become kind, gentle and positive. He has learned to better master the fire of his mind and spirit. His new clothes reveal the purification of his aura and relationship dynamics.

Why do new children need to be acknowledged so much? When someone manifests love to them, they sense the exact quality, all of the hues and tinges of this love. Every time their parents say, "I love you," these children feel all that this love conveys. They perceive its positive and negative aspects. They perceive it on the metaphysical level. The things these children perceive unconsciously may cause them to speak and behave very incoherently. They don't understand the phenomenon of resonance and haven't mastered the forces that emerge from their unconscious. Consequently, they constantly try to attract attention because unconsciously they are seeking harmony in their relationships with others.

Whenever they feel that their parents' attitude isn't right, they will jostle, bother, annoy and upset them to make him change, to incite him to correct their behavior. New children seek authenticity, true well-being, and right, just, qualitative expansion of emotional abundance. They sense when the energy emitted is tinged with hypocrisy, falseness, superficiality, lies, and corruption.

When our daughter Kasara was young, she demanded a lot of attention. Her questions were multi-dimensional, and she was always asking what was going to happen the following day; she was always way beyond the present moment. New children are very collective, very virtual. They want to know the deep meaning of life so as to nourish all of their dimensions. When we look after them well, when we listen to them attentively, patiently, with unconditional love, when we take our time to accompany them in their need to understand the physical and metaphysical realities of life, they then feel wholly and completely recognized, acknowledged, accepted and loved. In time, over the years, that makes them well-balanced, solid, autonomous people.

Here is another example of difficult, repetitive behavior. A woman in her 30s, who has been working with Traditional Angelology for a while, told us she still has the same fear as she had as a child. Wherever she is in the shower, in bed, or in the dark, she has a feeling that someone is going to stab her.

This woman also had rebellious behavior revealing her rebellion toward authority. At the beginning of her work with Angelology, applying the Law of Resonance allowed her to become aware of numerous things. And simultaneously, she undertook to deep-cleanse her memories.

One night, in a dream, *she was told she had been stabbed in 1975 at 11 o' clock.* In this life, she was born in 1976. Through this message, it is possible that she was being told how and when she died in her previous life. Lots of people have violence in their unconscious and died a violent death. In this woman's case, the dates of her death in her previous life and her birth in this one were very close, so we may ask, 'Did this event really take place at 11am in 1975?' Not necessarily, because, if so, the exact day and month would also have been specified. However, the mention of 1975 indicates that these two lives were indeed in very rapid succession. This woman looked up Angel Calendar 3 (*cf.* page ??), which is related to the intellectual level, to find out which Angel corresponded to 11am. It's Angel 34 LEHAHIAH. The human distortions of this Field of Conscience include *war*, *violence*, and *dangerous anger*.

She wasn't sent this dream earlier because she wouldn't have understood it. Now that she knows the Divine Laws and Angel Teaching, she is able to understand things in depth. She doesn't adopt the victim role because she knows that in a previous life or lives, she herself engendered the violence she was subjected to. Thanks to the Law of Resonance, she understands that to have experienced such a death, she too must have sown violence in other lives. Since she has begun working with the Teaching of Traditional Angelology, her fear of being stabbed has lessened. However, there are still after effects and this dream incites her to concentrate her inner work on liberating them. As soon as she thinks of this dream, her spirit is automatically connected with her memories of violence, and with Angel Mantra Recitation and the intensity of her intention, she can cleanse them all.

Gradually her fear will fade and diminish until one day it will completely disappear.

In the following example, we shall see why some people find it so difficult to change, to take steps to set change in motion, to start out and advance on a spiritual path. What causes their blockages?

A woman shared with us that since she has been working with Traditional Angelology, she has seen the people around her change, including her son and daughter-in-law. This couple have a one-year-old daughter – a beautiful child with luminous eyes, according to her grandmother. This child's father who is logical and rational, didn't believe in reincarnation and past lives. However, before his daughter's birth, he received a dream *wherein she came up to him and said, 'I've just died. I haven't been dead for very long. I'm coming to reincarnate in your home to...'* and just then, he was cut off and left yearning for more information. It was intentional! He didn't need to know more.

It was already a lot! Just imagine all the reflection such a dream may set in motion in a rational mind! The arrival of his daughter opened his heart to the concept of reincarnation. There was a lot to think about! After such a dream, even the most rational mind couldn't stop wondering about the possibility of previous lives. The fact that in his dream his daughter didn't tell him why she was incarnating with him and his wife gave rise to even more reflection!

Later, when his daughter was only one year old, her father gave her a pencil and paper and in her drawings, he could make out a little character with Angel's wings. This man was very moved! Despite all this, he delayed opening his deeper layers of conscience. He refused to advance spiritually because he didn't want to change.

Then, one day, he phoned his mother because a dream had deeply upset him. *He saw himself at a funeral meeting where there were several tombstones. He knew there was a bomb in one of them and that it was going to explode. He was terrified and wanted to run away. His daughter was in his arms. Someone wanted to stop him leaving so he pushed his eyes out and left. There was also a red owl. Then he found himself in a room with a woman he doesn't know in concrete reality. Although he was aware of being married, he lay down on the bed with this stranger, who masturbated him and he ejaculated.* When he woke up from this dream in bed beside his wife, he really didn't feel good!

It's a good sign that he was able to tell his mother his dream. His mother has a beautiful openness and this man knew she would understand what he was going through. If this trust exists between them, it's because this woman never imposed her spiritual path on her son. That's wisdom.

What does this dream mean? Well, of course, it could be sent to many people who don't want to walk a spiritual path, i.e. who refuse to cleanse their unconscious and transform their distortions. It could be sent to people with solely rational, logical minds who sometimes try to aggressively impose their atheist point of view. Let's take a close look at this dream.

The tombstones symbolize death and rebirth. We have to die to our human weaknesses and flaws before we can be reborn to Angelic Qualities. This is very often experienced on an initiatic, spiritual path. It also reveals that we are in contact with very ancient behaviors or aspects of us that are not finished. We have to solve and let go of a lot of things before we can feel Divine Light steadfast within us.

In this dream, the bomb in the tombstone reveals parts of the dreamer that harbor explosive forces related to ancient forces in him that are still alive. These negative memories of other lives may be so strong and difficult that the person really doesn't want to face them but they are resurfacing right now.

Putting out a person's eyes symbolizes refusal to let part of us see, and at the same time, refusal to let others see us as we really are. This is what may happen with atheists. They often become hypersensitive and explosive. The Law of Resonance whereby the other person is part of us is too difficult for them to accept. An atheist doesn't anticipate problems; he only lives in the world of consequences. Concretely, this man could meet people who talk about spirituality and he'd declare, "Rubbish! I don't believe in all those spiritual things!" Hence, he would prevent others from seeing because he himself refuses to look in depth.

What does the red owl mean? An owl is a nocturnal bird, and birds are related to the air element, which represents the world of thoughts. The owl represents the dreamer's hidden, unconscious thoughts. Owls see in the dark, symbolically in the unconscious. What's more, in the dream, the owl is red. Red symbolizes action, matter, so this man only wants to see and think about action and matter; he can also hide his way of seeing things and people, keeping his true opinion to himself, *in the dark*, so to speak. These forces are also in connection with anger, with the bomb of the tombstone.

In the final scene with the unknown woman, he is aware of being married, which indicates infidelity. His great need for sexuality and corrupt love confuses, fogs up his conscience and prevents him from advancing. Given these criteria, we understand his blockage; these are all aspects of himself that he doesn't want to see. This is what is behind his fear of knowing his past lives and other dimensions. He doesn't want to remember and think deeply about his hidden secrets. He prefers to continue to secretly nourish his unhealthy needs, without wanting to think that it is not right to do that. With such an attitude, a person may live a double life on the inside. He may seem to be a good family man, a good father, and simultaneously have instinctual, primary sexual urges that cause him to visit pornographic websites on the Internet.

It really isn't easy to face the multiple facets of ourselves. That's why we are sometimes so surprised to see a well-brought up, polite, mannerly person become coarse and vulgar and behave inappropriately under the influence of alcohol. A sweet, kind, gentle person – man or woman – may even become mean and spiteful after a few drinks.

With the dream he received, this man is on the right path. Especially with a very evolved young daughter who comes to talk to him in his dreams! In his present life, this man has a wonderful evolutive path ahead of him.

New children, also called children of Truth, indigo or crystal children, change the people around them. Each at his own pace of course, but they certainly stir things up! Many of these children function in the vibration of Angel ANIEL. Hence, they break the old structures and circles of dependencies, facilitating the passage for new currents. That is the role of these children in their families and in society. Of course, their presence creates a lot of disturbances, but it's for the greater good of all!

Here is another example of repetitive phenomena experienced by a young man in his 20s. At the age of 8, he received a dream that greatly affected him, so much so that he still remembers it. He told me that in his dream, *he saw a sofa explode. The explosion was so powerful that everything exploded into tiny, minuscule particles that he then picked up to rebuild the sofa, one particle after another until the very last one was in place. And then, everything exploded all over again.*

This dream is important! To understand its symbolic meaning, we need to think about what a sofa is used for. Usually it is found in a sitting-room, which is a place for encounters and exchanges with others. It is used to sit on, and so is a symbol of receptivity to others. Since we settle comfortably in it, it also represents rest, comfort and relaxation in social intimacy.

The explosion of the sofa reveals memories that blow up, that destroy his relationships and his social comfort. Even though he may want to be receptive and calm with himself and others, all of a sudden he explodes, which engenders relationship problems. The fact that he rebuilds the sofa from scratch, particle by particle, shows that this man has great potential to reconstruct. His efforts reveal great qualities, a lot of merit. But, once rebuilt, the sofa explodes all over again!

How many people reproduce the essence of this repetitive dream through their behavior, without even realizing? When things don't work, some people say, "Ok, we've had difficulties, but let's roll up our sleeves and start again!" Such people begin again; they rebuild, they set up a business again, or they buy a new house. Others work really hard at their relationship to finally realize it doesn't work. Symbolically everything blows up! Everything explodes!

Unconsciously, these people repeat the same pattern without understanding the deep cause, i.e. the hidden memories buried deep in their unconscious.

By cleansing our deep, hidden memories, we avoid a lot of wasted time and energy. As long as they haven't been transformed, these forces at work in our unconscious will continue to sabotage and destroy everything we undertake. Understanding these dynamics helps us take a step back – two steps back like in the Tai Chi example. Whenever we notice that our projects don't work out, that in spite of all our efforts, we always end up back where we started, we need to take two steps back, we need to return to the past to discover and work on the memories hidden in our unconscious. If we want to advance, we simply have to cleanse our memories. Although we may feel we aren't advancing at all, or that we are only advancing extremely slowly on the outside, on the inside, we are making great strides, that's for sure!

Here is a final example of one of these new children imbued with the Energy of Angel 37 ANIEL. It's an example of a teenager whose parents follow the Teaching of Traditional Angelology. When this girl was visiting her grandparents for a few days, she received the following dream: *She sees her grandmother in a camp site where she has a really small bed. Then she sees her dig in the ground under her bed where she finds a skeleton. Terrified, her grandmother exclaims, "I'll never dare sleep in this bed as long as there's a skeleton underneath it!" Just as frightened, her grandfather tells her grandmother to throw the skeleton as far as she can and it turns into a little monkey, that resembles Abu, the thieving monkey in a Walt Disney film; only the hands were transformed, the rest was still a skeleton.*

This girl is used to receiving dreams and she knows they contain messages and teachings that Cosmic Intelligence sends to us in the form of symbols. She understood the broad outlines of her dream and she knows the effect dreams can have on us. This time, however, she didn't feel any effect at all; nothing particular manifested in her or in her day. Knowing that we can visit other people's soul in dreams, while also receiving lessons for ourselves, she spent the day on the lookout for signs and incidents. And, by first referring the dream entirely to herself, she carried out inner work via Angel Mantra Recitation.

That day, during a meal she shared with her grandparents, she felt a surge of love for her grandmother. She reached out to give her a warm hug saying, "Oh! lovely, loving grandma; I love you!" Her grandmother looked at her and said, "Hmmh! You want something, don't you?" At that moment, the girl understood her dream. Her grandmother's reaction to her loving gesture revealed that her grandmother found it difficult to receive, because the girl had no intention whatsoever to ask her for something.

That evening, when her grandmother settled down to watch a TV program called *Skeletons in the Cupboard*, the girl understood even more clearly that her dream concerned her grandmother.

For those of you who don't know this very popular TV program in Quebec (Canada), it's a program where famous people – singers, actors, comedians, and others – are invited to play a kind of game. The audience tries to discover some hidden thing these people did in the past that no one knows about. The skeletons that come out of the cupboard are old, hidden things we'd prefer to keep buried. The girl immediately understood. This was confirmation that she had indeed visited her grandmother's soul.

Let's analyze the other symbols in the dream. A camp site: what purpose does this serve? It's a place in the countryside, mountains, or by the sea where we go to allow ourselves to relax, renew and replenish ourselves. And what did the girl see in this restful place? She saw her grandmother's bed, which was very small. We've already seen that when something is smaller or bigger than the norm, it indicates a complex of inferiority and superiority respectively. In this case, it was a complex of inferiority. This girl was shown that her grandmother doesn't allow herself the right to rest well and renew and replenish herself. Moreover, in concrete reality, she has dark circles under her eyes, a sign which proves this. This goes hand in hand with the skeletal hands we analyzed a little earlier, which reveal that her grandmother isn't capable of receiving love.

Her grandmother digs under the bed; this is related to what is unconscious, what is hidden in relation to her intimacy. She finds a skeleton that frightens her. There is something in her that she doesn't know about. Since it was a skeleton, she thinks this aspect is death and gone. But it hasn't been transcended. Her grandfather also represents part of her grandmother's energy, part of her inner man, who wants to get rid of the skeleton by throwing it away. But it transforms into a little monkey because the memories it represents are still alive. Instead of bringing about necessary changes – a new way of thinking, a change of mentality, for example – her grandmother prefers to continue copying others, just like monkeys do, with an instinctual, animal conscience. Many people behave like others merely to please and to be loved.

Let's have a look at the symbolism of monkey hands. We can see that it's on the level of her capacity to give and receive that this grandmother needs to work. Abu, the thieving monkey, symbolizes that, to get what we want, we have to take, we have to steal. A person may choose to function like this because it means he won't have to thank anyone, or give back, or be involved with the other person in any kind of relationship. Even if we don't actually steal in concrete reality, we may steal on the energy level, extracting from others the energy we want so much for ourselves. We take a great step forward when we understand this!

This teenage girl, who lives in France, told us that she has never seen her grandmother without heavy makeup. In fact, she goes to bed without removing it. When she was young, this girl sometimes slept in her grandparents' bedroom. She saw her grandmother, who always got up first, go and lock herself in the bathroom, where she took off her makeup and reapplied it immediately. It was the first thing she did on getting up. For years, no one had ever seen her grandmother without makeup, not even her grandfather!

This young girl is very wise. When she visits her grandparents, she doesn't talk about Angel Teaching. She doesn't show off the knowledge her parents have taught her about dream & sign symbolism. She knows her grandparents aren't yet ready to receive this information. She loves them as they are, and she respects the fact that they are transforming themselves at their own pace. Her love for them helps her not to make any comments that could hurt them; for example, by mocking her grandmother's makeup and her dependency on it. She has deep respect and understanding for her grandparents.

We might wonder why this girl received such a dream wherein she was allowed to visit her grandmother's soul. First of all, the messages and teachings it contains help us avoid reproducing behavior that isn't right. But above all, such dreams inspire compassion and help us understand what others are going through, like in the example of Aurore, the child martyr.

This girl has seen what her grandmother experiences. She understands the reason for all her makeup and why she isn't able to receive her I love yous. She feels deep compassion for her grandmother's incapacity to do inner cleansing. These are character traits of these new young people whose Mission is to help us break out of our old patterns.

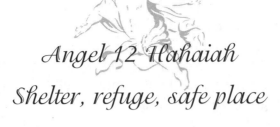

Angel 12 Hahaiah
Shelter, refuge, safe place

A woman who had worked for 32 years as a community psychotherapist found herself out of work for health reasons. She had to rely on social assistance. Life led her to the end of her physical resources so that she would get in touch with her deep inner being. This woman told Kaya – really joyfully actually – about the changes that had come about in her life since she'd started working with The Traditional Study of Angels.

Among other things, she told Kaya that she had recently had to give up her apartment and look for other accommodations. As she had very limited financial resources, she knew that she was starting out with a serious handicap. But she didn't feel discouraged. First of all, she started seeking answers through meditation. She meditated with her Guardian Angel, Angel 42 MIKAËL, for several days. She asked Him to guide her to the right place. As the days went by, she received visions of the ideal place to live: she saw a little garden, a specific door and a perfectly clean bathroom. She was even told the price she'd have to pay – which was, in fact, the maximum she could allow herself to spend on rent. After that she started her concrete search for a new apartment.

After a great many visits, she began to feel discouraged because nothing she saw in concrete reality corresponded to the visions she'd received. But her discouragement didn't last long; very quickly, she refocused and began to meditate with Angel MIKAËL once again. The very next morning, she opened up a newspaper at the classified ads and one of the ads immediately caught her eye. When she read the word garden in the ad, she knew it was a key word. She knew –her impressions were clear and precise – that this was the place for her, so she called the number and left a message on the answering machine. Needless to say, she awaited the return call rather feverishly; she kept wondering if her inner images were really going to materialize.

A little later, a man called to arrange a visit. When she arrived at the apartment, she was amazed by the beauty of this little corner of paradise. It was all there exactly as in her meditation; she couldn't get over it. She was even more impressed when the owner introduced himself. He said, "Hello, I'm Mikael." Just imagine! She'd been invoking Angel MIKAËL for days and here He was in the form of the owner called Mikaël.

And that wasn't the last of her surprises. After he told her he was very interested in astrology and that he believed in Divine destiny, they exchanged their dates of birth only to discover that they had the same birthday. She could only conclude that this man's Guardian Angel on the physical level was Angel MIKAËL too. AAH! She was truly impressed. She couldn't help saying to him, "It's amazing you called me when you'd received more than 30 calls."

She went home really exalted but also rather anxious as she had to wait for the owner's decision. He called her and simply asked for a co-signature to guarantee the rent. Everything was in order and the apartment was hers. She was so happy! Since that day, she's experienced real transformation in this apartment. For her, it is really favorable for meditation, inner harmonization and self-reassessment. This place has allowed her to begin a new life.

Angel HAHAIAH helps us find beautiful places that are favorable for meditation, but He does more than that. He helps us discover these ideal conditions in our inner home, on the inside. No matter what happens on the outside – whether there are physical storms, emotional upsets or any other sort of problem – an atmosphere of calm serenity continues to bathe our inner temple. Our own self becomes an ideal refuge. Now that's quite a goal!

Looking through the list of this Angel's Qualities, we can see many qualities related to refuge, meditation and interiorization.

What is interiorization? Interiorization consists in going within, going into our inner being. And of course, when we do so, we expose ourselves to experiencing all sorts of sensations. When our dreams are activated, when we begin to reflect on our attitudes and behavior, we are interiorizing and reassessing ourselves.

We shall see how certain conditions are necessary or certainly favorable to such interiorization. Generally speaking, exterior events and material thoughts and considerations continually attract our attention to the outside. We remain caught up in the outer aspect of things. Our vision is limited to what we perceive with our 5 senses and we are not aware of the other dimensions. In contrast to this, Work with the Angelic Energies, this great purification work, leads us to one day create and act while remaining in continual contact with the other dimensions, with the causal world. One day, it becomes a way of life. But to get there requires a lot of practice.

All sorts of negative forces within us, forces associated with memories of this life and of past lives prevent us from interiorizing. They prevent us from reflecting like this:

'Gosh, such and such an incident occurred today and I was put out by such a thing. Now here I am sitting peacefully in my car trying to meditate and aah! the same thought keeps coming to mind, the thought of that exterior incident... what could it mean? Let me try and analyze it symbolically. With Angel Work, we learn to use what bothers us and refer back to ourselves. Because we clothe all kinds of outer events in all sorts of ways when really they are only inner sensations.

We must always refer everything that happens to us back to ourselves. That's what interiorization is.

To face all these memories requires a lot of courage, of course. Well, Angel HAHAIAH is one of the Angels that gives us just that. Angel HAHAIAH gives us the necessary courage, strength and vigor. People in an ordinary conscience always project on the outside: what seems important to them is to be continually doing things, and they act without really being conscious. They hide their feelings of unease and lack of well-being so as to feel it less, but this only works for a while. Indeed, once a person finds himself unoccupied–for example while having to wait in line or before falling asleep–all of a sudden, he feels bad, he feels ill-at-ease. He feels a need to move, to do something. This is because he does not have a calm, peaceful place within himself where he can seek refuge.

That's why we encourage active meditation and especially Angel Mantra Recitation. The aim of the Traditional Study of Angels is to marry Spirit and matter. This means being active while remaining connected to the parallel worlds, the causal world. Used regularly and as constantly as possible, Angel Mantra allows us to begin the work of self-reassessment. We say to ourselves, 'I'm feeling put out. Ah! It's a part of me. I have that within myself. That's why I feel bothered,' and we breathe in the Name of the Angel to cleanse this aspect of ourselves. We can do this with our eyes open or closed.

In general, work with Angelic Energies facilitates interiorization, but Angel 12 HAHAIAH – and a few others – especially activates the capacity to go within, to interiorize and meditate. (*Cf.* The 72 Angels, page 353, Angel 12 HAHAIAH, page 365) This Angelic Energy momentarily isolates or neutralizes negative energies, thereby facilitating interiorization. It's as though we had Warriors of Light all around us, protecting us and allowing us to keep our vibratory level high. This is very useful, because if we want to begin meditating, we have to feel sufficiently well from the start.

Otherwise, if we are too caught up in emotions, which may include aggression, fear and anxiety or anguish, we simply can't.

To use another image, until we manage to attain the highest levels of Enlightenment, it's as though with Angel HAHAIAH we are granted a neutral country, a war-free country. All the other countries, to continue with this image, are also part of our conscience, but we have at our disposal a field of consciousness that allows us to begin interiorization. We say to ourselves, 'Wait a minute, hang on! Instead of ruining my life by being impulsive, I should think about this... Look! Such a thing has happened. OK. So, what does it mean?' That's what interiorizing is. From the moment we do this, we can change concepts and ways of thinking. It's the beginning of self-reassessment.

Actually, fear is the greatest aggression a person can be subjected to and fear is probably the root cause of impulsivity. It's the same for phobias. With Angel HAHAIAH, we are equipped to face the deep anxieties and phobias that dwell in us as long as we haven't completed our work on the purification of our conscience.

As I suggested earlier, when we work with the Angelic Energy HAHAIAH, it's as if we were surrounded by Warriors of Light that provide us with a peaceful place, safe from aggressive forces so as to allow us to begin to change certain concepts. And in changing these concepts, we eventually succeed in transforming aggressive forces. This is how these forces end up neutralized for good.

Now I'd like to talk to you briefly about the symbolism of the number associated with this Angel. The symbol 12 is very important because, among other things, it represents the completion of a cycle. There are 12 months in a year, aren't there? There are also 12 signs in the zodiac. In an astrological birth chart, there are 12 Houses and the last House, the 12th one, represents ordeals, suffering and initiations.

One day, we no longer speak of ordeals or suffering because we have finished a cycle. We've become complete. The number 12 is greatly used in various traditions to symbolize, as I've just said, the completion of a cycle. In Greek mythology, there's mention of the 12 Labors of Hercules. In the last one, Hercules had to go to the underworld, to hell, to liberate his beloved. Of course this story is symbolic. What does it mean? The feminine polarity, present as much in men as in women, symbolizes matter. This myth means that we have to liberate the materializations we've produced that aren't right. In order to do so, symbolically, we have to go to *hell*, i.e. into our own underworld, to visit the distorted parts of our unconscious. We have to liberate these memories so as to become complete and to rediscover harmony in and around us.

We also speak of Jesus and the 12 apostles and the 12 sons of Jacob. The number 12 has also got its physical component in the 12 pairs of ganglions in the sympathetic nervous system situated along the spinal column. When we know that our vital energy, the kundalini, must one day awaken and rise along the spine to enlighten and nourish the superior centers of our being – which is one of the aims of meditation – we can imagine the influence of this awakening on our physical body. By association, 12 symbolizes this awakening that we find within. It helps us understand why our physical body sometimes plays up during initiations.

The number 12 also comes up frequently in *The Apocalypse*, the last book of the New Testament. The term apocalypse comes from the Greek word *apocalypsis*, which means revelation. Hence its other name, *The Book of Revelation*. This book deals with initiations. The term apocalypse is often wrongly used to refer to the end of the world. In actual fact, it means the end of *a* world that exists within us which leads to rebirth. The apocalypse is the stage of revelations.

And we receive revelations via dreams and signs, via the understanding that everything that exists is symbolic.

The number 12 appears in numerous passages of *The Apocalypse*. One of the passages mentions 12 pearls, which are 12 doors, the 12 doorways into the Celestial City, which represents very evolved fields of consciousness, which we are all called to experience one day.

To analyze a symbol, we meditate on it, and we ask what it consists of and what purpose it serves in the tangible world. What use is a pearl? How is it formed? Where does it come from? A pearl is formed by a pearl oyster. When a foreign substance – a parasite or grain of sand – penetrates an oyster, rather than chasing it out in a movement that would empty it of its liquid, the oyster proceeds quite differently. Symbolically, an oyster is a great alchemist, a great philosopher. It reacts by secreting a liquid that will coat the foreign substance. This is how, from an unwanted element, it creates something very beautiful that it can then offer the world.

Oysters belong to the animal world. One day, we have to transcend this animal part; we need to raise our vibratory level by connecting with our Divine nature and developing Divine actions and reactions. Oysters also belong to the world of water; they generally live deep down in the sea, a symbol of the emotional unconscious. Hence the liquid they secrete symbolizes our unconscious emotions. This leads us to the emotions we secrete when, symbolically speaking, we are penetrated by a foreign substance; that is to say when we are confronted with something we don't know. Often, our reaction when faced with the unknown is fear. Well, the only way to no longer have any fear whatsoever is to acquire Knowledge.

How can we manage to behave like a pearl oyster, i.e. to integrate what bothers and scares us and turn it into something beautiful rather than expelling it? If we feel disturbed by a person or a situation, it means they represent a distorted part of us, to varying degrees of course, but one that shares the same *department*, the same type of content. That's the Law of Disturbance, a corollary of the Law of Resonance we talk about in all of our lectures. To apply it, we say to ourselves, 'Ah! This person isn't correct here. I feel put out. Ok. He represents part of me; I have this in me. So I'm going to transform this part.'

However simply managing to say, 'It's a part of me; I have that in me,' Sometimes it's so difficult! Because the more we open up – or rather the more Up Above opens our unconscious – the more on edge and easily irritated we become. We become very sensitive because these inner contents that bother us were previously camouflaged, veiled, and we didn't feel them. That's why a spiritual path is so difficult. We feel anger, for example, rising in us so often and we wonder, 'How come I feel like this? Why am I feeling so angry?' At times like this, if we invoke Angel HAHAIAH, the resonating negative forces are neutralized so to speak. They lose the power to annoy us, which enables us to go within and say to ourselves, 'Wait a minute! Stop! I'm not going to lose my temper and add another karma to my collection. This person represents part of me. I'm going to refer back to myself and make a pearl, just like an oyster. I'm going to accept what this person presents to me instead of expelling him from my life and emptying myself of my energy.'

Imagine what would happen to an oyster if it emptied its liquid every time a little grain of sand got into it. Well, that's exactly what happens when we feel disturbed or annoyed. We empty ourselves, and what's more, we feel it. You can see that a pearl is a truly great symbol; it symbolizes Angelic perfection, not bestowed on us but acquired through a phenomenon of transformation, of alchemy. Each of us must succeed in integrating this process one day.

Initiates don't spend their days lounging around in reclining chairs. On the contrary, they regularly experience all sorts of aggression and they put them to good use. They use evil, wrong, what hurts to make pearls. And they become very rich. That's why they can then share their wealth with others; they are very generous. You see, we could meditate on the pearl for days; as a symbol, it is so rich in teachings. One day, our conscience is constantly attracted to the deep meaning of the symbols we encounter in our dreams and everyday lives.

Speaking of pearls, I'd now like to tell you a true story. While I was preparing this lecture, a man I'd spoken to several times before told me about one of his experiences. I spoke about this man in another lecture, the one on Angel NELKHAEL. He's the man who used to go to the races and bet on horses, remember? I told you about the difficulty he'd had with a ticket machine and I ended the anecdote with what Kaya had told him, "When you're able to use the money you now spend at the races to help someone become a better person, you'll see, you'll touch on high sensations. Altruism is incomparable! No other feeling reaches the heights altruism gives us."

What we said slowly but surely sank in, and the following month, this man told me what had happened to him. He told me, "I went to bet and won again. On my way out, I saw a man I'm acquainted with. He's a very poor man, who's not quite a tramp but almost. I decided to share my winnings by inviting him to dinner. We went to a good restaurant where we had a top class meal. When we finished, I asked him, 'Well then? Did you enjoy your meal?' He answered, 'No, not really.' Oh! I was shocked!"

Along the same lines, he went on to tell me, "My wife and I have begun to sell natural products and I offered some to my mother. I told her they'd do her good. Well, some time later, I called in to see her again and she hadn't even touched them! They were still there on the shelf. Once again, I was shocked."

I told him, "Yes but through these two examples, you were being given Teachings. Up Above wanted to teach you to give well, not to give pearls to pigs. When we know the Law of Karma and the Law of Reincarnation, we know a person isn't poor just by chance; there are things he needs to understand. Cosmic Intelligence is generous. God is Generosity in its purest state. He'd never leave a person in poverty without good reason. It's always to help that person evolve. The person himself engendered his situation and he finds himself deprived in order to wean him off certain distortions so he can have the chance to learn the value of things, so as to no longer waste the resources he's been given, but rather to truly use them well. So you were being shown it wasn't yet time for that man to experience abundance. You saw his ungrateful attitude... you should refer this back to yourself. Since you were put out by his reaction this means that somewhere in yourself, you too nourish parts that shouldn't be nourished, that should be weaned."

How do we stop giving pearls to pigs? It's very easy but the path is long. We must recognize and purify those parts in us that are little pigs, so to speak. We experiment, we observe how and to whom we tend to give, and we note their reactions. Then we come back to ourselves and we identify the attitudes we need to change. Up Above wanted to give this man a little sign. They wanted to tell him, "Look, you keep on betting at the races; you continue to nourish certain parts of yourself that you shouldn't nourish. You give pearls to the pigs within yourself, to your inner pigs. You waste your time, your energy and your money instead of helping humanity improve."

Then, regarding the other example, I said to him, "You gave to your mother, but you had expectations. In a way, you were imposing something on her; you didn't really give generously. We don't experience altruism when we give like this."

His wife, who was listening to our conversation, said, "It's interesting that you should mention pearls and say we shouldn't give pearls to pigs, because recently I dreamed about pearls." And she told me her dream.

"In my dream," she said, "*I was on the bed in my bedroom. And from there, I could see a little blond-haired girl under my bed, playing with toys. And on the other side of the bed, I could see an aggressive, threatening man and I was afraid of him. Then, I was holding pearl bracelets and necklaces in my hands. And I was so frightened he'd come and steal them! So I hid them in my mouth. Then I very quickly realized that it wasn't a great place to hide them, that I might swallow them. So I took them out again and put them in my shoe, in the heel of my shoe. Suddenly a new scene appeared. I saw a kind of church and on the edge of the roof, there were gargoyles* (gargoyles are those famous half-animal, half-human sculptures that sometimes appear to be demonic). *And the gargoyles came alive. I was so frightened! I was panic-stricken. Then, at one point, I found myself above the gargoyles and I was no longer afraid. Then I found myself back down on the ground and, overcome with panic, I started to run. Just then I heard a voice say, 'Gargoyles can enter the mouth, especially through saliva.'* And I woke up."

The theme of the dream is indicated in the opening scene. Every time we see a house in a dream, we know it's about certain facets of our inner refuge, because when we go into a house, we can interiorize there, even more so when we are in a bedroom. A bedroom is a more private, intimate place than, for example, a sitting room where we welcome people. We usually rest and sleep in a bedroom, and when we dream or daydream, we visit our inner world and the parallel worlds. Hence it's very conducive to interiorization, to going within. Moreover the dreamer was on a bed, which also represents intimacy. So this dream was about the intimacy of her refuge, and in the rest of the dream, she was shown why she found it difficult to go within, to interiorize.

There was a young blond-haired girl surrounded by toys under the dreamer's bed. The space under a bed represents the unconscious aspect of intimacy. Furthermore, a girl symbolizes the inner world, and blond represents a person's solar, sunny aspect related to confidence, to shining, to success on the positive level. And what purpose do toys serve in concrete reality? They are used for learning. When a little girl plays with dolls, she is not only playing, she is learning to be a mother. Basically, toys have an educational role in life. This means that the dreamer is learning something—we'll see what that is as we analyze.

Then she was shown a threatening man. This character represented a part of her in the active world, in her actions. He represented memories of aggression that are lodged in her unconscious and that prevent her from learning and growing healthily, and she was afraid of this man. At that point she was holding pearls in her hand. Hands symbolize manifestation, giving and receiving. She was afraid of losing the pearls. Well, when we are afraid of losing something, it means we haven't really got it, that we haven't integrated it yet. We've already seen that a pearl is a great symbol of the purification-transformation process. One day, there is purity in every corner of our being, in every cell we have, and from then on, we are no longer afraid anything will be taken from us. However this woman is going through the learning process: with the toys, she was learning, experimenting. And she's only in the very early stages. For the moment, she is like a little child who is learning, who is experimenting intimacy, but still on the unconscious level. And it's because she hasn't yet integrated purity within herself that she's afraid of someone stealing her pearls; she has forces in her that are too superficial, too attached to matter. The superficial aspect of pearls are related to people who think they are pure, perfect and wonderful because they are rich or wish to be. And as we've already seen, she was shown what prevents her from learning and growing healthily in her intimacy: parts of herself that are aggressive and threatening, that create insecurities because the person is too materialistic.

So what did she do? She hid the pearls in her mouth. When we receive a dream, we should always try to see how it will materialize. Is it logical to react like that? This dream will have an effect on hundreds of materializations and manifestations in her life. How will it materialize? When this woman manifests in her intimacy, her energy will be like negative pearls, based on superficial aspects, ready to do anything to look pure and perfect. She will have difficulty speaking out, she will be like a doll, even her sexuality will be fake and superficial. She will also be very materialistic because the worst thing is that she will not be able to help the blond child. The man can hurt the child and she will not be able to say anything because all her energy is based on needs to nourish herself with elegance and riches. What is also crucial in this dream is that she could be the kind of woman that might close her eyes to the abuse of her children because of a bank account. This is a very important dream for her that says that matter is more important than justice and protection. A dream like that can go far in terms of personality. Of course it depends on the percentage of memories in her regarding this situation. If it is only 1%, then it is an influence in her but no actions will occur, but if it is 10-25% or more, she will attract major ordeals to help her stop eating pearls and to learn to protect a child from a dangerous man. She could also say beautiful words, talk about beautiful things – spirituality, for example – and it will all sound beautiful and perfect. But, behind what she says, we'll feel negativity and aggression, a need to obtain something, profound superficiality. That's why later on in the dream, she was told that gargoyles – the negative aspect of gargoyles – *went in through the mouth, especially through saliva*. Since saliva is a liquid, it calls to mind the emotional aspect. So when this woman speaks, she'll say beautiful things but we'll sense superficiality, a fake, non-authentic attitude and aggression behind her words, which are really only spoken to ensure she gets and keeps her materialistic castle. Just imagine how important it is to Work on ourselves one day with dreams! Only one dream opens a whole dimension in us that could become real if we do not cleanse the memories, the hidden intentions we nourish everyday. There is a depth in dreams whose beauty and splendor in terms of evolution touches the soul very deeply.

Then the dreamer moved the pearls; she placed them in the heel of her shoe. Shoes symbolize action and behavior in social life. The heel of a shoe, a feeling of elevation, and, in the negative aspect, a complex of superiority. Thus, as with her attitudes, this lady's gestures and actions will give an impression of refinement, beauty, purity and elevation, but the need for glory, money, and power will be tainted with frustrations, with energy that is ready to do anything to succeed, to look good and pure. And her inner aggression – also revealed by the gargoyle symbol – will be perceived. This is a very serious dream. This person could have major problems in the future because her aggressive parts will attract the same thing in her concrete life; she'll feel aggression projected toward her or she herself will be assaulted, or someone like her own child could be molested, abused by a man. That's why she was also shown an accumulation of symbolic aggression – first the aggressive man, then the gargoyles that are very dangerous, demonic forces that exist in terms of conscience and behavior. We should never take these forces lightly; we should always take them very seriously.

Gargoyles are a very interesting but very negative, dangerous symbol. I'd like to take a few minutes to talk to you about them to help you understand their symbolism in depth. Historically these sculptures date back as far as Ancient Rome, but the fashion for gargoyles had its hour of glory in the Middle Ages. At that time, huge numbers of gargoyles were made and installed on civilian and religious buildings. Originally these half-human, half-animal were linked to religious buildings. If we see any in a dream, we know they relate to our spirituality, but in a negative way, of course.

What purpose did gargoyles serve? From a mythological point of view, they were used to frighten away evil spirits – that's what people believed. From a practical point of view, they played much the same role as present day drainpipes. They were usually found on the edge of roofs and they collected rainwater to prevent it from running down the building and damaging the facades and foundations, which is why, originally, they vomited out water that could destroy buildings and foundations. In most cases, these half-animal, half-human representations had a deformed appearance to symbolically express people with negative needs, needs linked to animal instincts, needs that lead to problems. Hence they represented the distortions of our animal as well as human facets because they were half-animal, half-human. Many of them even looked like little devils. Evil is all kinds of thoughts and emotions that aren't right; evil simply represents the opposite of good.

Over time, a certain confusion set in as to the meaning of gargoyles; superstition played a role too. Whenever we lose sight of the essence of the significance of something, it only takes a few generations before the meaning of an object or phenomenon is misunderstood and mistaken and this is what superstition is. You may have noticed that whenever we analyze a superstition, whatever it may be, we invariably find a little bit of Knowledge in it. Over time, as we end up no longer taking into account anything other than the outer form of the phenomenon – since we've lost touch with its essence – its real meaning fades into the background and only the superstition remains. That's why Cartesian or scientific minds say that superstitions are nonsense. And they will continue to do so as long as they don't refer back to the essence, to their essential meaning, as long as they don't admit that everything that exists is first and foremost symbolic.

Let's examine the symbolism of gargoyles in detail by returning to their essence, to the very origin of these sculptures. As they were usually installed on the edge of cathedral and church roofs, they concern thoughts related to spirituality. When, all of a sudden, we have certain thoughts related to spirituality which aren't right, our emotions become involved, take over, and... overflow! We lose all discernment. We need to evacuate this negative water, this flood of emotions. This is what evil is. That's what evil is used for: to flood or break what isn't right so that it can be evacuated. It has its rightful place in the Universe.

Understanding the symbolism of gargoyles helps us truly grasp the usefulness of evil. If we think, feel and act right, we won't engender any distorted force. Hence, our soul won't need to call on a force of destruction to counteract the effects of these distortions. On the contrary, the forces engendered will actually have a beneficial effect; they'll procure great vigor for us that will be used constructively and positively. They'll give us strength and courage. That's why I said that, one day, when we truly understand good and evil, we are no longer afraid of evil. Like God, we are above good and evil because we have completely transcended evil.

The church is a symbol of spirituality. Well, there are all sorts of stages in a person's spiritual evolution. We could even say that there are different spiritualties, different ways of seeing and considering ourselves in the world of the Spirit. For a person who hasn't integrated Knowledge, who hasn't gone through initiatic stages, belonging to a religion signals the beginning of a spiritual path, and from this point of view, the church is a positive symbol. However, the more we evolve, the deeper we integrate Knowledge, the more the church appears as a symbol of an old, former or ancient spirituality because we become more universal in our Knowledge, we no longer relate only to one place or tradition, but we are inspired by the positive and Divine aspects of all traditions, religions and cultures all over the world. One day, we live a spirituality that embraces the wonderful opening of conscience that our present era is enjoying. Consequently, whenever a church appears in a dream, it may symbolize the positive or negative aspect of this symbol; everything depends on the context and what the dream scenario reveals.

Thus, the church can be a symbolic reminder of what the Church did in the past when it lost touch with the message of the great initiates. We only need to think of the atrocities it committed that were motivated by a struggle for earthly power. For successively long periods over centuries, initiates were persecuted – even tortured – whenever they spoke of dreams and symbolic language. It is really wonderful to see the present day mutation of consciences; more and more, spirituality is becoming a spirituality of initiates. In this spirituality, people become spiritually autonomous; they recognize the expression of spirituality in their daily life and they consider a person's evolution over several lives and not only one life.

When we visit religious edifices built during those dark periods, we can sense a greed for earthly power much more than Universal Love or Wisdom. That same greed led the Church to its downfall; its dark history, better known today, reveals it as an institution that deliberately occulted the teachings of Jesus and other initiates in order to establish and maintain its power. Moreover, the major part of the teaching occulted concerned the Law of Reincarnation, which has been transformed into the concept of Eternal Life. Nevertheless, having said this, the Church has its rightful place too. Symbolically, people go there like children go to kindergarten; it is useful for those who aren't ready to find *Jesus* inside themselves, which means integrating initiatic Knowledge. The church is a beautiful place for sharing, helping, and being involved in the community, and it is also a first step for people who still need limits and boundaries.

So, to go back to the dream, the gargoyle symbol was used to say to the dreamer, "This is why you are sometimes afraid; you resonate with this ancient spirituality, this old conception of evil, according to which a person has to struggle and fight against evil."

When fear is irrational and disproportional to the situation experienced, it's called a phobia. The Angelic Energy, HAHAIAH is truly the ideal Angel to work with when we suffer from a phobia. In the light of the Law of Reincarnation and the Law of Resonance, we can easily understand the origin of phobias. I shall give you several concrete examples to illustrate this, this evening. First of all, I'd like to say that we must never associate a phobia with a degree of evolution. In other words, one person may suffer from a major phobia and another have none whatsoever, but in no way does that mean that the person with a phobia is less evolved than the other one. The difference between these two people is that an initiatic process has been set off in the person who has the phobia. His unconscious is open and he is visiting certain memories. A certain type of exterior event plays the trigger-role that activates and regularly re-plunges him into memories marked by excessive fear. Hence the phobia.

Here's the first example. While we were preparing this lecture on Angel HAHAIAH, my husband had a phone call from a woman volunteer for UCM in Europe. This woman shared a personal problem she was struggling with; she told him she suffered from claustrophobia.

There are several types of phobias. In fact, there's quite a long list. Among the most common, is claustrophobia, fear of closed spaces; when a person is in a closed room, he feels great anxiety. Agoraphobia is the other extreme; it is fear of open spaces. As for xenophobia, it is fear of and hostility toward everything foreign.

In a way, before attaining high degrees of Enlightenment, we are all xenophobes to a certain extent. Xenophobia is the opposite of the pearl oyster: instead of transforming foreign bodies, it expels them. When the attitude of rejecting foreigners has descended right down into the physical body, then a person is literally xenophobic. He rejects everything he doesn't know or understand, thus he refuses to evolve. Hence, until we learn to transcend what bothers us, we manifest a certain degree of xenophobia.

To go back to this lady's story, she told my husband she worked with the handicapped and when she was obliged to take the elevator, she went through terrible anxiety. Whenever a person is in the grips of his phobia, he breaks out in a sweat and feels extremely anguished and he experiences this as a real assault. Indeed, this is the same for all great fears and anxieties. She told him, "I don't know what to do anymore. I've even thought I should give up my work because of the elevators. But I know very well if I do that, it'd be running away; I wouldn't be facing my fears. What's more, I receive recurring dreams about this. I have a dream that always comes back, the same one, where *I'm in my bedroom, asleep in bed with my husband. Then, in my dream, I wake up and I'm suffocating; it's unbearable.* And I wake up to concrete reality. It takes me two days to get over it and during those two days, my claustrophobia increases."

A bedroom symbolizes the inner world and intimacy. Therefore, this recurring dream reveals to this woman what is in her intimate life. It is interesting to note that in her dream, when she's sleeping, she isn't suffocating; it's only when she wakes up that she suffocates. Well, in a dream, when a person is asleep, this means their conscience isn't awake. Consequently, as the impression of suffocation occurs on awakening, it corresponds to an awakening of conscience, a connection and new awareness of being bothered, of what we need to transform. That's why I said we should not compare people suffering from phobias to those who don't. The latter may suffer from a phobia later on, when their unconscious opens up and it will open up one day or another, that's for sure.

When this woman's conscience awakens, she plunges into certain memories characterized by suffocation. These are memories of things unsaid, unspoken. Everything that was locked up, closed in and veiled in a person's unconscious while they experimented other things – and didn't suffer from any phobia – is suddenly revealed. They visit memories related to fear, assault, aggression and all sorts of distorted behavior that had been sealed up, locked away up until now. They touch on the very essence of confinement, of suffocation. This is actually what the opening of our unconscious consists of: memories that were previously unconscious become conscious.

Thus, when a person visits these memories – previously sealed up and locked away – and they find themselves in a closed in, restricted space such as an elevator, the difficulties related to their state of conscience are amplified. Their feeling of suffocation is exacerbated. This is the essence of claustrophobia.

After giving this explanation to the lady on the phone, my husband added, "I suggest you invoke Angel 12 HAHAIAH, that's the ideal Angel for phobias. But you mustn't expect the phobia to disappear immediately. Because Angel Recitation will cause the memories you sealed up and locked away to re-surface." With Angel Work, we can feel all sorts of difficult soul-states and we really don't feel very nice sometimes. It takes courage to go deep within to encounter our memories. However, whenever Up Above has decided the time is right for us to plunge into the depths of our unconscious memories, we have no choice. In we go, in spite of ourselves; because we have tried to avoid our unconscious for so long, it quite naturally bursts open. Remember, there is no punishment in the Universe. We always naturally create who we are.

When we have a phobia, we can see just how important it is to go to the essential meaning – i.e to the causal world – and visit those memories that are the root cause of the present phobia. But we can also work in the world of consequences. For example, while continually doing Angel Mantra, this woman can use elevators to gradually eliminate her claustrophobia. She can adopt the homeopathic method. This consists of injecting a tiny, tiny dose of evil to set the immune system working, so that it gets used to it, and hence strengthens and develops its own defense mechanisms. This is the great secret of the method Cosmic Intelligence uses to help us evolve. We are injected with tiny doses of evil. Then, as Work gradually progresses, we are submitted to greater doses, until we have transcended all our distortions and we no longer have any resonance with evil. At this point, we truly move on to another stage.

So my husband advised this woman to proceed very gradually. First of all, to enter an elevator – this is a huge effort for claustrophobics – hold the door button open, stay there for a few seconds and then step back out. Then do it again. A second step would be to close the door, and after that, when she felt ready, to go up and down one floor. This is to get used to being closed in. Through this method combined with Angel Mantra, the person can act on both levels – cause and consequence. It is very important not to always avoid elevators because with time, the problem of being closed in will increase and increase until you can become paralyzed, really handicapped and trapped in your body. This is what happens to handicapped people. They wait and wait too long before working on themselves and eventually they can no longer escape their memories and negative forces.

All sorts of techniques exist – most of them based on conditioning – that aim to reduce phobias. In many cases, however, there's a lack of depth. If we condition ourselves through visualization, for instance, by repeating over and over again, "I'm not afraid of elevators," and imagine ourselves relaxed and at ease in this restricted space, we can of course succeed in no longer being afraid of elevators. But if we haven't cleansed the distorted memories that are the root cause, the origin of the phobia, we've only acted on the consequence. The cause remains. We've taken an escape route or found an outlet for this ill-being, which became a phobia whose purpose was to serve as a warning. It will inevitably reappear in another form, as an illness or another phobia for instance. Therefore it is important to go to the root cause, to the essence of the problem, to reflect deeply on the question: 'Why am I claustrophobic?' and tell ourselves, 'I can do Angel Mantra with HAHAIAH and I will receive dreams and signs that will explain the root cause.'

Now I'd like to tell you another true story also related to a phobia, zoophobia this time – arachnophobia to be more precise, which is the phobia of spiders. It's a story about a woman who told my husband she very often dreamed about spiders and that she was really scared of them in concrete reality.

She said to him, "When I have a spider dream, the darker the spider, the more unbearable my migraines are the following day. What can I do about this phobia?" "You need to analyze the symbolic meaning of a spider," answered Kaya. "How does this insect behave? Of course, for all insects – as is the case for everything – there are always both positive and negative sides. Here we'll look at the negative symbolism. A spider is possessive and controlling and its attacks are premeditated. It sets traps. It weaves its web in very specific places. Sometimes near a light because it knows that insects are attracted to light and then it waits for them to be caught in its trap. So there's a whole *setting up to waylay and ensnare* aspect. And of course the darker the spider, the more its dark, negative aspect is represented."

This woman's unconscious had been opened and she was visiting certain memories. What sort of memories? My husband told her, "In other lives, you may have had a lot of power and used it solely to satisfy your personal needs. And now, you are visiting this kind of memory. Of course, if we didn't behave correctly and our actions weren't right, when we visit such memories, we feel anguish and emptiness on the inside. That's all it is. So all we need to do is to rectify our memories."

He added, "It's not only in other lives: it's in this life too."

"You're right; I've behaved like that even in this life. I've always gotten what I wanted. I wanted a millionaire...I got him. But he ordered me around; he was domineering and, one day, he threw me out. I found myself destitute. Ever since, I've always had difficulties with my husbands. The last one was an alcoholic. As a matter of fact, I come from a family of alcoholics myself. Sometimes it's so difficult I could easily be interned in a mental hospital."

One day, Up Above could release this woman from her spider-phobia even before she has transcended all her memories of misused power. However, should this happen, if she doesn't work on changing her power-related behavior, her phobia will come back; she'll be haunted by a fear of spiders once again. This will re-incite her to use her power better until, eventually, she has transcended all the distortions situated in this particular *department*.

Here's a story concerning phobias, which allows me to touch on a very interesting aspect. It's the story of a retired teacher who told me one of her dreams. In her dream, *she was going to a Christmas party and her cousin was driving the car. Then she saw a little girl fall into an abyss. After that she saw rebellious children making a mess. Then she found herself with a hen stuck to her body and overcome with fear, she wanted to scream but no sound came out.* She woke up with this dream.

What does this dream mean? Let's begin at the beginning, that's how we interpret dreams. The beginning of the dream – where the dreamer was going to a Christmas party – announces the theme. Christmas is a celebration of the birth of a Christ. Among other things, it symbolizes a capacity to experiment generosity and to receive gifts, which can be beautiful states of conscience. So, this woman was heading toward these beautiful states of conscience, toward a new spiritual birth. The remainder of the dream shows her the path she needs to travel so that, one day, she can stabilize these states, so that she can receive the Divine within herself.

As she was being driven by her cousin, I asked her, "What does your cousin represent for you?"

"Ah! When he was young, he was a very turbulent child. But now he's an adult, he's changed a lot. He's become really nice; he's really gentle."

"Well then, you were being shown that in your manifest action, in your social behavior or conduct, you advance with parts of you that have improved. You have worked well and these parts allow you to advance. But Up Above also wanted to show you other parts, to explain that when things are going well in your advancing, when you have access to abundance, to generosity, when you receive gifts from providence, you tend to fall into an inner abyss because abundance creates emptiness in you instead of joy."

What is an abyss? An abyss represents emptiness. What creates emptiness? Distorted memories, memories of disconnection from the Divine. Each time we didn't respect a Divine Law, it's as though we disconnected ourselves from God, and thereafter, when the time comes to visit these memories, we find ourselves facing emptiness, facing a region

Angel 12 Hahaiah

of our conscience that has no spiritual principles. Needless to say, it's very frightening and it's very powerful. You have memories in you that are connected to a very negative relationship with matter and abundance. It is sure that in a past life, you did not use resources well and that's why, when you have access to it, it creates chaos. A lot of spiritual people are like that. They tend to reject matter instead of learning to use it well.

In the following scene, she was shown that she still has rebellious parts that create havoc because of Christmas and abundance, and that she needs to cleanse them, to rectify them before going to a Christmas celebration.

Then in her dream, she was excessively afraid of a hen that was stuck against her. I asked her what hens represented for her. She replied, "Ah! I'm terrified of birds! It's a phobia. I've tried to get rid of it for years but I can't; I still have it. But I've worked hard trying to understand it, that's for sure. It dates back to my childhood. When I was 4 years old, just after her brother's suicide, I heard my mother say, "Ah! It's because of that bird of misfortune striking the window last night." That really marked me. Then, when I was 7, I went into a henhouse where there were laying hens and the cock attacked me."

Let's go back to what this woman experienced at the age of 4, i.e. the association she made between what her mother had called a bird of misfortune and her uncle's suicide. People from previous generations are often heard to say, "When a bird strikes against a window, it's a sign of death." Once again – like with gargoyles – it's a superstition. People have lost Knowledge and have only kept the outer form.

If, at the age of 4, this little girl had been in contact with the suicide of a close relative, it's no coincidence. Up Above wanted her to be deeply marked by the expression about the bird of misfortune. In other lives – because at that early age, she had only accumulated a very small amount of the baggage of her present life – she'd had links with suicide. She may have committed suicide herself or experienced certain unfortunate situations related to suicide. Through her mother's words, the image of the bird was engraved on those memories. I said to her, "A bird concerns the air element. So it's sure that your bird phobia is there to help you change your way of thinking."

If a soul is linked to suicide, it means that there was a time when memories of deep despair caused all of their horizons to be blocked. And if that happened, it's because it had previously committed acts or engendered materializations based on a non-respect of the Laws. The soul had excessively intense needs, wanted to obtain its desires at all costs, and behaved like that for a long period of time. Only old souls can commit suicide because, with time, after not making good use of the life force and resources they receive, then their soul naturally and gradually accumulates too many limitations and sufferings and they become empty, angry, lost in darkness because they can no longer see the *Light*. They don't understand the true purpose of evolution; as a result, their horizons feel blocked. They are no longer connected – well actually, we are always connected, but these souls no longer feel their Divine connection. This condition is what pushes people to commit suicide. So I said to her, "In a way, yes, the bird of misfortune is an appropriate symbol, in the sense that if you think in a certain way, it will bring misfortune into your life. It will inevitably bring you problems. That's an absolute fact." We can see that this woman really needed to change something on the level of her thoughts.

As a cockerel is a bird, it too, symbolically, concerns the world of thoughts. But it doesn't fly very high, does it? So it symbolizes thoughts that don't really help raise us up. On the other hand, in the Bible, it appears as a symbol of vigilance; it watches over the henhouse. As for its negative symbolism, this bird is reputed to be possessive, a bit like, "Hey! Hands off my chicks!" It's also got a belligerent temperament, which means it's very often aggressive. And a cockerel also represents a polygamous aspect: it has several hens.

Having explained this symbolism, I said to the lady, "You know, we don't get attacked by chance or coincidence. There's always a reason. You had resonance with the negative aspect of the cock. Many people go into henhouses without being attacked, don't they? How come you were attacked?" There was something this woman needed to understand about aggressive thoughts and attitudes concerning polygamy.

I went on to say, "That cock represented part of your inner man. You have unconscious memories..." This very serious lady was thinking as she listened to me and, all of a sudden, with a sense of humor, she blurted out, "Ah! That's true! When I think about it, my ex-husband was quite a cock!" She had just found a clue, understood an aspect that would help her rediscover the parts of herself that resonated with the negative aspects of a cockerel. Being afraid of a hen also means that our life, our behavior, feelings, thoughts and actions are too based on matter, on results, and, in this case, that she no longer wants to submit to what is not right. Submission is something that is so beautiful, and it is not only for women, it is also for men. We should always submit to what is right and Divine.

Now I'd like to tell you another story that is to do with aggression, but which is a good illustration of how the feelings attached to it sometimes prevent us from going within, meditating and thinking well. It's the story of a doctor, a GP, who has been working intensively with the Angels for quite some time now. He was sent a dream in which he was shown where he was on his spiritual path and what he needed to work on.

This man told me, "In my dream, *I met a man who was over 70 and he made a pass at me – he was a homosexual. I categorically refused and he became very aggressive and threatening. So I went back home to get a gun to kill him. When I went into my house, I saw my wife, like her usual self but much smaller; she was really tiny. Then I found myself in a butcher's shop in front of a great display of red meat and the butcher asked me if I wanted meat. I refused him very nicely, saying, 'No, thank you, I'm a vegetarian.'"*

During initiations, when the unconscious opens, the theme of homosexuality may be presented in our dreams, even if we have no conscious preoccupation with homosexuality nor any homosexual activity. What did this dream mean? It indicated that the person – not the whole person but certain parts of him – over-identify with matter and that he has a tendency to love action and the masculine energy too much. Normally a person seeks to integrate the two principles, the masculine and the feminine, in perfect equilibrium; it is the Mission of each and every one of us to succeed in achieving this balance.

We know both principles are necessary to create a child, even to create electricity. The symbol of homosexuality in a dream shows that the person has given priority to matter; he grants it too much importance. If the homosexuals are men, it's in manifestation, in action that these misplaced priorities manifest themselves. If they are lesbians, it's on the inside that they manifest themselves and it is linked more to a lack of softness, of feminine energy. So, in this dream, the man who made a pass at the dreamer represented part of the dreamer that materializes with such a state of mind, i.e. based too much on action, on outer manifestation.

When the dreamer refused the man's proposition, the man became aggressive and threatening. This part of the dream is a good illustration of why, when we begin a spiritual path – when we choose new, more spiritual directions for our life – it can be difficult to put these new spiritual aspirations into practice because we harbor all sort of memories that do not want to have balance in our life. Angel 12 HAHAIAH can really be of great help to us at this stage. We succeed in telling ourselves, "No, I can no longer do this. Such behavior or such an outing is no longer right for me." And we do as the dreamer did: we refuse.

The distorted parts of ourselves that we've nourished unconsciously and silently – sometimes whole lives long – suddenly find themselves weaned, cut off from their regular supply, and so they get angry and that's normal. It's as though we had wild animals on the inside that certain thoughts, emotions and behavior of ours regularly fed. This man wanted action, action, and action! He loves action so much that his whole life was based on gaining success and renown as a doctor, and having a self-centered attitude, which is the negative aspect of homosexuality, since it is too focused on satisfying and refining personal needs. When our stomach is full, we are usually relatively gentle, we aren't too aggressive. But when we say, "No, no more food! I won't feed you any more; that's enough! Stop! I've learned from the inside what I need to do. I'm giving up such negative, involute behavior!" Then, those needy parts of us suddenly become very aggressive and awaken our animosity. That's why we can then feel memories of aggression emerge. We can even become aggressive ourselves and we wonder, "How come? Why am I being so aggressive now? I know I wasn't perfect before, but what's emerging at the moment really isn't nice at all." It's because this process of change has been activated.

In those moments when we suddenly feel aggression and all sorts of impulses that aren't very nice, we can invoke the Energy of Angel 12 HAHAIAH to stop this animosity and aggressiveness. This allows us to isolate and block the movement of these parts that can cause havoc and wreck our lives. We build a life, step by step and with one word, one single word or action, we can wipe out all our work, our whole life. It can shatter our relationships and have virtually irremediable consequences in our job or in our life as a couple. Whenever we allow these forces to manifest, they can easily wreak havoc. However, with Angel 12 HAHAIAH, we prevent them from exteriorizing and we work on them. So HAHAIAH really is an ideal Angel for this kind of situation.

What is particularly interesting in this dream is that the dreamer was shown where he was on his spiritual path, what stage he had reached. He wanted to kill the aggressive, threatening part but killing is not right. However, it is a stage. One day, we no longer seek to kill evil; we transform and transcend it. We behave like the oyster pearl. We say to ourselves, 'That's a part of me. With meditation, interiorization and understanding of the Laws, I'm going to be able to make a beautiful pearl out of the ill-being I feel inside. So I no longer want to kill it.' Killing in a dream means that the person doesn't understand evil. And if he tries to kill it, he can expect it to re-surface: he'll be served up the same difficulty in one form or another because the problem hasn't been solved, only repressed.

The dreamer's wife represented his inner woman. But she was smaller than in concrete reality. What was he being shown through this detail? He was being told he had a superiority complex in his masculinity. And how is this complex applied? Some parts of the dreamer have no consideration for women, even including his wife, like homosexuals that have no attraction to women. He thinks they are inferior because his inner woman is diminished in his eyes. He doesn't have enough consideration for softness, interiorization, all the qualities of feminine energy. He is more attracted to action than to the inner world. For homosexuals, how they shine, what they do, the bank account that they have, the knowledge they have about art, sculptures, etc., is more important than a wife, children, and a family. They give priority to society. That is the main problem of homosexuals even if they also have beautiful qualities. But, most of them, on the unconscious level (not consciously, of course) consider the family, taking care of a child, etc., as a form of limitation of their personal needs. This example is a good illustration of how important it is that we are shown the characteristics of our hidden polarity.

All sorts of characters are featured in our dreams and they are all parts of ourselves. It is important to encounter these parts because we project them on the outside with all of their distorted aspects – automatically, without realizing, without knowing we do so.

This is why, with the evolution and purification of our soul, one day we are shown that our two polarities are united. And on that day, we truly understand the complementarity that exists between male and female, between a man and woman. We understand that they each have their place, and when each of them finds their place – when each of them understands his role as a man or her role as a woman – the result is fusion. First of all this fusion takes place on the inside, within ourselves, and that's why in this teaching, we often tell women, "The way you behave toward your husband is merely a reflection of how you behave toward your inner man." And vice versa – for men and their inner woman. It is very useful to understand this, because then we are better motivated to put an end to certain attitudes.

Now I'd like to tell you a true story that a woman shared with me during the period I was meditating on the various aspects of a refuge. This woman teaches Qi Gong–a martial art that is becoming more and more well known. It was just after her return from China where she'd been to perfect her art. She had tried to understand certain incidents she'd experienced and came up to ask me a few questions during the intermission. She said to me, "I understand that all the students who come to my courses represent parts of me. But I must have particular resonance with one of my students because I spend a lot of time with him. This man has serious heart problems. Recently I was invited to his island – he owns an island. When I went there, I saw certain things and I made certain links. I received signs and I'd like to understand them a bit better.

"On the island, I saw a nest with 12 duck eggs in it. I wondered what these eggs meant, why I saw them, what this meant for me. Shortly afterwards, I saw something wrapped up in a cloth; it was a cat that had been drowned. It'd clearly been wrapped up and thrown into the water. And this man – my student – was afraid; he didn't want to see it. He was really upset at seeing that. So that night, before going to sleep, I meditated on what had happened that day.

"During the night, I received a dream. *In my dream, I was in a bedroom and I saw a chest of drawers. When I opened the first drawer, I saw a nest with 12 duck eggs in it – but this time, the black and white contrast was starker. Then, when I opened the second drawer, I saw the same thing except the eggs had hatched and the ducks were gone. Then I saw something wrapped up* – exactly like what had happened in concrete reality – *but this time, it was alive. Something inside the cloth was moving. It was a very, very colorful, flamboyant parrot, a really beautiful parrot. But it gripped onto my hands with its claws and became very aggressive. It wouldn't let me go.* What does this mean?"

We can see here how, in many respects, Up Above matched waking, concrete experience with the dream. This is not unusual; our dreams often resemble what we experienced during the day. In such cases, if we don't understand dreams, we may say, "Oh! That's normal! I saw that yesterday and so I dreamed about it, even though it's not quite the same." However, when we understand dreams, we know this is not a valid explanation. Up Above uses the same symbols – whether by day or by night, there's no difference – to show us that they represent parts of us.

Let's begin by examining this woman's job. Doing martial arts is very good; it's very positive because we work on the martial aspect that we need to cleanse one day, on all the aggressive forces that prevent us from stabilizing a meditative state. Beyond their differences, all martial arts resemble each other in that they all marry the meditative state and the expression of strength. It is no coincidence that this woman teaches a martial art. After hearing my interpretation of her dream, she admitted, "Yes, I know there's something I need to understand, because both my father and my husband were verbally aggressive. So I know I have resonance with aggression. I know that there's something for me to understand about this aggression so that one day it can become strength and vigor and I'll be able to reach elevated meditative states."

What can give us a clue as to whether we have resonance with someone or not? If we feel either upset, annoyed or bothered by them, or indeed if we feel attracted to them, then we have resonance. This woman has a strong resonance with her student and she was shown this clearly in her dream. That man – who represents that part of her that is interested in martial arts, among other things – suffers from heart problems. If this problem manifests itself, if it has come right down into the physical level, it's because the person forced things too much. When we force, there's no room for gentleness. In a way, to force to get results, to achieve what we want, when we want it, is a form of aggression. Every time we force, vigor is manifested in the form of aggression. In the case of this man, this ended up affecting his heart. I said to this woman, "You see, you are really being directed toward work with Angel 12 HAHAIAH. With a dream like that, I suggest you invoke this Angel while you are doing Qi Gong."

With the island symbol, Up Above wanted to touch on the aspect of an emotional refuge. The dreamer was being shown which emotional attitudes prevent her from finding true refuge within herself.

So I said to her, "The man owns an island, but he may use it to flee certain situations which he really ought to face."

"Yes, it's true that in a way he flees his responsibilities. The island is an escape for him."

"It's no coincidence that you were brought there," I told her. "Up Above wanted to show you that you have certain *fleeing* aspects in you. Instead of the island being a source of meditation, of positive interiorization, it can sometimes be escapism."

This situation is not rare for therapists; some spiritual people flee material responsibilities because they find them too difficult, they feel antagonized by them.

Duck eggs. Let's briefly analyze the behavior of ducks. Ducks get together and––to use the rather strong term used in an article I read on this subject––they go and rape the female duck. That's not very noble, is it? In a group, the male ducks isolate a female duck and rape her. It's quite a barbaric show. So, we notice ducks tend toward rather vulgar behavior. Ducks are birds so symbolically they relate to thoughts. And they also live mostly on the water, which represents the world of emotions. Consequently, in the symbolism of this bird, two dimensions are touched on: thoughts and emotions.

Ducks also symbolize gossip, the habit of gossiping, because of their incessant quacking as soon as they are together. The dreamer was therefore being shown that in her efforts of introspection, in her attempts to go within, certain memories intervene and prevent her from finding refuge because the duck eggs were not in the right place in her dream. Without even being aware of this link, the thoughts and emotions that disturb her introspection are linked to memories where the person indulged in gossip. Cleansing such memories is quite a task. It's like in the dream about the pearls that we analyzed earlier: the woman spoke beautiful words, but behind them there was aggression, personal needs that may not have been very nice at all.

We have the right to evaluate others and symbolic language helps us to understand in depth, provided we do it without criticism or judgment, of course. We must always remember that what we perceive can always change and evolve; all the time. It's part of the power of discernment that, as a spiritual person, we sometimes lose because most of the time we avoid talking about others. Where is the limit then between good and evil, between right and wrong when we talk about someone? What turns our conversation into gossip? If two people talk about a third person, one of the two may be in a quality, i.e. simply evaluating, whereas the other person is in a distortion. This is the whole aim of our Work. Without love, knowledge – in this case, knowledge of the details of other people's lives – without love, knowledge is poison. One of the aims of this Work is to succeed in purifying ourselves enough so that, one day, the same words can be spoken with love and wisdom at all times. However, it is this very capacity to evaluate that allows us to integrate the understanding of good and evil, of right and wrong. So we must evaluate. Interpreting dreams inspires us to do so too. In the beginning, when people come to us to ask for a dream interpretation and we ask, "What does the person in your dream represent for you?" some people don't know how to answer. They find it difficult to evaluate even the negative aspect when it is present. We need to get used to evaluating.

To go back to the story of the woman with the 12 duck eggs both on the beach and in the drawer. This number isn't there just by chance. As this woman works with The Traditional Study of Angels, this number was used to suggest she should work with Angel 12 HAHAIAH, so as to lead her to visit certain parts of herself that are well hidden, stored away in her unconscious and which are linked to the symbolism of ducks. The black and white on the eggshells was also used to indicate that she should study her behavior in relation to good and evil, right and wrong, dualities, as well as priority granted to spirituality vs. that granted to materiality. She was being told, "Watch out! Be vigilant!"

Next the woman found a drowned cat wrapped in a piece of cloth on the beach. This symbol is very important; cats feature in so many people's dreams. While this animal was venerated in certain civilizations such as the Egyptians, it was feared in others. What's more, it is often associated with witches. Cats like to lie on telluric line crossings, those electro-magnetic lines organized in a crisscross network that are found on the Earth's surface. Zones with a very low vibration, much lower than elsewhere, are to be found at their junctions. Cats like to settle on these very zones as though they nourish themselves on low frequency, on evil, in a way. Of course, if there's a sofa or cushion nearby, comfort may win the day, but generally speaking, cats will choose places of low frequency.

However, their capacity to feed on negative vibrations exists only up to a point. That's why when we don't understand this phenomenon, we can often find cats capricious; our cat has only just come over wanting to be petted, and whoops, all of a sudden, off he goes again! And if we try to catch him, he may scratch us. This is because he's had his dose for the moment and knowing that, we understand that a cat's main quality is independence and its distortion is the opposite, i.e. over-independence.

A cat has other symbolic meanings too. As a symbol, it represents the feminine polarity and receptivity. From a negative point of view, it represents hypocrisy, a lack of receptivity, aggressiveness, egotism and individualism. And generally speaking, like all animals, it also represents our instinctual needs regarding independence.

Since the cat had been drowned, this woman was being shown that, on the emotional level, she drowned certain parts of herself – those parts represented by a cat linked to independence; she preferred not to see them. And we see that these contents had re-surfaced. As for her student, who also represented a part of herself, and who had a tendency to flee and to force things, he didn't want to see the drowned cat. He rejected this part of himself. We can see that a program has been activated in this woman to lead her to confront certain memories regarding difficulties in connection with too much or not enough independence. Whenever we begin to visit our memories, control no longer works. This woman seemed to have a certain degree of self-command and mastery, but in actual fact it was just a controlling attitude that allowed her to keep certain memories repressed under the veil. All sorts of things may occur in her now that she has access to these memories.

Since she asked Heaven to help her understand her experiences on the island, she was sent a dream which featured the same symbolism as events during the day. At the beginning of the dream, she was in a bedroom, a symbol of intimacy, as we've already mentioned. So what is in her intimacy, her private, intimate life? First of all, she saw a chest of drawers. What is a chest of drawers used for? What do we put in it? Well, generally speaking, we put clothes in it and we only open it from time to time. Clothes represent our aura. So, the contents of this chest of drawers indicate what this woman emanates.

Then she was shown the duck eggs. Through this image, she was being told, "Look at what's in your aura. This is the energy that emanates from you. Thus she was being shown what she needed to rectify; she needed to avoid gossiping and nourishing the other attitudes represented by duck eggs. Up Above sent her this dream so she can be aware of the kind of gossiping she indulged in with her student. She was probably impressed by his wealth and during their conversation gossiped with him about life and others. Then she was shown a nest where the eggs had already hatched and the ducklings were gone. Through this symbol, she was not being given the promise of a future flight; it was rather a case of her being told, "Acts have already been committed, deeds have been done and karmas have been inscribed. You must stop gossiping when you talk to other people, especially with men of power and wealth."

Next, the duck symbolism was used again but through a different representation: the parrot. A parrot, like a duck, is a bird and it symbolizes the world of thoughts and of communication because of its particularity, its ability to talk like humans, to repeat good or bad things. However, it doesn't fly very high. What a parrot does – the way it always keeps repeating what people say – is essentially what makes people in an ordinary conscience laugh. Hence, this woman was being told that she simply repeated what this man, or other people, told her, that she didn't submit what she was told to her inner truth. One day, we listen to people's declarations, to what they say, but we also say to ourselves, 'Hold on a minute. These people – my parents, society, this man – say such and such a thing,' and we go within, we interiorize and ask, 'In the Light of which Divine Law is it right?' Consequently, when we express the idea or adopt the behavior in question, we aren't merely repeating what was said, what others proclaimed to be true. We'll have received Knowledge from within and it will manifest itself one way or another.

Even the way this woman repeated what she had learned as a Qi Gong teacher, without submitting it to her inner truth, forced, *bullied* her into manifesting in a particular way. So I said to her, "You need to learn to go within, to interiorize and to stop repeating and gossiping." And very firmly and seriously, she said aloud, "I must be more authentic, I must be more authentic." Her soul knew she tended to repeat, that she wasn't always authentic, and that this affected the way she taught, especially when she found herself with people who have material abundance. It is easy to get caught because of our hidden needs and envy.

Angel 12 Hahaiah

In the past, a master transmitted the skills of teaching martial arts and he was the one who authorized his disciple to teach what he had been taught. Nowadays, this is no longer the case. This woman teaches what was transmitted to her, and Up Above has told her, "You're repeating." Furthermore, in her dreams and behavior, we can see this woman has quite a lot of repressed aggression. Well, one of the aims of martial arts is to master the expression of our force, our power, and yes, even gossiping because if we gossip, we can create major conflicts with others. One day, the person has no more aggression and no more the tendency to talk behind people's backs. And when we are ready to teach, we receive the message that it's time to do so. How? Through our dreams, where we are told, "Yes, now you are ready to manifest."

Often, people receive something and want to materialize immediately, instead of going within and carrying out the necessary purification and waiting to be given the go-ahead. But parrot behavior is also apparent when people just repeat what they've seen in the media, not just regarding fashion, but also concerning ideas and behavior. They don't let Knowledge received on the inside filter the impurities of the collective unconscious.

Now I'd like to tell you a very interesting true story that shows us another aspect concerning refuge. It's the story of a woman who had a recurring dream that she asked my husband to interpret for her. Sometimes, when people tell us their dreams, we can subtly feel that they don't really want to know the solution or the interpretation because that would mean being confronted with the need to change behavior. This was the case for this woman. So, while he was listening to her, my husband wondered how he was going to go about answering her.

She told him, "In my recurring dream, *I'm in a house*. From one dream to the next, it's always the same house. It's a house that I actually lived in for 5 years at the beginning of my marriage. It was out in the country and it was old and there was often water damage. Repair work often had to be done. And I didn't like this house for several reasons. First of all, I was brought up and had always lived in town and I really didn't like living out in the country like that. What's more the house was old; it wasn't nice. But as for my husband, he really liked it because he's a man of the woods. All he needs is a simple sleeping-bag and he can sleep out in the open, whereas I need comfort. If I haven't got a certain comfort, I don't feel well. And if I don't sleep in my own bed, I don't sleep well. What can I do? I don't want to see that house anymore, not even in my dreams."

She went on to explain to my husband that after living in that house for 5 years, she managed to convince – she used the term *force* – her husband to move into town. In an exchange I had with her, she told me, "There's an event that tarnished that move. My son fell ill. And a little later, he died. But still, I feel better in town." She persisted in rejecting life in the country.

Well, when my husband spoke to her, he said, "Madam, what you're experiencing is called the princess syndrome."

"What's the princess syndrome?" she asked.

"In your dreams, you are being shown parts of yourself, of your own inner habitat and you don't want it. That's why the dream often recurs. You don't want to visit this kind of memory because when you are brought there, you don't feel comfortable. But comfort always comes from the inside. There's nothing wrong with being comfortable – comfort isn't a distortion. But, if you feel uncomfortable as soon as exterior comfort is missing, that's a distortion. Your being sent this repetitive dream is truly an invitation to cleanse those parts

Angel 12 Hahaiah

of you where there is water damage, where it's old and not nice. It's symbolic. It represents memories that you need to cleanse and that you keep trying to flee from."

A town has both positive and negative symbolism. From the positive aspect, it represents a lot of activities and a certain feeling of expansion. From the negative aspect, the same abundance of activities attracts us toward the outside; it relieves us of the necessity to go within, to interiorize – i.e. to think about our life, our acts, our reason for living, the meaning of life. My husband told this woman, "When you were in the country, you could have taken the opportunity to interiorize. But you preferred to be surrounded by the activities found in town. You were allowed to flee that time. But if you don't do the Work that needs to be done in this life, you may find yourself in a really remote region, far from everything, with no comfort at all, not even running water. And there, you'll have your work cut out for you. But for Up Above, it wouldn't be a question of punishment. They always act with great understanding and the wisdom to reproduce what you have within you, and They do that with Pure Love and Wisdom."

Why does Up Above sometimes take away resources so drastically, to such an extreme extent? What's the aim of this? Here are a few examples to illustrate this principle. When I was in Europe, I used to take part in group hikes lasting several hours in very high mountains. Sometimes the weather conditions were very difficult. So, when we reached the refuge hut, what bliss! At night 20 or 30 of us shared the same dormitory. The blankets were often rough, itchy against our skin, or didn't smell very good, not to mention other inconveniences. I can tell you nobody dreamed of complaining. In ordinary circumstances perhaps, I'd have said, "Oh, these blankets don't smell good and they're itchy and ugh! some people are snoring!"– there are all sorts of inconveniences when we share a dormitory with lots of people. But it was paradise! Ah! It was so good to eat a bowl of hot soup and to have shelter for the night. We appreciated it because we'd experienced extreme conditions all day long.

When up Above removes our resources and leads us to experience extreme conditions, it's to help us appreciate the simple things in life. Later, when we regain comfort and resources, we realize those difficult moments were actually gifts, because we are able to truly appreciate what we'd have rejected before. We are grateful rather than discontent and disagreeable.

Let me give you another example. One day a man who's in the army told me he'd had to sleep in a mud-filled trench once during an important training exercise. I asked him,

"And did you sleep well?"

"Oh yes, really well!" he replied, explaining, "I was so exhausted!"

Just imagine, sleeping in mud! Ever since this experience, this man can sleep anywhere. It's the same for me. When I first began doing yoga many years ago, ah! I needed soft music and incense...if I heard the slightest noise, oh! I'd say, "Hey, don't make any noise, I'm doing my yoga." I needed certain external conditions to be able to go within. At that time, I hadn't yet understood that if external elements bothered me, it was because there was a noisy din on the inside. And ever since doing intensive Work with the Angels, there's been a great change.

Most of the time, before giving a lecture, I take time to interiorize and I usually go into a little corner or room at the rear of the hotel. And you know, it's not always very clean at the back of hotels. Often there are bins and all sorts of smells, and people coming in and out. I've got a little floor mat that folds up so the inside stays clean and the outside can be washed. No matter what the conditions are like – sometimes it can be a real squeeze – I open up my mat and settle down and I immediately feel good! I've gotten used to being able to meditate in all conditions. I go within, do my postures, and I feel really good. I've had to do intense purification work to develop this capacity because, as I've just mentioned, I tended to be quite fussy in the past.

Sometimes we wonder, "Why all these initiations? I experience suffering and nightmares and the following day, I feel uncomfortable, ill-at-ease, all out of joint. And what's more, I have to try not to project my ill-being onto others. What's the point of all this?" Once we understand that all this serves to liberate us, we're happy to go through initiations. If we don't feel well when we can't sleep in our own bed, just imagine how Up Above must feel on receiving our requests asking Them, "Please let me travel in the parallel worlds, throughout the Universe." We can imagine Their reply, "Yes but if you don't feel well when you haven't got your own bed, how do you think you could travel in the parallel worlds, in the Universe? Do you know that in the parallel worlds, there is as much darkness as Light, as much evil as good? Work on your discomforts and annoyances before asking for Angelic Powers. We'll open other doors for you after that." Often we want to have everything immediately, without taking time to do inner work, to prepare. We hear talk of other dimensions and think, 'Oh! Me too, I'd like to see that!' But we forget that it's thanks to all sorts of little annoyances as well as some big, intense ones – i.e. it's thanks to daily Work that isn't very gratifying at the time - that one day we are able to cross borders into other worlds. Our discomforts and annoyances are only the tip of the iceberg, but they lead us into the heart of the Universe.

Some people wish for the opposite situation of the woman who wanted to live in town. They'd love to live in a remote area, far from all the hullabaloo, because the slightest noise bothers them. But if these people have noise on the inside, they'll hear the whine of a chain saw or even the chirp of a cricket and they'll feel 100% annoyed. Or if a neighbor puts on some music, they'll feel aggressed and claim it's an artificial sound. It can be really calm in the outside world, but the slightest little noise sounds like a great big din to their ears. Why? Because whatever noise they hear resonates with their own inner din. So, every time we're bothered or annoyed by the noise of our neighbors, by restless children, or when any other outer element irritates us, we need to refer back to ourselves. One day, when our inner refuge is calm, no matter what happens on the outside, we feel good. And the Work which allows us to achieve this inner calm can be carried out with the Angelic Energy of Hahaiah.

I'd like to tell you another true story that concerns interiorization. It's the story of a lovely woman who's about 80 years old, who regularly comes to lectures and who asked my husband Kaya to interpret a dream for her. In her dream, *she saw her mother* – in concrete reality, her mother is no longer alive – *about to go down into the basement to tidy away some large boxes. She saw her head down the stairs and all of a sudden, she heard her fall on the stairs.* She asked my husband, "What does this mean?"

All the elements in this dream represented parts of the dreamer. Her mother symbolized her inner world, and the basement, her subconscious. So my husband told her,

"The fact that your mother fell on the stairs when she wanted to tidy away some boxes shows that Cosmic Intelligence is telling you it's time to stop overloading your unconscious with all sorts of memories. It's time you detached yourself from memories of your youth and events you've experienced in your life. It's time to do some cleaning."

"It's so true that old people live in their memories!" she exclaimed with lovely spontaneity. "I do too. From now on that's going to change. There's no age limit for change." Imagine, this woman is 80 years old!

"It's better to live in the present moment and prepare for our next life," my husband said.

This issue concerns old people in particular but – as you probably know well – it can be found in people of all ages. How can we interiorize and use our memories to help us advance? An important distinction needs to be made here. We can return to old memories and say, "Ah! When I was with so and so and did such and such... ah! It was so good!" and we let ourselves be lulled by a wave of nostalgia and sugary well-being. We curl up in a sort of cocoon and we nourish certain memories of lacks. That is not good interiorization; it's interiorization that leads us to flee the present moment. In the past, we experienced a certain well-being, but since we've never tasted a superior well-being – I'm referring to high states of conscience – when we stagnate, we feed on our negative memories and inner lacks. We say to ourselves, "Ah! when I had my own company...or when I was working..." or "When I lived with so and so..." But in the meantime, no Work is done.

When we work with the Angels, we inevitably open the past and think about people we've known, but we do this in a different manner. We reconsider ourselves. We meditate. We say to ourselves, "When I was there..." and, all of a sudden we feel certain emotions. Thinking of this past moment causes certain sensations to re-surface and we ask ourselves, "What was going on at that particular moment? Let me apply the Law of Resonance. What is there for me to understand here? What do I need to cleanse?" And we take advantage of this moment of introspection to cleanse distorted memories. This is how we live the present moment. All the memories of our present life are part of our personal library and if we need to take out a particular event and have a look at it, needless to say, it isn't taboo – we have the right to think and talk about it. But by reconsidering ourselves, we don't feel any nostalgia because there's nothing in the past that we regret, whereas nostalgia creates isolation; it has nothing in common with universality and altruism. By being satisfied with the sweet, sugarcoated aspect of our memories, being lulled by them, we more or less languish in artificial fields of conscience, which we believe procure a certain well-being for us.

Now I'd like to tell you a very interesting dream that illustrates one of the Qualities of Angel HAHAIAH: *gives access to occult mysteries*. A woman who's been coming to lectures for many years received this dream and she asked my husband for an interpretation. In her dream, *she was in her house, it was night-time and she was getting ready to go to bed. She went in to see her 11-year-old son who was asleep and, all of a sudden, she saw a rather negative shadow come through the window. Then she realized it was the shadow of her son when he was about 3 or 4 years old. She flew over it and blessed it. And from that moment on she felt that the negative aspect of the shadow had disappeared.*

In this dream, it is obvious that this woman visited her son's soul. She was shown what he was really going through so she could better accompany him and do real energy healing in dreams, which we call *Angel Healing*. It is a natural extension and expansion of personal Angel Work that leads us to develop Qualities, Virtues and Powers in their purest state. Her son is currently entering the adolescent phase, which is a program of important mutation where the teenager visits certain negative memories, and certain accumulations from his past also. The dreamer was being warned, "Look, a negative energy is on its way for him. He's going to experiment certain things." The fact that the shadow was a child's shadow meant that it wasn't all that negative. If the dreamer had seen the shadow of a giant or an adult holding a dagger, that would have announced an extremely negative situation – the symbolism would have been crystal clear. The day after the dream, this woman could have noticed that her son was in very bad humor and that he was going through a very difficult period. We can see why dreams are so important. They allow us to see what's coming and so to better anticipate the near future. It's so much easier to bring up our children when we can follow the movement of their soul.

Now I'd like to tell you a final true story which also relates to access to occult mysteries, but which, in addition to this, relates to strength, vigor and aggression. It's the story of an 83-year-old man I talked about in another lecture (Angel 14 MEBAHEL). We'd gone to visit him during a lecture tour accompanied by his daughter – a UCM volunteer worker – and we'd had a lovely conversation with him. In the lecture I explained that from time to time he heard his daughter's voice during the night but in actual fact it wasn't his daughter who was trying to communicate with him (even if that is possible): her voice was used because she represented spirituality for him and also because a familiar voice wouldn't frighten him as much as another voice might.

Since our encounter, this man has experienced a real opening regarding his dreams. And there's now wonderful communication between himself and his daughter. They live in different towns but he often calls her to tell her his dreams and to share his thoughts and reflections. His daughter is impressed by the vividness of the memories he shares with her — our memory becomes so vivid when dreams and multi-dimensions awaken it! She was particularly moved by a dream he told her; it took her two days to get over it. You'll see why he receives this kind of dream. Needless to say, this man is truly at the end of his life. These openings of conscience are seeds sown for his next life. They also serve the purpose of showing those close to him: "Look what happens when we do Angel Work," to move them and encourage them on their own spiritual path. In this rather detailed dream, this man was shown what happened at the moment of death.

In his dream, *he knew he was dead and he was looking everywhere for Saint Peter, but he couldn't find him. All of a sudden an Angel appeared to him in the form of a cloud and He spoke to him in quite a firm, authoritarian tone of voice. He said to him, "I'm going to bring you on a visit to the various Heavens." And the Angel took this man to the third Heaven. There was a magnificent garden there with colored flowers and a light we don't ever get on Earth.*

He said to his daughter, "It was so beautiful! What we see here is only a pale reflection. The light and the flowers were so beautiful!" This man, who has serious eyesight problems – he is almost blind and can only see out of the side of his eye – described the beautiful sights to her.

Then the Angel said to him, "Let's continue the visit, but you must read all the signposts very carefully." They went down into an inferior Heaven, into the hot-dog heaven. There was a menu serving hot-dogs, poutine (a typical French Canadian dish, consisting of French fries topped with cheese and gravy) and French fries. So the dreamer asked the Angel,

"Can I eat?"

"Yes, you can," replied the Angel.

"Can I have some more?" asked the man because he'd only had a little piece of hot-dog, three or four French fries and a tiny helping of poutine.

"No, you can't," replied the Angel.

And they continued the visit. The Angel brought him to an even lower Heaven. The man told his daughter, "It was the wife-batterers' heaven. It really wasn't a nice sight. They were fighting among themselves...," and he quickly skipped over the details. Feeling that this episode contained a lot more, his daughter asked him about it, but he replied, "No, no, I'll spare you the details," and he went on with his tale.

Next the Angel brought him lower again, this time into the rapists' heaven. There there were men who'd had their penis cut off; their penises were just tiny little stumps. Then the Angel brought him even lower, into the murderers' heaven. There there was a man who told another man, "You killed two men." The Angel intervened and said, "No, no, you didn't kill two, you killed four," and at the same time, the dreamer saw four men hanging by their feet. He said, "It really wasn't a nice sight."*

Then the Angel brought him back to the third Heaven, the one with the beautiful flower garden. But this time it was all withered. Surprised, the dreamer asked the Angel,

"What happened?"

"It's because you didn't read the signposts," the Angel replied. "In the hot-dog heaven, there was a sign up saying not to eat but you ate. You ate but you didn't really eat. You're going to have to work very hard to restore your garden to its former beauty. And you know, there are people praying hard for you down on Earth."

"Yes, yes, I'll work really hard to repair my garden!" cried the dreamer.

And instantaneously, the garden regained life and color; it became as beautiful as it had been when they first visited it. The dreamer tried to draw close to the Angel to touch Him. At that moment, he saw my face in the Angel cloud. Then the Angel said to him, "Up Above is the 7ᵗʰ Heaven." And raising his eyes up toward Heaven, the dreamer saw his mother's face all lit up; she was wearing a crown and looked more beautiful than he'd ever seen her. From Up Above – from the 7ᵗʰ Heaven – his mother told him, "One day, you too will come up to the 7ᵗʰ Heaven. All you have to do is to pray really hard and to work on your spirituality. You'll manage to get here." And he woke up with this dream. Quite a dream!*

Needless to say not everyone receives such revealing dreams before leaving this world. The symbols were perfectly adapted to suit this man. He was shown what happens the moment we leave our physical body. In the Bible, it is written, *You will live where your heart lived.* This means that at the moment of death, we'll find ourselves in whatever states of conscience we have integrated. In this dream, the man was shown certain states of conscience he had lived in and was connected to through resonance.

Such a dream can only lead a person to reconsider what he has learned, to completely change certain inculcated, indoctrinated concepts. First of all, the dreamer was looking for Saint Peter. As there was no Saint Peter, this man realized that things don't happen the way he'd been taught in church. Instead he saw an Angel in the form of a cloud. Up Above used this symbol because this man had heard about Angels. But what was really behind that cloud? It was a Guide who had taken on the form of a cloud. Even toward the end of the dream, when the dreamer saw my face, it wasn't me: it was a symbol that Up Above used because this man knew me and associated me with Angels. It was used to inspire confidence in him. It is true that sometimes I'm given dreams where I go and help others, but in this case, I knew it wasn't me, because I hadn't had a dream about this man at that time. It was a Guide helping him.

In his dream, as commanded by the Angel, this man was given a super-protected, guided tour. In dreams, there are various degrees of penetration into fields of conscience. At one point in the dream, the Angel said to the dreamer, "You ate, but you didn't really eat." This means that he was shown areas of his own conscience, but, in a way, he'd been protected, as if he'd observed the scene from behind a protective glass window. If he had truly tasted all those states of conscience, he'd have blown a fuse. Indeed, if a person were led too quickly too deep into negative fields of conscience, it would be too concentrated, too difficult for him. That's why we are given homeopathic doses of evil in our initiations and the veil is lifted very gradually. The day comes when we are ready to plunge into fields of conscience with highly concentrated levels of distortions and we manage to transcend them. So, as this man isn't yet ready to face so many distortions directly, he was given a protected tour. Besides, this visit was to serve those close to him much more than himself, because it didn't motivate him to start doing active meditation.

Let's analyze the guided tour. First of all, we can note that among the various heavens, the third and seventh were referred to by number. These numbers represent the chakras. In reality the heavens were fields of conscience. The third one, featuring the garden, was used to show the dreamer the contrast between the pure aspect of a field of conscience and its distorted aspect: in one case, the garden was beautifully vibrant and in the other it was all withered and lifeless. This is exactly what we experience when we work with an Angelic Energy: when we begin, we go through states of conscience that give us the impression of being in a beautiful garden and we have very powerful, beautiful dreams and mystic experiences; but we are not yet that pure Light. Up Above, They are great educators. They understand that *illusion is educational* and often necessary, and They make good use of it.

Hence, the dreamer was brought to visit an inferior heaven, the *hot-dog* heaven. Of course if the man had been a European, there wouldn't have been the symbol of *poutine*. Another symbol of very ordinary food would have been used. Later, when the Angel brought the dreamer back to the withered garden, He explained to the dreamer that it was in such a state because he had ignored the signposts. The Angel said to him, "You didn't read the signs; you shouldn't have eaten." You may ask, "But when the man asked if he could eat, why did the Angel say he could if it was forbidden?" This shows that people keep their free will. But notice that when he asked for more, the Angel didn't allow him to eat any more. Why not?

Because it would have made him too aggressive. Whenever we see ourselves eat in a dream, it means that energy descends right down into our physical body. Food is very powerful in a dream. That's why the dreamer was only given a very small helping. Also, the Angel said "Yes" because that man, in his spirituality, in his way of living it, always does whatever he wants, and he is very authoritative. So the Angel became him when he said yes. He became a part of him. That's the way it works in dreams. We are always all of the symbols, even if we are in the illusion mode.

The man was shown what kind of food he nourished himself on. The way he imagines Heaven. We can eat French fries and poutine, but we don't eat this kind of food every day and not in Heaven, that's for sure! It isn't very nourishing and it doesn't have many vitamins. As for hot-dogs, they generally come from animals – a symbol of our instincts – and their form represents emissivity, and again for this man, being in Heaven is eating hot-dogs. So we see the total illusion that man was visiting. It was his idea of heaven that he was visiting. It was not the Heaven of the Angels. Hot-dogs – at least those which are not vegetarian – are not very nourishing food. Indeed, they may contain rather unhealthy pork and other meat elements. Animals that have been killed, that have suffered. So the man was being shown that what he nourished himself on favored a very ordinary conscience and awakened an aggressive instinct, which is an animal instinct. Hence, already in this particular heaven of his, we can note numerous examples of non-respect for certain Divine Laws.

Then followed the descent into more and more inferior heavens. Through his visit to the wife-batterers' heaven, the dreamer was shown that he was connected to this type of energy. There are various degrees, of course. But if we could see into people's unconscious, in many cases, we'd see all sorts of memories where violence is firmly inscribed. Even if the person doesn't beat his wife physically, he can do so on the verbal and energy level, which was the case for this man.

It was terrible how he treated his wife and children when they were young. Just the way he demanded his coffee in the morning, the tone of his voice was really scary sometimes.

How often we can be told in dreams – and that's the beauty of dreams – "Look at the situation you experienced yesterday," and we are shown that we slapped or even beat the other person. We didn't do or say anything, but we had negative thoughts and words that contained a certain dose of aggression. We are shown how we affected the other person energetically and emotionally.

Consequently, each time we behave like this, we are linked to wife- husband- or child-batterers. This links us to a whole negative egregore. That's why it is so important to cleanse and purify our memories. Whenever we rectify memories pertaining to this *department*, even if we see aggression, we don't feel put out because we no longer have any link or connection with this energy, even on the level of our thoughts. Before this purification has been completed, even if we think we are a nice, kind, gentle person, just the sight of someone becoming aggressive can suffice to reconnect us to this egregore and we become aggressive too. Our inner garden can change in a fraction of second.

Then, when he reached the rapists' heaven, the dreamer saw that the rapists' penises had been cut off. A penis represents emissivity. This man was being shown that he had a blockage in both his emissivity and in his sexuality, and that he felt frustrated by this. He no longer committed certain acts or gestures, but this was because he'd been prevented from doing so because this force had been halted and deeply repressed. The energy, however, hadn't been transcended, and, of course, he is 83 years old now. Although his sexuality has probably been over for a long time, he continued to nourish so much need for sexuality when he looked at women, for example. Once again – as in the case of the wife batterers – when a person receives this kind of dream, it doesn't necessarily indicate that he literally raped someone. A rape is to force another person to do something, and this man has done this intensively in his mind for years and years, that's for sure. So, every time we force a child, or anyone else, to do something by trying to intimidate them, or by any other means, even if it's only on the energy and emotional levels, doing this constitutes a rape. Hence, in a way, or to a certain degree, we are linked to the rape egregore until we have transcended these forces in us.

I mentioned that this man's dream was to help toward activating an opening among those close to him. His son-in-law was affected, but his daughter was deeply affected; she truly experienced an opening after her father told her this dream. Some time later, while I was working with Angel HAHAIAH in preparation for this lecture, and as often happens to people who attend these lectures, she received a dream that related to this Angel. In this dream, which referred to the number 12, the Work she was about to undertake as well as certain important hidden contents of her unconscious were revealed to her. To be given such revelations, we need to have attained a certain degree of Wisdom and Love. Otherwise, we feel demolished and we might hold a bitter grudge against certain people. She told my husband her dream.

In her dream, *she saw herself as a little girl. She was in bed, when all of a sudden, she saw the door open. Her parents came in and her father pointed his finger at her and said, "I want her."* When she told her dream, she was clearly at a loss. She asked my husband, "What do I do with this dream?" because she had absolutely no memory whatsoever of having been sexually abused. She simply said, "It is true that when we were kids, my father drank and he was aggressive sometimes. He could get very bossy and point his finger at us."

No matter the extent of the aggression or on what level it occurred – if it were energetic, verbal or physical – it was revealed to this woman because she was going to continue to feel the same love for her father. My husband said to her, "If you were abused – there's no such thing as coincidence –, it's because you had this in you." Considering things in this light is the only way not to project onto others, not to hold it against them. We simply say to ourselves, "If I was subjected to such behavior, it's because I too abused or assaulted others in past lives. And now I need to cleanse these memories. I thank the person for helping me understand that."

It was the first time this *department* had been opened for this woman because she was ready and willing to cleanse her memories. When we are able to face our memories while remaining loving and grateful toward the other person – who has actually helped us to become aware of our resonance – we make great progress on our Life Path.

Needless to say this doesn't mean that in confirmed cases of sexual abuse human justice has no role to play, no lesson to give. But before undertaking judicial procedures - human, terrestrial procedures, I mean –, we need to ask Cosmic Intelligence if such a procedure is God's Will and, if we receive a yes in dreams, then we need to have the courage to activate the process of justice.

When the dreamer visited the murderers' heaven, one man accused another of having killed 2 men and the Angel retorted, "No! You killed 4 men." This scene showed that the Angel speaks the Language of Truth, that when we rise up into another dimension, we can longer hide anything; everything is brought out into the Light. Earlier we analyzed a dream where the person wanted to kill someone. We saw that when we reject evil, wrong-doing, what hurts, because we don't understand it, we are afraid and we become aggressive. Therefore, if a character in one of our dreams attempts to kill, this means that, to a certain degree, we are linked to an egregore of extreme violence. By the simple fact that this man eats meat every single day of his life, we can imagine the degree of violence he has ingested. When we are carnivores, we do not only eat the animal's flesh; we also eat the animal's conscience. Among other things, Angel Work serves to understand such links.

Then when the dreamer returned to the garden, he was shown, "Look, when you are in these states of conscience – wife-batterer, rapist or murderer – your garden becomes all withered, you no longer have any beautiful thoughts or feelings. Everything has withered within you because there's no love anymore."

Then the Angel added, "You're going to have to work very hard." That's exactly what contact with Angelic Energies leads to: it brings out our distortions and we realize that we have a lot of Work to do. And what's interesting — and the following scene showed this – is that just the mere intention to work on ourselves manages to modify the state of conscience all by itself. All of a sudden the dreamer found himself back in his educational illusion, in a beautiful garden, he was filled with lovely feelings. Heaven is so good to us, so pedagogical! This is how it works in the parallel worlds. It's so beautiful! Everything can change in a millisecond. This is a good illustration of the fact that when we take a step in the right direction, Divine Intelligence momentarily grants us Grace. Cosmic Intelligence creates realities for us that, at first, are artificial, in the sense that they are only scenarios, but It does so for educational purposes. No one has only negative aspects; we all have positive aspects to experience and experiment too. Moreover, as soon as we transcend our negative parts, they become positive aspects that are ours for good.

Finally, the Angel mentioned the 7th Heaven and the dreamer looked up and saw his mother. It wasn't really his mother: she was used as a symbol to represent his inner world. He was shown this image as an indication of what he'll experience on the inside one day. His mother was lit up and wore a crown. A crown represents the crown or seventh chakra, whose opening corresponds to the establishment of a permanent connection between Heaven and Earth. Through this image, the dreamer was being told, "Once you have cleansed all your inner being, you'll be able to rediscover your Royal, Celestial Origin. One day, you'll attain 7th Heaven." It was a message of hope for the dreamer and for all of us. This is true for everyone. He was told, "All you have to do is pray, work hard on yourself, work on your spirituality."

Such a dream leads us to great reflections. It helps us become aware of just how lucky we are to have access to a Teaching that – through our dreams – allows us access to our memories. This man is 83 years old. Through his recently awakened awareness, a little seed has been sown in his soul. However, we can see he's still got a lot of Work to do regarding his inner *hot-dog, poutine, etc.* concept of heaven. Cleansing just one of the negative heavens he visited may take one, or even several lives full of very difficult experiences and illnesses caused by not eating well. That's quite something, when we think about it!

Some people who begin the initiation process often say, "It's nightmares and difficulties and it's been like this for years!" My reply to such comments is, "Yes, but years aren't much compared to lives and lives of misactions. And if you don't work on aggression and all the other distortions that you're shown in your dreams, you'll have to go though a concrete, physical scenario: you'll be born to a father who beats or abuses you and all sorts of other difficult experiences. You'll have to experience them in your physical body."

When we know and put the Teachings of the Traditional Study of Angels into practice, we cleanse the memories of numerous lives in one single life. Of course it isn't easy. But, now we have a wonderful key: the Energy of Angel 12 HAHAIAH, an Angel who truly helps us go through these stages and understand that we are here on Earth for one reason and one reason only, to rediscover pure states of conscience within ourselves, i.e. to rediscover qualities, virtues and powers in their purest state.

One day we shall all attain these very highly elevated states, these Angelic states of conscience. This Teaching leads us to accept responsibility for what we materialize – not to flee materialization – and, above all, this Teaching teaches us to materialize divinely. The key is our intention, remember that. It all starts from our intention, which is why meditation with Angel Mantra is such a great help to reprogram ourselves. Instead of waiting for a consequence to receive and understand a lesson, we can analyze our life deeply and improve in every sector of our conscience and unconscious. And one day, like an automatic reflex, we always ask ourselves, "Ah, when I materialize here, am I reinforcing a link with negative egregores, and thereby accumulating karmic consequences? Or have I included a beautiful intention in my gesture, my action, my words. It doesn't matter what the result of our materialization is, what counts is the Divine intention with which we materialize.

Angel 32 Vasariah

An End to Feeling Guilty

A woman who follows the Teachings of the Traditional Study of Angels shared a dream that really affected her.

"In my dream," she said, "*I was being chased by bad men. To flee them, I ran into an elevator. I went very far down, about 100 floors, and I managed to get away from them. The same thing happened several times in my dream. Each time, I ran into an elevator and went down about 100 floors, and managed to escape. But after several times, the bad men caught me. The minute they caught me, I saw myself on beautiful green grass, and I started screaming, 'I'm bad! I'm bad! I'm bad!' I kept screaming non-stop, 'I'm bad!' My husband was there and he had a ball of white light in his hands. He threw that ball of light over to me, lighting up my whole being, my inner and outer body. I was completely liberated.*"

What does this dream mean?

This dream is announcing a new stage for this woman. Henceforth, she will be able to acknowledge her own negativity and no longer project it onto the outside. Consequently, she will no longer blame others when she is going through something negative. She will have this capacity thanks to a greater, deeper understanding of her own actions.

Let's analyze this dream in detail. All of the elements in this dream – the bad men, the elevator, the floors she went down, the grass, her husband, the ball of light – all of these elements symbolically represent parts of the dreamer. She didn't visit anyone in this dream but herself.

The bad people chasing her were men so they represent memories of aggression and negativity in action. A man symbolizes action in the outer world, and a woman represents the inner world. At the beginning of the dream, we see that the dreamer has difficulties facing negativity in her thoughts, in the upper floors. She flees *the bad guys* and this is mainly related to bad ways of behaving on the thought level, thoughts that are too emissive, too masculine that emanate a possessive attitude and abuse of power. In her flight, she gets into an elevator and goes down about 100 floors. The depths symbolize the different layers of the unconscious and access to the memories lodged therein. On the contrary, going up in an elevator symbolizes elevation, access to the mental level, and also a tendency to be too *up in the air*, unsubstantial, impractical from a negative point of view. Going up to high floors also symbolizes the causal world and understanding. This woman may sometimes tend to engender very negative thoughts and over-controlling forces when she thinks about something. She is also very sensitive and she will have all sorts of interactions with people who are like that sometimes, and this could create intense moods or soul-states in her of hyperactivity as well as anxiety, worries and fears. This is symbolized by the bad guys who represent distorted memories and attitudes. Now, with the opening of her conscience and her spiritual path, this is no longer possible. Now she has to face these aspects of herself that are responsible for creating in the causal world what manifests in her concrete life.

The elevator symbol. To understand this symbol in depth, we ask ourselves what an elevator is used for. It enables us to go up and down more easily and rapidly, and is usually found in large buildings and apartment blocks. From a positive point of view, an elevator indicates states of conscience that allow us to raise ourselves up more easily and also to descend into matter and into the unconscious. Elevators are usually found in public places and are accessible to a certain number of known and unknown people; they are also related to the social aspect. Since in this dream the elevator appears in a negative context, a context of flight, it reveals difficulty maintaining an elevated state of conscience and manifesting in social life in a right, just, qualitative way. Whenever this woman is in the presence of negative, aggressive people, who reflect aspects of herself, she flees them. But her flight leads her to descend deeply into her unconscious where she encounters her negative memories. The aggressive forces harbored within her end up catching her and that bothers her.

Through this dream, Cosmic Intelligence is showing this woman that a new program has been activated for her. The fact that she keeps screaming, 'I'm bad!' when the bad men catch her, means that she has just experienced a deep awakening regarding the Law of Resonance. She understands that the bad men she is afraid of are, in actual fact, a manifestation of her own memories. This woman was put in touch with the negative, aggressive memories that exist in her. This is what happens during great openings of the unconscious. And that's why, when the unconscious opens, it is vital to work with the Angelic Essence, VASARIAH, which helps us develop clemency. Clemency is essential so as not to be too harsh on ourselves when we discover our distortions. This woman tended to be very harsh on herself. It is her severity toward herself that made her repeat, 'I'm bad! I'm bad!' in the dream. It is not good to do this, to repeat negative criticism over and over. It creates a negative program in us and this woman often behaved like that; it had become a *behavioral-thought pattern* she kept activating when she was not happy about something.

It is important to understand that Angels are not little winged cherubs but States of Conscience that represent the Creator, Cosmic Intelligence. These Angelic States of Conscience also exist in each of us. They constitute our Divine nature. Angel Work helps us rediscover Qualities, Virtues and Angelic Powers that we all bear, thanks to which we can transform our human flaws and weaknesses. Thanks to Angel Work, through our dreams and visions, we can also travel in Universal Conscience and explore the multi-dimensions of Creation. Combined with symbolic language and reading signs, this Work also allows us to acquire a deep understanding of our daily life.

This example is a good illustration that clemency is necessary to evolve healthily. First of all, we have to learn to be clement with ourselves. For lives and lives, we projected negativity onto the outside, onto others, onto our entourage. But as soon as we begin to apply the Law of Resonance, we stop projecting onto the outer world the negativity we bear within us. Clemency toward ourselves helps us accept that we are not perfect, but we are perfectible, we all have negativity that needs to be transformed.

Here are a few explanations regarding the Law of Resonance, because it is very important to know how this Law works in our life. To understand this great Cosmic Law, we first need to know how our conscience works. The image on page 335 is a diagram of Consciousness. Above the veil are the conscious aspects of ourselves, what we usually consider as our identity. But below the veil, a great number of unconscious memories are hidden. They contain all of the thoughts, emotions, and acts we have engendered throughout the course of our many lives. We are constituted of memories and each of these memories has its own vibration frequency. Well, according to the Law of Resonance, which applies to the physical and metaphysical levels in all circumstances, we attract the people and situations that resonate with the totality of what we are.

Consequently, this Law also applies when we feel put out, bothered, annoyed or upset by anyone or any situation when we can't feel compassionate and understanding. Even if it is a very negative situation or person that we have nothing in common with, our being put out clearly indicates that, recorded in our unconscious memories, there are things in us that resonate with that negativity. Instead of blaming the other person or the outer world, we refer back to ourselves and use the annoyance we feel to cleanse and reprogram our corresponding negative memories. How do we do this? By Angel Mantra Recitation. It consists in repeating the Name of an Angel like a mantra, in silence or out loud, with great intensity in our intention.

The woman who received this dream is working with The Traditional Study of Angels and she does intense Angel Mantra. In the past, when she encountered aggressive, critical people, she tended to flee them. That's what she was shown in this dream. Then she began to systematically apply the Law of Resonance, as best she could. As soon as she encountered a negative, critical, annoying or aggressive person, she said to herself, 'If I'm bothered by this person, it means that my spirit is visiting memories that resonate with him. On one level or another, I resonate with him, I am not only that but I do have a small percentage of this in me. I'm going to recite an Angel Mantra and cleanse these memories thanks to the Power of the Angel.'

Proceeding like this gradually leads us to enlightenment because it brings the light of understanding to the totality of our memories. In her dream, this woman was shown that she is capable of touching on States of Conscience of Light. Her husband, who throws her a ball of light, also represents part of her. Through this symbol, she was being told that when she encounters negative aspects, she is capable of receiving Divine Light, which provides her with understanding right down into the concrete action level. Her whole being was lit up, hence simultaneously, thanks to understanding, deep transformation occurred and it stemmed from her masculine intimacy. We see that this part is more evolved than the social part represented by many men. It is very good thing that her husband did that. It means that she has this capacity to renew herself with the most important representation of her masculine energy, which is her husband. The key consists in recognizing and acknowledging the negativity in ourselves and accepting it without rigidity, without condemnation, without being harsh on ourselves. We need to love ourselves first and she succeeded in achieving this by receiving help from her husband. A dream like this is a huge step of evolution for her. Her life program has completely changed; her life will never be the same. We acquire this key of renewal by integrating the Angelic State of Conscience, VASARIAH. By working with this Angel we develop clemency, kindness and magnanimity, without self-indulgence or laxity.

Going down into our unconscious means having access to our memories. In our example, not only does going down in the elevator symbolize descent into matter, but also an encounter with unconscious memories. The soul-states we go through on our path always depend on our memories.

Like stairs, elevators are omnipresent in the lives of people who live and work in cities. These two symbols often feature in films. Sometimes we see glass elevators. In such an elevator we can observe what happens during the descent. It's as though Cosmic Intelligence has taken away the veil. It removes the veil and this allows us to see how we descend, and where we are in terms of conscience, which is positive. Using symbolic language, it is very interesting to analyze stair and elevator scenes in films as well as the accompanying music, and to observe the thoughts and emotions they activate in us.

Music is a symbol of atmosphere and ambiance, and plays a major role in films, even though we don't see the musicians. If an elevator scene is accompanied by music that awakens fear, anxiety or panic, it may activate these emotions in people who have such resonance. This shows how revealing and important ambiances are as tools for understanding. They allow us to penetrate into the subtle essence of actions, and also into dream interpretation in order to recognize what we or others emanate in our daily lives.

Even if we don't express ourselves verbally, each of us engenders an ambiance. This is part of the metaphysical dimension of the gift of oratory. Our radiance and emanation *speak*. In Angel Work, we analyze both symbols and ambiances as though we were in a dream. We know that outer reality is only a consequence, and that the true cause always stems from our memories.

Angel 32 VASARIAH grants us the *gift of oratory*. Generally speaking, when people see this quality, they associate it with being a good public speaker. But that is only an infinitesimal part. The gift of oratory is also all that we emanate on the metaphysical, energetic level. Our memories trigger interferences beyond words. Everything is related to memories. Angel VASARIAH also activates *Memory, Knowledge of good and evil, and Understanding of the meaning of ordeals.*

The more open our unconscious, the more memories are awakened, unfrozen and activated. Visiting our negative memories requires a lot of clemency toward ourselves. As the cleansing and reprogramming of our memories is gradually carried out, we may also be clement toward others, no matter what experimentation they are going through.

When we work with the Angels, we learn to feel, to sense the multi-dimensions behind words, people, objects, and events. We manage to guess and detect people's often unconscious, hidden intentions and motivations. While we are invoking an Angel, we are more specifically focused on the Field of Conscience that particular Angel represents, even though the 71 other Angelic Essences are also expressed through us.

The main theme of this lecture is guilt and a tendency to blame others, wanting them to feel guilty. Here is an example. Several people share an apartment. At one particular moment, one of them can't find his hairbrush, and asks, "Where's my hairbrush?" Of course, one of the others may have used it. The question is asked in order to find the brush, but the way it is asked, the tone of voice may be accusatory and reproachful. When asking this question, the hairbrush owner may want to blame the others, accuse them of using his hairbrush, when in actual fact, his brush may simply be in his bag or left somewhere he can't remember. With Angel 32 VASARIAH we become more and more aware of the intentions behind gestures and words. That's what clairsentience and clairaudience are. Focusing on Angelic Essences allows us to gradually come to perceive the multi-dimensions.

A tendency to blame often goes hand in hand with puritanical, moralist behavior. We may have memories of religious lives or ill-used power in our unconscious. Religions sometimes thought it good to use guilt to help people evolve, telling them, "If you do this, if you don't do that, you'll go to Hell!" Angel Mantra with Angel 32 VASARIAH will also awaken such memories in us so that we can become aware of them and reprogram them. Nevertheless, guilt does have a role to play. It should be first considered as a signal attracting our attention to something that isn't working, something that needs to be rectified or changed. Guilt has its usefulness. It is an indicator of memories to be cleansed. Blaming others momentarily, but in a distorted way, procures us a feeling of liberation. However, when we apply the Law of Resonance, there is no longer any point in blaming others and wanting to make them feel guilty because instead of blaming others, we refer back to ourselves.

What happens when we tend to blame ourselves? And what happens when we become aware that we ourselves are to blame, like the woman in her dream, first trying to flee the bad guys by taking the elevator and finally realizing and understanding that she herself was the bad person? When we have access to Knowledge, we don't limit ourselves to merely blaming ourselves and feeling guilty. We know what we need to do: we recite an Angel Mantra to cleanse our distorted memories thanks to the power of the Angels. We say to ourselves, 'Yes, I feel guilty, but I know that if I've experienced this, it means that I too have this kind of behavior. I'm going to cleanse these memories with the help of an Angel. Hence, I'll transform these negative parts in me and I'll be able to move on to another stage in the evolution of my soul.'

Now I'd like to share with you another true story that is related to Angel VASARIAH. It's the story of a woman who accompanied us on a 3-month German lecture tour in Germany, German–speaking Switzerland and Austria.

Since I was already preparing for this lecture, she heard me doing Angel Mantra with Angel 32 VASARIAH from the very beginning of the lecture tour. During a discussion about the characteristics of this Angel, she said to me, "I think it would do me good to work intensely with this Angel because clemency is not my strong point. I also think it would be beneficial for me to emanate this Angelic Energy when I'm in Germany." As the history of the German people was marked by wars, concentration camps and genocide, there is a major accumulation in their unconscious of unexpressed guilt regarding their heavy past.

To better understand the impact of Work with Angel 32 VASARIAH on this woman's destiny, here are the broad outlines of her life. She was born in Romania, where she lived until she was 16 years old, at the time of Nicolae Ceaucescu, the great megalomaniac, communist dictator. The Romanian people were greatly oppressed, as were most of the Eastern European countries during the communist regime when people couldn't freely leave their country. This woman spent her childhood and adolescence in Romania, but she always knew for certain that she wouldn't spend her whole life in that country. She was sure that, one day, she would leave. At that time, she didn't have access to Knowledge, and, in her entourage, no one was in the least spiritual. She herself didn't believe in God at all. Although very young, she understood that in the communist system, two things made survival easier and allowed a certain liberty of movement: intelligence and performance in sports. She therefore focused all her concentration on these two opportunities, all the more so since her daily, family life was in a state of survival, as much on the material as on the emotional level. This woman developed a very powerful intellect and great intelligence. She told us, "I used to do sports every day until I was exhausted. I realized that whenever I passed a certain degree of exhaustion, everything became possible in my mind and spirit. In those moments, my body was a mere machine that functioned according to my will. And at school, I made myself excel in all subjects, without exception."

Hence, by training her body and mind relentlessly, she developed an iron will and consequently, great emissivity. But as her intention wasn't yet qualitative – it was her survival instinct that drove her to advance – not only did she record the positive aspects of this behavior in her memories, but also the negative, distorted aspects. We can develop great qualities in sports and studies, but in her case, there was a lot of competition to be the best so as to be able to escape the country that held her captive. In such conditions, there was no room for clemency. Whenever we are in survival mode, when we are striving to escape difficult life conditions, and we are not yet on a conscious spiritual path, the qualities of clemency, kindness and gentleness are not *on the menu*, so to speak.

I am always deeply moved by the soul's path, from one life to another, both in qualities and in distorted experimentation. This woman really touched my heart.

During the lecture tour, I saw her alternate between her qualities and her distortions sometimes. Her great intelligence, powerful willpower and determination had led her to develop remarkable organizational skills and great practicality, but she could also manifest harsh intransigence, which became very intense. However, thanks to the new awareness and deep understanding Knowledge has offered her, she always rectified herself very quickly and regained a certain light-heartedness.

She had been on a spiritual path before encountering The Traditional Study of Angels and she knew the Cosmic Laws, including the Law of Reincarnation and the Law of Karma. She had assimilated those Laws on the intellectual level, but she hadn't yet integrated them on all the levels of her being. Regarding this, I said to her, "Angel 32 VASARIAH will help you experience right, just expansion, that isn't over emissive; Angel 32 VASARIAH will help you become more receptive and to work on your feminine polarity."

Although she had understood theoretically, she wanted to understand in depth the profound reason why she had been born in Romania. By applying the Law of Resonance, she understood that if she had been born into an oppressive dictatorship, it was because in other lives, she herself had oppressed, imposed things, and imprisoned people, not necessarily on the physical level, but emotionally or intellectually.

Eventually, this woman was able to leave Romania with her mother and sister. She then lived in the Federal Republic of Germany (West Germany) for 16 years, where she studied languages and linguistics to become a translator and interpreter. During her professional career, she worked for the European Parliament, an important seat of international politics. At that time, she didn't know the Law of Resonance and she was very put out by what she saw, heard and observed, all of which activated scorn and arrogance in her. These distortions sometimes caused her to abuse the power her skills conferred on her, leading her to behave like a little dictator herself. Her intense Work with Angel 32 VASARIAH helped her become aware of her numerous programs of survival as well as her dictator-like attitudes and behavior.

Very slowly and gently, she began to develop more receptivity and modesty.

When she said to my husband, "I often wonder why I was born in Romania," intellectually she knew the answer, but, her addressing the question to Kaya meant that she was ready to receive the reply on other levels. It was like the example of the woman in the elevator trying to escape the bad men. With Angel 32 VASARIAH she was now able to say to herself, 'I was born in that country because I bear memories of dictatorship in me. I have already imposed on and oppressed others.' It's quite a step, and it needs to be taken, otherwise we may tend to play the role of victim and martyr. By taking this step, this woman very gradually developed different dynamics. She began to understand and emanate modesty and to integrate acceptance of her distortions. Work with Angel 32 VASARIAH gave her access to other, deeper degrees of understanding.

This woman has been living a life of voluntary simplicity for many years now. She told us that when she worked for the European Parliament, she'd had at least 60 pairs of shoes. We sensed that shoes were very important for her. In symbolic language, shoes represent the way we advance and protect our advancement on the social level. A person who attaches a lot of importance to shoes, or who has a compulsive need to possess a great number, needs to understand and rectify a lot of aspects on this level. She told us, "I always bought good quality shoes, sometimes two pairs at a time, and often in the same store. They knew me there. They knew I wasn't content to simply try on the shoes in the store and walk up and down a little. I used to insist on running to test them. I did this for all the shoes I bought, not only sports shoes, but city shoes too." The way she told us this made us laugh happily. We could imagine her running in the store while trying on various pairs of shoes. This woman can be very funny; she has a good sense of humor.

At that time, she thought she was testing those shoes because, since she was very sporty, she was determined to wear comfortable shoes she could run in at any moment and in all circumstances. This woman really loved running. She told us that for many years, she ran almost every day, and always to the point where she felt so elated it was as if she were outside her body, running alongside it. This occurred when her body switched onto automatic pilot and she ran on in an elated, trance-like state of mind, wherein she felt great lightness, wonderful elation.

Kaya explained to her that hidden behind her need to test shoes by running were her survival programs. "On the metaphysical level, what pushed you to run when you were buying shoes? It was your survival memories and wishes to escape your difficult outer and inner life." In a way, it was if she had to be ready to flee at any moment, as if she were being hunted by her memories. That was the deep reason for her test running in the shoe store.

This example shows us how powerful memories are. The survival instinct and training were very developed in this woman. Her present life context has allowed her to develop great qualities and to put an end to the cycle, so to speak. She is presently in an Angelic, evolutive stage where her soul has known both sides of the medal. After lives in which she experienced dictatorial attitudes, wherein she imposed on and crushed others, she lived lives where she had to be subjected to what she had subjected others to. Both these stages are essential. They correspond to the Law of Karma, that great Cosmic Law whereby we always reap what we sow. When a person reincarnates, his soul is marked by all its past experiences, even if it doesn't consciously remember them.

Now I'd like to share with you a dream this woman received during the lecture tour that we did with her help as a translator and coordinator; she worked intensively with Angel VASARIAH throughout the tour. *In my dream, I'm on tour in Germany with Christiane, Kasara, a volunteer helper, my niece, and my sister. We are at the seaside in the North of Germany, looking out at the distant sea. Suddenly, I see the water and the landscape begin to freeze at top speed. The temperature plummets and everything freezes over instantaneously. I say to the group, 'We've got to leave here quickly before we get caught in the ice.' Kasara wants to stay and wait for her father, who has gone to organize things for the UCM Mission in the United States. I say to Kasara, 'No, no! We can't wait; he'll know I've led you to safety.' I turn right and begin walking in that direction, alternately repeating very intensely the Name of Angel VASARIAH and the prayer 'Gott, bitte zeig mir den Weg.' (Please God, show me the way.) As we advance, the path opens up before us, free from ice and frost, while the landscape all around us continues to freeze over rapidly. The path leads us to a mountain. On reaching the rock wall, I am able to quite simply keep on walking through the rock with the whole group. We find ourselves in a large room inside the mountain and there is a beautiful hearth fire burning brightly. I know this fire will save us. I begin to tear up some of the books that were in the room and put them on the fire to keep it burning. The volunteer helper accompanying us asks me, 'Why don't you use the logs from the pile beside the fire? They would give more heat.' I reply, 'These books are of no value anymore, they'll do fine for the moment. We'll need the logs later.' I think of Kaya and tell myself he'll know we are safe and he'll know where to find us.*

All of the elements in this dream represent parts of the dreamer. Her intense Work with Angel 32 VASARIAH had led her to visit a concentration of distorted memories. We see she was on tour in Germany, not only in concrete reality, but also in metaphysical, soul reality, in her dream. The symbols in her dream are related to her spiritual dimension regarding the Angel Mission, to the way she diffuses this Teaching to parts of herself. She could have seen herself in Canada, France, or any other country, but her dream takes place in Germany.

So we need to analyze the + and − of the German egregore. As mentioned earlier, this woman left Romania at the age of 16. She immigrated to The Federal Republic of Germany with her sister and mother, who was originally German, whereas her Romanian father remained in Romania. For her, Germany was a welcoming host country, and she lived there for 16 years.

The positive aspects of Germany are great practical intelligence, reliability, a great capacity for work, a lot of willpower, perseverance, order, structure, and discipline. All of these qualities are essential if we wish to attain very high levels of conscience. Among the negative aspects of the German egregore are rigidity, severity, the will to advance by physical or intellectual force, which engenders too much discipline, will power and emotional coldness. Because to be able to force in action or on the idea level, we have to freeze our feelings and emotions. Those are the broad outlines of this egregore. However, all populations can express all the qualities that exist as well as those that are particularly associated with the country they come from.

Angel Mantra with Angel 32 VASARIAH had activated great inner work in this woman. Her dream shows that she is capable of visiting extremely difficult areas of her conscience. The warm clemency bestowed on her by Angel VASARIAH allows her to advance in these zones without *freezing up*, and enables her to reprogram the corresponding memories.

When we work with the Angels, it is recommended to invoke the same Angel for at least 5 days. This allows us to focus on this particular Field of Conscience. During these 5 days, the dreams, signs, and teachings contained in daily events, will correspond to the Angel invoked. Angel Mantra also increases the frequency and clarity of our dreams and we gradually acquire the ability to remember and interpret them correctly. Beautiful dreams correspond to the Angel's

Qualities, and difficult dreams and nightmares show us the human distortions we need to rectify and transcend.

Through this dream, Cosmic Intelligence was telling this woman, 'We are going to let you visit memories wherein you have inscribed behavior that freezes everything, memories where love and clemency no longer exist. You see, in such conditions, everything freezes over within you and all around you, and you cannot advance anymore.' Then, she was shown the effect of her intense spiritual work with Angel Mantra. By intensely focusing her faith on the Power of AngelVASARIAH, a path opened in front of her, allowing her to advance through the ice and frost. The presence of her inner Kasara, who represents for her a very advanced spiritual soul, also explained that she has now a huge potential of Angelic Energy in her to advance. This path went up a mountain, which also represents part of the dreamer. The fact that she was able to walk through the rocky mountainside showed her another aspect of her inner spiritual work. She and the accompanying group found shelter inside the mountain. The room with the saving fire indicated that this woman is able to rediscover the saving power of the Divine Spirit, symbolized by the fire, within herself. The books she tore up to feed the fire with, reveal that she is in the process of liberating her mind, her intellect from all the erroneous teachings and beliefs she accumulated over the course of her many lives, which caused the sea and her inner landscapes to freeze over. But we can also say that it is not right to use books to create a fire to warm herself. This gesture is linked to memories of survival where she has to establish and maintain her inner warmth when there are problems with intellectual, virtual information. Now that she has access to real multidimensional Knowledge, now that she has effective tools to apply in her daily life, she can work on her blocks of frozen memories and transform them. However, to truly change, to completely transform the way she functions is a long path. Slowly but surely, Angel Work will gradually help her infuse Angelic Qualities in all parts of herself, in her whole being, and she has willingly undertaken this journey with all the beautiful, powerful intensity of her heart and soul.

In her dream, Kaya represented part of her that is related to Angelic spirituality in action, and that part was in the USA. It is true that, in concrete reality, this woman knew that Kaya and I were preparing another lecture tour to diffuse this Teaching in the United States. Hence, at that time, while immersed in a German atmosphere, she was also immersed in the ambiance represented by the egregore of the USA and the English language.

While Kaya was in the USA, everything began to freeze over. What was this woman being told by this element in her dream? Before answering this question, we first need to analyze what the US represents. From a positive point of view, this country symbolizes expansion, success in matter, a great capacity for materialization and the power that this leads to. The negative aspects include seeking success and power solely in matter, using power to dominate others as well as superficiality and overconfidence in matter. Regarding the dreamer, this meant that when her masculine principle becomes active with a view to expansion and great success, it awakens and reactivates her memories that are marked with coldness and everything begins to stiffen and to freeze up.

In this dream, she was shown the negative aspects of the German and American egregores together that she bears in her memories. Memories where, in past lives, she may have sought expansion, success and power in matter in an unjust way. She was shown the consequences of this kind of behavior that these forces create in her. That means that as soon as her mind and spirit are connected to whatever is related to expansion, power and materialization, she stiffens and her emotions completely freeze up. She can then become very tough so as to maintain her social status as we see rich people behave when they are not right. This woman speaks

6 languages and this was the first time she admitted that English was the only language she had difficulties with, not with learning or understanding it, but in speaking it. Whenever she found herself in an English-speaking situation, she felt an inner blockage. This woman is a perfectionist and language is really important for her. Regarding her feelings about the English-speaking egregore, one day she said to us, "I have to admit that I find it very difficult to like Americans and the United States."

Why did she not like this country? Because as soon as the subject of the United States came up, she connected with the distorted aspects of this egregore within herself. It awakened her own memories of when she didn't use power, expansion and matter well. Before knowing the Law of Resonance and symbolic language, she projected onto the outside what she rejected on the inside. The problems we may have with a language go far beyond the words and technical aspects of the language in question. A gift for languages goes hand in hand with the affinities we have with a country and its people.

She was shown this phenomenon that she already knew intellectually. With the help of Angel 32 VASARIAH, she can go down into her distorted memories more consciously, and with clemency and gentleness toward herself, she can continue to advance and find her way. She is in the process of aligning her own will and the fire of her spirit with Divine Will. This was shown when in her dream she alternately repeated the prayer, *'Please God show me the way'* and *Angel VASARIAH's Name.* The books she burned symbolize her liberation from old knowledge that is no longer useful for her. She recycles it and uses the energy to warm herself. Hence, she is also gradually acquiring the capacity to accept difficulties and remain confident and warm in contexts where the energies are stiff and cold while also having memories related to extreme attitudes regarding knowledge because that was how she used her ultimate will power to get out of poverty and limitations.

This dream clearly shows what was being prepared for this woman. It was very moving to see her. She heard us working in English as we were getting ready for the USA tour, and one day, she came along with a collection of magazines called *Spotlight*. They are language magazines to help people learn and perfect English. She had found them in a bookstore in one of the towns we visited during the lecture tour in Germany. As soon as she'd understood the reasons for her difficulties with English, she suddenly felt like learning it again. She also decided to cleanse her negative resonance with the US. Thanks to reconciliation with her inner United States, she was able to reconcile with all that this country symbolizes on the outer level.

When we proceed like this, one day we manage to no longer project onto a country, population, or language, and what they represent. We feel love and compassion for all countries because we have worked on our various inner populations and countries. One day, we become Universal Citizens and we integrate the qualities of all countries and we transcend all their weaknesses.

During the German tour, while we were in Berlin, we visited a concentration camp. During the visit, I invoked Angel 32 VASARIAH to help us remain clement when faced with horrors such as genocide, torture, and the worst possible experimentations. To help us remain clement, no matter what we see, no matter what we feel. To help us listen to our resonance and always remain capable of asking ourselves, 'What does this awaken and activate in me?' This subject led us to reflect on the following question, 'Is it positive to preserve such places? Isn't it focusing on bad memories and human distortions?' We may even wonder if maintaining these memories isn't a way to continue blaming the Germans.

In actual fact, preserving this kind of site is very positive. When we enter this former concentration camp, we feel the presence of a very special energy, an energy of deep reflection. No matter how open visitors are, no matter the level of their conscience, the great concentration of negativity emitted by these places automatically leads visitors to go within and reflect deeply. Such places allow us to study the past and help humanity never to begin such experimentations again. They have great educational value, not only for the Germans, but for all humanity. In this concentration camp, everything is divulged, nothing is hidden. We feel the great openness and honesty of the German people. For the visit, an audio tape is provided that explains the life of the prisoners in the different sectors. Survivors' testimonials are heard. As visitors advance through these places, they feel steeped in the energies of these memories and the worst human suffering. When we have developed multi-dimensional perception, we feel the karmic effect of the atrocities of concentration camps right down into our very body. From this point of view, preserving such places is very positive and educational.

Now I'd like to talk about a film that is specifically related to guilt regarding this very context. It's Steven Spielberg's film, *Schindler's List*. The film shows how a German man evolves from corruption to altruistic assistance and aid, by trying to save a maximum number of Jews from the concentration camps. It is a true story and a very beautiful, initiatic film. Even if you've already seen it, I recommend you watch it again and observe what sort of memories and emotions it arouses in you.

The following dialogue is an extract from the end of the film, when Oscar Schindler is presented with a gold ring with an inscription to thank and honor him for having saved so many Jews. While reading it, I suggest you imagine it's a dream that you are receiving.

— It's Hebrew, it's from the Talmud. It says, *Whoever saves a life, saves the world entire.*

— I could have got more out; I could have got more. I don't know... if I'd just... I could have got more.

— Oscar, there are 1100 that are alive because of you. Look at them.

— If I'd made more money. I threw away so much money...you have no idea. If I'd just... (Mr. Schindler breaks down and cries)

— There will be generations because of what you did.

— I didn't do enough!

— You did so much.

— This car. They would have bought this car. Why did I keep the car? 10 people right there, 10 people. 10 more people. And this pin, 2 people. This is gold, 2 more people. They would have given me at least one for that... one more person, a person... for that! (He cries) I could have got one more person and I didn't... I didn't... I didn't. (He sobs inconsolably)

This dialogue is very moving. Mr. Schindler, the man in question, is experiencing a great opening of his unconscious. At the beginning of the film, we see his distorted intentions. He wants to exploit the Jews' situation to make money. Then he gradually changes. He starts using his influence and all his resources to save as many Jews as possible. He succeeds in saving 1100 people from the concentration camps, but he blames himself for not saving more. Nazi politics and behavior toward the Jews becomes a trigger element to awaken a great number of distorted memories in this man's unconscious. Memories marked by pride, arrogance, vanity, presumption, waste, greed, avidity, abuse of power, absence of humanity. Developing awareness leads him to change his attitude. He becomes vulnerable, humble, modest, and begins behaving altruistically. However, it isn't true altruism just yet. He isn't yet aware that others represent parts of himself. First he acts to ease, to salve his conscience. The intense feeling of guilt he feels for not having saved more people comes from his distorted memories and the inhuman acts he committed. In the grip of these memories, he cannot see the good he did. This man doesn't have Knowledge to help him understand what is going on inside him, and correctly relate it to what occurs in the outside world.

We sometimes observe people who are materially at ease or prosperous begin a spiritual path and suddenly want to help others. That doesn't mean that they have become altruistic overnight. The apprenticeship of altruism necessarily involves the cleansing of memories and the understanding that other people represent parts of ourselves. Cosmic Intelligence always places us in contexts that correspond to our soul Program of evolution, as well as the karmic *luggage* we have accumulated throughout the course of our many lives. If we created negativity in certain lives, we also were subjected to it so as to finally arrive in a life where Up Above puts us in a situation where we can help others, thereby offering us an opportunity to close the cycle. Putting us in situations where we can settle our karmas and simultaneously cleanse our memories that resonate with these situations, that is also clemency.

Here is another example that is related to the Field of Conscience of Angel 32 VASARIAH. A woman who does Angel Mantra following the Annual Angelic Calendar shared the following dream with me, which she received during the reign of Angel VASARIAH. *I see myself inside a dark apartment. My father is there too. But because it's dark, I can hardly see him. He is sitting on a chair and there is an open window. I look out the window, and although it's also dark outside, I can see the head and chest of a huge giraffe. This giraffe isn't well. It's got a headache on the level of its third eye and its ears are all blocked. It's also got teeth problems. Someone is coming to fetch it to look after it and heal it.*

The next day, this woman felt like that giraffe. Her head hurt on the level of her third eye and her ears were all blocked. She couldn't see the link between this dream and Angel 32 VASARIAH so she asked me to interpret it for her.

What does this dream mean? How does it relate to the Angelic Field of Conscience of Angel VASARIAH? Let's begin by analyzing the symbolism of a giraffe. As it represents the animal world, a giraffe is a symbol of instinctual, vital energy related to our needs. Its main characteristic is its long neck, which allows it to see very far. Unlike a far-sighted bird that belongs to the air element, which represents thoughts, a giraffe is connected to the earth element, which represents the world of actions. A giraffe's coat is yellow with brown spots. From a positive point of view, yellow mainly symbolizes confidence, and brown represents connection with the earth. However, since the giraffe in the dream isn't well, and everything is dark, we have to look at the negative aspect of giraffe symbolism, which is haughty energy and over-confidence, a tendency to look down on and disdain others, believing ourselves to be superior. This indicates difficulty bringing our thoughts down to the heart level, difficulties linking the intellectual level with the emotional level. Alongside curiosity, the following attitudes are also to be found among the human distortions of the VASARIAH Field of Conscience: presumptuous, proud, materialistic, always thinking about and wanting to buy, to possess something, etc.

Through this dream, this woman was being incited to work on these aspects of herself, which reveal a major superiority complex since the giraffe was huge. The dreamer was in a house and she saw the giraffe through the window. A window represents our capacity to see outside and vice versa. Through windows, we can see what is going on outside, and people outside can look into our interior. The dreamer needed to change her vision of others, her memories of haughty, pretentious behavior.

The giraffe was ill. It had a headache and teeth problems. Teeth symbolize structure related to basic needs. They serve to nourish us, to satisfy vital needs. Through the giraffe symbolism, this woman was being told, 'Look what happens when you find yourself with a concentration of memories marked by pride and presumption. It gives you a headache, which symbolizes the way you think, and toothache, which represents the structure of your primary, basic needs. You need to change your vision of things, the way you consider others. Your third eye is blocked. This means that you are no longer able to see and understand in depth. Such an attitude also blocks your ears and prevents you from hearing and listening to others.'

Sometimes God, the great Cosmic Intelligence reactivates an accumulation of negative memories and we feel the effect of this right down into our physical body.

During a lecture tour in France, we saw a great number of giraffes in Paris. There were all over the city in the form of a new advertising campaign for Orangina. I looked up Orangina and learned that Orangina – the third largest seller of soft drinks in France – had chosen this particular advertising campaign using a *Moulin Rouge* show style in order to improve its turnover after a downturn. The advertisement in question shows a very seductive giraffe drinking Orangina with a straw, while stimulating sexual energy with a suggestive visual.

What effect does such an advert have on people? Whenever we analyze advertisements with symbolic language and a vertical conscience, we quickly realize that everything that looks beautiful and attracts people's attention is not necessarily positive. Advertisements very often aim at and nourish people's unconscious distorted memories. Hence, the giraffe symbol presented negatively activates memories of pride, presumption, and superiority in people's unconscious. If we present such a symbol on gift wrap, for example, it's as though we were saying to a haughty person, 'You are the best, you are the most beautiful, you are marvelous, and since you are all that, the whole planet will desire you.' By flattering a person's pretentious, haughty, proud ego, we ease his conscience; he will more easily consume the product in question and won't feel any need to change. As we know, the negative aspect of Paris is linked to a haughty attitude; it is very common there to meet people behaving arrogantly. This advertisement was specifically done to target wealthy, rich or intellectual people with a superiority complex, who think they are the best in the world. Of course, having said this, there are many wonderful, very evolved souls in Paris – always the plus, always the minus.

The animals we see in our dreams, or that manifest in one form or another in our daily life, always symbolize aspects of our instinctual needs, vital energy. And like all symbols, they have positive and negative aspects. The negative side of animals is the fact that they always act in the grip of their instincts, which seek to satisfy their needs at all costs. They can even kill for that. We human beings cannot attain high levels of evolution without carrying out deep work on our inner animal, instinctual world. This means that we have to succeed in transcending their negative aspects and integrating their qualities.

When we talk about our animal, instinctual side – which includes sexuality – some people quickly display a puritanical, moralistic attitude, whereas sexuality, which represents a natural, vital aspect of our being, can be very beautiful when experienced in a right, just, qualitative manner. In this Orangina commercial, however, it's the negative aspect that is highlighted. In this advertisement, we see a giraffe sitting on an ice cube. A cube is a symbol of structure, and ice symbolizes frozen emotions. Transposed onto human level, this indicates a person whose emotions and sexuality are frozen and repressed, but which, simultaneously, have very passionate, distorted aspects. It's as though the person is saying, 'I'm frozen but I want you!' This attraction-repulsion duality exists in many people's unconscious. In the example of this Orangina commercial, the message would translate as follows: 'Look, I'm haughty and I repress things so I drink Orangina to defrost, to unfreeze my seductive passion.' If we were to add the slogan 'All haughty people drink Orangina!' it's sure that no one would buy this drink.

This example shows us how important it is to know symbolic language. Understanding symbolism quite naturally leads to a different kind of advertising and healthier products for mind and body.

Now I'd like to continue with another true story that is related to the subject of sexual abuse and incest.

A woman who works with Traditional Angelology received the following dream while she was invoking Angel 32 VASARIAH. *I'm in a house, getting ready for a social evening. I switch on the hot water heater to have a hot shower and I turn up the heating. The house is bright and luminous. Then I see myself in another house that is a little darker and my sister is there along with Catherine Laborde, the weather announcer on a French TV channel and author of the book entitled: "La douce joie d'être trompée", which means, 'The Sweet Joy of being Betrayed.' My sister, who is a journalist in concrete reality, points out my astral theme, and reads out, 'You mope too much on your past.' Then I see myself in a third house, which is even darker.*

This is a very interesting dream that takes place in three phases. Through the three houses – first a bright, luminous one, then a dark house, and finally, an even darker one – the dreamer was being led deeper and deeper into her unconscious. The more she advanced, the darker it became. This dream announced a greater but gradual opening of her unconscious. The dreamer would have to face and meet the dark memories she has within herself.

This woman, who is now in her 60s, emanates discretion, simplicity, and a certain class. In the first scene of her dream, *she found herself in a bright, luminous house*, which represents part of her inner world. This part has a certain understanding because light represents understanding. *She was getting ready for a social evening, getting ready to meet other people*, so other parts of herself. *She switched on the hot water heater to have a hot shower and she turned up the heating*. This means that she is capable of putting warmth into the purification of her emotions.

In the second scene, *she found herself in a darker house where she encounters two feminine, collective symbols: her journalist sister and a TV announcer and author*, both of whose work reaches a large number of people. I asked this woman what Catherine Laborde represented for her. Here is what she said, "I think she is superficial and hyperactive. I was particularly affected by her book."

Whenever collective symbols appear in our dreams, it concerns a great many parts of ourselves, and the effect of the dream is even more powerful. The weather forecast symbolizes our inner climates. A weather announcer announces what the weather will be like, hence, symbolically, what ambiances there will be in us. As for journalists, they inform us as to what is going on in the world. In the case of this dream, since it was a female journalist, it announces what is going on inside the dreamer.

The journalist pointed out the dreamer's astral theme. For the dreamer, when deeply studied and well interpreted, astrology can reveal the potentialities of our future based on what we have created in the past and our present choices. Symbolically then, this represents her being informed as to her Program. The dreamer was told, '*You mope too much on your past.*' She was being told she focused too much on bad memories. She needed to work on that aspect. Then she was led to even darker parts of her unconscious.

Let's go back to Catherine Laborde and her book, *The Sweet Joy of being Betrayed*. Without reading any reviews of this book, the title alone indicates that she was being shown parts of herself that enjoy being betrayed and that are great multiplying forces. Here is how the author herself sums up her book. 'I've written this book for grieving, betrayed, abandoned women. I know, I've shared their lot. I too was cheated on, betrayed, and abandoned. I know, I've known sorrow, pain, hatred, humiliation, solitude, silent screams, nausea, a heavy heart, stomach, shoulders and neck, total indifference to the world and its appetites. The brutal aging of the body, the useless youth of the heart, and the mad, frantic desire for impossible embraces. I know and yet I still want to suffer all of these horrors, not because I've learned my wisdom from them, not because the pain becomes a habit and wears off, only because the incredible happens. In the solitude of grief and sadness, slowly, very slowly, sweet joy is born, and it's the very same cause that produces pain and joy.'

In this book, the author only expresses her own experience. We see that she hasn't yet found a key to solve her problems. She goes around in circles in her memories of suffering, solitude and abandon, and doesn't know how to purify and transform these memories. She doesn't know the Law of Resonance, and consequently, she continues to nourish her memories and to attract the same kind of situations. The title of her book reveals that she has created the illusion of taking pleasure in her difficulties, even finding joy in them.

We have seen how complex our unconscious is. Our unconscious memories may interfere and create pleasure and enjoyment via suffering. An extreme example of this is the case of an aggressor seeking sensations and the satisfaction of his affective needs in rape. The Law of Resonance helps us understand this phenomenon. A person may be attracted by negativity because, without realizing, he harbors the same kind of memories in himself.

I explained to this woman, "Through this dream, you are being told that you need to be very vigilant. You are being warned that there are memories in you that engender sadness, which are going to attract difficulties in your life. You need to transform these memories. That's part of your astral theme in the dream, so it is an integral part of your Program."

After interpreting her dream, this woman confided in me, "I've been wanting to talk to you for a long time, but it's very private and there are always people around. I've never really had an opportunity to talk to you about certain painful aspects of my life. When you have time, I'd like to talk to you about this." We were on a lecture tour in France, and that day, as usual, Up Above orchestrated things very well. I had to go to a public laundry to do our washing and this woman, who is a volunteer helper, offered to drive me there in her car. It was the perfect opportunity. Since we were alone, she was able to tell me her story.

She told me that from early childhood, her father tried to abuse and rape her, but she managed to prevent him. Later, she was subjected to unwanted sexual fondling by other members of her family.

Let's analyze the symbolism of sexual abuse and incest. First of all, we need to know that sexual abuse and incest are not only distorted manifestations of vital energy on the sexual level and the physical body. On the metaphysical levels, this behavior, and its corresponding energy dynamics, are also found in many domains, including the business world and others. Each time a person uses his authority, force or power to impose the satisfaction of his needs on someone else, there is abuse. When such acts are committed on a child, it means that we are violent toward, that we assault a young, growing part of ourselves that represents our future.

Whenever there is an accumulation of this kind of memories over several lives, Cosmic Intelligence may decide the time has come for the abuser to reap the consequences of his acts and behavior. He will then have to experience on the physical level what he subjected others to. This experience will help him understand and decide never to do so again. It requires a lot of clemency toward ourselves, not only to recognize ourselves in the person abused, but also in the abuser. When we know that Divine Justice is absolute, and that we always reap what we have sown, we acquire deep understanding of the victim-aggressor, abused-abuser relationship, and we stop blaming the other person or people. Forgiveness can then become true, authentic forgiveness. Angel Work with Angel Mantra allows us to purify and reprogram all forms of memories of abuse and incest.

This woman told me that when she was 8 years old, while she was playing a game in a children's holiday camp, she swore on her brother's life. At this same time, her 12-year-old brother was killed in a fatal accident. She didn't tell me what kind of accident, and when I'm not told, I don't ask questions. For years, this woman blamed herself. She told herself it was her fault her brother had had this accident.

Why is it that one person blames himself in such a situation and another doesn't? And what does it mean when a child or adult swears on someone's life?

Everything is in our intention. The events a person has to go through are orchestrated by Cosmic Intelligence in accordance with his life program. If certain memories of past lives are awakened at a precise moment, it always corresponds to the soul's program. This means that the guilt this woman felt about her brother's fatal accident went far beyond the concrete context of his death. The accident was a trigger element that awakened in this woman's unconscious memories of behavior when, wanting to be right at all costs, she may have gambled with other people's lives. Memories when she did not use her power correctly, and that created accidents. Not necessarily accidents in concrete reality, but accidents in her relationships. We have to get used to analyzing concrete incidents, events and situations in the same way as we analyze dreams. This allows us to understand the multi-dimensionality of accidents, as well as the thoughts, intentions and kind of behavior that engenders them. This event was also a huge understanding that we cannot play with people's lives for personal goals.

This woman continued her story. "When I was 12, the age my brother died at, I had a reaction. My ears began to fester and I lost my hearing in one ear." She didn't specify which ear. "I'm deaf in one ear, "she told me. This reaction also goes far beyond her brother's death. It is a sign indicating the awakening of a great number of unconscious memories accumulated in other lives. As she wasn't able to encounter these memories that caused a lot of guilt to resurface, she reacted by refusing to hear them. In the past, she had inscribed in herself, behavioral patterns of reactions where she closed in on herself so as not to hear or say anything. It was her way of fleeing, of not reacting in the face of adversity. But with such an attitude, we let others do whatever they like, even when it isn't right. If Cosmic Intelligence plans such events for a person's life program, it's because they serve the evolution of the person's soul. This woman's story showed this: her suffering – which was only beginning – forced her to find and follow a spiritual path, and to finally hear what she had repressed for lives and lives.

"At the age of 17, I discovered I was pregnant and I had a little girl. I married the child's father. He was an extremely violent man and he used to beat me and keep me locked up in the house. It was very difficult." In the light of the Law of Resonance, this explains that this woman had memories of violence inscribed in her. If a person is physically assaulted in a life, it's because he has repressed memories of violence within. In other lives, he too behaved violently. Divine Justice is absolute. Some people may wonder, "Yes, but what about great beings such as Jesus or others who were martyred?' The example of Jesus is not the same as someone who is subjected to karmas from other lives. Jesus had premonitory dreams so he knew what he was going to go through and he accepted his suffering in order to help Humanity and to bear witness to the fact that Love transcends the worst calumny. By accepting his Mission, Jesus simultaneously moved on to another stage in his own evolution.

What followed in this woman's karmic *calvary* showed her how many of her past actions were reactivated.

Three years after her daughter was born, this woman discovered that her husband was her mother's lover. While she was visiting her mother, she found a love letter her husband had written to her mother in a drawer. She was completely shocked! But she never said anything to her mother or her husband. She kept this painful discovery secret. In addition to her ear problems, over the years she developed throat problems. To a large extent, she was repressing and denying reality.

This woman told me, "My mother died 8 years ago. On her death bed, I forgave her, but I never talked to her about it." I sensed that the forgiveness she mentioned was only on the surface. There was still resignation and fear in her that prevented her from truly forgiving. Whenever memories haven't been completely purified, it only takes one incident or event for the frustration, rancor and anger the person still bears within to surge forth.

If Cosmic Intelligence allowed her to be betrayed by her own mother, allowed her to experience the infidelity of her husband with her own mother, it is because she herself did the same thing to others in other lives. She had accumulated this kind of behavior over several lives. A mother symbolizes our inner self as well as the emotional and affective side. I said to this woman, "If you really want to stop moping over your past, it is important for you to face up to things and not remain in the victim role. I suggest you work with Angel 32 VASARIAH to activate the qualities of clemency, loving kindness and magnanimity toward yourself, regarding your past experimentations." When we are capable of clemency for ourselves and others, our evolution is accelerated. The awakening of memories is set in motion and Angel Recitation helps us purify them. However, not everyone is ready for this stage. Indeed, if we begin it prematurely, it could be devastating.

That's why Up Above opens these doors very gradually. First of all, someone who has accumulated memories of violence in the course of his lives, will then find it's his turn to become a victim. That gives him a lot to digest. During this stage, he settles his karmas and learns to rectify his erroneous behavior. As soon as he understands the Law of Resonance and begins applying it to his life, he becomes capable of facing the blocks of memories that are the root cause of his situation. In other words, he can accept that he reaps what he has sown.

By working intensely with the Angels, we understand that dreams and signs can help us accelerate our evolution. Indeed, we can cleanse karmas in dream reality instead of having to experience their effects in concrete, physical reality. Everything is possible. But most of the time, people don't work enough on themselves. They only do it superficially, and very often, they only invoke Angelic Energies and Powers when things are going badly in their life, or when they want something.

Let's continue with this woman's story. Life became so difficult with her violent husband that she decided to leave him. She separated from him and took their 5-year-old daughter with her.

Her husband was an electrician, but he also had clandestine activities. He was a pimp. He exploited prostitutes and made a lot of money from this activity.

So this woman had attracted a man who was both an electrician and a pimp. Symbolically speaking, what does that mean?

We don't work in a particular field by chance, just as the work or activity we do is no coincidence. No matter what logical reason we may give, the true cause always stems from our inner work program. To know the symbolic meaning of any job, task, or activity we do, we analyze it with symbolic language, as if we saw this job or activity in a dream. We can then come to an in-depth understanding of the soul's apprenticeship program, with both its positive and negative aspects. Then, every activity, even if it may not seem very interesting, spiritual or right, takes on a whole new dimension.

What does the job of electrician symbolize? An electrician is a person who is a specialist in electric materials and installations. He has to know the phenomena caused by electric current and shocks. He learns how to wire, to *electrify* a house, an installation, etc., i.e. how to make things work using electric energy. Electricity plays an important role in our daily life because electric energy allows us to heat our homes and keep warm, to have lighting, and most of our machines and devices run on electricity. It's often during breakdowns and blackouts that we realize how important and how omnipresent electricity is in modern life; we also realize how dependent we are on it. Nowadays, we are also beginning to become more aware of how we human beings tend to waste and make poor use of this energy.

Now let's see what electricity and its related professions correspond to on the metaphysical level. Expressions referring to electricity, such as *the atmosphere was electric*, or *a powerful speech or performance that electrified the audience*, or *there was electricity in the air*, or *electric colors*, reveal how the phenomenon of electricity concerns very often both the fire and air elements, which represent our spirit and our thoughts. Whenever a person is attracted to electricity and makes it his job, it means that the person needs to learn to harmonize and use the power of his spirit and his thoughts correctly. Right down onto the emotional and physical levels, symbolized by water and earth. We know what happens when we manipulate electricity without appropriate knowledge, or when we are simultaneously in contact with water. We are electrocuted and may die. Generally speaking, electricity mainly represents our vital energy, the life energy that animates matter and makes it alive. It is a great symbol.

The case of this man, who was both an electrician and a pimp, reveals that he continued his apprenticeship through distortions. He was experimenting his vital energy through evil, through wrong. There are no positive aspects to being a pimp. Its + only exists in the capacity to transcend its negative aspects. This requires deep understanding and a lot of compassion for people who experiment this distortion, and who, for the sake of survival or money, become affective slaves. When we are spiritually evolved, we may also acquire angelic judgment or evaluation regarding people who sexually abuse others or who exploit prostitutes. We understand how right decisions taken for their re-education are, including prison sentences, without any feelings of rancor, bitterness or revenge.

We need to know that prostitution is not only related to the physical body. On the symbolic level, it means that, to varying degrees, but also in the name of matter, the person is prepared to fuse with all sorts of unhealthy energies to make money, to get rich. Prostitution may appear as a symbol in our dreams even though it is not at all present in our life on the concrete level. In such a case, we are being shown aspects of ourselves that give priority to matter.

Let's go back to this woman. Even if she is far from such behavior in this life, henceforth, thanks to the Law of Resonance, she understands that she harbors memories that resonate on a certain level with her ex-husband. He represents aspects of her inner man, aspects that come from previous lives.

He made a lot of money with his clandestine activities. This allowed him to employ a lawyer of repute, but not necessarily an honest one, and he was granted shared custody of their daughter. This woman told me, "The first time I sent my daughter to stay with her father, she was 6 years old. She came back destroyed, devastated. She used to scream during the night and I gradually realized that when she stayed with her father, he raped her. It was terrible what I went through. I tried to intervene by appealing to the law. I tried to have the shared custody decision revoked, but to no avail; I couldn't do anything. He denied everything and his lawyer was very convincing. For years, I had to send my daughter to stay with her father knowing that she was raped every time she went. And I couldn't say anything; I was incapable of expressing myself."

Imagine what this mother went through knowing what was happening to her daughter and not being able to help her! She told me, "My daughter became very disturbed. As the years went by, she became extremely aggressive. She got married and had 2 children, who are now in their 20s. But she was so disturbed she became schizophrenic and had to be interned. She now stays regularly in psychiatric institutions. Sometimes she gets out. I feel so guilty: guilty regarding my daughter, guilty regarding my grandchildren, guilty regarding my daughter's husband. They are separated now. I feel so guilty. I tell myself, 'It's my fault! It's all my fault!' I pay for an apartment for my daughter, but she keeps asking me for money. She's 47 years old. What should I do? Should I give it to her even though she's mean to me and makes irresponsible choices? I feel so guilty." This woman is so submerged by guilt that she is no longer capable of discerning true from false. She doesn't know how to say no to her daughter. She doesn't know when she should help her or how to truly help her. Sometimes the best way to help someone is to say no.

This woman added, "I was in therapy and the therapist advised me to write a letter to my ex-husband, sending back all his violence, all his aggression, telling him that I had nothing to do with all that, that it didn't belong to me." She said, "At that time, I didn't know the Law of Resonance and that's what I did. I got it all off my chest. I wrote it all down and I sent it back to him. And there too, I feel so guilty for sending that letter."

Whenever a lesson hasn't been learned and integrated, Destiny serves it up again. We'll see how in what happened after that. This man remarried and had 2 daughters with his new wife. One of these daughters discovered the letter this woman had sent her ex-husband to empty her soul of all its suffering. We can see here karmic similarities with what this young girl, who found the letter, was going through and what this woman experienced after finding the love letter her husband had written to her mother. However, unlike this woman who didn't dare say anything, the girl used the letter to accuse her father of rape, because he had subjected his two younger daughters to the same fate as his older daughter.

The two sisters wanted to bring their father to court for rape and incest. One of them eventually desisted but the other one persisted. And she came to ask her father's ex-wife for help. She said to her, "You have to come and testify for me; you have to help me. You have to testify to what you went through with your daughter, because I'm going to accuse my father in court." This woman told me, "I did testify to help this girl. I knew I had to do it. My ex-husband was sentenced to 18 years' imprisonment without parole for underage rape."

We see how Life led this woman to express herself. What she was unable to do for her own daughter, her life program set another similar karmic situation on her path, which pushed her to express herself and ensure the application of Divine Law here on Earth. Her program required her to learn to express herself in this life. She had to stop accumulating repressions and things left unsaid, which allow negativity to destroy and engender anger and inner violence, as she had done in other lives. It can be right to bring a case to our earthly, terrestrial court of law, but it is important to do so without any rancor, violence, or hatred. We must do so in a state of conscience where clemency is present.

This woman is in the process of putting an end to negative cycles. After 14 years of celibacy and abstinence, she remarried a good, kind, stable man. Remember she had ear and throat problems? She was deaf in one ear and had had to have an operation on her throat. Well, her second husband is a doctor; he's an ear, nose and throat specialist! He has also worked in Africa and operated on lepers. It was no coincidence this woman met such a man, who is also on a spiritual path. A new program has been set in motion. It reflects the great transformations that have been carried out in her.

This new program consists in helping others. She helps her daughter as best she can, but she really helps her grandchildren. When her granddaughter, who is in her 20s, comes to visit her, she asks her grandmother to interpret her dreams for her. Her grandmother told me, "I try and analyze as best I can, with the knowledge I have." She uses her opening of conscience and deep understanding of her life experience to help her loved ones.

She also helps her daughter's ex-husband. He was a butcher and he wanted to change profession. As mentioned earlier, we don't do a job just by coincidence. This job indicates that there is a certain degree of violence in the person's memories. A butcher's job is related to the animal kingdom, and the fact of killing animals and selling their flesh requires a certain degree of violence. This man wanted to change jobs, but he didn't have enough money to go back to full time studies and give up work at the same time. So this woman helped her former son-in-law by paying for his studies to become a nurse. This indicates a new program for this man whose aim is to help, care for and heal the wounded or ill parts of himself, and not only on the physical level.

If we consider that all these marvelous new elements in this woman's life represent parts of herself, what progress! She has been working with the Teachings of The Traditional Study of Angels for several years now. She told me, "It is very rare that I open up like this. I tell very few people my story."

I asked her permission to share her story in lectures and she said, "I agree if it can help people. If it can help, I'm very happy for it to be shared." This shows the great opening of conscience she was going through, and, at the same time, it is also a manifestation of her dream with the journalist and TV weather announcer. Henceforth, these two multiplying, collective symbols present in her will find it much easier to express themselves and diffuse positively. She will now be able to encounter her unconscious memories with greater stability and more Knowledge. I said to her, "You see, that's what your dream represents. The three houses where the light changes to become darker and darker show that you are now able to visit the obscure spaces within yourself."

When we had finished the washing in that laundry and were getting ready to leave, this woman said to me, "Well, that was quite a purification!" In both concrete and dream reality, washing clothes symbolizes purification of our aura, of what we radiate in the outside world. There was even a machine with number 32. I'll remember that laundry all my life.

Angel 43 Veuliah

Insecurity in Abundance

One day, a journalist interviewed Daniel Radcliffe, the young actor who plays the main role in the *Harry Potter* films, the film adaptation of the literary series that tells the story of a student wizard. During the interview, Daniel Radcliffe told the journalist about a dream he'd had one night. "In my dream," he said, *"I saw myself in a bookshop and nobody, absolutely nobody recognized me; not the book-keeper nor any of the customers!"*

All of the elements of this dream symbolically represent parts of Daniel Radcliffe. It reveals that this young man, who was 17 years old at the time, sometimes experiences a lack of acknowledgement of himself. Although it only lasted a few seconds, this dream may indicate a reservoir of memories wherein Daniel Radcliffe has inscribed behavior that engenders a lack of self-acknowledgement. No matter how much renown and fame he enjoys as an actor, in spite of the great material prosperity his celebrity provides him with, as long as these memories haven't been cleansed, his thirst for recognition and acknowledgement will never be quenched. This dream shows that, in spite of the international glory he has known for several years, in spite of his fortune valued at 22 million dollars, this young man sometimes feels insecurity regarding abundance. He may be afraid of losing it. But abundance and prosperity are first and foremost a state of conscience.

To better understand the true causes of this young man's insecurity, I suggest we analyze a few answers he gave when interviewed. We won't analyze these answers as people usually do, i.e. with an ordinary, horizontal, one-dimensional conscience; we shall proceed just as we do when analyzing a dream. Studying the symbolism contained in his answers will allow us to discover what may engender his feelings of insecurity.

Daniel Radcliffe said he loved reading. One of his favorite books is *Germinal*, a classic, 19th century French novel, by Emile Zola. This novel depicts the daily life of miners at that time: their labors, suffering, revolts, and strikes. It relates their anger with the rich bourgeois industrialists who exploited and abused them. Simply in mentioning his taste for this book, Daniel Radcliffe revealed part of his unconscious.

How can we understand this? Well, thanks to the Law of Resonance, the great Law that teaches us that we attract all that we are, both positively and negatively. Of course, this also applies to memories of our past lives.

The Law of Resonance also applies when we are attracted to a particular book, author, singer, or any other person or situation. Such an attraction indicates that we resonate with the book, person, or situation in question.

Likewise when we feel annoyed, bothered, put out or upset by a situation or a person's behavior, even if we apparently have nothing whatsoever in common with such behavior! As soon as we are not able to evaluate with understanding, compassion and neutrality, it means that, to a certain degree, we harbor memories that resonate with that situation or behavior. That's why we feel annoyed or upset.

Let's go back to *Germinal*, the novel, and Daniel Radcliffe. The fact that this novel is one of his favorite books shows that, in his unconscious, he harbors memories that resonate with rich bourgeois behavior that exploited others and misused their own wealth. He also harbors memories that resonate with the exploited, limited situation of the poor, angry, rebellious workers. To find themselves living life in such conditions means that, in other lives, those workers must have exploited others and abused their wealth.

How can we know if we have resonance with a given situation? Whenever we find ourselves confronted with injustice, does it mean we have to accept everything in the name of the Law of Resonance? No, not at all. However, we must act calmly and serenely, with absolutely no anger. We mustn't feel put out because as soon as there is anger or the slightest feeling of annoyance, it is telling us, 'If you feel angry about this injustice, it reveals that there are memories in you that resonate with this. What you are going through is a way of teaching you that, in other lives, you too behaved like this, even if you don't recognize yourself in this behavior."

This symbolic analysis based on a novel shows that Daniel Radcliffe has already known material abundance, but he didn't necessarily use it well. Thereafter, in other lives, he surely found himself in difficult situations where he was exploited. These memories may not have been cleansed and reprogrammed. As long as they exist, no matter how many millions or billions he has, he won't feel inner security. There will still be times when he feels gripped by fear of losing his abundance.

Needless to say, this doesn't only apply to Daniel Radcliffe. It's the same for all of us. No matter how many or how few millions we may have, quantity is of little importance. It's got nothing to do with quantity, but rather with all sorts of memories that dwell in us. It takes only one trigger element, which may be a simple word or a gesture, and our mind and spirit plunge into these memories. The insecurity then felt may be completely disproportionate to our material possessions.

Daniel Radcliffe also resonated with the author of this novel, Emile Zola. Indeed, as soon as we are attracted to a book, it means we also resonate with its author because the author imprints his work with all he is, positively and negatively.

Let's briefly study Zola's biography. Even if we don't know a person's life story, the Law of Resonance still applies. It's mathematical and completely and absolutely accurate.

In the last years of his life, Emile Zola was reviled and struck off the Legion of Honor. Most of his readers abandoned him. And yet, after his death, and still today, he is read by those who appreciate literature. Those last years of his life were difficult. And how did he die? In his study, suffocated by the heating system. It is not known if it were an accident, suicide, or a crime.

A symbolic analysis of the facts in concrete reality always reveals elements lodged in the unconscious. There is no such thing as coincidence. Let's analyze Emile Zola's case as we would analyze a dream. This allows us to go deep into the symbolism and understand the states of conscience behind the events.

Zola died in his study. This means it's related to his work. Not only the act of writing but also his inner work, the way he worked on himself. In addition to this, the fact that he died asphyxiated is related to two elements: fire and air.

In symbolism, the fire element represents the spirit. We must always consider both the positive and negative aspects of any symbol. At one moment, we can have a positive, luminous, constructive spirit, and at another, a negative, somber, destructive spirit. Air and gases generally symbolize the world of thoughts. In this context, the symbolism is negative because Emile Zola died asphyxiated, which reveals a mind and spirit that engendered destructive thoughts.

We can link this to Daniel Radcliffe's dream where no one in the bookstore recognized him. We know that at the end of his life, Emile Zola had lost most of his readers. Daniel Radcliffe may also fear losing his fans and popularity with the public. It's thanks to them that he lives in abundance and prosperity.

Daniel Radcliffe revealed another element in his unconscious when he declared that he loved *The Simpsons*. This American TV show has been very successful for many years and it is broadcast in many other countries. As we have already seen, the attraction we feel toward a book, film, or TV show reveals memories that resonate with what this book, film, or show emits through the attitudes, values, and behavior presented in it.

Let's analyze the contents of this series. The characters enjoy a rather crude, vulgar sense of humor. They mock other people's misactions. Their behavior is sometimes quite rebellious. One of the Simpsons' particularities is the fact that they only have 4 fingers and 4 toes. Well, every single drawing, sketch, and image emits a state of conscience. Everything has a profound, symbolic meaning.

What do hands and feet symbolize? What do we do with our hands? We give, we receive, we create and make things. Feet serve to advance. The fact that the Simpsons only have 4 fingers and 4 toes refers to animals. This means that when these characters give, receive, advance and do things, their conscience is more attached to instinctual, animal behavior. The animal world exists in human beings in the form of states of conscience, both in their + and their − aspects. In The Traditional Study of Angels (Traditional Angelology), we work with animal symbolism a lot; our aim is to maintain only their + aspects, their qualities. Animals' positive characteristics represent a powerful source of vital energy for us, thanks to which we can attain high levels of conscience.

Behavior such as observed in *The Simpsons* indicates an instinctual conscience. When an animal has a need, he doesn't think about it, he doesn't ask, 'Is it right or wrong to do this?' Pushed by its needs, it goes ahead and takes what it wants. That's how animals behave.

As long as we maintain aspects such as crude, vulgar humor, rebellion, and animal-like behavior, we won't use the resources given to us in a right, just, qualitative manner. This automatically engenders karma. Irrespective of the abundance we may have on the material level, our soul knows that the karma engendered will attract difficulties sooner or later. That's why we sometimes feel a strong sense of insecurity that is completely disproportionate with the external situation. It really depends on memories lodged within us.

Daniel Radcliffe revealed another important part of his unconscious when he played the role of Harry Potter. Although not perfect, this film does present beautiful aspects. First of all, it creates an opening into the parallel worlds and the topic of magic. It also takes symbolism into account, to a certain degree. It is very interesting to study films that have become world famous because they allow us to understand what is going on in the collective conscience.

If Cosmic Intelligence allows the materialization of success or a world event, it's because that success, that event corresponds to what is going on in the collective conscience. That's why some films (or books, or indeed people) with extremely negative or very positive contents, or some that have a little of both, become very successful. Each success always testifies to what is going on in the collective conscience.

The success of *Harry Potter* shows that there are more and more souls arriving on Earth with great openings of their unconscious, and also regarding the parallel worlds. The collective phenomenon that corresponds to *Harry Potter* has been evolving exponentially over the last 30 years. Some of these people will experience this opening positively, while others will experience it negatively, and the Law of Resonance applies in each case.

This film also shows people who can perceive the other dimensions, who can arrive in very materialistic, down-to-earth families that function with a very coarse, boorish conscience. It is sure that Daniel Radcliffe resonated with the role he played in this film. It is impossible for an actor to play a role if he doesn't have memories that resonate with it. Of course, this role doesn't represent his entire being. An actor doesn't experience in concrete reality what he experiences in a film, but the roles actors play always affect them because these roles nourish existing memories. This leads us to meditate on actors who play the role of the bad guy, who play aggressive, violent, extremely negative roles. They bear these aspects within themselves, and what's more, they materialize them. Needless to say, there will be consequences for their evolution, but everything is experimentation.

Daniel Radcliffe was born on July 23rd. This means that according to Angel Calendar 1, his Guardian Angel on the physical level is Angel 25 NITH-HAIAH. NITH-HAIAH is the Angel of magic *par excellence*! We see there is no such thing as coincidence.

The 72 Angels defined in Traditional Angelology represent States of Cosmic Intelligence that we all use, without exception, even if we aren't aware of Their Names, Qualities, Virtues and Powers. As explained at the end of this book, each person has 3 Guardian or Birth Angels. We can identify Them in the 3 Calendars according to the date and time of our birth. These 3 Angels represent the departure point and the physical, emotional, and intellectual framework of our present life. They also give us an indication as to the *luggage* accumulated during the course of our previous lives; the positive aspects in the Qualities, and the negative aspects in the distortions.

Now I'd like to talk to you about a woman who lives in Switzerland, who shared her life experience with us. "I had nothing when I was young but it seems to me I was freer. I felt free whereas now I have a certain amount, I'm afraid of losing it. I double lock the front door when I leave the house. I hold on tight to my handbag when I'm in town I'm so afraid someone will steal it. I'm not free like I was before."

This woman is certainly not a millionaire. She has some assets like many other people. So what is going on when someone finds himself in such a situation, behaving in such a way? As soon as this person thinks about money and resources, his mind and spirit go down into a *file* of unconscious memories marked by experiences of loss. He may not have experienced this in his present life. They may be related to other lives where the person experienced poverty and lack of resources. When his spirit is in contact with these memories, he feels afraid of losing everything again. His present possessions are not the cause of his fear, they are only a trigger element. The resulting fear comes from memories that are totally real on the metaphysical level. The freedom this woman felt in her youth was not true liberty. She hadn't yet transcended matter. We shall see what true liberty is.

We sometimes see people on a spiritual path rejecting matter and material abundance. They so want to raise themselves up and to live simply! It is beautiful to want to raise ourselves up. And simplicity is indeed important. However, these people don't realize that hiding behind their desire for simplicity are forces that reject abundance. This occurs on the subtle, energy level.

Why do people reject abundance? Because, in their souls, these people know they harbor negative forces in their unconscious that will push and encourage them to misuse abundance. They no longer want to create this kind of karma for themselves. Their soul knows that they need to seek the spiritual dimension. And at the beginning of their quest, they may manifest a certain rigidity and puritanism.

I know this process very well because I went through it myself. There may have been abuses and poor use of resources in other lives. To avoid a relapse, we become rigid. Sometimes this rigidity can be very intense but it doesn't indicate that we have transcended matter.

So what is the aim of this quest for simplicity? On the one hand, it is to become conscious of memories that reject prosperity; and, on the other hand, to learn right, just use of resources on all levels.

In this lecture, we are going to talk about Angel 43 VEULIAH, the Angel of Abundance and Prosperity. Angel VEULIAH helps us rediscover our inner prosperity, our inner riches. When we attain this state of conscience, we understand that abundance and prosperity are first and foremost a state of conscience, found on the heart level, in our feelings, and on the mind level, in our thoughts. VEULIAH, helps us continually feel and be receptive to Universal Abundance. This Angel also helps us make right, just, qualitative use of all forms of abundance. Hence, abundance, prosperity, and wealth on any level, is first of all a state of conscience, and at the same time a responsibility.

We all use the VEULIAH Field of Conscience or Energy, even if we don't know this Name. Even without invoking this Angelic Energy, we all express it. However, as we are all on Earth to learn, instead of expressing the Qualities, Virtues and Pure Powers of this Angelic Essence in Their perfection, we deform them. This creates a series of flaws and weaknesses that we call distortions. When we distort the potential of this Angel, we engender an abundance of thoughts, emotions, feelings, and behavior that are not noble. They impoverish our conscience and limit our perception of abundance to the material level only. We then experiment the illusion of prosperity, because it remains superficial. It is based on a materialistic philosophy. But illusion is educational. We'll see a few examples of this.

When we experience the VEULIAH state of conscience in a distorted form, instead of experiencing prosperity in its overall, global dimension, our life becomes poor, and not only on the financial level. How many people live in emotional, affective poverty that makes them arid and severe!

Another distortion related to prosperity is waste. When it's a question of wasting money, we quickly realize this because we soon see the consequences on our bank statement. However, when it's a question of wasting energy on the metaphysical level, in our thoughts and emotions, that's different. It's difficult to perceive this kind of waste because we can't see it. However, the consequences are present. We'll see that Angel 43 VEULIAH helps us manage abundance and prosperity well on the energetic, metaphysical level.

An extreme distortion is *miserliness, avarice.* We hold on and retain because of our fear of lack. This fear inhibits acts of generosity. We become incapable of behaving generously. Other distorted forms of this Angelic Essence are: *war, separatism, revolutions, destruction* and all that engenders these distortions. All of this creates poverty. Just think of countries at war. When we don't live in these countries, they may seem very far from us. But in terms of conscience, war affects a great many people. Each time we are discontent or aggressive, it means there is conflict, separatism, war and destruction inside us. This impoverishes us and prevents the manifestation of abundance and prosperity. When we think and speak in terms of conscience, we realize how far, how deep things go.

How do we work with an Angel? It's very easy. We do Angel Mantra Recitation (*cf.* page ?). This consists in repeating the Name of an Angel as often as possible, as soon as we have a moment. We can do this while walking, driving, doing any task that doesn't require concentration. We can either repeat the Name of the Angel, the Angel Mantra, on the inside or out loud, with great intensity in our intention: VEULIAH, VEULIAH, VEULIAH, VEULIAH... This is a very powerful action that connects us to the Angelic Field of Conscience and reactivate Its vibration in us. It is recommended to do Angel Mantra Recitation with the same Angel for 5 days. We then notice the signs, incidents, events, encounters, teachings, and dreams Cosmic Intelligence synchronizes for us in accordance with the Angel we're working with. We are then better able to perceive this Angelic Field of Conscience. For instance, someone may say something that doesn't seem to be related to insecurity, and yet, on hearing these words, we feel our own insecurity and others'. Even though we know the 71 other Angels exist and are expressed simultaneously in us, our attention is focused on this Angel in particular. This allows us become aware of what prevents the manifestation of prosperity and abundance in our life.

Whenever we do Angel Recitation intensely during the day, the frequency of our dreams increases. We remember them, and we gradually become better able to interpret them because their themes correspond to the Angel we are working with. Beautiful dreams reflect the Angel's Qualities and difficult dreams and nightmares reveal our human distortions of them.

Through the numerous examples presented in this lecture, we shall see that there are forces in us that we unaware of that are obstacles to prosperity and abundance. On the conscious level, we aspire to abundance, but it's the exact opposite in our unconscious. One of the greatest gifts Angel Veuliah offers us is the capacity to become aware of these obstructing forces. Here is the first example.

A woman who was unaware of harboring such forces, worked with Angel 43 VEULIAH. One of the Qualities of this Angel is *an opening of our conscience that sets us free from obscure motivations and vicious, pernicious habits that prevent abundance.*

This woman told us a dream wherein *she was offered a car that was worth $43 000, and she refused it.* She understood this dream very well. When we work with Traditional Angelology and we see a number, we usually associate it with the corresponding Angel.

Number 43 000 was easy; she immediately associated it with Angel 43 VEULIAH, the Angel of Prosperity. This dream wasn't a prediction that she would refuse a car of this value in concrete reality. The message it contains goes well beyond that.

This woman analyzed it. What does a car symbolize? What is a car used for? It is used to advance, to move from one place to another. With what state of conscience do I advance? I'm being shown the way I advance toward others, the way I behave and conduct myself. Through this dream, I'm being told, 'When you go toward others, when you advance, certain forces in your unconscious incite you to refuse the state of mind, the state of conscience that would allow you to experience great advancement, abundance and prosperity. As long as such forces dwell in you, you won't be able to emanate this state.' This woman knows that we attract people and situations that correspond to our state of conscience.

This dream that lasted only a few seconds indicates the presence of unconscious memories that prevent access to a state of conscience of abundance.

There are people who are rich on the material level and who seem to be luminous on all levels. However, this is very rare because it requires a very high level of conscience. When we approach most of them, we perceive the poverty and aridity their conscience emanates. They are often harsh, severe, critical, and poor on the inside. On the other hand, there are people who are materially much poorer but who emanate such a rich, prosperous disposition that we realize that abundance, wealth, prosperity is indeed a state of conscience.

Having understood the message she'd been sent through this dream, this woman said to herself, 'It's true that I have problems with prosperity. I'm going to work deeply and intensely with Angel 43 VEULIAH for several days.'

I'd just like to clarify something about Angel Work. If we are shown number 43 in a dream, it doesn't necessarily mean we are being told to change Angels and work with Angel 43. It's the same for signs in concrete reality; e.g. if we seem to see number 7 everywhere, it doesn't mean we have to work with Angel 7 ACHAIAH the Angel of Patience. We can be working with Angel 43 VEULIAH and see lots of number 7s. How do we interpret this? What does it mean?

We are simply being told, 'Ah! so you aspire to prosperity and abundance, do you? Be patient because you first have to work on your memories. You cannot be granted abundance immediately; you'd only begin to misuse it again. Be patient!' So, we take into account the figure we see and consider it as a supplementary sign.

Now let's go back to the story of the woman who refused the car worth $43 000.

During the period she was working intensely with Angel 43 VEULIAH, she received several dreams related to this Angelic Essence. One of them was really related to the opening of conscience that liberates us from obscure motivations. She was shown hidden aspects of herself that prevented access to prosperity on several levels. Here is the dream.

I saw myself in a kitchen. There was a table. My father and mother were there. I heard a voice saying, 'We are going to reveal a secret to you.' Immediately after this I found myself in another place. I was in a restaurant where I was offered a plate of healthy couscous. It was vegetarian couscous, and I refused saying, 'No thanks, what I'd like is 100g of potatoes.' Then, still in the restaurant, I saw a photograph album being passed around. The customers were looking at it and I was bothered by this. There were photos of me with a man in the album. The fact that the customers had seen me with this man bothered me.

What does this man represent for her in concrete reality? He's the man she is, or rather was, in love with. She no longer knows how to behave with him. She told us that he is very romantic, but she finds him a little intense. "He often puts little love notes on my windscreen. His intensity scares me. I've withdrawn from the relationship because I don't know what to do with him."

In this dream, this woman was being shown parts of herself that refuse love & abundance. Let's analyze the symbols in it. First of all, the kitchen. What do we do in a kitchen? We prepare food, so a kitchen is a symbol of preparation. Food symbolizes the energy we ingest. The way we prepare food and meals reveals the way we nourish ourselves. It also reveals the way we nourish others, and not only on the physical level, but also on the level of our thoughts, emotions, and feelings. And a table is a symbol of sharing, how this woman is preparing to share.

Her father was present. This is related to the way she prepares her actions concretely. The presence of her mother is related to her inner preparation and action. Parents represent also our origin and a more general, global symbol than a friend or colleague.

Then she heard a voice say, '*We're going to reveal a secret to you.*' What does the word *secret* refer to in this context? It refers to aspects of herself that she is unaware of, that she doesn't know exist. She is going to be shown her pernicious, unconscious motivations that prevent her from knowing abundance. That's what an opening of conscience is.

The dreamer was in a restaurant. As a public place where we go to eat, a restaurant symbolizes the energy of sharing on the social level. She was offered a healthy, vegetarian couscous, which she refused; she only wanted 100g of potatoes. Why was the symbol of couscous used? She could have been offered spaghetti, a Chinese specialty, or anything else, so why couscous?

A dream is very, very precise; it's as precise as a mathematical formula. Although couscous is known and appreciated all over the world, it specifically symbolizes the Arab aspect. Each nation, each ethnic group symbolizes positive and negative aspects. As it was a healthy, vegetarian couscous, it is the positive aspects of Arabs that she was offered. Let's analyze the + side of the Arab egregore. On the metaphysical, energy level, Arab people's first and second chakras are very open. This makes them beautifully intense and incarnated people. These two chakras affect our being rooted on the physical level, our capacity to materialize, to act in matter, as well as intensity of life, sensuality, sexuality and pleasure. The negative aspect is manifested by extremes such as obsession, fanaticism, fundamentalism, extremism.

The fact that the dreamer refused the plate of couscous has nothing to do with couscous itself. Nor does it mean she rejects Arabs. We need to consider her gesture on the symbolic level. This woman was being told that when she receives energy related to the first and second chakras, energy that would help her incarnate, have a great life intensity and materialize well, she doesn't want it. In the dream, she only wanted 100g of potatoes. Although potatoes are good food, they are usually an accompaniment to other food. Her refusal indicates austerity and a precarious life style of limitation; it shows that there are austere and severe parts in her.

In certain eras – and, indeed, in some areas of the world today –, abundance and variety of food products didn't exist. In many countries, particularly in the Western world, there were only potatoes for days on end! So this woman was being shown her poor, austere side on the social level, related to her relationship, because she was in a restaurant and that prevented her from accepting variety and beautiful energy of abundance on many levels. That was the secret that the dream revealed to her. Potatoes and couscous, we might think these details are insignificant, but when we transpose them onto the metaphysical level, we discover the attitudes and behavior of someone who refuses abundance. 100g also meant something interesting. 1 is the main number, so she is too self centered or she is creating limitation because probably in a past life she was too intense and misused abundance and resources. Now, like a fakir, monk or nun, she restricts herself too much in order to stop those forces of abuse and misuse.

Through the photograph album, she was given also a lesson regarding affective abundance. Let's analyze the symbolism of photographs. What does looking at photographs activate in us? Photos help us go back and study the experiences and events of our past. It is very positive to do this. The negative side is nostalgia for the past, regretting what no longer exists or what we have or have not done.

The dreamer was bothered because the restaurant customers saw her in the photos. Well, all of those customers represent parts of herself. Looking at the photos, these parts discover things about her past that she doesn't want to be known. She wants to keep certain aspects of herself hidden. She thinks the man is too passionate and that scares her. This woman is on a very intense spiritual path but there is still rigidity, extremism and puritanism in her. In the name of spirituality, we sometimes tend to set aside love, affective, emotional, and all kinds of abundance. We're scared; we tend to believe spirituality and physical love don't, cannot belong together. Since this woman has a tendency to extremism in spirituality, she attracted a person who is extreme on the emotional, affective and need level, i.e. a passionate man.

This analysis helps us understand that we are aware of only some of our behavior and attitudes. The veil of the unconscious hides innumerable memories from us that come from our multiple past lives. In our dreams we can see the memories and past behaviors we have in terms of percentage, i.e. as part of us; what we are shown is not all of us.

This woman's rigid, austere, arid behavior reveals parts of her unconscious where there are memories of passion and very intense, extreme attitudes. Sometimes, Up Above programs situations where we see extreme behavior. This is always to help us realize that this behavior represents part of ourselves and is there to help us rediscover balance.

To sum up, couscous symbolizes an energy of concentrated action and also forces, powers of the senses, intense love and manifestation because it is linked to the beautiful Arab energy and intensity. But this woman doesn't want this. In the photographs, parts of her saw her with the man whose behavior bothers her. Using this man as a symbol in the dream, Cosmic Intelligence wasn't telling her he was the man of her life. It was simply revealing some of her behavior that prevents her from experiencing good balance, abundance and prosperity on the emotional, affective level. By doing Angel Mantra, she will be able to cleanse these memories.

Rather than project onto the other person, we need to refer back to ourselves and work on whatever bothers us. Accompanied by an Angelic Energy, we gradually cleanse our memories; we reprogram ourselves. This Work is very powerful and effective. It isn't always easy; it takes a lot of perseverance, but it guides us to high levels of conscience.

Here is another example. It's the case of a woman who has abundance on the material level, but a certain degree of poverty on the affective level. She shared the following dream with my husband, Kaya. *She saw herself in the restaurant of the company her husband works for and her husband didn't want to sit beside her. Completely indifferent, he ignored her and behaved as though she didn't exist. She felt hurt.*

Kaya said to her, "I'm going to give you two possible interpretations of this dream. Either you were being shown parts of yourself, or you visited your husband's soul. A company restaurant symbolizes energy on the work level in the outer world. In the first case, you are being told that, in terms of conscience, you have memories related to work that prevent fusion on the relationship level, in your couple, regarding sharing and love. In the second case, you may have been shown some of your husband's behavior, when he may sometimes neglect you because work is his priority."

Tears in her eyes, the woman said to Kaya, "I recognize this behavior of his. We have two children but he's never home. All he thinks about is work. He abandons us, he neglects his family. Sure, we live in abundance, we have a big house, but, in a way, it's just a golden cage."

If she did visit her husband's soul, she must remember that her husband represents part of herself too. The Law of Resonance always applies. We don't live with someone just by chance or coincidence. It always means that we have resonance with that person. Even if this woman doesn't recognize herself in this kind of behavior, she attracted the husband she has. This means that she behaved like him in other lives. She too neglected her family and devoted all her time to outer work, even though she values the family and spirituality today.

What should we do in a case like this? In the Teachings of The Traditional Study of Angels, we always recommend referring back to ourselves. "You feel put out, bothered, annoyed, upset by someone or something? Don't flee what bothers you, refer back to yourself and work on your memories." So this woman can say to herself, 'OK. I'm upset and saddened by what I'm going through so that means my spirit is presently visiting a reservoir of memories stemming from my past lives. OK. I'm going to use this to work on myself, to cleanse and reprogram these memories and, one day, my life will improve.'

The Law of Resonance helps us to no longer waste our energy. Great cleansing is done in us each time we refer back to ourselves when we feel annoyed or bothered in any way.

Lots of people say to me, "You often talk about cleansing and reprogramming memories but how do we do this?" It's very easy. Of course, it's a long process but it is easy to understand and to do. When I feel in the least put out, when I don't feel well, it's because my spirit is visiting negative memories. No more scapegoats! I refer back to myself and I cleanse these memories by doing Angel Mantra. Eventually, more and more, I attract happy, positive people and situations and my life gets better and better as I evolve and become a better person, a better soul.

Here is how we work with Angel 43 VEULIAH to rediscover affective prosperity. For several consecutive days, we repeat the Name of the Angel as often as possible: VEULIAH, VEULIAH, VEULIAH... with great intensity in our intention. Simultaneously, we think about the behavior and attitudes we want to modify. This allows us to go down into our memories to cleanse them and to understand what is going on, until we eventually regain prosperity. Thanks to Angel Work, we can face our unconscious memories. Otherwise, it is so difficult! We all have a lot of distorted memories in our unconscious. But with the help of the Angels, we can encounter these memories and reprogram them with Angelic Conscience. It is very powerful, very effective, and so much easier than having to be subjected to difficult, karmic consequences.

In a couple, if one of the spouses always refers back to him or herself, he or she will do great deep cleansing in his or her memories. That person gradually acquires a capacity to communicate well with the other spouse and to inspire the other person to change. However, if the other person doesn't do this work, it is possible that over time, their destinies will differ and their paths separate. We should be aware of this. It may also be part of their respective programs. However, before making such a decision, we must always ask Up Above for signs and dreams! We keep asking about this, over and over again, for days, even weeks, 'Is this decision right for the evolution of my soul? Is it right for me to take another path?' If we have doubts, and there is no physical, verbal or moral violence, we abstain from all action and keep on working on ourselves, while doing our very best to be a good spouse on all levels.

How many people don't dare decide to go their separate ways because they have a house and other goods in common? This fear of material loss stems from a feeling of insecurity so we need to acknowledge it in ourselves, and tell ourselves, 'My fear and worry are holding me back so I'm going to work on them. I'm going to work on them with Angel Mantra, and when the time is right, I'll have the courage to take this step if it is part of my program!'

It is very important to always respect our own pace and rhythm of development and evolution. Each person has his own program. Always connect and remain connected with Up Above, that's what leads to spiritual autonomy!

Here is another case that is also common to a great number of people: the desire for possessions and access to great material wealth. Yet some people are simultaneously afraid. A woman told us one of her dreams that is a good illustration of this inner duality. *She saw herself on an ocean liner with her mother-in-law. Her mother-in-law was encouraging and inciting her to have a love affair with a Russian millionaire who was also on the ship. In the beginning, the dreamer told herself, 'No, there's no sense in that! I don't want to have an affair with this millionaire!' But after a while, she let herself be influenced by her mother-in-law and she began a love affair with this man. He had bodyguards and he said to her, 'You see, you are protected with me; I've got bodyguards.'*

As time went by, she realized this man wasn't nice. With his wealth, he treated people like slaves; he abused and misused his power. She felt bad in this situation and wondered, 'What am I doing here? What am I doing with such a man?' She was unhappy.

All of the elements in this dream represent parts of the dreamer. This dream shows that this woman is experiencing an opening of her unconscious that will allow her to set herself free from her obscure motivations. This type of dream is very important!

Let's see what she was being shown. She was on an ocean liner. That is related to the water element, so the world of emotions. A boat symbolizes emotional stability, the way we advance on the emotional level. Had it been a rowboat, the power and state of conscience represented would have been different. An ocean liner represents much greater potentiality than a rowboat. However, it also indicates that there may be a lot more things to be rectified on the emotional level.

Two of the symbols in the dream are presented negatively: the mother-in-law and the Russian millionaire. Both represent aspects of the dreamer. Behind these two symbols, there may be reservoirs of memories that come from previous lives. Symbolism is so rich, so vast, and multi-dimensional! In its pure simplicity, a symbol may speak to us of several lives.

Let's analyze this example. What does her mother-in-law represent for this woman? She told me, "In concrete reality, my mother-in-law got in the way of my relationship with her son. She put up a lot of resistance, but he married me in spite of it."

Some people declare, "My mother-in-law is really not nice, she's mean." But when we know the Law of Resonance, we know that it's no coincidence that we have such a mother-in-law. So we say to ourselves, 'Ok, I can't change my mother-in-law. If her behavior annoys, bothers, or upsets me, it means that a similar mother-in-law exists in a corner of my own unconscious. I'm going to take care of her with Angel Mantra.' By working on our inner mother-in-law, sooner or later, our outer mother-in-law will change one way or another. It's an absolute fact.

In this woman's dream, the mother-in-law symbolizes obstructive memories that resist and prevent love. Such memories push her toward relationships where material wealth is present, but which wasn't acquired and used in a right, just way. In such conditions, true love is impossible.

As a woman, the mother-in-law symbolizes aspects of the dreamer's inner world, forces that dwell in her and influence her. Then, there's the millionaire with his bodyguards. From a negative point of view, having bodyguards means that we are afraid of being attacked, robbed, and/or assassinated. We are afraid of losing our life, our wealth, etc. It is possible that it could be preventive and positive to have such security around a person for political reasons, or because they are very rich, famous, influential, etc. Having large-scale abundance can attract the attention of all kinds of people, and, of course, it doesn't necessarily mean that we are a member of a criminal organization.

But in this dream, why was she shown a negative *Russian* millionaire? She could have been shown an American, German, Chinese, or other nationality millionaire. So why a Russian?

Let's briefly analyze the symbolism of Russia, taking into consideration, as always, the + and – aspects. In this example, it's the – aspect that is shown because, in the dream, the symbol is negative. Let's think about the history of Russia. First of all, there were tsars and a lot of power struggles for domination. Then, there was communism, which degenerated into tyranny and dictatorship. Today, a majority of the society has been infiltrated by the mafia and widespread corruption, like in many other countries, with its retinue of illegal businesses, drugs, money laundering, alcohol and/or prostitution, etc.

This woman was being told, 'There are memories in you that push and incite you to misuse wealth and power as soon as they are yours. Moreover, there is also a hidden tendency for domination, a cold attitude and rude, unrefined energy.' That's what the Russian millionaire in this example represents.

This man treated others like slaves. And, after a while, the woman didn't feel good. She understood that such an attitude was not right. She acknowledged her unhappiness. 'I'm not happy. I'm rich but I feel so unhappy!'

This dream reveals aspects that influence her emotional life and can trigger certain difficult situations. This woman told us, "I haven't got great material wealth in this life but I know I've already had great wealth in other lives. I know what great wealth is."

In other lives, most of us have been more or less materially wealthy and rich. Having great material wealth at our disposal always corresponds to a program. Cosmic Intelligence decides when the time has come for a person to experiment and learn in a life context where he will have to manage a lot of resources.

Up Above knows that these people may become despotic, abuse and misuse the power material abundance provides them with, treat others as slaves, harm the environment, and neither share nor use their wealth altruistically. God, Cosmic Intelligence already knows how people will dispose of their abundance.

You might ask, "Why give such resources to people knowing they will be badly used?" The answer is: evil is educational. These people learn through negativity. They experiment through distortion. Of course, behaving as they do, they create serious karmas, especially when their behavior has collective, planetary repercussions. Everything they do is inscribed on their soul. Then, in this life or another, they will have to repair these karmas. They will have to settle them and rectify their behavior according to the program Cosmic Intelligence judges appropriate for their evolution. Hence, they could be born to a life where they will experience great limitations, extreme poverty, and even slavery.

Then, they will have other lives where Cosmic Intelligence will give them resources that they will use a little better until they understand that matter is temporal and educational, that what is most important of all is the development of Qualities and Virtues. But it's quite a task! It is a whole lot of work. In many cases, people whose life program includes an abundance of resources and material wealth live their life in great illusion. When we understand that, material wealth no longer impresses us. But in our society, wealth still impresses a lot of people!

Many people experience limitations in this life. They have few resources. Many experience extreme poverty and their life is very difficult. Let's analyze their situation symbolically. It means they have accumulated a lot of memories in their unconscious that correspond to the Russian millionaire in the dream we've just analyzed. Memories of past lives where many of them abused and misused the resources and power at their disposal. The forces contained in these memories push just like the mother-in-law in the dream. They incite these people to seek wealth and power. But their life program clearly says, 'No, in this life you won't have resources, you will be limited. This serves your evolution. These limitations will allow you to settle your karma and rectify your attitudes. And so the next time you have resources, you will know how to make better use of them.'

One day, by working on ourselves, we manage to understand this. But how do people who function in an ordinary state of conscience behave in the face of such forces? Well, they continue to nourish them. How? Sometimes, simply by watching TV! What purpose do you think all those reality TV shows serve? When people see all the characters – actors, actresses, singers, etc., – in various contexts of glamour, wealth and celebrity, they no longer feel their limitations. For a few minutes their inner millionaire is nourished. In such programs, they see waste and abuse, and against all common sense, they identify with those characters; they often criticize but give them a million dollars and we will see that, most of the time, they will behave exactly like the rich people they criticized. Via such TV shows and reading or hearing about rich, famous people in the media, they nourish those parts of themselves that lack success and celebrity; they lie to themselves by occulting the negative aspects they see.

This doesn't mean that we should avoid watching these programs, but we need to watch them with spiritual, vertical conscience and awareness. As we watch them, we need to observe ourselves so as to recognize the resonance we have with the characters and situations we see. If we are excited, we have these forces in us, and if we criticized them, thanks to the Law of Resonance, we can understand that we still have these aspects in our memories. That is why we are disturbed. We should ask ourselves, 'What emotions does this program arouse in me? Do I feel envy, am I angry? What does watching this program create inside me? Is it an expansion of conscience, more heightened awareness that leads me to realize that it isn't right? What aspects of myself are nourished by all this?' Doing Angel Mantra while watching these kinds of programs allows us to gradually cleanse distorted aspects in ourselves. Hence, we train ourselves to use all situations, without exception, to learn and know ourselves better and to reprogram our memories related to illusion and abundance.

As soon as a person begins to walk a spiritual path, he feels torn. We see in this woman's dream that unconscious forces pulled her toward abundance. This induced a feeling of ill-being in her. She realized that it wasn't good, that it wasn't right. In her dream, this situation made her feel bad.

This process is perfectly normal when we are on a spiritual path. For a certain length of time, we may be torn between the negative forces exerted by unconscious memories, that often date back to previous lives, and our desire to attain high levels of spirituality, fidelity to Divine Laws and Principles, and pure altruism. By working on ourselves, the undesirable forces gradually disintegrate and we find ourselves able to say, 'Now I feel that my soul is no longer in the grip of these past memories. Even if I don't know everything related to what I experienced in my past lives, I won't begin this kind of behavior again. I won't let myself be tempted by ill-acquired, misused wealth because I know what it involves and what it leads to. If I were to give in to temptation, Up Above would have to take everything away from me again and I'd be sad, unhappy and disconnected.'

There are people who use positive thinking methods. They suggest we formulate sentences constantly asking for and visualizing ourselves in abundance. However, with such methods, we don't necessarily become aware of the memories we need to cleanse and the abundance we attract may be illusory and karmic.

It is true that these methods work; they even work very well. But why do they work in some cases and not in others? It's because Cosmic Intelligence has decided this. It allows those for whom the method works to move on to another stage. They now understand that thought is creative because the request they continually repeated with great intensity materializes.

It's a first stage. Nevertheless, the negative aspect – the distorted memories corresponding to the mother-in-law and Russian millionaire in the dream – is still there. As soon as abundance or an ardent desire for wealth and riches re-emerges in these people, the forces and aspects in them that correspond to these two symbols will be reactivated. In the grip of these forces, they will continue to create serious karma for themselves. It remains an experience and lasts a certain length of time, until one day, it is finished.

That's why the time comes when Cosmic Intelligence decides that things won't work for these people any longer, and it is a great gift from Heaven! A true Godsend! They may persist in asking and repeating positive thought-formulae 10 000 times, but they will remain limited. Such methods no longer work because Up Above wants to help these people. Their limitations are an incitement to rectify both their *mother-in-law* attitudes that push them to seek material wealth and the *millionaire* attitude that abuses and misuses the power conferred by abundance. Hence, when resources are put at these people's disposal, they will no longer create negative karmas. They will know they need to use them in a right, just, qualitative way, and that will make them happy; they will then know true happiness.

So you see, everything is a gift, everything is a Godsend! We finally come to understand this. And this understanding incites us to work deeply and intensely with Angel 43 VEULIAH. We do this work because we know it's not only material prosperity that we need to focus our attention and motivation on, but, first and foremost, on the state of conscience of abundance.

It's a huge task that concerns all of the memories we have accumulated throughout all of our lives regarding prosperity. Thanks to this inner work, we understand that the wealth accumulated on the material level is nothing in comparison with the wealth of conscience and powers we rediscover within ourselves. This understanding becomes fully integrated when we use the creative power of our spirit and thoughts altruistically, in a right, just, pure way. That's what we aim for. It's exactly the same for abundance on the emotional level. True, right, pure love opens all doors. It is so powerful when we feel this love in us! We can then have material abundance too without the risk of creating serious karmas for ourselves. So we see that, above all, abundance and prosperity are a state of conscience. However, Angel Work with Angel 43 VEULIAH is not a question of waving a magic wand! It is important to know that we don't just invoke Angel VEULIAH and hey presto! abundance falls into our lap! That's not how it works. On the contrary, in fact, while we're doing this Work, we also have to face memories of behavior that engenders poverty.

Here is an example. A woman shared the following dream with us: *She moved into an old broken down cabin; it was poor. She moved in with her husband who looked like her ex-husband in concrete reality, and their children and grandchildren. They were all crowded together and very uncomfortable. There were 7 rocking chairs and an old church pew.*

Let's analyze what this woman was being told through this dream. All of the elements – the characters, the old cabin, the rocking chairs, and the church pew – all symbolize aspects of the dreamer. Moving house in a dream, like in concrete reality, indicates a change in state of conscience.

When we work on ourselves, when we are on a spiritual path, we often dream we are moving house. Sometimes we can see ourselves move into great big beautiful houses, in lovely natural, green landscapes, even if we actually live in a very modest apartment. In such dreams, we are being told, 'Look, there aren't only poor aspects within you; there are also beautiful states of conscience.'

However, we may also be moved into old, run down, poor homes. And it's as great a gift as the beautiful mansions! Of course we won't feel very well the following day. Whenever we see ourselves in a beautiful home in a dream, we emanate good energy the next day. However, after a dream like this woman had, we don't feel well. We will have feelings of insecurity. Consequently, the energy we emanate the next day won't be beautiful.

A lot of people who still live in an ordinary conscience visit this kind of memories in their dreams, but it is occulted. Very often they don't even remember what they dreamed, but the following day they don't feel good. The least thing makes them feel insecure because the memories visited in their dream reactivate a great many emotions: fears, anxiety, insecurity, etc. But they don't understand what is happening to them.

On the other hand, when we work with The Traditional Study of Angels, as soon as we find ourselves in difficult moods, in difficult soul-states, we ask ourselves, 'What's the matter with me? What did I dream about last night? Ah! I see. A large block of memories has been activated. Up Above has increased the dosage because it corresponds to my program at the moment, so it's normal I feel like this. I'll do intense Angel Recitation each time emotions re-surface. As soon as I have time, I'll reflect on my dream. And I'll remain connected to this block of memories and cleanse it layer by layer.'

One day, we are very happy to receive this kind of dreams because they allow us to become aware of and rectify our distorted memories. Otherwise, if not cleansed and transformed, sooner or later, in this life or another, they will create a situation of poverty. It's an absolute fact.

This woman has already experienced poverty in her present life. She told us that she came from a big family and spent her childhood in poverty. Now, everything is fine so she is taking time to work on herself, to cleanse her memories of poverty and misused wealth. One day, we do this, we work like this. Even though what we are shown about ourselves may be ugly and difficult to accept, we are happy and we consider it a great gift.

Now let's see the symbolic meaning of the rocking chairs the woman saw in her dream. From a positive point of view, a rocking chair symbolizes comfort and consolation. The fact that there were 7 shows that, even in poverty, this woman is capable of finding consolation on the 7 levels, represented by the 7 main chakras and it also confirms that she has a tremendous inner capacity to create comfort and consolation in difficult times.

And what does a church pew symbolize? To find its symbolic meaning, we analyze its use in concrete reality. What is a pew used for? It is used as a seat to sit on to listen and pray in a church, which is a spiritual place, a place of prayer and contemplation. Hence, a church pew symbolizes receptivity and contact with the spiritual levels.

It's an old church pew. Consequently, it refers to old spiritual concepts of praying to want something, without understanding the Law of Karma, that we always reap what we sow. Although prayer is a magnificent tool, the way we pray may be based on old beliefs that don't take the Law of Reincarnation into account. Like in the past, many poor people today pray and pray, wondering, 'How come I pray all the time and yet I'm still poor, while all those other people don't pray, aren't nice, are real crooks, and they are rich? After all, we have only one life and they are rich, whereas I pray all the time and I'm poor. Why?' These people continue to pray all the same but they eventually tire because they don't have Knowledge, which allows us to understand the deep, true cause of this situation. As soon as we know the Cosmic Laws, we know that our existence on Earth is not limited to only one life. We understand that the reason why we are poor in our present life is because we are reaping what we sowed in our past lives.

However, we must never ever evaluate a person's spiritual evolution on the fact of his being born into either a poor or rich family! Being born into a wealthy family doesn't necessarily mean that we used resources and wealth well in previous lives. A soul may incarnate in a family of millionaires and be extremely spoiled. Subsequently, through his attitude and behavior he may create a great many serious karmas. Another soul that has already attained a certain degree of evolution may arrive in a poor family. Up Above decides this is best for him because he still has memories of past lives to rectify, memories of lives where he wasted resources, or where his attitude and behavior weren't right and just. He is limited in order to be trained to use his resources well and to no longer waste. Such a life program may guide the person in question to high levels of conscience. Of course, the person has to accept it. He needs to be able to say to himself, 'My being born into a poor family, and having to deal with a lot of limitations, is no coincidence. There's a reason and meaning behind all of this. I accept it even though I don't know how I created this. Since I'm now reaping it, I must have sown it. From now on, I'm going to pay attention to what I do and how I behave with my resources. I know I can rectify and repair.' We are often happily surprised when we know materially poor people who live exemplary lives of wonderful, cheerful generosity and contentment. They are evolved souls who, usually entirely unconsciously, know this program is good for them and that poverty on any level is a state of conscience.

Here is another example. As I explained, when we work with an Angel, when we do Angel Mantra Recitation regularly, then situations related to the States of Conscience of that Angel occur during the day.

When I was preparing this lecture on Angel 43 VEULIAH, I recited this Angel Mantra for several weeks. During that period, we attended a family reunion in Quebec (Canada). There were grandmothers and grandfathers, great uncles and aunts, as well as lots of aunts and uncles and cousins. During this reunion, some family members began to talk about old age pensions, saying, "If the decrease in population continues at this rate, who'll pay for our retirement?"

Quite a topic of discussion! Of course, there was a certain truth to it, and it may be interesting to talk about it, but it needs to be talked about objectively, with detachment. However, Kaya and I could feel that, for the people present, this topic had aroused great anxiety.

One day, we are able to feel, to sense in depth. We perceive what lies behind the spoken words, what is happening on people's metaphysical level. We understand their worries, their soul-states, even in a conversation that may seem to be very neutral.

For these people, the topic of their old age pension was a trigger element because in concrete reality, they don't have financial problems; in fact, they live in a certain abundance. This discussion had plunged their mind and spirit into memories that had nothing to do with old age pensions, memories where they had recorded insecurities and fear of lack.

In such situations, Kaya and I always respect people's level of evolution. We never impose Angel Teaching or our Knowledge. We do Angel Mantra and we listen to what is said in symbols, analyzing the conversation just like a dream. We know that the vibration we emanate in doing this may be a trigger element for others. When this happens, it is not a coincidence; it is always related to the program of the people present.

As the conversation on this topic continued, Gabriel, our 3-year-old nephew, got up from the children's table, went over to his father, and said, "Daddy, I want to tell you a secret!"

Gabriel's father was very surprised because this was the first time his son had ever behaved like this. When the grandparents heard the word *secret*, there was a great silence. Secrets usually interest everyone! (laughter) So they all went silent and listened. Gabriel's father leaned down and Gabriel whispered a few words in his ear. The curious grandparents then all asked, "What did he say? What's his secret?" Gabriel's father replied, "He said that we are eating mice!" "What does that mean? What does he mean by that?"

Gabriel, very mischievously, danced back to his place singing, "We're eating mice! We're eating mice!" It was funny to see him dance around, and then he sat down again.

His father, who works with The Traditional Study of Angels, knew his son had just spoken in symbols. He hadn't said that for no reason. We weren't eating mice at this family reunion; we were having a delicious meal!

To understand the message contained in Gabriel's secret, we have to analyze the situation using symbolic language, as if it were a dream. This 3-year-old was speaking about their energy, the metaphysical ambiance engendered by the discussion about old age pensions. He was saying, 'Your discussion is making us eat mice, that is to say, you are feeding us with the worries, anxieties, and little, gnawing fears on the inside.'

In one very short sentence, Gabriel had summed up the energy emitted by them. If we had been shown this situation in a dream, i.e. on the metaphysical level, behind his words, we could have clearly perceived the energy present during the discussion. We could even have been shown people eating mice!

Let's analyze the symbolism of mice. The energy emanated by a symbol always reflects a state of conscience. As for all symbols, we need to analyze the + and – aspects. A mouse is an animal. Hence, it refers to instinctual vital energy. This is very important energy and we need to learn to educate it well. What negative behavior does a mouse symbolize? In general, it's a very fearful animal.

Of course, the energy would have been very different if Gabriel had said, "We're eating lions." But he didn't; he said, "We're eating mice." This means, 'There's anxiety in your vital energy. You are emanating little worries and fears!' A lot of insecurity could be felt among the grandparents. Let's see how symbolism works and you'll understand how perfect it is!

What does a mouse do? Sometimes it gets into people's houses through little cracks and fissures, especially at night. Let's analyze this as if we saw it in a dream; we go from concrete reality to metaphysical, symbolic truth. A house represents our interior, inner self, and walls represent our structure. If there are cracks and fissures in our structure, then little fears and worries can get in. And what will these little anxieties do? They will gnaw at us. Mice are rodents that nibble and gnaw on resources, food, and sometimes even clothes. A mouse symbolizes energies that cause minor damage by nibbling on and chiseling away our resources. Mice may also carry disease.

Some people may say, "A little mouse doesn't cause much damage, it's not a major problem!" That's true, but a mouse is very prolific! A female mouse can have more than 100 baby mice in a year! That means that a mouse emits a state of conscience of proliferation. It's not like a hippopotamus, which is not at all prolific like a mouse. So we need to be careful of the little fears and worries we sometimes let in. They may seem harmless, but if we let them, they will multiply and engender serious damage, great worries and strong feelings of insecurity.

That's what Gabriel meant! See how right he was! Of course, he wasn't aware he was conveying a message, but his soul knew. His soul was saying, 'Stop this conversation, you are nibbling and gnawing at us! Stop being so insecure!' Through his simple intervention, Gabriel changed the conversation! Even if the elderly adults didn't all understand the message consciously, their souls did; their souls received the message.

Gabriel is not exceptional. Listen to your children and grandchildren like this! You'll see they all speak in symbols. All we have to do is listen to them. That too is a form of abundance. A lot of people seek sensations. Well, simply listening to a child in symbols can give us access to the amazing, extraordinary sensations created by contact with the multi-dimensions!

As soon as we listen to a person in symbols, we do a lot more that a simple intellectual task. We open up to the other multi-dimensions, because behind each material form, there is a thought-form, a state of conscience. One day, this becomes a way of life. Hence, we are constantly connected to the multi-dimensions. However, it takes quite an apprenticeship before we master this capacity!

While I was preparing this lecture, I also meditated on the symbolism of mice. And one day during that period, Kaya came home and told me, "I bought a mouse today." Of course, he didn't mean a live mouse but a computer mouse, the small device that allows us to move the cursor. By clicking on this device, we activate programs and various functions. It is a very practical device. All it takes is one click! Having meditated deeply on the symbolic meaning of a mouse, I said to Kaya, "Why is it called a mouse? We could change the name and call it a clicker." "Good idea!" was his immediate reply.

I looked up the Internet to find out where the name had come from. The original device was invented in 1964 by an American called Engelbart. Even if some people think the flex connecting it to the computer resembles a mouse's tail, this device has no resemblance whatsoever with this animal. Our perception of things is very subjective!

Regarding this name, Mr. Engelbart said, "I always thought that once the product was on the market, it would have a much more dignified name than that! It happened in spite of me!" We'll come back to this shortly.

During an interview, a BBC journalist asked Mr. Engelbart, "How does it feel to have invented a device that is used by thousands of people every day? You have transformed man's interaction with the machine. How does that make you feel? Do you feel you have accomplished something important?" Remember this was more than 50 years ago. At that time, people were far from the current situation. They couldn't have imagined the expansion of computer technology. Today, computers aren't used by thousands of people, but millions, billions! However, in spite of improvements, the concept remains the same.

Here is Mr. Engelbart's answer. "It's strange because I had aimed at a much larger project that was to go far beyond the mouse. In a way, it's disappointing that we didn't manage to go further."

To understand this man's answer in depth, let's go back to the symbolism of a mouse. This name alone reveals unconscious memories. Mr. Engelbart was an engineer, who made several inventions that led to a certain prosperity and renown. However, the name given to this device indicates that, at times, fears and worries gnawed at him. That's what we can experience when we click on the computer mouse. We may become impatient and anxious when our file delays opening or for other reasons.

You may be thinking, 'But Engelbart didn't choose that name! He even thought it was undignified.' You'd be right, but it was no coincidence that Mr. Englebart had the colleague he had! The colleagues we have are never, ever a coincidence! Everything is orchestrated with great precision. Everything is mathematic. That's why we compare Cosmic Intelligence to an immense Living Computer that calculates everything with infallible precision. We have such and such a colleague because we resonate with him, both positively and negatively.

Let's analyze the situation as if it were a dream. The colleague who named the device a mouse represents part of Mr. Engelbart himself. The answers Mr. Engelbart gave the journalist also reveal aspects of himself. In actual fact, whenever we talk about someone or something, we are always talking about ourselves.

Sometimes on seeing a cloud, a person may say, 'I see a flower,' while another person may say, 'I see a dragon.' Both people see the same cloud and yet their associations with it differ. Why? Because the contents of their respective unconscious are different. Consequently, what emerges on seeing the cloud cannot be identical. Whenever we talk about the sunshine, the rain, or the climate in general, we are always talking about our inner climate. In our example, if Mr. Engelbart's colleague associated the invented device with a mouse, which means it corresponded to what emerged from his unconscious at that precise moment in time. It's the same for us, all the time!

This device is related to computers. The next step is to question the symbolic meaning of a computer. A computer allows us to deal with, manage, record, safeguard (save), receive, and send a vast amount of information, not only on the physical level here on Earth, but also on the metaphysical level, i.e. in the parallel worlds and dimensions. As a symbol, a computer

is related to the multi-dimensionality of our being, to the workings of our conscience, and the management of all the memoires recorded on our soul, and on the various levels of our unconscious. Hence, every time we physically click on a computer mouse in concrete reality, we simultaneously activate corresponding memories and programs – our inner, personal software – on the metaphysical level.

In the Teachings of Traditional Angelology, we talk a lot about memories that are reactivated and interact in our life. That's what a computer symbolizes, as do all inventions. They symbolize a collection of processes related to the states of conscience that are about to materialize.

Let's go back to Mr. Engelbart. He said, "In a way, it's disappointing that we didn't manage to go further." What does he reveal to us in this sentence? This man was fascinated by the capacities of our intellect. Moreover, he did a lot of research in the computer field. When a person is able to receive an invention, he is a genius. He has access to a certain level on the mental, intellectual level, and he receives the information required to materialize this information on the physical level. In Mr. Engelbart's case, his karmic *luggage*, his unconscious memories prevented him from going further. His soul knew that there were still things in him that created an obstacle to the achievement of even greater works and inventions.

Of course, what he invented is good, efficient, and useful, bearing in mind, of course, that everything depends on the use we make of it! On the soul level, this person knew that he had a collective program to realize. Indeed, to invent such a device, he had to have a collective program. But in his soul, he also knew that he could have gone much further. He could have invented and created objects or circumstances that would have been so much more enriching for all humanity! However, he wasn't able to do so because the contents of his unconscious memories blocked him on certain levels. That's what the mouse symbol reveals: fears, worries, anxieties, and feelings of insecurity that nibbled and gnawed on the inside.

Let's analyze a few details of Mr. Engelbart's biography.

Engelbart was an engineer who began his career in the US Navy. So here we see the water element, which symbolizes the world of emotions and feelings. He did research on radars. What does this indicate? Every job, every activity that we do in the outer world always corresponds to work we need to do in our inner world, on the level of our conscience. Engineering and research work indicate that Mr. Engelbart needed to work on concepts regarding structure. Naval radars allow us to detect objects, obstacles and potential dangers in the water. If we transpose this to the metaphysical level, it shows that he needed to develop his own inner radar, his subtle perception, so as to discover the cause of obstacles on his emotional level. The military aspect of the Navy is related to protection and defense. When a person's life program is related to the military field, it means that the person needs to put an end to inner and outer conflicts and wars.

His unconscious, distorted memories prevented his access to abundance on the conscience level, which would have allowed him to share lots of other things with humanity! That's why he was disappointed. His disappointment was related to other dimensions!

What's more, he was called Engelbart! This man was American, but his name is of German origin. There is the word *Engel* in this name; Engel is the German for Angel. Well, the name we have is never a coincidence. This name meant, 'If you want to achieve great things for humanity, you need to seek and develop an Angelic Conscience because with an Angelic Conscience you will be able to attain lots of other dimensions.'

The simple fact of knowing the symbolic meaning of a mouse allows us to understand what sort of memories this man had in his personal unconscious. We also understand that it was also related to a program on the level of collective conscience. It is no coincidence that this little device has been called a mouse, in all languages, for over 50 years now.

Every time we click on a computer mouse, metaphysically, we open a window onto our unconscious memories and we go into inner research mode. The thousands, millions, billions, trillions of daily clicks all over the world reveal that, for the last 50 years, humanity has been experiencing an immense opening of conscience, exploring the individual and collective conscience. The great worldwide success of the *Harry Potter* film mentioned in the introduction is an example of this.

Work with The Traditional Study of Angels helps us understand in depth the complexity of the processes presently being experienced in the collective conscience. Up Above, They too click, and each time They do, a human being receives one dream, then another and another and another, etc. Thus, we are led to visit our unconscious memories – our inner millionaires that treat others like slaves, our poor inner worlds, our uncertainties, our mice, our aggression, our wars, etc. There is quite a stock of things in our unconscious! Traditional Angelology allows us to experience these processes consciously. It offers us keys to open, encounter and transform our memories. However, this isn't the case for everyone. For some people, the time hasn't yet come for their access to Knowledge. Nonetheless, we can say that in general the collective unconscious has been opened and is continuing to open. Each time we click, a memory emerges. There are quite a number of clicks every day! And it's increasing.

A mother said to me, "We are all on an intense spiritual path in my family. I have 3 children and they all do Angel Work. But my 5-year-old boy is really very open! He experiences all kinds of very positive and negative, metaphysical manifestations. I allow him to spend an hour on the computer. I choose the games he can play – no war, no fighting or aggression. But when the hour is up, he is all upset! So much so that I've now forbidden him to play on the computer." "You know," I said, "That's not the solution. Continue to choose games but teach him to manage his emotions and soul-states. Teach him not to click impatiently or aggressively, or nervously and anxiously, with feelings of insecurity. Explain to him what happens when he uses the computer. His unconscious is so open that what he sees on the screen automatically plunges his spirit into reservoirs of memories. His whole being is upset by what he perceives in his unconscious. Explain to him very gradually what he is experiencing. Teach him symbolic language. Ask him how he feels. Accompany him in this work, do it with him; don't forbid him to use the computer!"

Whenever anyone, child or adult, is open like this, it is important to explain to him that everything he sees on the outside is only a trigger element and a consequence, that such a gesture produces such an effect, etc. Understanding the positive and negative effects helps us evolve.

We began with the declaration, "We are eating mice." And see where it has led us! Symbolism is so vast! With Angel Study, everything interests us. Even if has nothing to do with a mouse on the concrete level, it's very important to understand and remember this state of conscience. We need to understand that the behavior symbolized by a mouse or mice, such as fears, worries, anxieties, and doubts, proliferates, multiplies. That's what a mouse means! And it corresponds to the collective conscience.

Understanding symbolism and the symbolic meaning of everything on the individual and collective scale is a source of great abundance on the conscience level. This leads to our pronouncing the word *mouse* and immediately perceiving the state of conscience it emits. I suggest you do this very simple exercise. Close your eyes for a few seconds and then imagine you are touching a computer mouse. Think of the word mouse with all of your conscience, with full awareness, and observe what happens in you.

Between ourselves, my husband and I have decided to call this device a clicker. We know the effect is different. There's nothing wrong with calling it a mouse; it's just another state of conscience. And of course, if I had to buy one, I wouldn't say to the salesman, "I'd like a clicker." He might think, 'She's got a problem, maybe she's a simpleton. Why is she asking for a clicker?' I could ask for a computer pointer device or an electronic cursor device, but the salesman would probably think, "What's the matter with her? Isn't she rather high and mighty? Doesn't she know it's called a mouse?' We must always respect common usage. Respect is very important! However, we can change lots of things when we understand what is behind a word. For example, in a restricted circle, among close family and friends, we can call a computer mouse a clicker. Mr. Engelbart certainly wouldn't mind since he himself thought the name mouse lacked dignity!

Here is another example a woman shared with us. In concrete reality, she suffered several thefts. First, her bank card was stolen, then she was mugged, and her handbag was snatched with her wallet in it. This woman works with The Teachings of Traditional Angelology and she knows these thefts were not coincidences. She is aware that anyone who is robbed has something to understand and learn. Cosmic Intelligence would never let us be robbed unless there were something for us to learn. She also knows that the thief has created karma for himself.

This woman used these experiences to ask herself a few questions. 'OK, my bank card has been stolen. A bank card is related to money and money is energy. Am I being shown that I still steal energy sometimes? I'd like to know a little more about this!' That evening, before going to sleep, she recited an Angel Mantra and she asked God why she'd had to experience these thefts. She wanted to know the deep reason, the true cause of them.

During the night, she received a dream. *She saw herself with an ex-boyfriend, whom she'd lived with 20 years ago. She noticed her wallet was empty.*

We asked her what her real-life ex-boyfriend represented for her. She replied, "Miserliness! He was so mean and miserly it became unbearable. That's why I left him." But this woman knows that all of the elements in our dreams represent parts of ourselves. Through what this ex-boyfriend symbolizes for her, she was being shown that she still harbors miserliness in herself. Even if she has evolved and undertaken deep-cleansing of her memories. She was shown why she experienced those two thefts.

Miserliness! When we are with someone who has no financial difficulties, who has got money and wealth and yet is mean and miserly, we may wonder, 'How come he is so mean? It doesn't make any sense!' What happens in such a case? What makes a person mean and miserly? It's because of his unconscious memories. They may date back to previous lives where he experienced poverty and hunger; lives where he may have been poor, homeless, and permanently struggling to survive. But these memories have been occulted. He isn't aware of the fact that every time he thinks about money, his spirit plunges down into these difficult memories. This reactivates his past experiences and emotions as well as the fear of losing all he has now in his present life. Understanding this process helps us have compassion for mean, miserly people.

This woman might think, 'I don't see where the resonance is, I'm not mean or miserly; I'm actually quite generous.' Yes, that may be true, but miserliness may be situated on another level, not necessarily on the material level.

Her ex-boyfriend experienced miserliness on the physical, material, financial level. In this woman's case, it may be situated on the affective, emotional level. Miserliness also exists on the level of feelings. Her behavior may resemble her ex's behavior, but on the emotional level. As soon as there's question of offering her feelings, her spirit may visit memories of betrayal, infidelity, abandon, sorrow, grief, and all sorts of affective, emotional difficulties. So she thinks, 'No, no, no! I can't give my feelings. I'm afraid of losing and suffering. It's better if I retain them.'

No matter what level it exists on, miserliness is always a retention mechanism. Hence, the mean, miserly person automatically prevents free circulation of giving and receiving. And even though he may feel rich because he keeps his money, he continues to impoverish himself on other levels. The poverty he feels on the inside, on the emotional, mental and spiritual levels will push and force him to steal these energies on the outside, even though he may be materially wealthy. One day, we are able to admit without any embarrassment, 'Yes, I realize I steal energy; I need to work on these aspects of myself.'

Energy stealing is common behavior among people who live in an ordinary conscience. They take other people's energy on one level or another. This lasts until they acquire Knowledge, which allows them to transcend their memories.

That's why this woman had those experiences of theft. She was being told, 'You were robbed because there is still miserliness in you. You are being helped to understand that at a certain level, you too steal from others, you take their energy!

The resonance may also relate to the other extreme: waste. This is not necessarily waste of money. A person may manage his affairs very well. It may be waste on the thought and feeling level. For example, when the person becomes excited and over exalted. He may then scatter and disperse his energy in all directions. Such behavior naturally attracts the other extreme, which is miserliness. This may not be situated on the same level, as in the case of this woman who attracted a man who was mean and miserly on the material level. Whenever a person manifests one extreme, we can be sure that the complementary extreme is also present in his life and in himself. Everything has its complement.

However, we must never judge and say, 'How can this be? I've been working on these aspects for 20 years! How come I've been robbed again?'

We must never evaluate a person's level of evolution according to the fact that he has been robbed. It depends on the degree the person has attained and the memories he is cleansing. Up Above may say, 'We are going to help this person evolve by marking his conscience profoundly! We will synchronize a theft in concrete reality so that he will go further on his spiritual path, so that he will take a step toward unconditional giving and cleanse the last block of memories where there are still a few worries and fear of lack.'

The empty wallet symbolizes the energy and resources this woman retains on certain levels of her being because of her fear of lack. She needs to move on to another stage and to get there, she needs to cleanse her memories. As soon we have an in-depth understanding of how we work, we are always happy, in all circumstances, because we know that whatever experiences we go through are all teachings made to measure for us by Up Above. We know that Up Above can orchestrate a theft just to help us work on our miserliness or to learn to put in place a better protection structure in our life or company for example. Sometimes a small incident will become a great lesson that helps us improve and protect future development. And more than that, we can say that normally an initiate will be informed through dreams that something is going to happen so he can understand why the Universe has created this incident. The level of awareness we receive when we attain a high level of evolution with our angelic conscience is beyond anything that we can imagine. On the other hand, of course, with an ordinary conscience, if we get angry with whatever experience that has been organized for us and we refuse to accept or live it to evolve, then we impoverish ourselves on the inside, whereas if we understand the deep meaning of a situation and we accept it and decide to cleanse the memories that engendered it, we advance very rapidly.

To convey the message to this woman in her dream, the symbol of a mean, miserly person she knew was used. It was quite easy to decode. However, if Up Above had wanted to give her a more specific teaching about her vital, instinctual energy, she could have been shown an animal that symbolizes meanness and avarice. What animal is that? It's the rat.

A rat symbolizes an almost identical state of conscience to a mouse, but to a stronger degree. Rats have almost the same behavior as mice. They live in groups and are generally nocturnal. They are also very proliferate! The frequency of reproduction is very high. Theoretically a female rat can have approximately 1000 descendants in one year and 250 000 in a lifetime. Imagine! However, we are not going to analyze the life of a rat. What particularly interests us is the symbolic state of conscience that is emanated, i.e. proliferation. Of course, there is always a positive and negative aspect to every symbol.

Field rats can also be very destructive but we will analyze the symbolism of town rats because, on the one hand, this symbol is related to extreme waste, and on the other, extreme avarice.

In towns and cities, rats very often live in the sewers and water pipes. They feed on excrement and rubbish produced by human beings. Symbolically this indicates that on the level of vital energy, we nourish ourselves on other people's leftovers and remainders. That's a miser's behavior. That's what he does unconsciously.

It is said that in the sewers in Paris rats eat 800 tons of rubbish per day. Without their presence in big cities the sewers and water pipes would very often be blocked. Citizens living in cities would have to seriously revise their way of life because without rats, it would be impossible to continue to live as they do.

Angel 43 Veuliah

Physically and symbolically, the presence of rats in big cities indicates that people consume excessively. There is overconsumption and waste. But it is also an indication that the state of conscience of miserliness is also widespread since extremes always attract each other. We mustn't judge this state of things since it is experimentation. Evil is always educational. The aim of its manifestation is not to harm what is positive, beautiful and good. Its role is to create a reaction so that negativity is transformed.

We sometimes hear people say, "I feel drained! That person completely sapped my energy!" Well, feeling drained by someone indicates that there is waste in ourselves because the other person represents part of us; other people always represent parts of ourselves. Feeling drained indicates that on some levels, we drain ourselves. In other words, we have resonance with people who act like this otherwise they wouldn't have any effect on us. It would be impossible.

Let's go back to rats. They have their place in the scheme of things. Human beings would have to change their lifestyle so that the reason for the existence of rats would disappear. In the collective unconscious rats do not have a good reputation. Indeed, the sight, sound, image, or mention of a rat may recall memories of previous lives possibly dating back to Antiquity or to the Middle Ages when rats were believed to spread the plague and cause terrible epidemics. This belief strongly marked the collective conscience.

In actual fact, it isn't rats as such that set off epidemics! It is the fleas they carry sometimes. When a rat is sick and has fleas, the fleas jump onto other animals, and onto human beings too. A flea is a tiny insect that lives off its hosts, i.e. the animals and people it bites. It nourishes itself on their blood.

In French-speaking countries, the word *flea* is very often used as a term of endearment, but if we analyze it symbolically, such a name expresses a particular state of conscience that is not very positive, is it? In a way, when people use this word to address their child, they are declaring that their child drains them of vital energy just like a blood-sucking flea – blood symbolizes vital energy. When they call their child this, they also drain their child's energy!

Calling a child a flea also reveals a complex of superiority. Every country and language has its own pet names. The very term *pet* name, which refers to both a gentle, kind caress or stroking gesture and the domesticated animals that we keep as pets, also reveals a complex of superiority, as well as an emanation, and even solicitation of instinctual, affective energy, and encouragement of emotional dependencies. In the United States, pre-school children are sometimes called *rug rats*. There are many other terms of endearment, of course. Before knowing symbolic language, I too used these kinds of terms of endearment. That was before I realized that such terms revealed my own resonance and states of conscience. It was never a coincidence I had chosen such a pet name for that particular person.

During the intermission at a lecture, a woman came up to me and said, "I call my daughter *my little weasel*, is that ok? Can I call her this?"

"Madam, you can call your daughter whatever you wish! But do analyze the state of conscience emitted by the term you choose!" (laughter)

"Can I call her *my sweetie-pie*?"

"You can call her that if you like. But in that case too, think about the state of conscience that exists behind the name you've chosen."

That's what spiritual autonomy is: we begin to think and reflect deeply as soon as we know there are hidden meanings. There are dimensions beyond mere concrete, physical reality! When we begin to ask ourselves, 'What lies behind the words

I use, behind the gestures I make, the things I do?' this creates an opening into the multi-dimensions. One day, we understand that each word we use bears multiple essences that stem from its origin, accumulate through the ages and emanate in its energy today, simultaneously conveying many of our + and – memories.

To conclude with the rat symbolism, let's see how this animal is considered in other countries.

In some traditions, such as in Southern China, rats are rice bearers, and in Japan, rats bring good luck. "But that's only superstition," you may say to me. Yes, indeed it is. It's as though knowing that rats can cause great damage, people try and get on their side by soft-soaping and flattering them! Hence, they pray to negativity and nourish superstition. Such an attitude is understandable as long as we have no knowledge of symbolic language or the Law of Resonance. But one day, we go beyond superstition. We begin to question ourselves, to reflect, study and analyze in depth, which inevitably leads us to symbolism.

We'll see the symbolism of credit cards in the following example. One day, a woman told me that in a dream, *she had lost all her credit cards*. What is the symbolic meaning of this dream? First of all, let's analyze what a credit card is used for in concrete reality. It allows us to receive credit, money, forms of energy that allow us as card holder to create, invest, elaborate and realize projects. Some people might say, "Credit cards can be very negative because a lot of people use up all the credit granted to them and end up in terrible debt." It's true that a credit card can indeed lead to very negative results. After a while, our bank statement shows us the consequences quite clearly. However, what is essential in having a credit card is the way we use it, the intention, state of mind and conscience with which we benefit from the credit granted. We must always remember that what we do on the physical level, we also do on the metaphysical level.

If we are afraid of using the credit we are granted, it means that there are forces in us that tend to overspend and to waste. On our soul level, we know that God, the Cosmic Intelligence, will no longer grant us either physical or metaphysical resources if we continue to make poor use of the credit granted to us. Hence, the way we use credit cards teaches us a lot about our memories related to abundance, prosperity, and the management of our resources.

The great facilities credit cards offer us on the physical level, we also receive on the metaphysical level. Cosmic Intelligence constantly gives us gifts of credit. If Up Above were to grant us human beings the life conditions and spiritual, intellectual, emotional, and physical resources according to the merits of our past lives, and the qualities we developed during those lives, everyone on the planet would be very, very poor! Life would be extremely difficult; there would be poverty everywhere. But, in Its infinite Kindness and great Wisdom, Cosmic Intelligence constantly grants us credit so we can continue our apprenticeship and develop qualities and virtues so as to be able to learn sometimes even through the worst distortions. Evil is always educational! Hence we continually receive opportunities to change, to develop qualities and virtues, in order to recognize abundance and prosperity on all levels, and to make good, right, just use of it.

Here is another true life experience in which a woman was shown she harbors unconscious forces that prevent her from appreciating and savoring the prosperity and abundance she has on several levels.

This woman told my husband, Kaya, that herself and her husband wanted to buy a plot of land to build a house on. She specified that she lived in Switzerland, in a beautiful little town surrounded by mountains, and that they didn't really know where to buy a plot. Should they buy one near the small town they lived in, or should they choose another region? She added, "We did our research and nothing seemed to flow!

What's more, I didn't feel good about looking for a plot. So, one evening, I asked Up Above to show me where we ought to buy a plot of land for our future home."

During the night, this woman received a dream that she thought contained the answer: it wouldn't be in the small town where they were living. She said to Kaya, "I'd like your opinion on this. I'd like your interpretation of it, please."

Here is the dream she had. *I saw myself in the small town where we are living at the moment and I was on a motorbike. One of my girlfriends was driving it. Then we were riding along a street in this small town and I saw 2 houses that were under construction. Suddenly there was an earthquake. The 2 houses shook and collapsed! Then I saw myself phone my husband and tell him that the hotel in Italy where we usually go on vacation had also collapsed. I was in a terrible panic!*

Kaya began by asking her a few questions first.

"What does your friend who was driving the motorbike represent for you? What does she symbolize for you?"

"She sometimes finds it difficult to commit and she is dissatisfied with what she has. When she has one thing, she wants something else. It's as if she is never satisfied, never content."

And what about the town you live in, what does it represent for you?"

"It is surrounded by mountains. Sometimes I like the mountains, but at other times, they really get on my nerves!"

"And the hotel in Italy that collapsed in your dream, what does it represent for you?"

"My husband and I often go to this hotel to renew and replenish our energy; I meditate there."

These answers reveal that the dream was not a premonitory dream. Cosmic Intelligence was not announcing events that would actually occur in concrete reality. Through this dream, this woman was not being told, 'Look! We are showing you 2 houses that collapse in this town, so you mustn't buy land here.'

Through this dream, she was given information about her inner world. She was shown what the earthquake activated in her; she was shown aspects of herself that she needed to work on. Very often Cosmic Intelligence answers our questions like this. For Up Above, it's not the land purchase or the construction of a house that is essential, but rather our soul journey, the path we walk, the inner work we accomplish while carrying out such and such an activity. Through the events and symbols used in this dream, this woman was being told, 'Look! This is why you have difficulty materializing. Look at what you need to change if you want to accomplish your projects. Rectify on the inside and then things will flow on the outside.' Dreams are very educational!

Everything that happens on Earth, all our programs, are actually scenarios to help us evolve, develop qualities, to understand human nature, to experiment. Sometimes we experiment in negativity that we then have to correct. As soon as we know how Up Above thinks, we understand a lot of things!

The discussion between Kaya and this woman continued. "Your friend who was driving the motorbike represents a part of you. On the inside, you have memories that resonate with her dissatisfied, never content side. In the dream, you are with your friend on a motorbike. As a means of transport, a motorbike symbolizes the way we advance. From a positive point of view, it's advancing with a feeling of freedom. From a negative point of view, it's the rebellious side, and this applies in your case. You're advancing in a rebellious manner with a force that is never content. You don't know how to recognize and appreciate the things you have. That's what Up Above wanted you to understand through this dream.

"As for the 2 houses that collapse after an earthquake, they also symbolize parts of you. There were 2 houses and there were 2 of you on the motorbike. The number 2 is present; it is related to your relationships, to your associations with others. The earthquake shows that you sometimes have great worries, deep needs that create fears that destroy what you have built with the other person, or other people, right down onto the physical level. These include frustrations, a haughty attitude regarding abundance, fear of losing, of lack, of not succeeding, fear that things won't work, etc. In addition to this, the hotel in Italy reveals that there are aspects in you that prevent you from renewing and replenishing your energy and from meditating. This takes away your capacity to appreciate, recognize and acknowledge love and the abundance that you already have in your life. We can even see that you are exactly like your dissatisfied friend and you do not see it."

After hearing these explanations, the woman said, "I didn't understand this dream like that at all, but I do recognize myself in what you've said. It's true that I sometimes have feelings of dissatisfaction and fears of losing or lack. I'm not content with what I have and this even extends to my husband. Sometimes I'm afraid he'll leave me. So what do I do? I pretend to be indifferent." Kaya explained, "You see, it is important for you to cleanse your memories. You asked Up Above a question and you were shown what aspects of yourself you need to work on. The mountains surrounding the little town you live in are absolutely beautiful! The fact that they sometimes get on your nerves shows that there are rebellious forces in you that reject what is beautiful, harmonious, and represents elevation and grandeur. It goes beyond, way beyond the mountains! These negative, rebellious forces go wherever they want, they are afraid and this fear leads to destruction. It is related to your associations, to your relationship with others. You have a certain abundance on the physical and emotional levels. But as long as you haven't cleansed these memories, you won't be able to truly appreciate it. Whatever you have, you will never be content and this might be the reason why your husband could leave you. Because you are never really happy whatever he does."

So many people aspire to abundance and prosperity. However, as long as they have this kind of memories in their unconscious, their experience of abundance will remain ephemeral and unstable. The recipe or prescription for cleansing these memories consists in working with Angel 43 VEULIAH because this Angelic Energy helps open our conscience to set us free from obscure motivations and vicious, pernicious habits. And the more we cleanse our distorted motivations and memories of insecurity, etc., the better our chance of forming a divine couple, whose shared aim is to love and help each other evolve and become a better person, a better soul.

Now, let's have a look at a final example of a 17-year-old girl who lives in France. She told us the following dream. *I saw myself in a school, a senior high school, where I felt like a prisoner. It was a square building. There were giants outside and I was scared of them. At one point the giants arrived and they were looking for me. And to find out if I was in the school, they started throwing money, throwing coins. If the coins hit an obstacle, they'd know it was me! Then they reached the room where I was. One of the coins landed on my head. I said to myself, 'That's it, now they know I'm here!' I put the coin on a cushion, thinking, 'Now they'll think it hit a different object.' Then I flew out the window and high, high up into the sky. I didn't want to come back down to Earth again. Then I realized that I had a mobile device in my hand, it was a Nintendo game. The giants were only a game! All I had to do was to remove the batteries to make them disappear!*

This is a very interesting dream! All of the elements in it represent parts of this young woman. She is in a school, which means she is being shown the way she learns in terms of conscience. It shows what she needs to learn related to giants, which are also parts of her. They represent the way she perceives the outer world. They were throwing money, coins. Money here symbolizes matter, a form of energy that allows us to act on the material level.

She is afraid of the giants and feels like a prisoner in that school. We also learn that she is capable of raising herself up very high, but this elevation is actually escapism, a means to flee her difficulties, her fears. And then she no longer wants to come back down to Earth.

When we talk to this young woman, we see that she is not only beautiful on the outside, but she is also beautiful on the inside. Her eyes reflect great purity. She is 17 years old and has been working intensely with The Traditional Study of Angels since the age of 15. She has already been on a spiritual path in other lives and she is really very intense in her work. We can also feel the presence of memories of lives as a Tibetan, Buddhist monk where she learned to concentrate her mind and spirit and be detached from matter.

Her dream reveals that in her present life, matter scares her. For example, the giants could be storeowners and salesmen she encounters when she goes shopping, very down-to-earth people whose conscience is limited to the material level. This young woman, who has meditated on the subtle level, on the mind and spirit levels, for lives and lives, feels this materialistic kind of energy when faced with *giants*, and it scares her. The fact that she is scared means that she resonates with this type of energy, that she harbors corresponding memories in her unconscious. At the same time, she has a great capacity to raise herself up. Her conscience is immediately capable of rising very high, but then she doesn't feel like coming back down again. This shows that she wants to flee matter, that she rejects it. She needs to learn to unite Spirit and matter.

At the moment, for many years already, a lot of people are arriving on Earth with a profile of past monastic lives. They find it difficult to feel good in the world of matter. They often find it heavy, coarse, and limiting. The Teachings of Traditional Angelology offer them keys to move on to the final stage, which consists in the synthesis of Spirit and matter, in feeling at ease in all circumstances and in all worlds.

However, to be able to attain and maintain the High Levels of Conscience represented by the Angels, we have to cleanse all of the memories we have accumulated in our different lives. This leads us to go through great initiations in which Cosmic Intelligence sometimes activates strong doses of negativity in us. Over time, we may encounter extremely negative, materialistic people while remaining open and receptive! We'll be able to perceive the different facets of these people, their memories as well as their learning programs, and feel compassion. That's mastery! But we attain it very gradually. Up Above respects each person's individual level and pace of evolution. We are always helped until we are able to work with our own psychic powers. We are helped until we have developed clairvoyance, clairaudience, clairsentience, and the ability to perceive and act autonomously in multiple dimensions.

See how far *reading vertically* leads us! It is true for everyone we encounter and for all situations. We no longer want to flee them on the physical or subtle levels. No, no! We remain present, well incarnated when confronted with a person or situation, no matter how negative or down-to-earth.

This young woman's dream reveals that she has just moved on to another program. This is revealed by the fact that she realizes it's only a game, that all she has to do is remove the batteries for it to stop. In The Teachings of Traditional

Angelology, we learn that matter is temporal and educational. If we take matter too seriously, then at any moment, Up Above can pull the plug out, remove the batteries and put a stop to it – game over! Illusion is shattered and we realize it is pedagogical, educational. We are all learning and we mustn't judge others. This young woman is heading toward this stage and she is also on the path of cleansing these giants forces of superiority that have misused matter in past lives; because she has not only lived as a monk in past lives. Before deciding to be a monk, we always need a few lives where we have lived in the illusions of matter. Being a monk is a reaction to an accumulation of too much matter not being used properly. The soul chooses a monastic lifestyle in order to radically turn the page to escape memories and ways of living that created chaos in us and in others. Evolution is a long journey! A very long intense journey!

We began this lecture with the young actor, Daniel Radcliffe, exploring the parallel worlds in the role of Harry Potter. This indicates a certain opening regarding magic and the metaphysical dimensions. But for the moment, it's only a role he's played! He has memories that resonate with the themes, characters and stories of the film. However, that doesn't mean he is able to consciously experience what he did in the film.

On the other hand, this young woman, who is the same age as this actor, has neither his glory nor his fortune. She has arrived in a beautiful family, but when faced with society, she sometimes feels a little like Harry Potter. This young woman radiates great richness of conscience and wonderful abundance on the level of her feelings! With her, we can easily feel and understand that abundance and prosperity are indeed a state of conscience!

There are a great many people like her on Earth. They don't make any noise, we don't necessarily recognize them, but they are here. They are arriving in greater numbers and they are going to succeed in restructuring society by integrating

Angelic Knowledge. It's a real message of hope! Through their presence and work, they will help so that, one day, we will no longer seek prosperity and abundance only on the material level, but we will experience it as reality on all levels of our being!

THE TRADITIONAL
STUDY OF ANGELS

Since time immemorial, Angels have been presented as Celestial Messengers, but most of the time without real knowledge of what They truly are, or what kind of messages They bring us. In actual fact, Angels are the representation of Divine Qualities, Virtues and Powers in their purest form; They are also a symbol for we human beings when we activate our spiritual faculties, our capacity to dream, meditate, and travel in the multi-dimensions of the Universe and our conscience.

Their origin is found in the ancient Kabbalah, more precisely in the Traditional Study of Angels, that speaks about the 72 Angels, the 72 facets of the Creator that our human conscience must gradually develop to become angelic and manifest our divine nature. When we succeed in integrating the Angelic Essences, we attain the highest levels of evolution, knowledge, and blissful happiness. It is a long journey that leads us to become angels, to live with true Spiritual Powers, and hence set in motion the next stage in the evolution of humanity on Earth.

It is essential to understand that Angels are pure Energies that also exist in human beings, whether we know these Essences or not. However, generally unaware of our own divinity and angelic potential, we tend to make poor use of them, thereby engendering, via our multiple experimentations, the human distortions, resulting in our human weaknesses, faults and flaws.

Whenever we pronounce the sacred Name of an Angel, out loud or within ourselves, a vibratory echo is produced, which acts directly on our cellular memory and activates our connection with Universal Conscience. Over time, reciting Angel Mantras gives us access to Divine Powers, activates and intensifies our dreams, and helps us recognize the signs through which Cosmic Intelligence constantly communicates with us.

The fact that a number has been attributed to each Angel, situating Him in the Celestial Hierarchy, allows us to discover that the structure of the Universe and its governing Laws are mathematical.

THE ORIGIN OF ANGELS

The Traditional Study of Angels, which represents Teachings related to the origin of Angels, is an extraordinary inheritance of knowledge, the legacy of evolutive research undertaken by man to reach the highest levels of evolution. The ultimate goal of this Ancestral Tradition is to guide us through numerous initiations that will enable us to rediscover our Celestial Origin and our full spiritual powers and capacities. (The Traditional Study of Angels may also be referred to as Traditional Angelology or Traditional Angel Study.)

THE KABBALAH

Kabbalah means *Hidden Wisdom* and *The Word Received*, and refers to a teaching that is transmitted by word of mouth. This initiatic science allows everyone to reach the highest spiritual levels through an in-depth study of his own conscience. Considered in its essence, this teaching, or philosophy, brings us the knowledge of physical and metaphysical experimentation. The study of its founding principles plunges us into intense introspection. This reaches its heights the moment we discover the profound nature of man, woman, Angels and Divine Creation and Divine Work, through the perfect union of Spirit and matter.

The Kabbalah brings together a set of methods that allows us to truly understand the Creation of the Universe.

It is difficult to trace with precision the historical origin of the Kabbalah because, like Traditional Angel Study, it goes back to oldest antiquity. According to the available sources, it originated in Egyptian, Phoenician, Indian and Babylonian civilizations and would have been recorded for the first time by scribes held in captivity in Babylon around the year 450 BC.

The Kabbalah has been, and still is, the greatest and most hidden esoteric mystery of Humanity and has influenced all religions and traditions of the world. That is why Angels are mentioned in the sacred texts of all religions and cultures. Angel Work is a Universal Philosophy and may be adapted to all religious and philosophical backgrounds.

Among the Teachings of the Kabbalah, those that constitute aspects related to Divine Powers, i.e. The Traditional Study of Angels, are the ones that were kept secret the longest. The States of Conscience brought about by the study of Angelic Energies give people so much force and power that there was a tendency to occult this science, even among the initiates themselves. Several great beings received this Teaching of Highest Knowledge that was only transmitted orally to those predestined to receive it.

The philosophical study of the Kabbalah, or the intellectual study of the great Principles of the Universe, is useful, but it will never replace the groundwork that each individual must carry out in order to rediscover his Angelic Origin and to acquire Knowledge, the key to peace and happiness. In fact, the most important aspect of this approach consists in discovering these secrets directly, within ourselves, through the in-depth study of the Angelic States of Conscience. This is commonly called The Traditional Study of Angels or Practical Kabbalah.

PRACTICAL KABBALAH

The Kahal – the first school to transmit Angel Teaching that we can date and document today (although, as mentioned above, this Teaching originated in ancient Eygptian, Phoenician, Babylonian and Indian civilzations) – was founded in 1160 AD, in Gerona, a little Catalonian town in North-Eastern Spain at Isaac el Cec's instigation. The students of this school worked out a way to apply Angelic Knowledge to everyday life. The Kahal flourished from 1200 to 1475, during which time the detailed structure of the Tree of Life and the list of the Angels' Qualities and their associated distortions were drawn up for the first time.

In 1492, under the Inquisition, the Angelic initiates of Gerona were forced to choose between conversion to Catholicism or exile. In the case of exile, they could take nothing but their personal belongings with them. The Kahal was closed by order of the Inquisitors, and the entire old quarter of Gerona was walled up. But the descendants of the Angelic initiates who had converted, and who had stayed close to their ancestral quarters in Gerona continued to transmit their oral tradition in secret. Then, in 1975, some of them reopened the walled-up district and discovered the Angel texts that their ancestors had hidden and sealed in a building that today has become a historical site.

WHAT IS AN ANGEL?

An Angel represents Qualities, Virtues and Powers of the Creator in their purest form. In the Ancient texts, the Angels are the 72 Facets of the Creator. When we manage to rediscover Them and to reintegrate Them in their Essence, we then attain wonderful states of conscience, happiness and bliss. This constitutes a long journey but it is our only reason for being here on Earth.

An Angel is pure Energy. But as humans, we are rather ignorant and we don't have a proper understanding of the Energy of God and we use it badly. We distort the Essential Aspects of the Creator. This gives rise to our faults and weaknesses, in other words, the human distortions associated with each Angel. The fact remains, however, that these Essences reside within everyone, whether we know the Names of the Angels or not.

As recorded in The Traditional Study of Angels, each Essence has a sacred Name and Vibration. When we pronounce this sacred Name aloud or in silence, it sets off a vibratory echo that acts directly on our cellular memory. Thus, we connect with the immense Field of Conscience designated by the sacred Name. Over time, the high levels of Conscience that we attain give us wings. A number is also attributed to each Angel, positioning Him in the Celestial Hierarchy.

THE ADVANTAGES OF THE TRADITIONAL STUDY OF ANGELS

We may wonder why pray to the Angels and not God Himself. The reason is because Angel Work provides us with bearings and a structured work method that enables us to gradually integrate Universal Knowledge. Indeed, deep work is carried out within us when we recite the sacred Name of an Angel – Angel Mantra –, which activates dreams and signs, and simultaneously purifies our memories and the personal data recorded in our inner computer.

Angel Work is distinctive in that it allows us to identify precisely what it is that we need to rectify. It gives us the means to carry out this transformation work. It also allows us to measure the extent of the changes that take place in our unconscious as our conscience gradually opens up.

Working with one Angel at a time also creates a personal *map* of our inner countries, of our conscience, that we can identify in our dreams and through the signs we receive. When we invoke one Angel in particular, the other Angels continue to exist within us, but we focus on one specific *department* or *ray* of the Great Cosmic Intelligence. In fact, all 72 Angelic Energies are interconnected.

WORKING WITH THE ANGELS

Essentially, working with the Angels – Angel Work – consists in reprogramming our unconscious memories. It is purification work: memories that have been tainted with distortions are rectified one by one by the Power of the Angel and by our intention. By invoking States of Angelic Conscience, we focus our willpower on purity. Thus, we learn to be centered and become very intense. In this work, the intensity of our intention is a very important aspect. Increased focus and concentration occur in everyone who discovers that spirituality is not a hobby, but actually an intense transformation process that leads us through many stages. These often become steps on the path to the detoxification of our conscience.

During our apprenticeship on Earth and throughout our various incarnations, all of our experiences are recorded in our soul, in the same way that a computer records its data. All of our fears, sufferings, limitations, qualities and potential are recorded in our subconscious and in the various layers of our unconscious. (cf. the Consciousness Diagram page 335) It represents our soul and its different strata. A veil, called the veil of the unconscious, separates the part of us that we are conscious of from the part we ignore, represented by the hidden memories in our subconscious as well as in the personal, family, ethnic, collective and biological unconscious.

Working with the States of Angelic Conscience makes this veil disappear. In other words, through our Work with the Angels, we create a passageway between our conscience, our subconscious and the different layers of our unconscious. We also gain access to our distorted memories and we reprogram

THE CONSCIOUSNESS DIAGRAM

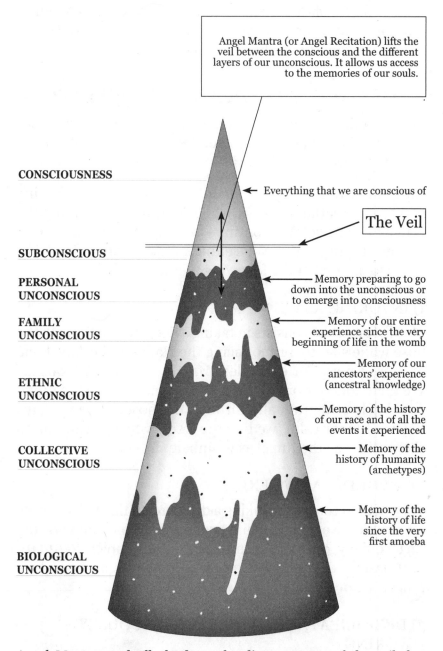

Angel Mantra (or Angel Recitation) lifts the veil between the conscious and the different layers of our unconscious. It allows us access to the memories of our souls.

CONSCIOUSNESS

← Everything that we are conscious of

The Veil

SUBCONSCIOUS

PERSONAL UNCONSCIOUS

Memory preparing to go down into the unconscious or to emerge into consciousness

FAMILY UNCONSCIOUS

Memory of our entire experience since the very beginning of life in the womb

Memory of our ancestors' experience (ancestral knowledge)

ETHNIC UNCONSCIOUS

Memory of the history of our race and of all the events it experienced

COLLECTIVE UNCONSCIOUS

Memory of the history of humanity (archetypes)

Memory of the history of life since the very first amoeba

BIOLOGICAL UNCONSCIOUS

Angel Mantra gradually leads to the disappearance of the veil that separates our consciousness from our subconscious and the different layers of our unconscious, hence providing access to the memories inscribed in our soul.

335

Angelic States of Conscience within. This work aims to purify our soul and to help us acquire full conscience so we can rediscover the Knowledge that is inscribed therein.

ANGEL MANTRA OR ANGEL RECITATION

Many traditions recommend the repetition of sacred names or phrases called mantras. Angel Recitation or Angel Mantra is at the heart of Angel Work.

Angel Mantra is very easy to do. Standing, sitting, or lying down, we breathe naturally while continually repeating the Name of an Angel. We continue for as long as we can and at our own rhythm. We invoke either in silence or out loud. We can also use one of the following methods:

1) INVOKING AS WE INHALE

This first method consists in taking a deep breath through the nose while silently pronouncing the Name of the Angel one or more times. For example: "MIKAËL, MIKAËL, MIKAËL..." We then hold our breath for a few seconds before breathing out slowly and gradually through the nose. Once we have regained inner calm, we breathe freely while continuing to silently invoke the Angel as we inhale.

2) INVOKING AS WE EXHALE

This method consists in taking a deep breath through the nose after which we exhale while pronouncing the Name of the Angel quietly, out loud, or in silence. For example: "VEHUIAH, VEHUIAH, VEHUIAH..." We inhale deeply once again and we repeat the process.

3) DEEP BREATHING WHILE CONTINUOUSLY INVOKING

This third method consists in repeating the Name of the Angel continually and silently while fully inhaling and then completely exhaling the air from the lungs. For those unaccustomed to deep breathing, this may cause dizziness. If so, the breathing rhythm can be slowed down or alternated with another method of invoking. It is important to respect our personal rhythm.

4) INVOKING WITH AN INTENTION IN MIND

This method consists in repeating the Name of the Angel quietly or silently, according to one of the methods above, while adding a message to the Angel. This message shares with Him our intention to develop a quality or a particular ability, to rectify or transcend a distortion. For example: *"Angel HARIEL, purify my soul and guide me towards purity. HARIEL, HARIEL, HARIEL. Help me become pure and help me integrate Wisdom within me. HARIEL, HARIEL, HARIEL. Purify me and teach me what I need to understand. HARIEL, HARIEL, HARIEL. Purify my soul. HARIEL, HARIEL, HARIEL..."*

5) INVOKING WITH A QUESTION IN MIND

This method consists in helping us find the answer to a question. First of all, we formulate a clear question, then we invoke according to one of the first three methods, all the while incorporating the question and the request so as to be enlightened and guided towards the answer. For example: *"Angel JELIEL, is it right for me to marry this person? JELIEL, JELIEL, JELIEL. Help me sense whether this is the right person for my evolution. JELIEL, JELIEL, JELIEL. Enlighten me. JELIEL, JELIEL, JELIEL. I wish to follow the Will of God. JELIEL, JELIEL, JELIEL. Is it right for me to marry this person? JELIEL, JELIEL, JELIEL..."*

When we do Angel Mantra with a question, we must call upon the same Angel for at least five days or until we receive an answer. By focusing on the question, for 5 days or more, the desired transformation may manifest itself and we gain access to the program that Cosmic Intelligence has prepared for us. This will activate dreams and signs that will answer our question.

Whichever method we choose, Angel Mantra remains a simple exercise that can be practiced in any context and in any of life's situations. It can be done while walking, driving, meditating, relaxing, doing sport or housework. It can be done before falling asleep or upon wakening. It can be done in difficult times or happy times. We must, however, remember that it is important to respect our own rhythm and to invoke with a sense of sacredness.

The intensified energy that occurs while working with an Angel manifests through intuition, dreams, signs and synchronicities or so-called coincidences encountered in our daily lives. It is fascinating to see the relevance between the Qualities of the Angel and what is shown to us in dreams and in everyday life, as much in their pure form as in their distorted form. Angel Mantra activates or intensifies the initiatic process. In that sense, the Name of the Angel serves as a magic formula. Working with Angels is an initiatic adventure that immerses us in the contemplation of multiple realities.

A wonderful way of optimizing the benefits of Angel Mantra is to do it throughout Angelica yoga exercises. These exercises are the subject of other publications under the designation *Angelica Yoga*, also published by Universe/City Mikaël (UCM), (for further information, we invite you to visit our website: www.ucm.ca).

CHOOSING AN ANGEL

In choosing the Angel to be invoked, it is suggested that a person follow Angel Calendar 1 (cf. pages 344-345). This is also called the Annual Angel Calendar. The use of this Calendar has the advantage of allowing us to familiarize ourselves throughout the year with the 72 States of Angelic Conscience. It provides us with a good work structure and allows Cosmic Intelligence to plan the many steps of our apprenticeship in advance and with precision.

Although the use of Angel Calendar 1 establishes an extraordinary work method, the choice of Angel remains a personal one and may very well be determined in relation to a particular situation. In fact, any Angel may be chosen because of His affinity to a situation that we wish to understand or resolve. For this purpose, you will find at the end of this book a list of situations and common problems associated with the Angel to invoke.

It is suggested that we only invoke one Angelic Energy at a time and for a period of at least five days in order to truly activate this particular Field of Conscience. Needless to say, five days are not enough to integrate all the Qualities and Virtues of an Angel, but through the work we do with the Angels over the years we eventually come to a point where we have visited all the different *sectors*, *departments* or *rays* of our conscience. We advance methodically along the path that leads to Enlightenment.

We can work for more than five days with the same Angel if we wish to go further into this particular Field of Conscience. It is preferable however, to change regularly as our conscience needs to visit all aspects of the Essences of the Creator so that one day we can fully manifest Them.

SHORT-TERM EFFECTS

When we do housework in our daily life, we can naturally expect to find things we've lost, and also a lot of dust. If, for example, we do Angel Mantra with Angel 7 ACHAIAH, whose principal Quality is patience, we may suddenly become much more impatient than usual. This is because the Angel opens the door of our conscience and lets the memories connected to impatience emerge. Liberating ourselves from them may take several minutes, several hours, or even several days. If we have no expectations, as if by magic, we suddenly feel good again because certain memories of our conscience corresponding to Angel ACHAIAH have been cleansed. During this period of adjustment, we will also tend to come across impatient people and go through situations that try our patience. This bears witness to the fact that we are directly linked to the essence or ray of the Angel chosen. So we should use these situations as sacred opportunities to get to know ourselves better.

Imagine that all of a sudden we discover a new room in our house, a room that we have never visited. Upon opening the door, we notice that it is full of dust, rats, etc. Simply opening the door lets so much dust into the other rooms that a full, top-to-bottom cleaning of the house has to be done. When we work with the Angels it is as if we choose not to close the door but to extend our house. We continue to clean until the entire house is completely clean. While doing the housework, we discover treasures and books in the new room. These represent knowledge and we decide to include them in our library.

During this period of intense cleansing, we alternate from one extreme soul-state to another. When we have an important dream or a nightmare, or when a particular event activates an opening of conscience, our entire being is perturbed. That is why we need to be aware and warn those close to us that we may display unusual behavior. In fact, we activate the Qualities of the Angelic Energy in ourselves, and this causes us to experience states of real bliss. But shortly afterwards, because we have to cleanse our distorted memories, we plunge into difficult soul-states and deep anxieties resurface. When we understand the process, we get used to it. Eventually, great stability is established. We rediscover our Angel wings and we feel good all the time. This, however, may require years of inner work.

All the while we are led to dream and to notice signs that are present in our environment. This occurs with irregular frequency. The symbolic study of dreams and of signs is complementary to the Work we do with the Angels since symbols are the words, the vocabulary of the language of the unconscious and of the soul. Thus, we learn to read signs in our daily life and we realize that coincidence does not exist.

GENERAL EFFECTS OF ANGEL WORK

When carried out on a daily basis, the Work we do with the Angels creates a gradual opening of our subconscious and of our unconscious that manifests in several ways:

- ⊙ As mentioned above, a first occurrence may be that we experience extreme mood swings. For example, we may go from a profound state of well-being to deep anxiety;

- ⊙ The keenness, the acuity of our five senses (sight, hearing, smell, taste and touch) is considerably increased and this leads us to develop clairvoyance, clairaudience and clairsentience;

- ⊙ The frequency and intensity of our dreams are gradually increased and we can better interpret them;

- ⊙ The interpretation of dreams and the reading of everyday signs will bring about deep, mystical experiences;

- ⊙ We acquire great spiritual autonomy, because the study of signs and dreams helps us to gradually learn the various steps of our initiatic journey;

- ⊙ Our soul acquires the capacity to leave our body and to visit the different dimensions of time and space, thereby discovering the secrets of the Universe.

Working with Angelic Energies takes us well beyond time and space. The Angels enable us to travel through the numerous dimensions of the Universe.

GUARDIAN ANGELS

At birth, a person receives three Guardian Angels. Their Qualities and associated human distortions show us the strengths and weaknesses that we are to transcend in this life.

1. The 1st Guardian Angel corresponds to our physical body. He guides the world of actions. We can identify Him in

Angel Calendar 1, according to our date of birth.

2. The 2nd Guardian Angel corresponds to our emotions and our feelings. He shows us the potential and virtues that we need to work on from an emotional point of view. We can find His Name in Angel Calendar 2, according to the day we were born.

3. The 3rd Guardian Angel corresponds to our intellect and is related to the world of thoughts. We can identify Him in Angel Calendar 3, according to our time of birth.

As with astrology, we use the time of birth as a simple indicator and starting point that also depends on our country of birth. It is important to note that these calendars were inspired by ancient astrology. However, their meaning goes much deeper in that they correspond to the symbolic aspect of daily life. For example, children normally go to school at 8 o'clock in the morning, eat at noon and go to bed early at night. In whatever country we were born in, we find a symbolic way of living that is similar. It is the same with our time of birth. In accordance with this universal behavior we take into account local time to find our third Guardian Angel. This is the One that corresponds to our intellect. The Angel calendars are universal and can be applied in every country.

The goal of Working with the States of Angelic Conscience consists in integrating not only our three Guardian Angels, but also the entire Knowledge represented by the 72 Angels of this Ancient Tradition.

ANGEL CALENDARS

ANGEL CALENDAR nº 1
Physical Level

March 21	to	March 25	1	VEHUIAH
March 26	to	March 30	2	JELIEL
March 31	to	April 04	3	SITAEL
April 05	to	April 09	4	ELEMIAH
April 10	to	April 14	5	MAHASIAH
April 15	to	April 20	6	LELAHEL
April 21	to	April 25	7	ACHAIAH
April 26	to	April 30	8	CAHETEL
May 01	to	May 05	9	HAZIEL
May 06	to	May 10	10	ALADIAH
May 11	to	May 15	11	LAUVIAH
May 16	to	May 20	12	HAHAIAH
May 21	to	May 25	13	IEZALEL
May 26	to	May 31	14	MEBAHEL
June 01	to	June 05	15	HARIEL
June 06	to	June 10	16	HEKAMIAH
June 11	to	June 15	17	LAUVIAH
June 16	to	June 21	18	CALIEL
June 22	to	June 26	19	LEUVIAH
June 27	to	July 01	20	PAHALIAH
July 02	to	July 06	21	NELKHAEL
July 07	to	July 11	22	YEIAYEL
July 12	to	July 16	23	MELAHEL
July 17	to	July 22	24	HAHEUIAH
July 23	to	July 27	25	NITHHAIAH
July 28	to	August 01	26	HAAIAH
August 02	to	August 06	27	YERATHEL
August 07	to	August 12	28	SEHEIAH
August 13	to	August 17	29	REIYEL
August 18	to	August 22	30	OMAEL
August 23	to	August 28	31	LECABEL
August 29	to	September 02	32	VASARIAH
September 03	to	September 07	33	YEHUIAH
September 08	to	September 12	34	LEHAHIAH
September 13	to	September 17	35	CHAVAKHIAH
September 18	to	September 23	36	MENADEL

ANGEL CALENDAR nº 1 (cont.)
Physical Level

September 24	to	September 28	37	ANIEL
September 29	to	October 03	38	HAAMIAH
October 04	to	October 08	39	REHAEL
October 09	to	October 13	40	IEIAZEL
October 14	to	October 18	41	HAHAHEL
October 19	to	October 23	42	MIKAEL
October 24	to	October 28	43	VEULIAH
October 29	to	November 02	44	YELAHIAH
November 03	to	November 07	45	SEALIAH
November 08	to	November 12	46	ARIEL
November 13	to	November 17	47	ASALIAH
November 18	to	November 22	48	MIHAEL
November 23	to	November 27	49	VEHUEL
November 28	to	December 02	50	DANIEL
December 03	to	December 07	51	HAHASIAH
December 08	to	December 12	52	IMAMIAH
December 13	to	December 16	53	NANAEL
December 17	to	December 21	54	NITHAEL
December 22	to	December 26	55	MEBAHIAH
December 27	to	December 31	56	POYEL
January 01	to	January 05	57	NEMAMIAH
January 06	to	January 10	58	YEIALEL
January 11	to	January 15	59	HARAHEL
January 16	to	January 20	60	MITZRAEL
January 21	to	January 25	61	UMABEL
January 26	to	January 30	62	IAHHEL
January 31	to	February 04	63	ANAUEL
February 05	to	February 09	64	MEHIEL
February 10	to	February 14	65	DAMABIAH
February 15	to	February 19	66	MANAKEL
February 20	to	February 24	67	EYAEL
February 25	to	February 29	68	HABUHIAH
March 01	to	March 05	69	ROCHEL
March 06	to	March 10	70	JABAMIAH
March 11	to	March 15	71	HAIAIEL
March 16	to	March 20	72	MUMIAH

ANGEL CALENDAR nº 2
Emotional Level

JANUARY	FEBRUARY	MARCH
1: #65 DAMABIAH	1: #25 NITH-HAIAH	1: #53 NANAEL
2: #66 MANAKEL	2: #26 HAAIAH	2: #54 NITHAEL
3: #67 EYAEL	3: #27 YERATHEL	3: #55 MEBAHIAH
4: #68 HABUHIAH	4: #28 SEHEIAH	4: #56 POYEL
5: #69 ROCHEL	5: #29 REIYEL	5: #57 NEMAMIAH
6: #70 JABAMIAH	6: #30 OMAEL	6: #58 YEIALEL
7: #71 HAIAIEL	7: #31 LECABEL	7: #59 HARAHEL
8: #72 MUMIAH	8: #32 VASARIAH	8: #60 MITZRAEL
9: #1 VEHUIAH	9: #33 YEHUIAH	9: #61 UMABEL
10: #2 JELIEL	10: #34 LEHAHIAH	10: #62 IAHHEL
11: #3 SITAEL	11: #35 CHAVAKHIAH	11: #63 ANAUEL
12: #4 ELEMIAH	12: #36 MENADEL	12: #64 MEHIEL
13: #5 MAHASIAH	13: #37 ANIEL	13: #65 DAMABIAH
14: #6 LELAHEL	14: #38 HAAMIAH	14: #66 MANAKEL
15: #7 ACHAIAH	15: #39 REHAEL	15: #67 EYAEL
16: #8 CAHETEL	16: #40 IEIAZEL	16: #68 HABUHIAH
17: #9 HAZIEL	17: #41 HAHAHEL	17: #69 ROCHEL
18: #10 ALADIAH	18: #42 MIKAEL	18: #70 JABAMIAH
19: #11 LAUVIAH	19: #43 VEULIAH	19: #71 HAIAIEL
20: #12 HAHAIAH	20: #44 YELAHIAH	20: #72 MUMIAH
21: #13 IEZALEL	21: #45 SEALIAH	21: #1 VEHUIAH
22: #14 MEBAHEL	22: #46 ARIEL	22: #2 JELIEL
23: #15 HARIEL	23: #47 ASALIAH	23: #3 SITAEL
24: #16 HEKAMIAH	24: #48 MIHAEL	24: #4 ELEMIAH
#17 LAUVIAH	25: #49 VEHUEL	25: #5 MAHASIAH
25: #18 CALIEL	26: #50 DANIEL	26: #6 LELAHEL
26: #19 LEUVIAH	27: #51 HAHASIAH	27: #7 ACHAIAH
27: #20 PAHALIAH	28: #52 IMAMIAH	28: #8 CAHETEL
28: #21 NELKHAEL	29: #52 IMAMIAH	29: #9 HAZIEL
29: #22 YEIAYEL		30: #10 ALADIAH
30: #23 MELAHEL		31: #11 LAUVIAH
31: #24 HAHEUIAH		

How to find the Guardian Angel that governs your emotions

It is very easy to find this Guardian Angel. In Calendar nº 2, shown above, the first figure corresponds to your date of birth. The second figure corresponds to the number of your Angel. For example, the Angel that governs May 5 on the emotional level is Angel 45 SEALIAH. **Particularities: 1)** The asterisk (*) included with seven of the dates means that from midnight to midday of that day the

346

ANGEL CALENDAR nº 2 (cont.)
Emotional Level

APRIL	MAY	JUNE
1: #12 Hahaiah	1: #41 Hahahel	1: #71 Haiaiel
2: #13 Iezalel	2: #42 Mikael	2: #72 Mumiah
3: #14 Mebahel	3: #43 Veuliah	3: #1 Vehuiah
4: #15 Hariel	4: #44 Yelahiah	4: #2 Jeliel
5: #16 Hekamiah	5: #45 Sealiah	5: #3 Sitael
6: #17 Lauviah	6: #46 Ariel	6: #4 Elemiah
7: #18 Caliel	7: #47 Asaliah	7: #5 Mahasiah
8: #19 Leuviah	8: #48 Mihael	8: #6 Lelahel
9: #20 Pahaliah	9: #49 Vehuel	9: #7 Achaiah
10: #21 Nelkhael	10: #50 Daniel	10: #8 Cahetel
11: #22 Yeiayel	11: #51 Hahasiah	11: #9 Haziel
12: #23 Melahel	12: #52 Imamiah	12: #10 Aladiah
13: #24 Haheuiah	13: #53 Nanael	13: *
14: #25 Nith-Haiah	14: #54 Nithael	14: #11 Lauviah
15: #26 Haaiah	15: #55 Mebahiah	15: #12 Hahaiah
16: #27 Yerathel	16: #56 Poyel	16: #13 Iezalel
17: *	17: #57 Nemamiah	17: #14 Mebahel
18: #28 Seheiah	18: #58 Yeialel	18: #15 Hariel
19: #29 Reiyel	19: #59 Harahel	19: #16 Hekamiah
20: #30 Omael	20: *	20: #17 Lauviah
21: #31 Lecabel	21: #60 Mitzrael	21: #18 Caliel
22: #32 Vasariah	22: #61 Umabel	22: #19 Leuviah
23: #33 Yehuiah	23: #62 Iahhel	23: #20 Pahaliah
24: #34 Lehahiah	24: #63 Anauel	24: #21 Nelkhael
25: #35 Chavakhiah	25: #64 Mehiel	25: #22 Yeiayel
26: #36 Menadel	26: #65 Damabiah	26: #23 Melahel
27: #37 Aniel	27: #66 Manakel	27: #24 Haheuiah
28: #38 Haamiah	28: #67 Eyael	28: #25 Nith-Haiah
29: #39 Rehael	29: #68 Habuhiah	29: #26 Haaiah
30: #40 Ieiazel	30: #69 Rochel	30: #27 Yerathel
	31: #70 Jabamiah	

Angel of the preceding day presides, while the Angel of the following day presides from midday to midnight. For example, Angel #27 presides all day on April 16 and until midday on April 17, while Angel #28 presides on April 17 from midday until midnight and all day on April 18. **2)** Where dates refer to two Angels – i.e. January 24 and December 27 – the first Angel governs from midnight to 6 pm, and the second from 6 pm to midnight.

ANGEL CALENDAR nº 2 (cont.)
Emotional Level

JULY	AUGUST	SEPTEMBER
1: #28	1: #57	1: #15
2: #29	2: #58	2: #16
3: #30	3: #59	3: #17
4: #31	4: #60	4: #18
5: *	5: #61	5: #19
6: #32	6: #62	6: #20
7: #33	7: #63	7: #21
8: #34	8: #64	8: #22
9: #35	9: #65	9: #23
10: #36	10: #66	10: #24
11: #37	11: #67	11: #25
12: #38	12: #68	12: #26
13: #39	13: #69	13: #27
14: #40	14: #70	14: #28
15: #41	15: #71	15: #29
16: #42	16: #72	16: #30
17: #43	17: #1	17: #31
18: #44	18: #2	18: #32
19: #45	19: *	19: #33
20: #46	20: #3	20: #34
21: #47	21: #4	21: *
22: #48	22: #5	22: #35
23: #49	23: #6	23: #36
24: #50	24: #7	24: #37
25: #51	25: #8	25: #38
26: *	26: #9	26: #39
27: #52	27: #10	27: #40
28: #53	28: #11	28: #41
29: #54	29: #12	29: #42
30: #55	30: #13	30: #43
31: #56	31: #14	

How to find the Guardian Angel that governs your emotions

It is very easy to find this Guardian Angel. In Calendar nº 2, shown above, the first figure corresponds to your date of birth. The second figure corresponds to the number of your Angel. For example, the Angel that governs May 5 on the emotional level is Angel 45 SEALIAH. **Particularities: 1)** The asterisk (*) included with seven of the dates means that from midnight to midday of that day the

ANGEL CALENDAR nº 2 (cont.)
Emotional Level

OCTOBER	NOVEMBER	DECEMBER
1: #44 Yelahiah	1: #3 Sitael	1: #33 Yehuiah
2: #45 Sealiah	2: #4 Elemiah	2: #34 Lehahiah
3: #46 Ariel	3: #5 Mahasiah	3: #35 Chavakhiah
4: #47 Asaliah	4: #6 Lelahel	4: #36 Menadel
5: #48 Mihael	5: #7 Achaiah	5: #37 Aniel
6: #49 Vehuel	6: #8 Cahetel	6: #38 Haamiah
7: #50 Daniel	7: #9 Haziel	7: #39 Rehael
8: #51 Hahasiah	8: #10 Aladiah	8: #40 Ieiazel
9: #52 Imamiah	9: #11 Lauviah	9: #41 Hahahel
10: #53 Nanael	10: #12 Hahaiah	10: #42 Mikael
11: #54 Nithael	11: #13 Iezalel	11: #43 Veuliah
12: #55 Mebahiah	12: #14 Mebahel	12: #44 Yelahiah
13: #56 Poyel	13: #15 Hariel	13: #45 Sealiah
14: #57 Nemamiah	14: #16 Hekamiah	14: #46 Ariel
15: #58 Yeialel	15: #17 Lauviah	15: #47 Asaliah
16: #59 Harahel	16: #18 Caliel	16: #48 Mihael
17: #60 Mitzrael	17: #19 Leuviah	17: #49 Vehuel
18: #61 Umabel	18: #20 Pahaliah	18: #50 Daniel
19: #62 Iahhel	19: #21 Nelkhael	19: #51 Hahasiah
20: #63 Anauel	20: #22 Yeiayel	20: #52 Imamiah
21: #64 Mehiel	21: #23 Melahel	21: #53 Nanael
22: #65 Damabiah	22: #24 Haheuiah	22: #54 Nithael
23: #66 Manakel	23: #25 Nith-Haiah	23: #55 Mebahiah
24: #67 Eyael	24: #26 Haaiah	24: #56 Poyel
25: #68 Habuhiah	25: #27 Yerathel	25: #57 Nemamiah
26: #69 Rochel	26: #28 Seheiah	26: #58 Yeialel
27: #70 Jabamiah	27: #29 Reiyel	27: #59 Harahel
28: #71 Haiaiel	28: #30 Omael	#60 Mitzrael
29: #72 Mumiah	29: #31 Lecabel	28: #61 Umabel
30: #1 Vehuiah	30: #32 Vasariah	29: #62 Iahhel
31: #2 Jeliel		30: #63 Anauel
		31: #64 Mehiel

Angel of the preceding day presides, while the Angel of the following day presides from midday to midnight. For example, Angel #27 presides all day on April 16 and until midday on April 17, while Angel #28 presides on April 17 from midday until midnight and all day on April 18. 2) Where dates refer to two Angels – i.e. January 24 and December 27 – the first Angel governs from midnight to 6 pm, and the second from 6 pm to midnight.

ANGEL CALENDAR nº 3
Intellectual Level

Midnight	to	0:19 am	1	VEHUIAH
0:20 am	to	0:39 am	2	JELIEL
0:40 am	to	0:59 am	3	SITAEL
1:00 am	to	1:19 am	4	ELEMIAH
1:20 am	to	1:39 am	5	MAHASIAH
1:40 am	to	1:59 am	6	LELAHEL
2:00 am	to	2:19 am	7	ACHAIAH
2:20 am	to	2:39 am	8	CAHETEL
2:40 am	to	2:59 am	9	HAZIEL
3:00 am	to	3:19 am	10	ALADIAH
3:20 am	to	3:39 am	11	LAUVIAH
3:40 am	to	3:59 am	12	HAHAIAH
4:00 am	to	4:19 am	13	IEZALEL
4:20 am	to	4:39 am	14	MEBAHEL
4:40 am	to	4:59 am	15	HARIEL
5:00 am	to	5:19 am	16	HEKAMIAH
5:20 am	to	5:39 am	17	LAUVIAH
5:40 am	to	5:59 am	18	CALIEL
6:00 am	to	6:19 am	19	LEUVIAH
6:20 am	to	6:39 am	20	PAHALIAH
6:40 am	to	6:59 am	21	NELKHAEL
7:00 am	to	7:19 am	22	YEIAYEL
7:20 am	to	7:39 am	23	MELAHEL
7:40 am	to	7:59 am	24	HAHEUIAH
8:00 am	to	8:19 am	25	NITH-HAIAH
8:20 am	to	8:39 am	26	HAAIAH
8:40 am	to	8:59 am	27	YERATHEL
9:00 am	to	9:19 am	28	SEHEIAH
9:20 am	to	9:39 am	29	REIYEL
9:40 am	to	9:59 am	30	OMAEL
10:00 am	to	10:19 am	31	LECABEL
10:20 am	to	10:39 am	32	VASARIAH
10:40 am	to	10:59 am	33	YEHUIAH
11:00 am	to	11:19 am	34	LEHAHIAH
11:20 am	to	11:39 am	35	CHAVAKHIAH
11:40 am	to	11:59 am	36	MENADEL

ANGEL CALENDAR nº 3 (cont.)
Intellectual Level

Noon	to	12:19 pm	37	ANIEL
12:20 pm	to	12:39 pm	38	HAAMIAH
12:40 pm	to	12:59 pm	39	REHAEL
1:00 pm	to	1:19 pm	40	IEIAZEL
1:20 pm	to	1:39 pm	41	HAHAHEL
1:40 pm	to	1:59 pm	42	MIKAEL
2:00 pm	to	2:19 pm	43	VEULIAH
2:20 pm	to	2:39 pm	44	YELAHIAH
2:40 pm	to	2:59 pm	45	SEALIAH
3:00 pm	to	3:19 pm	46	ARIEL
3:20 pm	to	3:39 pm	47	ASALIAH
3:40 pm	to	3:59 pm	48	MIHAEL
4:00 pm	to	4:19 pm	49	VEHUEL
4:20 pm	to	4:39 pm	50	DANIEL
4:40 pm	to	4:59 pm	51	HAHASIAH
5:00 pm	to	5:19 pm	52	IMAMIAH
5:20 pm	to	5:39 pm	53	NANAEL
5:40 pm	to	5:59 pm	54	NITHAEL
6:00 pm	to	6:19 pm	55	MEBAHIAH
6:20 pm	to	6:39 pm	56	POYEL
6:40 pm	to	6:59 pm	57	NEMAMIAH
7:00 pm	to	7:19 pm	58	YEIALEL
7:20 pm	to	7:39 pm	59	HARAHEL
7:40 pm	to	7:59 pm	60	MITZRAEL
8:00 pm	to	8:19 pm	61	UMABEL
8:20 pm	to	8:39 pm	62	IAHHEL
8:40 pm	to	8:59 pm	63	ANAUEL
9:00 pm	to	9:19 pm	64	MEHIEL
9:20 pm	to	9:39 pm	65	DAMABIAH
9:40 pm	to	9:59 pm	66	MANAKEL
10:00 pm	to	10:19 pm	67	EYAEL
10:20 pm	to	10:39 pm	68	HABUHIAH
10:40 pm	to	10:59 pm	69	ROCHEL
11:00 pm	to	11:19 pm	70	JABAMIAH
11:20 pm	to	11:39 pm	71	HAIAIEL
11:40 pm	to	11:59 pm	72	MUMIAH

THE 72 ANGELS

When we travel in an unknown country, geographical maps are very useful, if not indispensable. The same applies when we explore our conscience. The latter is so vast that when we wish to work on it, we need markers so as not to get lost. Each *ray, sector* or *department* of our conscience is specific, and the Work we do with the Angels provides us with a list of the Qualities of each Angel as well as the associated human distortions so we can better understand the structure of our conscience and visit the memories that constitute who we are. This is what you will find in this chapter. Regular consultation of these lists familiarizes us with each of the 72 Angels and structures our Work.

These very ancient lists are the product of centuries of rigorous research and work on conscience. As presented here, they have been adapted to our contemporary era with a view to universal use.

How do we use these lists? If we invoke an Angel for at least five days, we focus on this Angel. In other words, we focus on this specific *ray* or aspect of our conscience. It is then possible to observe the manifestation of the Angel. Depending on the contents of the memories lodged within the chosen *department*, the Angel manifests in all Purity or activates our distortions. One thing is sure, He does manifest. Thus, and this is what is extraordinary, in our dreams and in everyday life, we encounter the exact characteristics of the Angel invoked. By paying attention to our dreams and to the situations we experience, we can recognize in them the contents of the lists presented here. This allows us to consciously participate in the work the Angel is doing.

NB: It is important to interpret the qualities and human distortions first and foremost in terms of conscience. In other words, they are not to be taken literally.

1 VEHUIAH

Qualities

- Divine Will
- Brings the Primordial Creative Fire
- Capacity to undertake, initiate, begin
- Success for all new creations
- Guides toward innovative work in an avant-garde field
- Sets an example, serves as a model and a leader
- Enables us to get out of an impasse and confusion
- Renewed energy that enables us to heal illness, ill-being and depression
- Abundance of energy, courage, audacity, bravery
- Loves as if it were the first time
- Understanding the importance of ourselves, hence the importance of others, individuality and intimacy
- Capacity to concentrate, to focus on an objective
- Helps us understand true success and leadership

Human distortions

- *Imposes one's will, tendency to force, counter or defy Destiny*
- *Stubborn, relentless, authoritarian, imposing*
- *Triggers anger, turbulence*
- *Intervenes in affairs that will end badly*
- *Rushes into things without thinking, dangerous passion*
- *Excessive reactions, impetuosity, violent situations, destruction of entourage*
- *Lack of dynamism and willpower*
- *Inability to decide on, to determine one's direction, one's orientation*

Physical: March 21 to March 25
Emotional: January 9, March 21, June 3, August 17, October 30
Intellectual: Midnight to 12:19 am
Residence: Kether / **Specificity**: Hochmah

2 JELIEL

Qualities

- ⊙ Love, Wisdom
- ⊙ Related to the couple, to relationships
- ⊙ Capacity to materialize and consolidate any reality whatsoever
- ⊙ Providential association
- ⊙ Grants reliability, tranquility and fertility
- ⊙ Grants the fidelity of one's spouse
- ⊙ Settles any dispute or conflict
- ⊙ Altruistic, seeks to manifest love everywhere
- ⊙ Mediator, conciliator
- ⊙ Unifies masculine and feminine principles
- ⊙ Conviviality, harmonious life
- ⊙ Powerful use of speech that inspires calm
- ⊙ Helps calm inner turmoil
- ⊙ Capacity to persuade, insight into theoretical analysis

Human distortions

- − *Lack of love, absence of wisdom*
- − *Difficulty in the couple and in relationships with others*
- − *Perverse mores and behavior, corruption*
- − *Bad associations*
- − *Perpetual conflict, quarrels, oppression, tyranny*
- − *Disagreement, separation, divorce*
- − *Problems with sexuality and intimate relationships*
- − *Selfish celibacy, refuses children out of egoism*
- − *Difficulty meeting a spouse*

Physical: March 26 to March 30
Emotional: January 10, March 22, June 4, August 18, August 19 from midnight to midday, October 31
Intellectual: 12:20 am to 12:39 am
Residence: Kether / **Specificity**: Binah

3 SITAEL

Qualities

- ⊙ Construction
- ⊙ Master builder on the inside and on the outside
- ⊙ High Science
- ⊙ Grants us the capacity to expand, the ability to make everything fructify
- ⊙ Planner, great strategist, gifted with a practical mind
- ⊙ Honest, upright administrator
- ⊙ Support which helps us overcome all difficulties and adversities
- ⊙ Capacity to engender a child, a project
- ⊙ Helps us become aware of our errors and transform our karmas
- ⊙ Nobility, magnanimity, generosity, clemency
- ⊙ Faithful to one's word, keeps promises, peacemaker
- ⊙ Work with important responsibilities
- ⊙ Architect and engineer in the service of the Divine
- ⊙ Gift for negotiating, enthusiasm
- ⊙ Social and political renown

Human distortions

- – *Destruction, collapse of structures, unfavorable period, ruin*
- – *Greed, excess, diabolic strategy*
- – *Error in preparation, planning, and evaluation*
- – *Difficulty conceiving a child, a project*
- – *Aggression, ungratefulness, boastfulness*
- – *Hypocrisy, emphasis placed on appearances, lack of authenticity*
- – *Reneges on one's promises, does not keep one's word*

Physical: March 31 to April 4
Emotional: January 11, March 23, June 5, August 19 from midday to midnight, August 20, November 1
Intellectual: 12:40 am to 12:59 am
Residence: Kether / **Specificity**: Hesed

4 ELEMIAH

Qualities

⊙ Divine Power
⊙ High Science
⊙ Fair, just, impartial authority
⊙ Rectification, discovery of a new path
⊙ Force that helps us take action, ability to make decisions
⊙ Participation in the creation of Destiny
⊙ Study and revelation of life plans
⊙ Discovery of professional orientation
⊙ Initiative, enterprise, commitment
⊙ Optimism, end of a difficult period
⊙ Disappearance of agitation and torment
⊙ Helps us identify those who have betrayed us so we can make peace with them

Human distortions

– *Diabolic power directed toward the satisfaction of personal needs*
– *Inertia, destructive tendencies*
– *Professional failure, bankruptcy, setbacks, period of destruction*
– *Pessimism, turmoil, dangerous discoveries*
– *Betrayal, existence of inner traitors*
– *Avidity and abuse of power*
– *Domination by others*
– *Exhaustion, stretched to the limit, out of resources*
– *Feelings of superiority and inferiority*

Physical: April 5 to April 9
Emotional: January 12, March 24, June 6, August 21, November 2
Intellectual: 1:00 am to 1:19 am
Residence: Kether / **Specificity**: Geburah

5 MAHASIAH

Qualities

- ☉ Rectification of errors
- ☉ Reforms, re-establishes Divine Order
- ☉ Rectifies what is growing crooked before it materializes
- ☉ Facilitates learning
- ☉ Capacity to live in peace and enjoy simple, natural things
- ☉ Success in exams
- ☉ Admittance into initiatic school
- ☉ Dream analysis, study of symbolic language
- ☉ Decodes everyday signs
- ☉ Aptitude for Initiatic science
- ☉ Improvement of one's character, a beautiful, happy life
- ☉ Aptitude for languages

Human distortions

- – *Difficulty rectifying, repairing, acknowledging, regretting one's errors or forgiving*
- – *Tendency to want or seek revenge, resentment, prejudice, arrogance*
- – *Wicked, pernicious*
- – *Ignorance*
- – *Licentiousness, sexual abuse*
- – *Denial of one's errors, bad-tempered, difficult to live with*
- – *Difficulty learning, poor choices, authoritarianism*
- – *Joining a spiritual movement to escape reality*
- – *Precarious health*

Physical: April 10 to April 14
Emotional: January 13, March 25, June 7, August 22, November 3
Intellectual: 1:20 am to 1:39 am
Residence: Kether / **Specificity**: Tiphereth

6 LELAHEL

Qualities

- ⊙ Divine Light that heals everything (Light of Love)
- ⊙ Insight, clear understanding
- ⊙ Renown, happiness, fortune
- ⊙ Embellishment, natural beauty
- ⊙ Mirror of the soul
- ⊙ Art of expressing oneself well in society
- ⊙ Celebrity through talent and achievements
- ⊙ Artist

Human distortions

- – *Lack of love, which prevents healing and understanding*
- – *Ambition*
- – *Masks, multiple personalities*
- – *Exterior beauty only*
- – *Believes oneself indispensable*
- – *Feelings of superiority and inferiority*
- – *Useless spending, wasting, squandering*
- – *Tendency to take everything for granted*
- – *Illicitly acquired wealth (dirty money)*
- – *Ruthless ambition, social climbing, pride*
- – *Focused solely on the material aspect of things and people*
- – *Uses one's charm for one's own ends, for selfish purposes*
- – *Lives beyond one's means*
- – *Unstable situation*

Physical: April 15 to April 20
Emotional: January 14, March 26, June 8, August 23, November 4
Intellectual: 1:40 am to 1:59 am
Residence: Kether / **Specificity**: Netzach

7 ACHAIAH

Qualities

⊙ Patience
⊙ Discovery of the role of patience in the Creation of the Universe
⊙ Exploration of the inner dimensions, helps discover Truth
⊙ Good use of waiting periods
⊙ Ease in the execution of difficult tasks
⊙ Beneficial force/energy in the use of computers and programming
⊙ Faculty of introspection and discernment, which enables us to discover hidden, occulted aspects
⊙ Propagator of Light (Knowledge)
⊙ Facilitates media diffusion through computers, television, radio, the press and publishing
⊙ Helps us pass examinations and solve difficult problems, inspires us with a taste for learning
⊙ Discovery of hidden secrets, helps find original solutions

Human distortions

− *Impatience, rebellion, resignation*
− *Laziness, negligence, thoughtlessness, heedlessness, recklessness, ignorance*
− *No desire to learn, does not study*
− *Failure in exams, bewilderment, consternation, distress in new situations*
− *Paralysis in the face of adversity*
− *Problems with computers and programming*
− *Excluded from positions of authority*
− *Media manipulation, seeks personal glory*
− *Lacks understanding*
− *Does not keep promises*

Physical: April 21 to April 25
Emotional: January 15, March 27, June 9, August 24, November 5
Intellectual: 2:00 am to 2:19 am
Residence: Kether / **Specificity**: Hod

8 CAHETEL

Qualities

- ⊙ Divine Blessing
- ⊙ Gratitude
- ⊙ Materializes God's Will
- ⊙ Conception, giving birth
- ⊙ Easy success, progress, helps to change one's lifestyle
- ⊙ Great capacity for work, active life
- ⊙ Material wealth
- ⊙ Fertile lands, abundant harvests, food for the soul
- ⊙ In harmony with the Cosmic Laws
- ⊙ Patron of the four elements: fire, air, water and earth
- ⊙ Sets us free from evil spirits

Human distortions

- – *Lack of gratitude*
- – *Self-interest, self-centered, predator*
- – *Material failure, ruin*
- – *Acts against Destiny, rebels against one's life plan and the Divine, Cosmic Program*
- – *Useless, sterile activities*
- – *Excessive willfulness, rigidity*
- – *Tyranny, pride, bad temper, blasphemy*
- – *Wealth used solely for material purposes*
- – *Torrential rains, floods, polluted waters*
- – *Catastrophic climate, fires*
- – *Confused, ambiguous feelings, aggression, transgression*
- – *Defies, violates and acts against the law, corruption, crushes others*

Physical: April 26 to April 30
Emotional: January 16, March 28, June 10, August 25, November 6
Intellectual: 2:20 am to 2:39 am
Residence: Kether / **Specificity**: Yesod

9 HAZIEL

Qualities

- ⊙ Universal Love
- ⊙ Divine Mercy
- ⊙ Gift of forgiveness, reconciliation
- ⊙ Good faith
- ⊙ Trust, sincerity
- ⊙ Goodness that absolves all evil
- ⊙ Powerful energy that transforms all negativity
- ⊙ Support, encouragement, friendship, grace, favors from those in power
- ⊙ Promises, commitment
- ⊙ Altruism, selflessness
- ⊙ Childlike purity

Human distortions

- – *Difficulty loving and being loved and/or absence of love*
- – *Possessiveness, jealousy, passion, fear of loving and being loved*
- – *Hatred, war, non-reconciliation*
- – *Hypocritical, deceives others*
- – *Manipulates to obtain favors from those in power*
- – *Resentment, malevolence, hostility*

Physical: May 1 to May 5
Emotional: January 17, March 29, June 11, August 26, November 7
Intellectual: 2:40 am to 2:59 am
Residence: Hochmah / **Specificity**: Hochmah

10 ALADIAH

Qualities

- Divine Grace that absolves and pardons all faults
- Dissolves all karma
- Spiritual and material abundance
- Innocence
- Reinsertion in society
- Great healing power
- Regeneration, flourishing health
- Helps the underprivileged
- New beginnings, a second chance

Human distortions

- *Attitudes and behavior that engender problems and difficult karmas*
- *Repeated errors and misactions*
- *Dangerous spirituality, false guru*
- *Waste, squandering*
- *Broken promises*
- *Hidden crimes*
- *Moral decadence*
- *Negligence*
- *Nonchalance, indifference, laxity*
- *Poor health, difficult karma*
- *Bulimia, sexual excesses, lust*
- *Wrong-doer, lawbreaker, prisoner*

Physical: May 6 to May 10
Emotional: January 18, March 30, June 12, June 13 from midnight to midday, August 27, November 8
Intellectual: 3:00 am to 3:19 am
Residence: Hochmah / **Specificity**: Binah

11 LAUVIAH

Qualities

⊙ Victory
⊙ Renown, celebrity, success
⊙ Expertise
⊙ Life of devotion
⊙ Altruism, goodness, kindness
⊙ Receives the Light of God
⊙ Confidence, enthusiasm, joy
⊙ Successful initiations
⊙ Exalted love for Divine Creation and Divine Work
⊙ Businesses that are useful and profitable for humanity
⊙ Can obtain all one wants from the great people of this world
⊙ Cosmic Organization

Human distortions

– *Difficulty succeeding and being successful, failure*
– *Plays roles in order to please, lack of authenticity, hyper-positivity*
– *Excessive focus on renown and celebrity; or, a tendency to reject them, to be satisfied with a humdrum life*
– *Aiming too high or too low*
– *Envy, jealousy, pride, slander, using trickery to succeed*
– *Extravagance, ambition, greedy for power*
– *Excessive materialism, only wanting to enjoy physical resources*
– *Emotional outbursts and dependency*
– *Lack of confidence and/or difficulty trusting others*
– *Perverse works*
– *Lightning, reprimanded by Cosmic Intelligence*

Physical: May 11 to May 15
Emotional: January 19, March 31, June 13 from midday to midnight, June 14, August 28, November 9
Intellectual: 3:20 am to 3:39 am
Residence: Hochmah / **Specificity**: Hesed

12 HAHAIAH

Qualities

- Refuge, period of calm, rest
- Meditation, interiorization, love of solitude
- Helps us sleep, replenish ourselves, renew our energy, and balance our intimate and social lives
- Inspires us to take care of our inner self and of our house, our home
- Appreciation of cleanliness and order
- Inner harmony through self-evaluation
- Transforms destructive attitudes
- Isolates negative tendencies in a circle of energy
- Examination of one's personal life
- Dissolves aggression
- Facilitates the interpretation of dreams, grants access to occult mysteries
- Grants peace and protection
- Increases psychic abilities
- Positive attitude, discretion

Human distortions

- *Tendency to withdrawal, isolation, self-isolation, alienation, escapism, flight, refusal to face one's responsibilities; or, hyperactivity to camouflage one's problems, worries, insecurities and emotional wounds or issues*
- *Over-independence, hermit attitude*
- *A period of stress, agitation, lack of time for oneself, incapacity to interiorize, to meditate*
- *Excess or lack of social life*
- *Unsociable, anti-social behavior*
- *Tendency to harbor, brood over and nourish emotional problems or refusal to face them, tendency to sulk*
- *Impulsiveness, aggression*
- *Addictions, dependencies*
- *Negativity, indiscretion*
- *Lies, breach of trust, betrayal, bitterness, resentment, resignation, grudge, rancor*
- *Hallucinations*
- *Deceitful practice and wild imaginings of an unbalanced medium*
- *Confusion between dreams and reality*
- *Phobias: agoraphobia, claustrophobia, etc.*

Physical: May 16 to May 20
Emotional: January 20, April 1, June 15, August 29, November 10
Intellectual: 3:40 am to 3:59 am
Residence: Hochmah / **Specificity**: Geburah

13 IEZALEL

Qualities

- ⊙ Fidelity
- ⊙ Reconciliation, affinity
- ⊙ Facilitates learning
- ⊙ Happy memories
- ⊙ Friendship, get-togethers
- ⊙ Faithful servant
- ⊙ Preparation for encounters
- ⊙ Faithful to Divine Principles
- ⊙ Gives life to unity, to union
- ⊙ Complementarity and balance of the masculine and the feminine
- ⊙ Order, harmony

Human distortions

- – *Infidelity*
- – *Enslavement, passion*
- – *Excessive focus on personal needs and social life*
- – *Wants to please everyone*
- – *Hurts children, destroys a marriage and family, separation, divorce*
- – *Engenders karma with heavy consequences*
- – *Ignorance, error*
- – *Limited mind*
- – *Tendency not to learn from the lessons of experience*
- – *Distance, alienation from loved ones*
- – *Lies, cheating*
- – *Does not want to learn*
- – *Negative influence on other people or situations*

Physical: May 21 to May 25
Emotional: January 21, April 2, June 16, August 30, November 11
Intellectual: 4:00 am to 4:19 am
Residence: Hochmah / **Specificity**: Tiphereth

14 MEBAHEL

Qualities

- Commitment
- Humanitarian aid, altruism
- Motto: Truth, Freedom, Justice
- Unconditional love
- Inspiration from Higher Worlds
- Liberates prisoners and the oppressed
- Helps those who have lost hope
- Equity, appreciation of exactitude, accuracy, precision, and right choices, re-establishment of natural order
- Respect for the environment
- Exorcism
- Mediation, arbitration
- Abundance, enrichment, elevation of the senses

Human distortions

- *Difficulty committing oneself, disengagement, withdrawal*
- *Reneges on, does not keep promises*
- *Helps others either too much or not enough*
- *Feeling of being disliked, ill-loved or rejected*
- *Problems with truth and justice, lies, false testimony, slander*
- *Lawsuits, accusations, captivity, imprisonment*
- *Lawbreaker, criminal*
- *Usurpation, inner struggle, adversity, oppression*
- *Diabolical forces*
- *Tyrant/victim dynamics*
- *Identifies with social rules and conventions*
- *Goes against the tide*

Physical: May 26 to May 31
Emotional: January 22, April 3, June 17, August 31, November 12
Intellectual: 4:20 am to 4:39 am
Residence: Hochmah / **Specificity**: Netzach

15 HARIEL

Qualities

- ⊙ Purification
- ⊙ Moral purity, innocence
- ⊙ Spiritual feelings
- ⊙ Discovery of new methods, useful inventions
- ⊙ Inspiration for scientists and artists
- ⊙ Absolves the conscience by simultaneously instilling Law and Knowledge
- ⊙ Procures great insight, awakens discernment
- ⊙ Re-establishes communication between individuality and personality
- ⊙ Liberates from paralysis, from anything that prevents action
- ⊙ Liberates from all forms of addiction and dependencies

Human distortions

- – *Puritanism*
- – *Excessive perfectionism, over focused on details, lack of global vision*
- – *A complicated person*
- – *Becoming an accomplice to the forces of darkness*
- – *Willing to die to impose or defend an unnatural truth*
- – *Terrorism, extremism*
- – *Sectarian mind*
- – *Failure, collapse*
- – *Fights against natural order*
- – *A desiccating mentality, a searing, blistering attitude, over-analytical mind, excessive tendency to dissect or scrutinize every detail*
- – *Erroneous discernment, mistaken judgment, inverted principles*
- – *Separatism*

Physical: June 1 to June 5
Emotional: January 23, April 4, June 18, September 1, November 13
Intellectual: 4:40 am to 4:59 am
Residence: Hochmah / **Specificity**: Hod

16 HEKAMIAH

Qualities

- ☉ Loyalty to Divine Principles
- ☉ Royal attitude
- ☉ Respects commitments
- ☉ Coordinator, pacifier
- ☉ Candor, nobility
- ☉ Granted responsibilities
- ☉ Liberator
- ☉ Universal Love
- ☉ Becomes a leader, a person in charge, a president
- ☉ Political and social organization

Human distortions

- – *Treachery, betrayal, war, rebellion*
- – *A lifestyle marked by arrogance, snobbery*
- – *Complexes of superiority and inferiority*
- – *Envy, jealousy*
- – *Excessive materialism*
- – *Agonizing struggle, torn by remorse or indecision*
- – *Obstructs the realization of our higher nature*
- – *Selfish, self-centered love, passion*
- – *Plotting, scheming*
- – *Provokes dissension in a group, discord, disagreement*
- – *Feeling of being diminished, servility*
- – *Irresponsible*
- – *Idolatrous, egocentric, megalomaniac*

Physical: June 6 to June 10
Emotional: January 24 from midnight to 6 pm, April 5, June 19,
September 2, November 14
Intellectual: 5:00 am to 5:19 am
Residence: Hochmah / **Specificity**: Yesod

17 LAUVIAH

Qualities
Revelations

- ⊙ Faculty for intuitive understanding, without analyzing or studying, telepathy, knows how the psyche works
- ⊙ Acts against torment and sadness
- ⊙ Permanent state of joy, spiritual ascension
- ⊙ Gift for transcendent, transcendental music, poetry, literature and philosophy
- ⊙ High science
- ⊙ Helps us perceive the great mysteries of the Universe and Cosmic Laws during the night, revelations received in dreams, daydreams and meditation
- ⊙ Penetrates the unconscious

Human distortions

- *Lives in illusions, not grounded enough*
- *Ignorance, false perceptions, erroneous behavior, atheism, reneges on, does not keep one's promises*
- *Torment, depression, sadness*
- *Insomnia, hyperactivity*
- *Existential anguish, anxiety, dropout, imposed or self-imposed marginalization*
- *Prophet of misfortune, unhealthy and misleading spirit*
- *Haughty, arrogant attitude*
- *Stubbornness, poor perception, material problems*
- *Lack of faith, enthusiasm, self-confidence and trust in others*
- *Discrepancy between body and spirit, gets lost in abstraction*
- *Science without conscience*
- *Difficulty expressing Knowledge*

Physical: June 11 to June 15
Emotional: January 24 from 6 pm to midnight, April 6, June 20, September 3, November 15
Intellectual: 5:20 am to 5:39 am
Residence: Binah / **Specificity**: Hochmah

18 CALIEL

Qualities

⊙ Absolute Truth
⊙ Eliminates all doubt, proves innocent
⊙ Divine Justice, karmic vision
⊙ Tribunal of conscience
⊙ Discerns what is right
⊙ Understands the interaction between good and evil
⊙ Respects Divine Laws
⊙ Perfect judgment, honesty
⊙ Judge, magistrate, lawyer, notary
⊙ Integrity, love of justice
⊙ Discovers Divine Truth, rediscovers the source of elevation
⊙ Capacity to see through intentions

Human distortions

– *Problems with truth and justice*
– *Condemnation*
– *Uses justice for the sole purpose of material gain, personal enrichment*
– *Seeks to win, rivalry*
– *False witness, false evidence, flattery*
– *Unfair trial, adversity*
– *Scandal, depravity, baseness, corruption, dishonesty, falseness*
– *Confused, entangled situation*
– *Moves away from the Truth, dark period*

Physical: June 16 to June 21
Emotional: January 25, April 7, June 21, September 4, November 16
Intellectual: 5:40 am to 5:59 am
Residence: Binah / **Specificity**: Binah

19 LEUVIAH

Qualities

- ⊙ Expansive intelligence
- ⊙ Memory of past lives, Cosmic Memory
- ⊙ Prodigious capacity for memorization
- ⊙ Gateway to Memory, Guardian of the Daath Archives (the Universal Library)
- ⊙ Mastery of feelings through reason, great patience
- ⊙ Communicative temperament, modesty, generous mentality
- ⊙ Enables us to bear adversity with patience and acceptance
- ⊙ Ready to help those in need

Human distortions

- – *Problems with intelligence, loss of one's intellectual faculties*
- – *Excessively perfectionist, only interested in material gain*
- – *Useless memories, amnesia, memory lapses*
- – *Atrocities committed in past lives*
- – *Grief, mortification, sterility, stubborn-minded, mistrust*
- – *Sadness, despondency, despair, a doleful, plaintive attitude*
- – *Subject to or causes losses, bitterness, complicated person*
- – *Accuses and makes others feel guilty*
- – *Manipulates via people's desires, seeks to impress*
- – *Absence of human warmth, inability to express one's feelings*
- – *Uses one's intelligence to serve the forces of evil*

Physical: June 22 to June 26
Emotional: January 26, April 8, June 22, September 5, November 17
Intellectual: 6:00 am to 6:19 am
Residence: Binah / **Specificity**: Hesed

20 PAHALIAH

Qualities

⊙ Deliverance
⊙ Transcendence of sexuality, divine sexual fusion in the couple, pure intimacy, fidelity
⊙ Awakening of the kundalini, of one's vital energy
⊙ Subjects concerning spirituality and morality
⊙ Knowledge of good and evil
⊙ Purity, consents to sacrifice in order to evolve
⊙ Rectification of errors caused by exalted desires
⊙ Establishes rules in one's instinctual behavior, rigor
⊙ Helps us undergo ordeals with courage and dynamism
⊙ Irreproachable moral behavior, great initiate,
⊙ Redemption, encounter with one's divine nature, one's higher self
⊙ Harmonious spiritual life

Human distortions

– *Abuse of power, fanaticism, extreme violence*
– *Relentless struggle, difficult destiny, rigidity*
– *Problems with sexuality and/or rejection of a sex life*
– *Repeated infidelities, short-lived affairs, debauchery*
– *Sexual abuse and squandering, prostitution*
– *Despondency, discouragement, fear, illness*
– *Does not believe in a Higher Power, transgresses Divine Laws*
– *Seeks material possessions*
– *Dogmatically religious, seeks to convert*

Physical: June 27 to July 1
Emotional: January 27, April 9, June 23, September 6, November 18
Intellectual: 6:20 am to 6:39 am
Residence: Binah / **Specificity**: Geburah

21 NELKHAEL

Qualities

- Facilitates learning
- Loves studying, successful in exams
- Omniscience
- Ability to go from the concrete to the abstract, from reality to ideas
- Gifted in science, technology and poetry
- Understanding of geometry, astronomy, astrology and mathematics
- Inspires scientists and philosophers
- Conscious of Cosmic Organization
- Good concentration, ability to understand the benefits of mantra recitation for access to Knowledge, to receive answers, and communicate with the parallel worlds
- Anticipation
- Protects against calumny, trickery, bewitchment
- Exorcism through Knowledge
- Teacher, excellent pedagogue

Human distortions

- *Difficulties in apprenticeship*
- *Problems with exams, tendency to feel stressed*
- *Wants to please others*
- *Seeks success at all costs, studies motivated by ambition*
- *Haughty attitude*
- *Complexes of superiority and inferiority*
- *Ignorance, learning without understanding*
- *Seeks and uses Knowledge for one's own ends*
- *Rejects learning and the learned, weak mentality, gets lost in abstraction*
- *Prejudices, vindictive behavior*
- *Erroneous mental structures*
- *Incapable of applying Knowledge*
- *Bewitchment through lack of Knowledge*

Physical: July 2 to July 6
Emotional: January 28, April 10, June 24, September 7, November 19
Intellectual: 6:40 am to 6:59 am
Residence: Binah / **Specificity**: Tiphereth

374

22 YEIAYEL

Qualities

- Renown, celebrity
- Patronage, philanthropy
- Political, artistic and scientific activities
- Great generosity
- Encourages goodness
- Leader
- Command, leadership, diplomacy,
- Fortune, wealth, business, commerce, altruism
- Enables us to make surprising discoveries
- Travel

Human distortions

- *Megalomaniac, tyrant, profiteer*
- *Slavery, repression*
- *Manipulation, relentlessness, competition*
- *Feels unacknowledged, wants to be rich and famous*
- *Difficulty recognizing oneself*
- *Greedy, grasping, insatiable, proud*
- *Loss of acknowledgement, of approval*
- *Contradictory feelings*
- *Unbalanced life, immobilism, resists changing, improving, progressing*
- *Difficulties in the field of business, enterprises, commerce, trade*

Physical: July 7 to July 11
Emotional: January 29, April 11, June 25, September 8, November 20
Intellectual: 7:00 am to 7:19 am
Residence: Binah / **Specificity**: Netzach

23 MELAHEL

Qualities

- ☉ Capacity for healing
- ☉ Doctor, healer, pharmacologist, scientist
- ☉ Naturopathy, herbalism, natural sciences
- ☉ Knows the properties and virtues of medicinal plants
- ☉ Ability to act like a medicinal plant
- ☉ Healthy food and cultivation
- ☉ Understands that healthy, well combined food is a form of true medication
- ☉ Knowledge of all the cycles and stages of the food chain
- ☉ Appreciation and gratitude for Divine Abundance, not taking it for granted
- ☉ Pacifies and soothes
- ☉ Masters one's emotions, adapts to every situation
- ☉ Faith that anticipates Knowledge
- ☉ Protection of the environment, respect for nature
- ☉ Initiated into the secrets of the Forces of nature
- ☉ Understands the multi-dimensional benefits of a healthy, well-balanced vegetarian or vegan diet

Human distortions

- – *Illness, disease, malaise, ill-being*
- – *Medicine without conscience*
- – *Uses medicine solely for material gain*
- – *Pollution that is harmful to vegetation and the environment*
- – *Corrupt feelings and businesses*
- – *Difficulty expressing one's feelings and improvising*
- – *Artificial agriculture and food*
- – *Polluting, destructive mind, unhealthy thoughts*

Physical: July 12 to July 16
Emotional: January 30, April 12, June 26, September 9, November 21
Intellectual: 7:20 am to 7:39 am
Residence: Binah / **Specificity**: Hod

24 HAHEUIAH

Qualities

⊙ Protection
⊙ Police, army, lawyer, judge
⊙ Warning of danger
⊙ Honesty, incorruptibility
⊙ Blocks evil, renders justice
⊙ Protects the exiled and immigrants
⊙ Protects against thieves and murderers
⊙ Protects against diabolical forces
⊙ Protects against harmful animals
⊙ Protects against bewitchment and evil spells
⊙ Helps us return to our Country of Origin
⊙ Sincerity, likes the Truth
⊙ End of a difficult period
⊙ Good intuition, capacity to anticipate, to know in advance
   what is going to happen
⊙ Helps accept one's sentence, understanding it is dispensed
   by Divine Justice
⊙ Activates the desire to repair one's karma

Human distortions

– *Problems related to protection*
– *Abuse of power, corrupted police, army officers or members
   of the judicial system*
– *Difficulty obtaining or applying justice*
– *Does not understand the meaning, the purpose of ordeals*
– *Instability, inconsistency, going astray*
– *Vengeful feelings, persecution, punishment*
– *Flees responsibility*
– *Indifference, emotional coldness*
– *Demonic forces*
– *Lives by illicit means, commits illegal actions*
– *Delinquent, criminal, reaps the fruit of violence*
– *Fraud, theft, imprisonment*
– *Victim of judicial rigidity*

Physical: July 17 to July 22
Emotional: January 31, April 13, June 27, September 10, November 22
Intellectual: 7:40 am to 7:59 am
Residence: Binah / **Specificity**: Yesod

25 NITH-HAIAH

Qualities

- ⊙ Bearer of Supreme Love and Wisdom
- ⊙ Mastery of spiritual forces
- ⊙ Study of metaphysics and the Kabbalah
- ⊙ Understands the notion of time
- ⊙ Hears the music of the High Spheres
- ⊙ Like an Angel
- ⊙ Can obtain everything
- ⊙ Discovery of the hidden mysteries of Creation
- ⊙ Revelations received in meditation and dreams, facilitates visions
- ⊙ Helps find a place in which to meditate
- ⊙ Loves peace, solitude and silence, a calm person
- ⊙ White magic, wanting other people's well-being
- ⊙ Spiritual charisma

Human distortions

- – *Illusory love and wisdom*
- – *Black magic, satanic pact*
- – *Ready to do anything to get what one wants*
- – *Fake psychic powers*
- – *Spiritual manipulator who behaves with a complex of superiority*
- – *Incapacity to perceive the magic of life and to accede to its multidimensions*
- – *Renounces God, the concept of a Universal Creator, atheism*
- – *Possession, bewitchment*
- – *Misfortune, despair*
- – *Material interests, egocentricity*
- – *Agitated, incoherent, impatient*
- – *Acts against Destiny and the Universal Laws*

Physical: July 23 to July 27
Emotional: February 1, April 14, June 28, September 11, November 23
Intellectual: 8:00 am to 8:19 am
Residence: Hesed / **Specificity**: Hochmah

26 HAAIAH

Qualities

⊙ Discretion
⊙ Capacity to structure power and abundance well
⊙ Wise advisor
⊙ Faculty to keep and manage State secrets, confidential government files, access to information and knowledge that needs to remain secret
⊙ Sense of organization and family
⊙ Contemplation of Divine Structures
⊙ Political science, harmonizes social life
⊙ Peaceful cohabitation
⊙ Respect for Divine Order
⊙ Ability to adapt to any situation
⊙ Scientific and political attitudes in accordance with Divine Science
⊙ Political and social leader, catalyst, administrator, decision-maker, diplomat, ambassador, dispenser of justice
⊙ Allows us to know how to behave in ambiguous situations
⊙ Seeks Truth through reason
⊙ Creator of positive, constructive atmosphere, inspires team spirit

Human distortions

– *Indiscretion, egocentricity, family and/or social problems*
– *Difficulties related to politics, decision making, administration, organization*
– *Motivated by ambition, jealousy, envy, covetousness, pride, vanity and passion*
– *Flees one's responsibilities, one's life-plan*
– *Desire for earthly power and glory, abuse of authority and power, competitive spirit, abides by the law of the jungle*
– *Social disorder, anarchy, conspiracy, treachery,*
– *Imposes one's point of view, does not listen to others*
– *Complexes of inferiority and superiority*
– *Negative consequences of disorderly actions*

Physical: July 28 to August 1
Emotional: February 2, April 15, June 29, September 12, November 24
Intellectual: 8:20 am to 8:39 am
Residence: Hesed / **Specificity**: Binah

27 YERATHEL

Qualities

- ⊙ Confidence
- ⊙ Inexhaustible Source of Energy
- ⊙ Propagates the Light
- ⊙ Creator of a positive atmosphere, optimism
- ⊙ Teachings through the spoken and written word, social broadcasting
- ⊙ Civilizes, sociability
- ⊙ Liberates from slanderers, from evil intentions
- ⊙ Liberates in the case of possession
- ⊙ Likes justice, science, literature and the arts in general
- ⊙ Liberates from those who are opposed to our development
- ⊙ Dissipates confusion, leads to success

Human distortions

- – *Lack of self-confidence and/or self-esteem; or, over-confidence, ego problems*
- – *Superficial activities*
- – *Hyperactivity, lack of concentration, focus and wisdom*
- – *Wants to please everybody*
- – *Prepared to do anything to succeed, to be acknowledged and appreciated*
- – *Dispersion, over-excitability*
- – *Possession, slavery*
- – *Squandering, waste*
- – *Addictions, dependencies, perverted habits, fanaticism*
- – *Compulsive desire to please, provocation*
- – *Compulsive gambler*
- – *Egoism, flattery, emphasis on appearances*
- – *Law of the jungle, meanness, ignorance, intolerance, slander*
- – *Destructive science and arts*

Physical: August 2 to August 6
Emotional: February 3, April 16, April 17 from midnight to midday, June 30, September 13, November 25
Intellectual: 8:40 am to 8:59 am
Residence: Hesed / **Specificity**: Hesed

28 SEHEIAH

Qualities

- ☉ Foresight
- ☉ Happy longevity
- ☉ Protection against lightning, falls, accidents, fires, and illnesses
- ☉ Miraculous healing, rehabilitation, health
- ☉ Providential Protection, Celestial Insurance
- ☉ Grants wisdom through the examination of past experiences
- ☉ Premonition, protective inspiration
- ☉ Caution, ability to foresee events
- ☉ Great calm

Human distortions

- – *Lack of foresight, carelessness, deep worry*
- – *Problems of longevity, fear of change and death*
- – *Anxiety, fear of the future*
- – *Compensation through superficial activities*
- – *Always afraid and worried for others, lack of confidence in Destiny and in the Life Program of all beings*
- – *Inconsistency*
- – *Falls, illness, accidents*
- – *Ruination, turmoil, turbulence*
- – *Triggers catastrophes*
- – *Impetuous, rash action, absent-minded, scatterbrained, thoughtless blunders*
- – *Whirling, swirling energy*
- – *Excessive willpower, angry temperament*
- – *Inner and outer paralysis*

Physical: August 7 to August 12
Emotional: February 4, April 17 from midday to midnight, April 18, July 1, September 14, November 26
Intellectual: 9:00 am to 9:19 am
Residence: Hesed / **Specificity**: Geburah

29 REIYEL

Qualities

- ⊙ Liberation
- ⊙ Loves wide open spaces, high mountains and nature in general
- ⊙ Leads to High Summits
- ⊙ Sets us free from evil, spells and bewitchment
- ⊙ Not linked to any particular credo (does not belong to a particular religious group or sect)
- ⊙ Improvement of life through meditation and self-study
- ⊙ Confidence, spreads the Truth
- ⊙ Free citizen of the Universe, global vision
- ⊙ Behavioral science
- ⊙ Seeks Truth, material detachment
- ⊙ Conception, accomplishment, production
- ⊙ Discovers the mysteries of Divine Work through meditation
- ⊙ Divinely inspired work, carried out in a high state of conscience
- ⊙ Establishes a connection with the Spiritual Guides

Human distortions

- – *Restricting situation, impasse, lack of freedom on different levels*
- – *Wanting to be number one and/or the best, at all costs*
- – *Ambition, greed, manipulation*
- – *Either too airy, unworldly or too down-to-earth, too wordly*
- – *Mistrust, fanaticism, hypocrisy*
- – *Propagation of false and dangerous ideas*
- – *Bewitchment, keeping bad company*
- – *Sectarianism, bigotry, religious struggle*
- – *Indoctrination, nationalism*
- – *Prisoner*
- – *Opposition to altruistic achievements*
- – *Materialistic philosophy, worldly pleasures*

Physical: August 13 to August 17
Emotional: February 5, April 19, July 2, September 15, November 27
Intellectual: 9:20 am to 9:39 am
Residence: Hesed / **Specificity**: Tiphereth

30 OMAEL

Qualities

- ⊙ Multiplication
- ⊙ Materialization, development, expansion
- ⊙ Production, achievement, application, planning
- ⊙ Patience, sense of responsibility
- ⊙ Re-establishes health, leads to healing, relates to the medical profession
- ⊙ Fertility, birth, concerns pregnant women
- ⊙ Fulfillment, joy, living antidepressant
- ⊙ Tonic, energizer
- ⊙ Patron of the vegetable and animal kingdoms
- ⊙ Favors plantation and harvests
- ⊙ Rediscovery of one's inner child

Human distortions

- – *Superficial success, materialistic philosophy*
- – *Ambition, greed, ready to do anything to win, worldly attitude*
- – *Sterility, lack of success, repeated failure, poverty*
- – *Corrupt materialization, lack of planning and organization*
- – *Impatience*
- – *Vivisection (dissection on the living)*
- – *Euthanasia, suicide, bearer of death*
- – *Genocide, extermination, monstrous experiments, devastating fury*
- – *Sadness, depression, despair*
- – *Poor harvests*

Physical: August 18 to August 22
Emotional: February 6, April 20, July 3, September 16, November 28
Intellectual: 9:40 am to 9:59 am
Residence: Hesed / **Specificity**: Netzach

31 LECABEL

Qualities

- ☉ Talent for solving life's enigmas
- ☉ Love of exactitude and precision
- ☉ Excellence, seeks order on all levels
- ☉ Lucidity, powerful intellect, finds practical solutions
- ☉ Emotional mastery through reason
- ☉ Strategist, administrator, engineer, architect, agronomist
- ☉ Decision maker, creator, designer, planner of the future
- ☉ Study of exact sciences, business management
- ☉ Luminous ideas generating abundance
- ☉ Revelation of Cosmic Processes through the observation of the infinitely small
- ☉ Respects stages and cycles, long-term planning

Human distortions

- – *Lack of talent, inspiration, ideas, and/or frustration regarding our talents that are not used to their full potential*
- – *Manipulates and exploits others*
- – *Insecurities, which lead obsession with success*
- – *Illicit means, shady deals, drug-trafficking*
- – *Opportunist, dishonest, greedy, miserly*
- – *Over-analytical management, dissatisfied perfectionist*
- – *Permissive, neglectful, wasteful, slovenly, slipshod*
- – *Poor use of capital and resources, business losses, bankruptcy, insoluble problems, acts too hastily*
- – *Possessive, places importance on results, seeks to force Destiny*
- – *Compulsive gambler*

Physical: August 23 to August 28
Emotional: February 7, April 21, July 4, July 5 from midnight to midday, September 17, November 29
Intellectual: 10:00 am to 10:19 am
Residence: Hesed / **Specificity**: Hod

384

32 VASARIAH

Qualities

- Clemency
- Capacity to forgive
- Great wisdom that helps us reflect, plan, find solutions and solve problems
- Planner, thinker, strategist
- Goodness, benevolence, magnanimity
- Modesty, kindness
- Understands the meaning of ordeals
- Helps free us from feelings of guilt
- Nobility, uprightness, elevated sense of justice
- Natural pardon
- Judge, magistrate, lawyer
- Gifted speaker
- Grants access to Cosmic Memory, Knowledge of good and evil
- Generous mentality

Human distortions

- *Lack of clemency, difficulty forgiving*
- *Lack of wisdom and goodness, difficulty or incapacity to plan, think, find solutions, solve problems*
- *Revenge*
- *Unfair, dishonorable, resentful, bears a grudge*
- *Guilt, accusation, condemnation*
- *Flees when faced with responsibilities, difficulty discerning good and evil*
- *Resists evolving, nourishes harmful intentions toward others*
- *Puritanical, moralistic, harmful influence*
- *Illness that can worsen*
- *Focuses on bad memories*
- *Presumptuous, impolite, ill-mannered*
- *Proud, materialistic*

Physical: August 29 to September 2
Emotional: February 8, April 22, July 5 from midday to midnight, July 6, September 18, November 30
Intellectual: 10:20 am to 10:39 am
Residence: Hesed / **Specificity**: Yesod

33 YEHUIAH

Qualities

⊙ Subordination
⊙ Good, right, just authority, leadership
⊙ Ability to work well with one's superiors, to create team spirit, and close collaboration with important people
⊙ Capable of globally understanding the structure of a situation, a business company, a mission, etc., capacity to plan important projects, honor one's commitments and assume great responsibilities
⊙ Appreciation and acknowledgement from one's superiors
⊙ Inspires confidence and loyalty
⊙ Capable of withstanding high tension, powerful initiations
⊙ Letting go, averts confrontation
⊙ Fidelity to what is superior, honesty
⊙ Capable of recognizing true Hierarchy
⊙ Conscious of one's place in the Cosmic Order
⊙ Enables us to unmask traitors and uncover schemes and plotting
⊙ Supports altruistic initiatives, leads to a sense of duty
⊙ Gives rise to scientific discoveries
⊙ A trustworthy person
⊙ Commitment, contract, alliance, philanthropic association

Human distortions

– *Insubordination, problems with hierarchy and authority*
– *Rebellion, confrontation, resistance or refusal to execute orders, aggression*
– *Cannot bear hierarchy, pushed aside or dismissed from positions of command*
– *Defies orders from Up Above*
– *Perversity, multiple desires, lack of moral fiber and strength to do what is right*
– *Dropout, quest for the useless, abandon*
– *Conflict, betrayal inscribed in one's genetic code, in the unconscious*
– *Contempt*
– *Feelings of superiority and inferiority*
– *Worldly pleasures, abuse of privileges*
– *Lack of loyalty, betrayal, treachery*
– *Ego problems*
– *Imposes one's will and presence, dictatorial behavior*
– *Rigidity, anger*

Physical: September 3 to September 7
Emotional: February 9, April 23, July 7, September 19, December 1
Intellectual: 10:40 am to 10:59 am
Residence: Geburah / **Specificity**: Hochmah

34 LEHAHIAH

Qualities

⊙ Obedience
⊙ Faithful servant
⊙ Trust and favor from superiors
⊙ Discipline, sense of order
⊙ Loyalty, devotion, altruistic acts
⊙ Obeys Divine Laws and the authority that represents them
⊙ Devotes one's life to the service of an established order
  (government leader, minister, president, director)
⊙ Intelligence, peace, harmony, at ease with ambiguity
⊙ Obedience without necessarily understanding
⊙ Understands Divine Justice
⊙ Incorruptible, upright, responsible
⊙ Accepts the rigors of one's destiny without protest

Human distortions

– *Disobedience*
– *Problems with authority*
– *Complexes of inferiority and superiority*
– *Disloyal, unreliable, untrustworthy*
– *Unfair laws, authoritarianism, dictatorship*
– *Lack of authority, incomprehension*
– *Competitive spirit, opposition, contradicts for the sake of being right,
  to have the last word*
– *Rigidity, frustration, conflict with one's superiors*
– *Dangerous anger, treachery, triggers ruination, destruction*
– *Discord, rebellion, violence, war*
– *Emotive nature, tendency to rebel against laws*
– *Rejection, impulsiveness, absence of receptivity*

Physical: September 8 to September 12
Emotional: February 10, April 24, July 8, September 20, September 21 from
midnight to midday, December 2
Intellectual: 11:00 am to 11:19 am
Residence: Geburah / **Specificity**: Binah

35 CHAVAKHIAH

Qualities

⊙ Reconciliation
⊙ Harmonious family relationships
⊙ Trust, family help and support
⊙ Aware of the sacredness of family bonds
⊙ Ability to bring out ancestral Wisdom
⊙ Brings people closer, re-establishes links
⊙ Humanities and social sciences
⊙ Loves peace, mediator, peacemaker
⊙ Loyalty rewarded, services appreciated
⊙ Inheritance, sharing possessions, donations
⊙ Return to lost paradise

Human distortions

– *Family problems, disputes, quarrels, disunity*
– *Difficulty and discord related to inheritance*
– *Jealousy, envy, treachery*
– *Excessive, unhealthy attachment, possessiveness, seeks to control others*
– *Problems regarding ancient family traditions*
– *Holding onto the past, perpetuation of outdated ancestral, family customs and behavioral patterns*
– *Forced marriage*
– *Wants to please the family at all costs, emotional and material dependency*
– *Lack of bonds, egoism*
– *Unfair trial*
– *Offence*
– *Ruin*
– *Bigotry, narrow-minded, sectarianism, racism, nationalism*
– *Hereditary illnesses*
– *Humanitarian problems*
– *Social disorganization and disorder*

Physical: September 13 to September 17
Emotional: February 11, April 25, July 9, September 21 from midday to midnight, September 22, December 3
Intellectual: 11:20 am to 11:39 am
Residence: Geburah / **Specificity**: Hesed

36 MENADEL

Qualities

- ⊙ Work
- ⊙ Vocation, cooperation, obliging, helpfulness, altruism
- ⊙ Foreman in the Divine factory
- ⊙ Helps find work
- ⊙ Provides us with the wherewithal to live
- ⊙ Truth and freedom found through work
- ⊙ Inner work, facilitates adaptation
- ⊙ Liberates prisoners and outcasts
- ⊙ Understands the meaning of work
- ⊙ Procures the willpower to set to work
- ⊙ Recuperation of one's potential
- ⊙ Dedication

Human distortions

- − *Problems related to work and professional activities*
- − *Does one's work in order to be loved*
- − *Excess or lack of work*
- − *Lives only for one's work, identifies mainly with one's social status and role*
- − *Materialistic philosophy*
- − *Slavery*
- − *Loss of employment, difficulty finding work*
- − *Exile, flight, laziness, avoids responsibilities*
- − *Lack of goals and intensity, scarcity of ideas*
- − *Too busy in matter*
- − *Exhaustion, coldness, isolation*
- − *Incomprehension of the inherent meaning of work*
- − *Tries to force, counter or defy Destiny, seeks success at all costs*
- − *Seeks personal glory*

Physical: September 18 to September 23
Emotional: February 12, April 26, July 10, September 30, December 4
Intellectual: 11:40 am to 11:59 am
Residence: Geburah / **Specificity**: Geburah

37 ANIEL

Qualities

⊙ Breaks old patterns
⊙ Helps us understand the cycles of life and evolution
⊙ Study of History, of causes and consequences
⊙ Understands the Law of karma, the fact that we attract who we are and that we reap what we sow
⊙ Change of mentality, new ideas
⊙ Develops an independent will
⊙ Helps cleanse, purify negative memories related to sexuality, emotional dependency and all kinds of addiction
⊙ Mastery when faced with intense intellectual and emotional impulses
⊙ Spiritual autonomy
⊙ Liberates us from negative forces and emotions
⊙ Bearer of new sciences and new conceptions of the Universe
⊙ Encourages novelty

Human distortions

– *Difficulty, refusal or fear of change*
– *Tendency to live in past memories*
– *Materialistic philosophy, excessive worldly mentality*
– *Does not understand or ignores the Law of karma, the fact that we reap what we sow*
– *Resistance to new currents*
– *Attachment to former structures, to what is old*
– *Subjection to matter*
– *Goes round in circles rehashing the same thoughts*
– *Relentless struggle to maintain the status quo*
– *Charlatan, perverted, misleading mind and spirit*
– *Fierce, unshakable traditionalist*
– *All kinds of addiction*
– *Talks about what one does not know*

Physical: September 24 to September 28
Emotional: February 13, April 27, July 11, September 24, December 5
Intellectual: Noon to 12:19 pm
Residence: Geburah / **Specificity**: Tiphereth

38 HAAMIAH

Qualities

⊙ Sense of ritual and preparation
⊙ Strategist, planner
⊙ Loves to make things, to cook, to look after and care for others, etc.
⊙ Leads to the highest human achievements
⊙ Transposes ritual into daily life
⊙ Science of behavior and conduct
⊙ Beauty, harmony, peace
⊙ Good manners, politeness, conviviality
⊙ High place of transcendence
⊙ Exorcism
⊙ Dissolves inner and outer violence
⊙ Helps find the perfect complement
⊙ Extraordinary love story
⊙ Divine sexuality
⊙ Rituals, ceremonies, initiation
⊙ Adores the Divine

Human distortions

– *Lack of involvement or difficulties related to preparation and rituals*
– *Poor strategist and planner*
– *Dislikes making things, preparing meals, nourishing and taking care of others, etc.*
– *Selfish person, lacks consideration for others*
– *Impatience*
– *Lack of politeness and kindness, ill-mannered*
– *Too perfectionist, driven by insecurity and fear of lacking resources*
– *Follows or submits to rituals to please others, to be accepted and loved*
– *Refuses or fears marriage, absence or lack of true love*
– *Lies, errors, refusal to respect the rules, manipulative behavior*
– *Absence of spirituality or false, non authentic spiritual concepts*
– *Worshipper of monuments*
– *Black magic cults, rituals and ceremonies*
– *Demon, evil spirit, possession, aggression, violence*
– *Guided by material interests*

Physical: September 29 to October 3
Emotional: February 14, April 28, July 12, September 25, December 6
Intellectual: 12:20 pm to 12:39 pm
Residence: Geburah / **Specificity**: Netzach

39 REHAEL

Qualities

- Submission, receptivity
- Great sensitivity
- Open conscience, deep awareness leading to profound understanding
- Respect for Hierarchy
- Capacity to listen to others
- Trust and confidence of one's superiors
- Perfect submission to fair parents and right, just authority
- Paternal love
- Obedience and respect
- Healing of mental illnesses, depression and anxiety
- Regeneration

Human distortions

- *Problems with submission, tendency to be either too submissive or not submissive enough, insubordination, rebellion*
- *Lack of receptivity and openness*
- *Hypersensitivity or insensitivity*
- *Difficulty listening to others, too self-centered*
- *Megalomaniac attitude*
- *Disrespect for hierarchy on all levels*
- *Crime against parents and children*
- *Parents projecting their failed ambitions onto their children*
- *Violence, hatred, cruelty*
- *Authoritarianism*
- *Imposes obedience with cruel severity*
- *Mental illnesses*
- *Emotional problems*
- *Anxiety, anguish, depression, suicide*

Physical: October 4 to October 8
Emotional: February 15, April 29, July 13, September 26, December 7
Intellectual: 12:40 pm to 12:59 pm
Residence: Geburah / **Specificity**: Hod

40 IEIAZEL

Qualities

- ⊙ Consolation, comfort
- ⊙ Appreciation, period of renewal
- ⊙ Consolation after effort
- ⊙ Restores and revitalizes the body, helps us recuperate fully
- ⊙ Prevents emotional outbursts and overspill
- ⊙ Helps us master passion and very intense energy
- ⊙ Sets us free from emotional conditioning and addictions (alcohol, drugs, etc.)
- ⊙ Sets prisoners free
- ⊙ End of a period of ordeals or difficult situations, beginning of an easier period
- ⊙ Brings peace, harmony and rejoicing
- ⊙ Beginning of a new creation
- ⊙ Concerns writing, editors, printing, bookshops, libraries, reading, music, painting and the arts in general

Human distortions

- – *Difficulty consoling and comforting others*
- – *Lack of intimacy and renewal*
- – *Pessimistic thoughts, sadness*
- – *Accumulation of problems, trials, ordeals, difficult period*
- – *Emotional outbursts, overspill*
- – *Addictions, dependencies, passion, tumultuous emotions*
- – *Discouragement, lack of confidence*
- – *Tendency to flee social life, reclusion*
- – *Illness that could lead to death*
- – *Unhappy, sad, pessimistic writing*
- – *Music and other forms of destructive art*

Physical: October 9 to October 13
Emotional: February 16, April 30, July 14, September 27, December 8
Intellectual: 1:00 pm to 1:19 pm
Residence: Geburah / **Specificity**: Yesod

41 HAHAHEL

Qualities

- ⊙ Mission
- ⊙ Faithful servant
- ⊙ Gives unconditionally
- ⊙ Shepherd of souls, missionary
- ⊙ Vocation in relation to spirituality
- ⊙ Heightens faith
- ⊙ Spiritual enrichment
- ⊙ Non-attachment to worldly things
- ⊙ Acts in an impersonal, detached manner on the invisible plane
- ⊙ Wards off enemies of spirituality
- ⊙ Reveals the Universal Creator
- ⊙ Capacity to sacrifice oneself, nobility of soul
- ⊙ Leadership, courage, capacity to make great efforts to help and support others
- ⊙ Understands the meaning and purpose of Life
- ⊙ Great Sage
- ⊙ Visionary, knows what needs to be done and when to do it
- ⊙ Active meditation, capacity to meditate even in action
- ⊙ Consecrates one's life to God
- ⊙ Spiritual Guide
- ⊙ Ability to marry spirit and matter

Human distortions

- – *Difficulty finding or recognizing one's mission, and understanding the meaning and purpose of Life*
- – *Materialistic philosophy, egoism, lack of altruism*
- – *Feels apart, cast aside, alone, nourishes discrepancies within oneself, feeling of separation, alienation from others*
- – *Rigidity, spiritual extremism*
- – *Exerts one's authority in a bad way*
- – *Seeks to convince*
- – *Identifies with martyrs, feels persecuted*
- – *Opposes what one cannot be*
- – *Scandalous behavior*
- – *Fails in one's projects*
- – *False virtue, based on appearances only*
- – *Denies one's divinity*
- – *Enemy of spirituality*
- – *Mockery, scorn, hatred*
- – *Inquisition, religious fanaticism*

Physical: October 14 to October 18
Emotional: February 17, May 1, July 15, September 28, December 9
Intellectual: 1:20 pm to 1:39 pm
Residence: Tiphereth / **Specificity**: Hochmah

394

42 MIKAËL

Qualities

- ⊙ Political order
- ⊙ Establishes the Laws of Heaven on Earth
- ⊙ Social and spiritual organization
- ⊙ Structures success and expansion
- ⊙ Plans wisely, with foresight
- ⊙ Helps us understands adversity
- ⊙ Knowledge of good and evil
- ⊙ Procures lucidity and global vision
- ⊙ Unmasks traitors
- ⊙ Allows us to discover secrets, mysteries
- ⊙ Natural authority, obedience, loyalty
- ⊙ President, leader, person in charge, minister, ambassador, consul
- ⊙ Teacher
- ⊙ Security and protection while traveling
- ⊙ Protects against accidents
- ⊙ Success in external relationships
- ⊙ Teaches and instructs during the night
- ⊙ Establishes absolute Power of the Spirit

Human distortions

- – *Political and social problems, disorder, difficulties on the organizational level*
- – *Abuse of power, or incapacity to decide, to be a good leader*
- – *Not planning wisely and in advance, getting lost in details, in technical issues*
- – *Envy, jealousy, betrayal*
- – *Bad teacher or leader, does not set a good example*
- – *Complexes of superiority and inferiority*
- – *Democratic system that legalizes the expression of base instincts*
- – *Double dealings, corrupt government*
- – *Speech, words that do not correspond to Divine Thought*
- – *Betrayal of ideals, propagator of false news*
- – *Lies, slander, defamation, conspiracy, treachery*
- – *Accident*

Physical: October 19 to October 23
Emotional: February 18, May 2, July 16, September 29, December 10
Intellectual: 1:40 pm to 1:59 pm
Residence: Tiphereth / **Specificity**: Binah

43 VEULIAH

Qualities

⊙ Prosperity
⊙ Wealth, abundance, joy, enriches our conscience
⊙ Abundance of noble feelings
⊙ Astute strategist, capable of overcoming inner and outer enemies
⊙ Understands that money is energy that may be used well or badly
⊙ Ability to use one's prosperity in a responsible, right, just, altruistic manner
⊙ Commerce, businesses, finance (banking system, accounting, etc.), administration, management
⊙ Makes everything fructify, helps others
⊙ Natural authority, trusted by superiors
⊙ Opening of one's conscience, which liberates it from obscure motives, pernicious, vicious habits
⊙ Peace, plenitude
⊙ Prepares the world's future patrons
⊙ Gives unconditionally
⊙ Visionary, capacity to foresee and plan in advance
⊙ Philanthropist
⊙ Understands that we reap what we sow

Human distortions

– *Artificial, illusory prosperity, materialistic philosophy*
– *Waste of money and energy, seeks artificial paradises*
– *Discord, loss of privileges, ruin, poverty*
– *Profound insecurity, worry about the future*
– *Greed, theft, wealth sought and obtained through illicit means*
– *Believes that money can buy everything*
– *Egocentric and egotistical*
– *Narrow-minded, blinded by personal power*
– *Complexes of superiority and inferiority*
– *Abuse of power, existential struggle*
– *Division, separatism, revolution, war, destruction*
– *Behavior, actions that engender karmas, future problems*
– *Damage, harm, destruction of the environment*
– *Lack of love and wisdom*
– *Megalomania*

Physical: October 24 to October 28
Emotional: February 19, May 3, July 17, September 30, December 11
Intellectual: 2:00 pm to 2:19 pm
Residence: Tiphereth / **Specificity**: Hesed

44 YELAHIAH

Qualities

- ⊙ Warrior of Light, Celestial Army
- ⊙ Universal Protector
- ⊙ Spiritual Guide
- ⊙ Application of Divine Justice
- ⊙ Ability to resolve conflicts created by our behavior
- ⊙ Helps us through initiations
- ⊙ Military talent in the service of just causes
- ⊙ Life oriented towards liquidation of karmic debts
- ⊙ Leads to victory and establishes peace
- ⊙ Frank, loyal, courageous, brave
- ⊙ Success in difficult situations
- ⊙ Acquired Wisdom
- ⊙ Understands the role and functioning of borders in the Parallel Worlds
- ⊙ Grants the Universal Passport
- ⊙ Benefits from the confidence and trust of one's superiors
- ⊙ Obeys what is right and just
- ⊙ Great capacity to help others

Human distortions

- – *Pretends to be a warrior of Light, spiritual extremism*
- – *Imposes one's will, convictions and beliefs, tries to control others*
- – *Evil, demonic mission, diabolical forces*
- – *Abuse of power, dictatorship, megalomania*
- – *Fanaticism, terrorism*
- – *War, scourge, brutal, aggressive, vindictive behavior*
- – *Massacre and merciless treatment of prisoners*
- – *Infringes the law, criminal, wrong-doer*
- – *Imprisonment*
- – *Injustice*
- – *Tendency to overwork*

Physical: October 29 to November 2
Emotional: February 20, May 4, July 18, October 1, December 12
Intellectual: 2:20 pm to 2:39 pm
Residence: Tiphereth / **Specificity**: Geburah

45 SEALIAH

Qualities

- ⊙ Motivation, purity of intention
- ⊙ Rediscovered willpower, concentration, focus
- ⊙ Ardor, enthusiasm, hope
- ⊙ Awakening, spring, motor of the Universe that awakens those who are asleep
- ⊙ Restarts what has become bogged down, stuck
- ⊙ Gives back hope to the humiliated and deprived
- ⊙ Confounds the proud and vain
- ⊙ Exalts our conscience
- ⊙ Return to well-balanced vital energy
- ⊙ Bearer of health and healing
- ⊙ Patron of the four elements: fire, air, water, earth

Human distortions

- – *Lack or excess of motivation and enthusiasm*
- – *Proud, conceited, excessive*
- – *Hyperactivity, or inactivity, idleness, lack of energy*
- – *Full of oneself, despotic, difficult to live with*
- – *Imbalance and unleashing of natural elements (earthquakes, floods, droughts, tornadoes, natural catastrophes, volcanic eruptions) and their inner correspondence*
- – *A difficult life, ordeals*
- – *Excessive or insufficient self-control and self-confidence, lacks mastery*
- – *Exaggeration, tendency to want to force Destiny*

Physical: November 3 to November 7
Emotional: February 21, May 5, July 19, October 2, December 13
Intellectual: 2:40 pm to 2:59 pm
Residence: Tiphereth / **Specificity**: Tiphereth

46 ARIEL

Qualities

- ⊙ Revelatory perception
- ⊙ Psychic abilities, clairvoyance, clairaudience, clairsentience
- ⊙ Discovery of hidden treasures
- ⊙ Revelatory meditations, dreams and signs
- ⊙ Discovery of nature's secrets
- ⊙ Acknowledgment, gratitude
- ⊙ Subtlety, discretion
- ⊙ Bearer of new ideas, inventor
- ⊙ Discovery of philosophical secrets that lead to the reorientation of one's life

Human distortions

- *False perception or difficulty receiving revelations*
- *Lack of spirituality, or spiritual illusions created and nourished by one's ego*
- *Psychic powers used without purity*
- *Problems due to false perceptions and/or psychic abilities used with bad intentions and/or in impure ways that are not right and just*
- *Weak mentality*
- *Incoherence, indecision, senseless behavior, tribulation*
- *Crippling shyness, chronic timidity*
- *Difficulty or incapacity to find solutions*
- *Useless activity*

Physical: November 8 to November 12
Emotional: February 22, May 6, July 20, October 3, December 14
Intellectual: 3:00 pm to 3:19 pm
Residence: Tiphereth / **Specificity**: Netzach

47 ASALIAH

Qualities

- ☉ Contemplation
- ☉ Glorification of the Divine, mystical experience
- ☉ Global perspective, overall view
- ☉ Contemplation from an elevated viewpoint
- ☉ Synthesizes information easily
- ☉ Initiate, supra-normal faculties
- ☉ Pedagogue, instructor, teacher
- ☉ Psychologist
- ☉ Finds Truth in little everyday things
- ☉ Revelation of cosmic processes
- ☉ Creative genius, strategist, talent for planning
- ☉ Intuitive, well-balanced, radiates discernment and integrity
- ☉ Great interest in esotericism
- ☉ Ability to accede to the Parallel Worlds, to be in contact with their inhabitants and/or deceased people
- ☉ Ability to attain high spiritual levels through meditation and visualization
- ☉ Develops mental power and the capacity to concentrate and focus thanks to mantra recitation
- ☉ Understands the importance of experiencing the fusion of both polarities and sacred, Divine sexuality
- ☉ Divine pleasures, pure intention
- ☉ High morals, true, authentic, pure values, respect and fidelity in the couple

Human distortions

- – *Lack of global vision, or tendency to get lost in mental structures and abstract concepts, disconnection from concrete reality*
- – *Materialistic philosophy, excessive focus on basic, primary needs, ego problems*
- – *Problems, worries, insecurities*
- – *Immoral, scandalous action*
- – *Inverted truth, dishonesty, charlatan, fake teacher*
- – *False beliefs, teaching erroneous, dangerous systems, blind admiration, idolatry*
- – *Excessively dissects and analyzes*
- – *Lies, error of evaluation, ignorance*
- – *Attributes the reincarnation of famous people to oneself*
- – *Sexual abuse and waste*

Physical: November 13 to November 17
Emotional: February 23, May 7, July 21, October 4, December 15
Intellectual: 3:20 pm to 3:39 pm
Residence: Tiphereth / **Specificity**: Hod

48 MIHAEL

Qualities

- Fertility, fecundity
- Marital peace and harmony
- Marriage, marital fidelity
- Reconciliation, fusion of masculine and feminine polarities
- Reproduction, growth
- Helps engender a great soul
- Divine sexuality
- Ease in associations and partnerships
- Gift of clairvoyance, improved perception
- Inner and outer peace
- Helps materialize Divine intentions
- Providential protection
- Wisdom in receptivity and listening

Human distortions

- *Sterility, difficulty engendering a child or conceiving a project*
- *Discord, disagreement between spouses, jealousy, inconsistency, infidelity*
- *Fear of losing the other, possessiveness, subservience, machismo*
- *Sexual problems and/or lust, passion, seeking sensual pleasures to compensate for the absence of a spiritual life*
- *Unproductive business*
- *Claims the place of another, competition*
- *Feelings of attraction and repulsion*
- *Multiple relationships, licentiousness, prostitution*

Physical: November 18 to November 22
Emotional: February 24, May 8, July 22, October 5, December 16
Intellectual: 3:40 pm to 3:59 pm
Residence: Tiphereth / **Specificity**: Yesod

49 VEHUEL

Qualities

⊙ Elevation towards Greatness and Wisdom
⊙ Meditation, visualization and mantra recitation
⊙ Ability to accede to the Parallel Worlds, to be in contact with their inhabitants and/or deceased people
⊙ Exaltation and glorification of the Divine
⊙ Enlightenment
⊙ Detachment from matter
⊙ Elevation through service
⊙ Great soul, lives devoted to great causes that are beneficial to humanity
⊙ Is related to great, key figures
⊙ Elaborates the seeds of human thought
⊙ Sensitive, generous mentality
⊙ Source of inspiration
⊙ Altruism, diplomacy
⊙ Frees us from the hold of instinctive desires
⊙ Feelings of fraternity, humanitarian aid
⊙ Aspiration to what is elevated
⊙ Great writer
⊙ Great devotion to others

Human distortions

– *Difficulty raising oneself up and manifesting wisdom*
– *Complexes of superiority and inferiority*
– *Spiritual extremism or lack of spirituality*
– *Does not meditate*
– *Atheism*
– *Self-abasement, enslavement to material impulses*
– *Egoism, hypocrisy, absence of principles*
– *Opposes feelings of fraternity*
– *Critical writer, person of negative influence*
– *Passion, hatred*
– *Escapism, flight*
– *Fear of matter*

Physical: November 23 to November 27
Emotional: February 25, May 9, July 23, October 6, December 17
Intellectual: 4:00 pm to 4:19 pm
Residence: Netzach / **Specificity**: Hochmah

402

50 DANIEL

Qualities

⊙ Eloquence
⊙ Great capacity to communicate and inspire people
⊙ Leadership, capacity to announce and explain important decisions
⊙ Efficient, well-thought out structuring, carried out gently and kindly
⊙ Ability to express things beautifully and pleasantly, to speak well so as to hurt no one
⊙ Speech that attenuates the rigor of Truth
⊙ Goodness, harmony, beauty
⊙ Enables us to perceive clearly
⊙ Enables us to perceive events as they are and to make the most appropriate decisions
⊙ Enables detachment from matter so as to perceive Truth
⊙ Capacity to materialize thoughts through deeds
⊙ Speeches, singing, music and the arts in general

Human distortions

– *Problems related to communication*
– *Eloquence used for personal gain*
– *Flatterer, deceiver*
– *Speaks artfully to fool the gullible, the naïve*
– *Elocution difficulties*
– *Deterioration of language*
– *Egoism and ego problems*
– *Shady deals, trickery*
– *Lives on illicit means*
– *Manipulates to obtain the support of influential people*
– *Negative speech, music and other art*
– *Hides behind masks and/or uses different masks to attain one's goals*

Physical: November 28 to December 2
Emotional: February 26, May 10, July 24, October 7, December 18
Intellectual: 4:20 pm to 4:39 pm
Residence: Netzach / **Specificity**: Binah

51 HAHASIAH

Qualities

- Universal Medicine
- Related to all medical professions (doctors, nurses, therapists, neurobiology, neurotechnology, etc.)
- Capacity for global, multi-dimensional understanding
- Enables us to detect and identify the cause of illnesses
- Great healer, bearer of universal remedies, leads to true healing, which touches all levels
- Infinite goodness, unconditional service
- Bestows the philosopher's stone
- Patron of High Science
- Grants access to the Truth, which enables us to understand the dynamics of the Universe
- Expert in esoteric knowledge (the Kabbalah, alchemy, metaphysics, etc.)
- A truly wise person, an elevated soul

Human distortions

- *Medicine that treats only physical symptoms and pains without searching for or understanding the real causes of illnesses; or charlatans, fake therapists that take advantage of people's naivety and ignorance*
- *Flatterer, swindler, imposter manipulator abusing other people's good faith*
- *Lack of spiritual knowledge and conscience in the medical professions*
- *Uses medicine solely for material gain, seeking power, ambition*
- *Victim of fraud*
- *Illusion*
- *Science without conscience*

Physical: December 3 to December 7
Emotional: February 27, May 11, July 25, July 26 from midnight to midday, October 8, December 19
Intellectual: 4:40 pm to 4:59 pm
Residence: Netzach / **Specificity**: Hesed

52 IMAMIAH

Qualities

⊙ Ease in recognizing one's errors
⊙ Enables us to expiate, pay for and repair our errors (karmas)
⊙ Ease in carrying out difficult tasks
⊙ Courage, ardor, great vigor and emotional strength
⊙ Great capacity to take care of, console, help and support others in difficulty
⊙ Charisma, leadership
⊙ Harmonious social life
⊙ Makes peace with one's enemies
⊙ Sets us free from inner prisons
⊙ Faithful servant
⊙ Humility, simplicity, patience

Human distortions

– *Tendency not to recognize one's own errors and/or to put oneself or others down*
– *Unstable, tumultuous emotional life*
– *Competitive love*
– *Passionate relationship, perverted desires*
– *Aversions, fights, quarrels, vulgarity*
– *Overly emotional, excessive willpower*
– *Tendency to criticize, anger, jealousy*
– *Hidden truth, dissimulation, double meaning, lip service, two-facedness, hypocrisy, insincerity*
– *Spitefulness, meanness due to lack of recognition of one's errors, offences and misdeeds*
– *Worsens one's karma, difficult destiny*
– *Conflicting, rebellious spirit*
– *Pride, blasphemy, rivalry, animosity*

Physical: December 8 to December 12
Emotional: February 28, February 29, May 12, July 26 from midday to midnight, July 27, October 9, December 20
Intellectual: 5:00 pm to 5:19 pm
Residence: Netzach / **Specificity**: Geburah

53 NANAEL

Qualities

- ☉ Spiritual communication
- ☉ Inspires meditation
- ☉ Knowledge of abstract science and philosophy
- ☉ Interested in spiritual life and teaching
- ☉ Fascinated by the contemplation of Higher Worlds
- ☉ Mysticism
- ☉ Loves solitude and meditative states
- ☉ Facilitates communication with the Divine

Human distortions

- – *Negative spiritual communication, spiritual extremism, tries to persuade and impose one's beliefs on others*
- – *Non-respect for other people's pace of evolution*
- – *Wants to convince and save everyone*
- – *Difficulty meditating*
- – *Abstract person, tendency to flee, to escape concrete reality, autistic behaviour, recluse*
- – *Rejects spiritual knowledge and communication*
- – *Ignorance*
- – *Errs frequently*
- – *Difficulty learning*
- – *May enter a religious order through fear of facing life*
- – *Difficulty achieving one's aims and communicating*
- – *Fear regarding daily tasks*
- – *Feeling of failure*
- – *Teaches spirituality without having acquired Knowledge*
- – *Seeks spiritual power*
- – *Melancholic temperament, isolation*
- – *Egotistical celibacy*
- – *Difficulty living as a couple*

Physical: December 13 to December 16
Emotional: March 1, May 13, July 28, October 10, December 21
Intellectual: 5:20 pm to 5:39 pm
Residence: Netzach / **Specificity**: Tiphereth

54 NITHAEL

Qualities

- ⊙ Eternal youth
- ⊙ Beauty, grace, refinement
- ⊙ Synchronicity, stability
- ⊙ Hospitality, warm welcome
- ⊙ Artistic and aesthetic talents
- ⊙ Celebrity, prestige
- ⊙ Childlike candor, freshness
- ⊙ Healing
- ⊙ Legitimate succession, inheritance

Human distortions

- – *Fear of growing old*
- – *Seduction to achieve one's goals*
- – *Focused on external beauty and appearances*
- – *Feelings of inferiority and superiority*
- – *Lust, ambition, blind admiration, idolatry*
- – *Wants to please everyone*
- – *Emotional dependency*
- – *Possessivity*
- – *Illegitimacy*
- – *Reversal, permanent conspiracy*
- – *Attitude that does not correspond to one's words*
- – *Illness, accident, ruin*
- – *Unstable situation*
- – *Takes for granted*
- – *Bulimia, anorexia*

Physical: December 17 to December 21
Emotional: March 2, May 14, July 29, October 11, December 22
Intellectual: 5:40 pm to 5:59 pm
Residence: Netzach / **Specificity**: Netzach

55 MEBAHIAH

Qualities

⊙ Intellectual lucidity
⊙ Clarity of ideas that allow goodness and kindness
⊙ Understanding through the senses
⊙ Adjusts and regulates desires
⊙ Harmonization of behavior
⊙ Sense of duty and responsibility
⊙ Opens the heart with discernment
⊙ Consolation born through understanding
⊙ Communicates the mystery of Morality to the intellect
⊙ Profound, mystical, spiritual experience
⊙ Example of Morality, exemplary behavior, commitment
⊙ Capacity to rectify on the collective level

Human distortions

– *Excessive logic, dry, analytical mind*
– *Lack of lucidity, mental opacity*
– *Lies*
– *Dissatisfied perfectionist*
– *Complexes of superiority and inferiority*
– *Difficulty expressing emotions, negates all sentimentality, denies one's feelings*
– *Destroys spirituality*
– *Acts against the principles of Morality*
– *Only interested in material things*
– *Failure*
– *Mistrust, opposes, fights positive ideas*
– *Capricious, selfish person, excessively focused on his appearance and exterior beauty, maintains a façade of harmony*
– *Lack of kindness and love due to an overly rational mind and false concepts*

Physical: December 22 to December 26
Emotional: March 3, May 15, July 30, October 12, December 23
Intellectual: 6:00 pm to 6:19 pm
Residence: Netzach / **Specificity**: Hod

56 POYEL

Qualities

- ⊙ Fortune, support
- ⊙ Modesty, simplicity, altruism
- ⊙ Providential gifts
- ⊙ Fortune on all levels
- ⊙ Creator of positive ideas and atmosphere, ambiance
- ⊙ Talents, renown and celebrity in complete humility
- ⊙ Health
- ⊙ Esteemed by all
- ⊙ Ease of elocution, expresses oneself clearly and simply
- ⊙ Agreeable disposition
- ⊙ Hope, optimism
- ⊙ Humor

Human distortions

- – *Poverty, problems related to abundance, lack of resources, support and/or lack of modesty, simplicity and altruism*
- – *Poor use of resources, excesses, exaggeration, squandering, worldly pleasures*
- – *Materialistic philosophy and lifestyle*
- – *Pride, ambition, wanting to rise above others*
- – *Boasting, display of material wealth*
- – *Feelings of inferiority and superiority*
- – *Criticism, controversy, disdain, puts others down, inhibition, mediocrity*
- – *Absence of happiness, an unhappy person, ill-humor*
- – *Illness*
- – *Elocution problems*
- – *Jokes that hide needs and judgments*
- – *False joy and fake smile or laughter*

Physical: December 27 to December 31
Emotional: March 4, May 16, July 31, October 13, December 24
Intellectual: 6:20 pm to 6:39 pm
Residence: Netzach / **Specificity**: Yesod

57 NEMAMIAH

Qualities

- ⊙ Discernment
- ⊙ Capacity to understand by simply observing
- ⊙ Gifted intellect, capacity for anticipation, foresight
- ⊙ Reveals the cause of problems
- ⊙ Strategic genius, decisiveness
- ⊙ Procures a sense of action
- ⊙ Devotion to great causes through one's ideas
- ⊙ Renounces material privileges to devote oneself to one's mission
- ⊙ Magnanimity, noble-minded
- ⊙ Non-attachment
- ⊙ Feeling of freedom
- ⊙ Liberates prisoners
- ⊙ Understands life-plans

Human distortions

- *Lack of discernment, of profound understanding and global vision, tendency to get lost in details*
- *Dark mentality, devoid of principles*
- *Complicated, obscure life*
- *Relationship problems, disagreement, discord*
- *Difficulty communicating, unable to open up easily*
- *Lack of free speech and freedom in general*
- *Betrayal, cowardice*
- *Indecisive, irresolute*
- *Naivety, tendency to believe anyone and everyone, anything and everything*
- *Bogged down, stalled in routine*
- *Does not engage, become involved in action*
- *Prisoner of the psyche*
- *Flees experimentation and the concrete world*
- *Chronic illness and fatigue*

Physical: January 1 to January 5
Emotional: March 5, May 17, August 1, October 14, December 25
Intellectual: 6:40 pm to 6:59 pm
Residence: Hod / **Specificity**: Hochmah

58 YEIALEL

Qualities

- ⊙ Mental power, high level of intelligence
- ⊙ Great logic, capable of disciplining one's thoughts
- ⊙ Capacity to discern with rigor
- ⊙ Helps develop intellectual faculties
- ⊙ Favors awareness, lucidity, clairvoyance
- ⊙ Ability to concentrate, seeks precision, exactitude, competence, patience
- ⊙ Beneficial force in the use of computers and programming
- ⊙ Neurotechnology
- ⊙ Masters passions and emotional impulses
- ⊙ Frankness, bravery
- ⊙ Sense of justice and order, rigor, unconditional loyalty
- ⊙ Understands Divine Laws and Structures

Human distortions

- – *Tries to control, thinks too much, obsessions, over focused on worries*
- – *Problems with love and emotions in general*
- – *Lack of intelligence, difficulty concentrating, focusing one's attention, energy and intentions; or, misuse of intelligence and intellectual faculties*
- – *Gets lost in virtual worlds (video games, the Internet, social networks, etc.)*
- – *Misuse of neurotechnology*
- – *Excessively perfectionist*
- – *Imposes one's ideas using cunning, trickery, manipulation*
- – *Bad intentions, lies, betrayal*
- – *Anger, revenge*
- – *Abuse of power, crime*
- – *Obstinacy, stubbornness, illogical*
- – *Rigidity, severity*
- – *Moroseness, sadness, pessimism*
- – *Lack of belief or refusal to believe in God, in a Higher, Superior Power, atheism*
- – *Megalomania*
- – *Abstract life*
- – *Excessively rational, logical person, who believes only what can be concretely proven*
- – *Discrepancies between the intellect, emotions and physical aspects*

Physical: January 6 to January 10
Emotional: March 6, May 18, August 2, October 15, December 26
Intellectual: 7:00 pm to 7:19 pm
Residence: Hod / **Specificity**: Binah

59 HARAHEL

Qualities

- ⊙ Intellectual abundance, access to Knowledge
- ⊙ Capacity to materialize through technology, advanced programming
- ⊙ Emanates Goodness, Beauty, Truth
- ⊙ Well-balanced intelligence in all fields
- ⊙ Likes learning, learns easily
- ⊙ Intellectual creativity, practical intelligence
- ⊙ Fecundity, productivity on all levels
- ⊙ Children who are obedient and respectful towards their parents
- ⊙ Ability to make a fortune thanks to one's intellectual qualities
- ⊙ Writing, journalism, publishing and printing

Human distortions

- – *Lack of knowledge, ideas or intelligence*
- – *Spends too much time on computers, lives in a virtual world, not grounded enough, lacks exercise, concrete action and contact with physical reality*
- – *Intellectual aberration*
- – *Destructive writings, broadcasts and influences that are negative for humanity*
- – *Mental opacity, incomprehension*
- – *Sterility, lack of productivity on all levels*
- – *Rebellious, disrespectful children*
- – *Fire, burns everything on one's path*
- – *Enemy of Light*
- – *Projects doomed to failure*
- – *Manipulation of the media for personal gains*
- – *Fraud*

Physical: January 11 to January 15
Emotional: March 7, May 19, May 20 from midnight to midday, August 3, October 16, December 27 from midnight to 6 pm
Intellectual: 7:20 pm to 7:39 pm
Residence: Hod / **Specificity**: Hesed

60 MITZRAEL

Qualities

- ⊙ Reparation
- ⊙ Understands obedience and authority
- ⊙ Rectification
- ⊙ Facilitates the practice of psychology and psychiatry
- ⊙ Great talent in the field of neurobiology, neurotechnology and technology in general
- ⊙ Heals mental illnesses
- ⊙ Reparation through awareness
- ⊙ Intellectual work and harmonization
- ⊙ Reunification of the physical, emotional, mental and spiritual levels
- ⊙ Simplicity

Human distortions

- – *Difficulty accepting one's mistakes and repairing one's life, tendency to abandon, to give up*
- – *Fear of change, non acceptance of the karma one has engendered, refusal to evolve*
- – *Fragility caused by discrepancies*
- – *Problems with authority, with one's father, father figure, or boss*
- – *Insubordination, disobedience*
- – *Vindictive, critical, complicated*
- – *Lack of mutual help and cooperation, everyone-for-himself mentality*
- – *Revolt, rebellion, persecution*
- – *Mental illnesses (paranoia, madness, schizophrenia, etc.)*
- – *Chronic fatigue, migraines*
- – *Medicine without conscience*

Physical: January 16 to January 20
Emotional: March 8, May 20 from midday to midnight, May 21, August 4, October 17, December 27 from 6 pm to midnight
Intellectual: 7:40 pm to 7:59 pm
Residence: Hod / **Specificity**: Geburah

61 UMABEL

Qualities

- ⊙ Friendship, affinity
- ⊙ Study and understanding of resonance
- ⊙ Aptitude for technology and neurotechnology
- ⊙ Helps penetrate the subconscious and the unconscious to discover our true motives
- ⊙ Physics, astronomy, astrology
- ⊙ Helps us understand the analogies between the Universe and the Earth, between all levels of Creation
- ⊙ Reveals the secrets of the mineral, vegetable and animal kingdoms
- ⊙ Helps develop deep awareness, conscience
- ⊙ Capacity to teach what has been learned
- ⊙ Instructor, teacher
- ⊙ Enables us to learn the unknown through the known

Human distortions

- − *Problems with friendship and affinity*
- − *Fear of solitude, afraid of being alone*
- − *Wants to please others*
- − *Seeks appreciation and renown*
- − *Does not understand the Law of resonance, the principle of attraction/repulsion*
- − *Licentiousness*
- − *Solitary heart, difficulty finding friends, self-alienation, loneliness*
- − *Problems with one's mother*
- − *Return to the past, nostalgia, attachment to outdated concepts*
- − *Problems with technology and neurotechnology*
- − *Narcissism*
- − *On the fringe, marginalization, acting against the natural order*
- − *Drug problems*
- − *Ignorance of the analogies between the different levels of Creation*
- − *Science without conscience*
- − *Difficulty teaching what has been learned*
- − *Fake or bad teacher, instructor, professor*

Physical: January 21 to January 25
Emotional: March 9, May 22, August 5, October 18, December 28
Intellectual: 8:00 pm to 8:19 pm
Residence: Hod / **Specificity**: Tiphereth

62 IAHHEL

Qualities

- Knowledge rediscovered
- Philosopher, mystic
- Enlightenment
- Procures Wisdom and a sense of responsibility
- Beneficial for retreats, facilitates going within, positive, constructive, fruitful introspection,
- Solitude, tranquility
- Modesty, gentleness
- Favors the encounter of a man and a woman
- Divine sexuality, pure pleasures
- Payment of karmic debts
- Pacifism
- Refines all the senses, including the most subtle (clairvoyance, clairaudience, clairsentience)
- Creator of positive, harmonious ambiances
- Likes quality, beauty, poetry
- Culinary art

Human distortions

- *Problems due to lack of Knowledge or tendency to appropriate Knowledge for oneself*
- *Swindler, imposter, pseudo-learned person*
- *Need for pleasure, scandal, luxury, vanity*
- *Materialistic, ambitious person*
- *Problems in the couple, difficulty in intimate relationships, separation, divorce*
- *Lack of modesty, kindness, gentleness*
- *Need for approval*
- *Jealousy, envy*
- *Creator of conflicts, aggression*
- *Fickleness, restlessness, incapable of remaining tranquilly alone*
- *Isolation*

Physical: January 26 to January 30
Emotional: March 10, May 23, August 6, October 19, December 29
Intellectual: 8:20 pm to 8:39 pm
Residence: Hod / **Specificity**: Netzach

63 ANAUEL

Qualities

- ⊙ Perception of Unity
- ⊙ Success in human relationships, ease in communication
- ⊙ Practical intelligence, logic, global vision
- ⊙ Initiator of projects and enterprises dedicated to the service of the Divine
- ⊙ Right understanding of the concept of money and exchanges
- ⊙ Ability to materialize in a right, just, fair manner with respect for each stage
- ⊙ Sense of organization and altruism
- ⊙ Capacity to generate great abundance with new concepts, new ideas, new technologies
- ⊙ Administrator, coordinator, planner, visionary
- ⊙ Retailer, banker, industrialist, entrepreneur in the service of the Divine
- ⊙ Expert in understanding mentalities, cultures
- ⊙ Emotional mastery
- ⊙ Great leader, inspirator
- ⊙ Citizen of the Universe

Human distortions

- – *Gets lost in details, grants too much importance to money, egoism*
- – *Incapacity to create unity in a group*
- – *Difficulty generating abundance, exchanging with others, succeeding in business*
- – *Problems with new concepts, ideas and technologies*
- – *Lack of knowledge and respect for other mentalities and cultures*
- – *Complex of intellectual superiority, believes one knows everything, arrogant mindset*
- – *Difficulty guiding and inspiring others*
- – *Travel limitations, incapable of receiving the Universal Passport and access to the Parallel Worlds*
- – *Absence of wisdom in business*
- – *Lack of common sense, of global vision and understanding*
- – *Corruption*
- – *Prepared to do anything to make money*
- – *False reasoning, manipulated by desires*
- – *Extravagance (spending more than one has), waste, ruin*
- – *Limited, too critical and/or excessively rational mind*
- – *Cold appreciation*
- – *Lack of or refusal to believe in a Higher, Superior Power, atheism*

Physical: January 31 to February 4
Emotional: March 11, May 24, August 7, October 20, December 30
Intellectual: 8:40 pm to 8:59 pm
Residence: Hod / **Specificity**: Hod

64 MEHIEL

Qualities

⊙ Vivification, inspiration
⊙ Intense, productive life
⊙ Intelligence, imagination, receptivity and profound understanding
⊙ Helps to find practical, innovative solutions
⊙ Develops mental faculties in harmony with the imagination
⊙ Beneficial energy for intellectual activity, for computers and programming
⊙ Helps to understand correlation between dream science and technology
⊙ Concerns writing, printing, publishing, distribution, bookshops, orators, as well as television and radio programs
⊙ Facilitates technological development
⊙ Helps reflect upon and understand personal experience
⊙ Antidote against the forces of darkness

Human distortions

– *Lack of energy, unable to think or do things; or, hyperactivity, over-excitement, wanting to please, to be appreciated and acknowledged*
– *Sterile, unproductive life, difficulty creating and/or carrying out projects*
– *Lack of intensity and inspiration, problems with creativity and imagination*
– *Either a lack or excess of aims, objectives, goals, aspirations*
– *Contradiction, criticism, controversy*
– *Distortion of reality, indulging or even wallowing in illusion*
– *Tyranny, megalomania oppression, falseness*
– *Destructive, tries to force, counter or defy Destiny*
– *Unable to understand one's life scenario*
– *Excess of rationality*
– *Plays a role, lacks authenticity*
– *Personality problems*

Physical: February 5 to February 9
Emotional: March 12, May 25, August 8, October 21, December 31
Intellectual: 9:00 pm to 9:19 pm
Residence: Hod / **Specificity**: Yesod

65 DAMABIAH

Qualities

⊙ Fountain of Wisdom
⊙ Purity, gentleness, goodness
⊙ Radiates great spiritual values such as altruism, devotion, generosity, detachment and unconditional love
⊙ Helps us advance the easy way
⊙ Success in enterprises that are useful for the community
⊙ Linked to water (springs, rivers, seas, etc.), emotions and feelings
⊙ Providential person capable of solving compromising situations

Human distortions

– *Lack of wisdom, purity, goodness, gentleness, devotion, generosity and altruism*
– *Egotistical, self-centered*
– *Failure in business linked to lack of love and respect for the community*
– *Chooses the difficult way to do things*
– *Incapacity to solve problems*
– *Excessive, compulsive behavior*
– *Tumultuous emotions, unstable feelings, or puritanism*
– *Anger, aggression*
– *Storm, shipwreck*
– *Fatalism*

Physical: February 10 to February 14
Emotional: January 1, March 13, May 26, August 9, October 22
Intellectual: 9:20 pm to 9:39 pm
Residence: Yesod / **Specificity**: Hochmah

418

66 MANAKEL

Qualities

- ⊙ Knowledge of good and evil
- ⊙ Transcendence of fears
- ⊙ Stability, confidence
- ⊙ Helps create a beautiful life
- ⊙ High morality
- ⊙ Calms, soothes, heals illness
- ⊙ Kindness, goodness, thoughtfulness
- ⊙ Liberates one's deeply buried potential
- ⊙ Neurotechnology
- ⊙ Dreams, daydreams, High Initiation
- ⊙ Reunification of the qualities of the body and soul

Human distortions

- – *Plays with negative forces, does not understand that evil attracts evil*
- – *Receptivity to dark forces*
- – *Instability, lack of faith and confidence, suicidal tendencies*
- – *Potential trapped in negative memories*
- – *Old soul that does not want to change, laziness*
- – *Feelings of superiority and inferiority*
- – *Megalomaniac attitudes*
- – *Dangerous, machiavellian manipulator, prepared to do anything to achieve one's ends, absence of principles and altruistic values*
- – *Physical and moral perturbation*
- – *Seeks only material pleasure and social prestige*
- – *In women: late development of personality*
- – *In men: belated encounter with a woman*
- – *Dangerous friendships*
- – *Destructive spirit, impulsiveness*
- – *Reneging on, not keeping one's promises*
- – *Refusal to apply Knowledge*
- – *Pernicious, malevolent use, abuse and misuse of technology*
- – *Anger toward God, revolt, rebellion*

Physical: February 15 to February 19
Emotional: January 2, March 14, May 27, August 10, October 23
Intellectual: 9:40 pm to 9:59 pm
Residence: Yesod / **Specificity**: Binah

67 EYAEL

Qualities

⊙ Sublimation
⊙ Science of mixtures and exchanges
⊙ Transubstantiation (changing one substance into another), transformation, mutation, metamorphosis, transfiguration, transfer
⊙ Understands Universal History, capacity to detect the origin and genesis
⊙ Archeology
⊙ Ability to observe, recognize and understand affinities
⊙ Understands the Law of resonance, the fact that we attract and create what and who we are
⊙ High, advanced knowledge in chemistry, physics, biology, biotechnology, neurotechnology, etc.
⊙ Study of the DNA, cells, atoms, fundamental structures
⊙ Study of High Science
⊙ Abstract truth transformed into concrete truth
⊙ Culinary art, painting, music
⊙ Joy
⊙ Likes solitude

Human distortions

– *Negative, harmful transformations and mutations*
– *Manipulations that engender bad experiences*
– *Excess or lack of exchanges*
– *Fear of change*
– *Error, prejudice*
– *Propagates erroneous systems, fake teacher*
– *Tendency to mix up everything, to create confusion*
– *Problems resulting from a lack of knowledge in chemistry, alchemy, biology, biotechnology, etc.*
– *Misuse of science*
– *Lack of light, morals and principles*
– *Goes from one experience to another without understanding*
– *Heaviness, absorption in matter, does not meditate*
– *Artificial food, painting and music that exert a negative influence*
– *Absence of joy, sadness, worry*
– *Isolation*

Physical: February 20 to February 24
Emotional: January 3, March 15, May 28, August 11, October 24
Intellectual: 10:00 pm to 10:19 pm
Residence: Yesod / **Specificity**: Hesed

68 HABUHIAH

Qualities

⊙ Healing
⊙ Concerns all medical and therapy professions as well as energetic, metaphysical, spiritual treatments and healing
⊙ Capacity to restructure, to adjust, and regulate desires
⊙ Adjustment to Divine Standards
⊙ Restores balance after phase discrepancies
⊙ Reharmonizes when out of synchrony
⊙ Loves nature, country life, open spaces
⊙ Agriculture, harvests, agricultural expertise
⊙ Fertile nature, creative power

Human distortions

– *Difficulty understanding illness and healing due to lack of knowledge, wisdom, and incomprehension of the original, metaphysical causes*
– *False healer, charlatan*
– *Lost in multiples desires and needs*
– *Discrepancies, out of synchrony, difficulty being in the right place, at the right time*
– *Double life, discrepancy between thoughts and emotions*
– *Discrepancy between what one wants to be and do and what one is and does*
– *In women: tendency to dominate*
– *In men: tendency to let themselves be dominated by women*
– *Reluctance to abandon old privileges*
– *Anti-life attitude*
– *Infertile soil, famine, misery, pollution, insect plagues*
– *Contagious diseases, epidemics*

Physical: February 25 to February 29
Emotional: January 4, March 16, May 29, August 12, October 25
Intellectual: 10:20 pm to 10:39 pm
Residence: Yesod / **Specificity**: Geburah

69 ROCHEL

Qualities

⊙ Restitution, grants each person what he is entitled to
⊙ Finds lost or stolen objects, thoughts and feelings
⊙ Succession, inheritance
⊙ Notary, magistrate
⊙ Intuition
⊙ Study of Law and Justice
⊙ Study of History
⊙ Universal Library and Archives (Daath)
⊙ Practical and theoretical science
⊙ Ability to give and receive with ease
⊙ Administration, accounting, secretarial work
⊙ Rediscovers the Divine self, Original Androgyny
⊙ Cleanses and transforms karma

Human distortions

– *Takes what does not belong to us*
– *Jealousy, possessiveness, egoism*
– *Spousal relationship based solely on sexuality and materialism*
– *Sexual abuse, licentiousness and multiple relationships*
– *Family problems*
– *Difficulties related to succession, inheritance, and the work of notaries, magistrates*
– *Problems with regard to administration, managing resources, accounting and secretarial work*
– *Over focused on practical aspects, excessively pragmatic*
– *Problems with giving and receiving*
– *Usurpation of goods, theft, cunning, trickery*
– *Existential fear, insecurity*
– *Vampirism, takes other people's energy*
– *Manipulation of historical facts*
– *Megalomania*
– *Legal issues, flagrant injustice, unending lawsuit or trial*
– *Ruin*
– *Lack of receptivity or emissivity*

Physical: March 1 to March 5
Emotional: January 5, March 17, May 30, August 13, October 26
Intellectual: 10:40 pm to 10:59 pm
Residence: Yesod / **Specificity**: Tiphereth

70 JABAMIAH

Qualities

- ⊙ Alchemy
- ⊙ Transforms evil into good
- ⊙ Understanding and application of the Law of resonance
- ⊙ Great receptivity and capacity to love in all circumstances
- ⊙ Healing
- ⊙ Regenerates, revitalizes, re-establishes harmony
- ⊙ Transforms, transmutes into spiritual gold
- ⊙ Transforms society with enlightened ideas
- ⊙ Masters instincts
- ⊙ Guides the first steps of the deceased into/in the other world
- ⊙ Helps us accompany the dying
- ⊙ Capacity to visit the Parallel Worlds, to understand the work of spiritual guides, to learn how to be one of these guides and how to become a divine healer

Human distortions

- *Difficulty transforming, transcending evil and negative energies, situations, aspects, etc.*
- *Blockage, retention, difficulties with digestion on different levels, obesity*
- *Health problems, incurable diseases, difficulty healing due to a surplus of negative memories, thoughts, feelings and behavior*
- *Unable, unwilling or refuses to be receptive*
- *Problems caused by unsatisfied instinctual needs*
- *Outbursts, excessive reactions, conflict, confrontation*
- *Rejects others, lack of love, accumulation of negative feelings*
- *Tendency to get bogged down, heaviness, incapable of setting objectives*
- *Ignorance of the Law of resonance or refusal to apply it*
- *Incomprehension of good and evil*
- *Atheism, disbelief*
- *Fear of change and death*
- *Difficulty accompanying people in their terminal phase*

Physical: March 6 to March 10
Emotional: January 6, March 18, May 31, August 14, October 27
Intellectual: 11:00 pm to 11:19 pm
Residence: Yesod / **Specificity**: Netzach

71 HAIAIEL

Qualities

⊙ Divine Arms
⊙ Discernment (sword symbol)
⊙ Luminous aura (shield symbol)
⊙ Divine Protection to make the right, fair, just decision
⊙ Receptive intelligence, protective spirit, strategist
⊙ Releases from one's oppressors
⊙ Protects and leads to victory, bravery and courage
⊙ New ideas and concepts that can change the world
⊙ Receptivity to Divine inspiration
⊙ Develops great energy
⊙ Leadership

Human distortions

– *Terrorist, activist*
– *Lack of intelligence and inspiration*
– *Dangerous person who uses negative forces and thoughts, dark, somber energy, black magic, satanic pacts*
– *Manipulator, liar*
– *Ready to do anything to win, to reach one's goal*
– *Vindictive, dictatorial, tyrannical*
– *Discord, betrayal*
– *Provides weapons for killing*
– *Bearer of internal contradictions*
– *Rupture (divorce, broken contracts, etc.)*
– *Criminal ideas, extremism*
– *Excessive rationality*
– *Non-respect of commitments*
– *War, continual conflicts*
– *Corrupt government*

Physical: March 11 to March 15
Emotional: January 7, March 19, June 1, August 15, October 28
Intellectual: 11:20 pm to 11:39 pm
Residence: Yesod / **Specificity**: Hod

72 MUMIAH

Qualities

⊙ Rebirth
⊙ Great receptivity, psychic abilities, mystical experiences
⊙ New beginning
⊙ High Initiations leading to major transformations and new knowledge
⊙ Sows the seeds of new life
⊙ Understands the Law of reincarnation and how affinities manifest on all levels
⊙ Beginning of Angelic transformation and mutation
⊙ Announces the end of one cycle and the beginning of a new one
⊙ Brings to an end, helps terminate what has been started
⊙ Concrete achievements, materialization
⊙ Concerns medicine and health
⊙ Terminal phase in which the seed of renewal is found
⊙ Accompanies the dying
⊙ Great experience of life
⊙ Opening of conscience

Human distortions

– *Difficulty ending a cycle and/or beginning a new one*
– *Fear of mystical experiences due to a lack of spiritual, metaphysical knowledge and understanding*
– *Fears initiations and the evolution of one's conscience, preferring to continue living in ordinary conscience*
– *Lacks knowledge, or refuses to believe in reincarnation and eternal life*
– *Despair, impasse, blocked horizon, depression*
– *Tendency to abdicate, to give up, to nourish negative ambiances and old patterns*
– *Difficulty opening up to spirituality and the Divine, developing and living in accordance with a new conscience, atheism*
– *Unconscious death, suicide*
– *Repudiates one's own existence, negative influence*
– *Bad health, disability*
– *Collapse, ruin, loss of employment, of one's spouse, friends, etc.*
– *Goes from one experience to the next without understanding*
– *Seeks to convince*
– *Acts against the natural order*
– *Forces materialization*
– *Knowledge and science without conscience*

Physical: March 16 to March 20
Emotional: January 8, March 20, June 2, August 16, October 29
Intellectual: 11:40 pm to 11:59 pm
Residence: Yesod / **Specificity**: Yesod

INDEX

Acknowledgements

Our heartfelt thanks to all the volunteers who have joined us to help spread knowledge of dream & sign interpretation, symbolic language, The Traditional Study of Angels, Angelica Yoga and Meditation throughout the world. Through your altruistic dedication, you inspire millions of people to apply this knowledge and help them develop an angelic, multi-dimensional conscience. Our wish is for everyone to one day understand that life is lived and decoded like a dream, that it is a true source of experimentation and evolution, enabling us to reach the highest levels of Love and Wisdom.

To contact us:

Universe/City Mikaël (UCM) gives workshops, seminars, webinars and training courses on symbolic language and the interpretation of dreams, signs & symbols, as well as lectures on The Traditional Study of Angels (Traditional Angelology) and Angelica Yoga and Meditation lessons.

Its Angelica Pratica Clinic offers physical and metaphysical treatments as well as help and support in personal and spiritual development. Consultations may take place at the clinic or on Skype.

If you would like to help organize activities in your region, or join our volunteer team, heartfelt thanks for contacting us via our website.

● UNIVERSE/CITY MIKAËL (UCM)
TEACHING & RESEARCH CENTER

53, Saint-Antoine Street
Sainte-Agathe-des-Monts, QC
Canada J8C 2C4

Email: publishing@ucm.ca
Website: www.ucm.ca

Universe/City Mikaël is a non-profit organization with no affiliation to a religious group or movement. Its teachings are universal and open to all.

OUCM

www.ucm.ca
org@ucm.ca

AVAILABLE FROM OUR PUBLISHING HOUSE

BECOMING AN ANGEL
THE PATH TO ENLIGHTENMENT
AUTOBIOGRAPHY
Kaya
ISBN: 978-2-923654-67-6
e-Book ISBN: 978-2-923654-72-0

THE BOOK OF ANGELS
THE HIDDEN SECRETS
THE TRADITIONAL STUDY OF ANGELS
Kaya and Christiane Muller
ISBN: 978-2-923097-54-1
e-Book ISBN: 978-2-923654-05-8

HOW TO READ SIGNS
THE ORIGIN OF ANGELS,
SIGNS & SYMBOLS
Kaya and Christiane Muller
ISBN: 978-2-923097-61-9
e-Book ISBN: 978-2-923654-06-5

DICTIONARY
DREAMS-SIGNS-SYMBOLS
THE SOURCE CODE
ISBN: 978-2-923654-25-6
e-Book ISBN: 978-2-923654-43-0

ALSO AVAILABLE WITH
UNIVERSE/CITY MIKAËL (UCM) PUBLISHING:

ANGELICA YOGA
INTRODUCTION
Kaya and Christiane Muller
ISBN: 978-2-923097-63-3

**HOW TO INTERPRET
DREAMS & SIGNS**
Kaya
ISBN: 978-2-923654-11-9

THE 72 ANGEL CARDS
DREAMS, SIGNS, MEDITATION
Kaya and Christiane Muller
ISBN: 978-2-923097-60-2

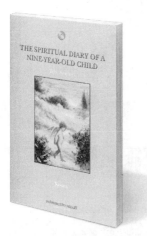

**THE SPIRITUAL DIARY OF
A NINE-YEAR-OLD CHILD**
Kasara
ISBN: 978-2-923097-66-4

**THE SPIRITUAL DIARY
OF A TEENAGER**
Kasara
ISBN: 978-2-923654-75-1
e-book: 978-2-923654-71-3

**IN THE LAND
OF BLUE SKIES**
Gabriell, Kaya
and Christiane Muller
ISBN: 978-2-923097-65-7

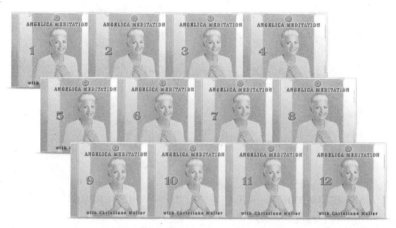

ANGELICA MEDITATION COLLECTION

CD 1: (Angels 72 to 67) ISBN: 978-2-923097-68-8
CD 2: (Angels 66 to 61) ISBN: 978-2-923097-69-5
CD 3: (Angels 60 to 55) ISBN: 978-2-923097-70-1
CD 4: (Angels 54 to 49) ISBN: 978-2-923097-71-8
CD 5: (Angels 48 to 43) ISBN: 978-2-923097-72-5
CD 6: (Angels 42 to 37)ISBN: 978-2-923097-73-2
CD 7: (Angels 36 to 31) ISBN: 978-2-923097-74-9
CD 8: (Angels 30 to 25) ISBN: 978-2-923097-75-6
CD 9: (Angels 24 to 19)ISBN: 978-2-923097-76-3
CD 10: (Angels 18 to 13) ISBN: 978-2-923097-77-0
CD 11:(Angels 12 to 7) ISBN: 978-2-923097-78-7
CD 12:(Angels 6 to 1) ISBN: 978-2-923097-79-4

ANGELICA MUSICA COLLECTION

CD 1: (Angels 72 to 67) ISBN: 978-2-923097-80-0
CD 2: (Angels 66 to 61) ISBN: 978-2-923097-81-7
CD 3: (Angels 60 to 55) ISBN: 978-2-923097-82-4
CD 4: (Angels 54 to 49) ISBN: 978-2-923097-83-1
CD 5: (Angels 48 to 43) ISBN: 978-2-923097-84-8
CD 6: (Angels 42 to 37) ISBN: 978-2-923097-85-5
CD 7: (Angels 36 to 31) ISBN: 978-2-923097-86-2
CD 8: (Angels 30 to 25) ISBN: 978-2-923097-87-9
CD 9: (Angels 24 to 19) ISBN: 978-2-923097-88-6
CD 10: (Angels 18 to 13) ISBN: 978-2-923097-89-3
CD 11: (Angels 12 to 7) ISBN: 978-2-923097-90-9
CD 12:(Angels 6 to 1) ISBN: 978-2-923097-91-6

BORN UNDER THE STAR OF CHANGE
Kaya
Production: Russ DeSalvo, New York, USA
Record Label: Golden Wisdom Records / Airgo Music
Genre: Adult Contemporary / Pop / Inspirational
Format: CD and MP3
# of songs: 13
Item number: 627843159308

ANGELICA MANTRA VOL. 1
Angels 1 to 12
Kasara
ISBN: 978-2-923654-35-5

ANGELICA MANTRA VOL. 2
Angels 13 to 24
Kasara
ISBN: 978-2-923654-36-2

ANGELICA MANTRA VOL. 3
Angels 25 to 36
Kasara
ISBN: 978-2-923654-37-9

ANGELICA MANTRA VOL. 4
Angels 37 to 48
Kasara
ISBN: 978-2-923654-38-6

ANGELICA MANTRA VOL. 5
Angels 49 to 60
Kasara
ISBN: 978-2-923654-39-3

ANGELICA MANTRA VOL. 6
Angels 61 to 72
Kasara
ISBN: 978-2-923654-40-9

GREETING CARDS
EXPOSITION ANGELICA
Artist: Gabriell
A collection of 65 greeting cards

NOTES

NOTES

NOTES

NOTES

NOTES

NOTES

NOTES